Cuba: Twenty-Five Years of Revolution, 1959—1984

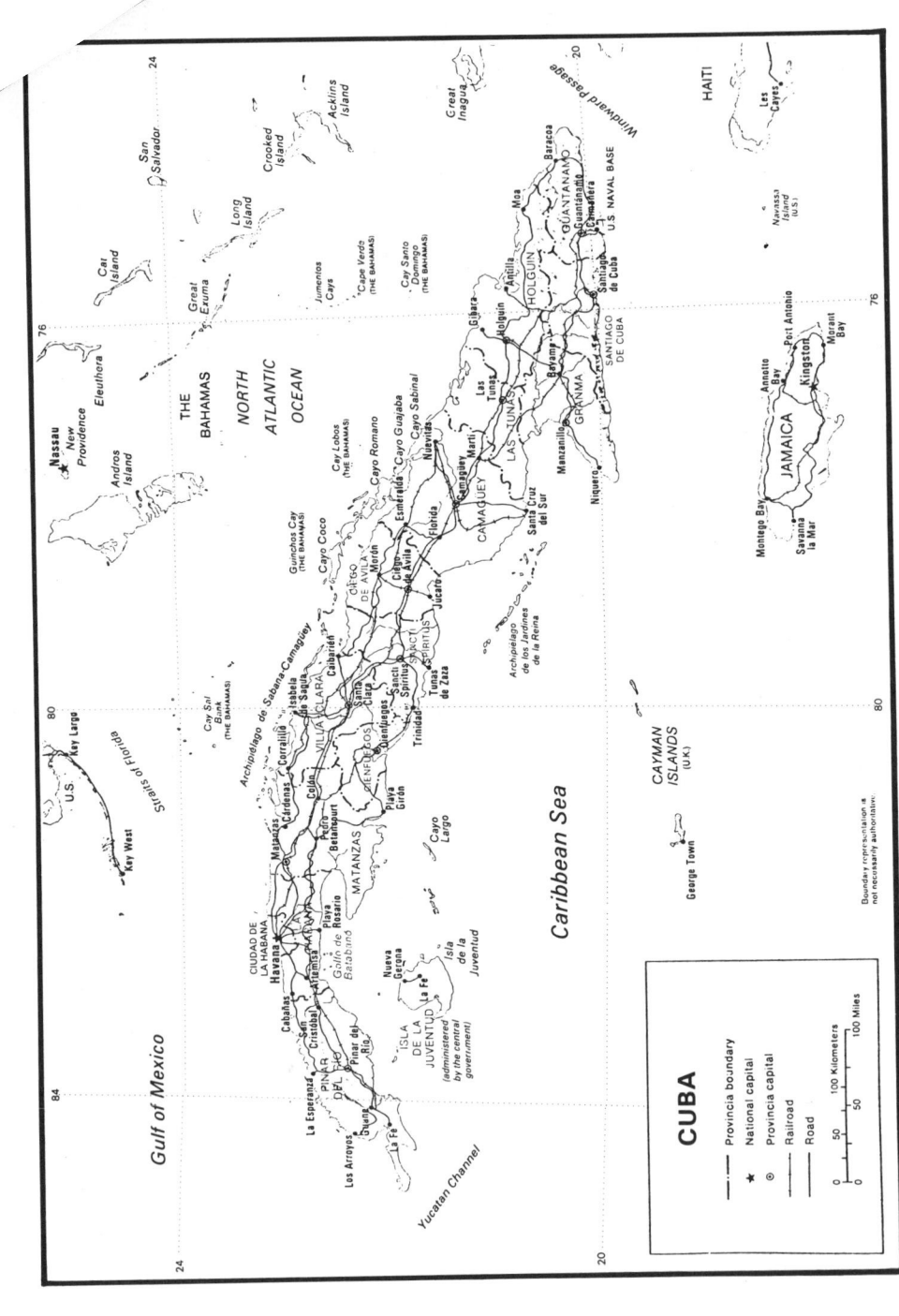

Cuba: Twenty-Five Years of Revolution, 1959–1984

edited by
Sandor Halebsky
and
John M. Kirk

PRAEGER SPECIAL STUDIES • PRAEGER SCIENTIFIC

New York • Philadelphia • Eastbourne, UK
Toronto • Hong Kong • Tokyo • Sydney

Library of Congress Cataloging in Publication Data
Main entry under title:

Cuba—twenty-five years of revolution, 1959–1984

   Bibliography: p.
   Includes index.
   1. Cuba—Civilization—1959-   —Addresses, essays,
lectures.   I. Halebsky, Sandor.   II. Kirk, John M.
III. Title: Cuba—25 years of revolution, 1959–1984.
F1788.C826   1985   972.91'064   84-26494
ISBN 0-03-071637-3
ISBN 0-03-071636-5 (pbk.)

Published in 1985 by Praeger Publishers
CBS Educational and Professional Publishing
A Division of CBS, Inc.
521 Fifth Avenue, New York, New York 10175 U.S.A.

© 1985 by Praeger Publishers

All rights reserved

56789   145   987654321

Printed in the United States of America on acid-free paper.

Contents

ACKNOWLEDGMENTS		ix
PERMISSION ACKNOWLEDGMENTS		xi
SECTION I.	**INTRODUCTION**	**1**
	Editors' Introduction	3
	25 Years of the Cuban Revolution *Fidel Castro*	19
SECTION II.	**SOCIAL REVOLUTION**	**25**
1	Cuba's Schools: 25 Years Later *Marvin Leiner*	27
2	Medicine in the Community *Ross Danielson*	45
3	Cuba's Food Distribution System *Joseph Collins and Medea Benjamin*	62
4	Women in Socialist Cuba, 1959–84 *Alfred Padula and Lois Smith*	79
5	From Counterrevolution to *Modus Vivendi*: The Church in Cuba, 1959–84 *John M. Kirk*	93
SECTION III.	**CULTURAL CHANGE**	**115**
6	The Emergence of Popular Culture *Judith A. Weiss*	117
7	Film and Revolution in Cuba: The First Twenty-Five Years *Julianne Burton*	134

8 Criticism and Literature in
Revolutionary Cuba
Roberto González Echevarría   154

SECTION IV.   ECONOMIC REFORM   175

9 Economic Policy and Development
Models
Joel C. Edelstein   177

10 Cuba: Redistribution and Growth
with Equity
Claes Brundenius   193

11 Cuban Economic Planning:
Organization and Performance
Andrew Zimbalist   213

SECTION V.   POLITICAL PROCESS AND CHANGE   231

12 Continuity and Evolution of
Revolutionary Symbolism in
Verde Olivo
C. Fred Judson   233

13 Cuban Political Structure: Vanguard
Party and the Masses
Rhoda Pearl Rabkin   251

14 The Organs of People's Power and
the Communist Party: The Nature of
Cuban Democracy
Archibald R.M. Ritter   270

15 Class, Organization, and *Conciencia*:
The Cuban Working Class After 1970
Marifeli Pérez-Stable   291

16 Socialist Legality and Practice:
The Cuban Experience
Max Azicri   307

| SECTION VI. | FOREIGN POLICY DEVELOPMENTS | 331 |

17 U.S.–Cuba Relations: Twenty-Five Years of Hostility
    Wayne S. Smith — 333

18 Cuba, the Soviet Union, and Third World Struggle
    Marjorie Woodford Bray and Donald W. Bray — 352

19 Cuban Internationalism
    Susan Eckstein — 372

| SECTION VII. | OVERVIEWS | 391 |

20 The Cuban Revolution Twenty-Five Years Later: A Survey of Sources, Scholarship, and State of the Literature
    Louis A. Pérez, Jr. — 393

21 Cuba: A Revolution of the People (November 23, 1960)
    A. Gunder Frank — 413

22 Why Is Cuba Different?
    Arthur MacEwan — 420

23 The Cuban Revolution: An Historical Perspective
    James F. Petras and Morris H. Morley — 429

24 Impressions on Twenty-Five Years of Change
    Philip S. Foner — 437

25 Cuba: A Personal Overview
    Margaret Randall — 442

INDEX — 447

ABOUT THE EDITORS — 457

ABOUT THE CONTRIBUTORS — 459

For the Cuban and Central American people struggling to create new futures and new societies, may they persevere over all threats.

Acknowledgments

The editors would like to acknowledge the assistance of Lynda Sharp, our editor at Praeger, the editorial assistance from the people at Publication Services, and secretarial help from Noreen Miller, Wanda Hebb, Joanne Sinclair, and Pat Kyle. Other who have helped in various ways are Jorge I. Domínguez, Sandra Levinson of the Center for Cuban Studies in New York, and Margo Kirk. Finally, gratitude should be expressed to our contributors who met deadlines with promptness, responded well to all suggestions and minor revisions, and who in general proved more cooperative than editors have a right to expect. On behalf of all, we hope this study will awaken the need among many for a fresh appraisal of Cuba for, with apologies to Franklin D. Roosevelt's famous discourse (crucially important in the context of the renewed Cold War): God made us neighbors—we should try at least *not* to be enemies.

Permission Acknowledgments

A number of the present chapters in part draw on earlier published essays. Appreciation is here gratefully acknowledged for permission to use some of this earlier material.

Fidel Castro: 25 Years of the Cuban Revolution
The complete speech from which this is excerpted originally appeared in *Granma Weekly Review,* January 7, 1984 and was reprinted in *Cuba Update,* vol. 5, no. 1, January/February 1984 published by the Center for Cuban Studies, New York.

Marvin Leiner: Cuba's Schools: 25 Years Later
This essay is an updated version of "Two Decades of Educational Change in Cuba," *Journal of Reading,* vol. 25, no. 3 (December 1981), pp. 202-214. Reprinted with permission of the International Reading Association.

Ross Danielson: Medicine in the Community
The author expresses his gratitude to Transaction Books of New Brunswick, N.J. and to the journal *Social Science and Medicine* 15 (1981), pp. 239-247, published by Pergamon Press, Inc. for permission to draw upon his earlier work, *Cuban Medicine.* He is also grateful to Margaret Gilpin for allowing him to review her work and for updated health statistics.

Joseph Collins and Medea Benjamin: Cuba's Food Distribution System
For a more detailed discussion of the points raised in this chapter see the forthcomin work by the authors (together with Michael Scott), *No Free Lunch: Food and Revolution in Cuba Today* to be published in early 1985 by the Institute for Food and Development Policy.

Julianne Burton: Film and Revolution in Cuba: The First Twenty-Five Years
This essay is a revised and updated version of a more extensive study published as "Cinéma Cubain" in Guy Hennebelle and Alfonso Gumucio Dagron, eds., *Les Cinémas de l'Amérique Latine* (Paris: Textimages), 1981, pp. 259–79, which appeared in an abbreviated English version as the introduction to a three-part special section, "Revolutionary Cuban Cinema," in *Jump/Cut: A Review of Contemporary Cinema* (Chicago and Berkeley), no. 19, December 1978, pp. 17–20; no. 20, May 1979, pp. 12–29; and no. 22, May 1980, pp. 25–34 also form part of the special section on Cuban cinema.

Roberto González Echevarría: Criticism and Literature in Revolutionary Cuba
This chapter is an updated version of an essay published in *Cuban Studies/Estudios Cubanos,* vol. 11, no. 1 (January 1981): 1–17.

Joel C. Edelstein: Economic Policy and Development Models
This is a revised version of an earlier article, "The Evolution of Cuban Development Strategy," published in *From Dependency to Development,* ed. Heraldo Muñoz (Boulder, Colorado: Westview, 1981), pp. 225–66.

Claes Brundenius: Cuba: Redistribution and Growth with Equity
Portions of this chapter are reprinted from the author's previous essay, "Growth with Equity: The Cuban Experience (1959–1980)," *World Development,* vol. 9, no. 11/12 (1981): 1083–1107. Reprinted with permission from Pergamon Press, Ltd.

Andrew Zimbalist: Cuban Economic Planning: Organization and Performance
Portions of this chapter are reprinted from "Cuba: Socialism Next Door," in Andrew Zimbalist and Howard Sherman, *Comparing Economic Systems: A Political Economic Approach* (New York: Academic Press, 1984). Reprinted with permission of Academic Press. The author wishes to thank Susan Eckstein, Arthur MacEwan, Nola Reinhardt, and José Luis Rodríguez for useful comments on earlier incarnations of this essay.

Archibald R.M. Ritter: The Organs of People's Power and the Communist Party: The Nature of Cuban Democracy

This essay is a modification and updating of an earlier essay entitled "The Authenticity of Participatory Democracy in Cuba," in Archibald R.M. Ritter and David H. Pollock, eds., *Latin American Prospects for the 1980s: Equity, Democratization and Development* (New York: Praeger, 1983), pp. 182–213.

Max Azicri: Socialist Legality and Practice: The Cuban Experience
An earlier version of this study was presented at the XIIth World Congress of the International Political Sciences Association, Rio de Janeiro, Brazil, August 1982.

Susan Eckstein: Cuban Internationalism
Portions of this chapter are reprinted from "Structural and Ideological Bases of Cuba's Overseas Programs." *Politics and Society* 11 (1982), pp. 95–121.

Section I
Introduction

Editors' Introduction

> It is to the *substance* of these matters that we are going, rather than to the forms.... It is a case of changing a nation's soul, their entire way of thinking and acting, and not just their external clothes.[1]
>
> *José Martí*

Writing in *Patria*, the journal of the Partido Revolucionario Cubano, in May 1892, José Martí expressed with his customary eloquence the need for a fundamental change in the Cuban political, social, and economic systems. He urged his fellow Cubans to be authentic radicals in the Latin sense of the term, as he noted the following year, "Really that is a true radical: someone who gets to the root." Some 60 years later a young and articulate lawyer, Fidel Castro, stormed the Moncada garrison and in his defense speech presented a searing condemnation of Cuban reality, claiming Martí as the "intellectual author" of his plans. The rest is history.

Few events in Latin American history have exercised as much influence as the Cuban Revolution—whether in international politics, educational reform, or cultural innovations. For this reason a discussion of the revolutionary process is a controversial matter. There are few neutral views about the Cuban Revolution: you are either totally opposed to the subordination of individual liberal values to the rights of the masses, or you praise the collective gains made by the vast majority at the expense of a minority. The result of this impassioned debate is a lack of understanding of the Cuban process, which, as Wayne Smith suggests in Chapter 17 has been exploited by several U.S. administrations.

This critical anthology addresses the general misunderstandings concerning the Cuban Revolution and attempts to provide a more balanced overview of the revolutionary process. While some essays by leading *cubanólogos* in the United States, Europe, and Canada highlight the dramatic advances and improvements gained by the Cuban people, others detail negative aspects of the process. Both viewpoints must be presented if we are to comprehend the nature of the Cuban phenomenon, which has had a major impact on the world. It is our hope that a more rational understanding of the Cuban experience will result.

BEFORE THE REVOLUTION

Since our contributors detail the evolution of the revolutionary process in their particular field of expertise since 1959, it is necessary for readers to examine the pre-revolutionary context in order to appreciate conditions prior to the revolution.

There is an old and somewhat racist Cuban joke that illustrates the need to set the historical context. A large international conference is studying the role and importance of the elephant in the modern world. The Japanese delegation, following group calisthenics, presents a study on the relationship between the microchip and the elephant. The French group's paper is a detailed examination of the elephant's sex life. The German delegates thoroughly analyze the economic mechanical design of the elephant's bone structure, while the American delegates, neatly attired in matching red, white, and blue sportscoats, present an inspirational essay—liberally sprinkled with quotations from the presidents of Amway and McDonald's corporations—on the market value and profitability of the elephant. The Cuban delegate finally arrives, a day late, and frantically begins to type his presentation. The following morning he strides to the podium, a chewed cigar perched between his lips, and begins, "Before the revolution...."

This story illustrates the need to examine life prior to the overthrow of Fulgencio Batista, since without such a context one is left with only an automatic acceptance or rejection of the revolutionary process since 1959. We would encourage our readers to explore this field for themselves, since it will provide an invaluable context for analyzing the positive and negative aspects of the quarter century of revolution experienced by Cuba. Useful suggestions for further readings can be found in Chapter 20 by Louis Pérez.

In their insightful study of the food distribution system in Chapter 3, Joseph Collins and Medea Benjamin confront the erroneous perception that results when one uncritically examines figures concerned with "development." Thus, while Cubans were seemingly better off than the vast majority of Latin Americans in the late 1950s, there were grave disparities between the apparent "norm" and reality. According to Collins and Benjamin, while the per capita consumption of meat was 70 pounds annually, actually only 4 percent of peasants ate meat regularly, and only 2 percent consumed eggs on a regular basis. In 1951 a World Bank team estimated that, at the very least, some 30 percent of urban dwellers and 60 percent of rural dwellers suffered from malnutrition.

Twenty years ago, Robert Scheer and Maurice Zeitlin emphasized the complex social differences in prerevolutionary Cuba: "There were really two splits in Cuban society. One was between the upper and lower classes; the other between the residents of Havana and the rest of Cuba, which the upper classes referred to as the 'interior,' as if it were another world."[2] Certainly Havana was in a far better situation than the rest of the island as far as employment, housing, education, health care, and nutrition were concerned.

Health care and education—the twin jewels in the revolutionary crown—were restricted in prerevolutionary Cuba, particularly for rural dwellers. The vast majority of hospital beds and medical personnel were concentrated in Havana and, to a lesser extent, in provincial capitals. As a result, "few rural families could afford medical care in those few localities where adequate care was available and... more than 13 percent of the rural population suffered from intestinal parasites, 14 percent had suffered at some time from tuberculosis, and 13 percent had suffered from typhoid fever."[3] Susan Schroeder notes that in 1958, "with incomplete information," some 2,784 children died of "enteritis and other diarrheic conditions" largely due to unsanitary living conditions and lack of access to appropriate medical facilities. In 1961 this increased to 3,009 but by 1974, the last date she provides, the number had dropped to 62.[4]

In his landmark studies on Cuba, Professor Hugh Thomas, a Latin American adviser to British Prime Minister Thatcher, provided a very clear picture of prerevolutionary social conditions. He indicated that the percentage of illiterates in 1953 was actually increasing—despite the facade of "development" in Havana.[5] Thus, while 30 percent of Havana's teenagers might go to school, only 7 percent of those in rural areas attended.[6] Citing a 1956 survey among peasant families, Thomas noted that in all of Cuba, "about 45% had never been to school and, of those who had been, nearly 90% had not got beyond the third grade. Batista was thus a good deal less successful than Machado in his schools policy."[7]

Living conditions in prerevolutionary Cuba, particularly in rural areas, should also be examined. The government's own census in 1953 categorized 15 percent of the nation's housing as *ruinoso* ("worthless") and 31 percent as "bad." Yet while these statistics are grim, it is worth noting that in rural areas some 75.2 percent of all dwellings were termed *ruinoso*.[8] Susan Schroeder's figures amplify these statistics and her "Comparison of the Standard of Living of Agricultural Workers, 1946 and 1957" notes that only 37.6 percent of houses in the countryside did not have dirt floors; only 36 percent of houses had toilets; only 5.9 percent had plumbing and running water; and only 7.3 percent had electric lighting. Moreover, while in 1946 some 29.7 percent of houses were termed "in good condition," this had decreased to 22.1 percent in 1957.[9]

In assessing the prerevolutionary historical context, one must also consider the following: unemployment and underemployment rates following the *zafra* ("sugar harvest"), the degree of racism, the police brutality, the political corruption on the part of the government,[10] the generally sordid atmosphere of prerevolutionary Havana and its reputation as a fleshpot and a place for business junkets to "sin in the sun," and the foreign control of key sectors of the Cuban economy. All contributed to the residents' frustration with the status quo and their desire for a profound change. It is not surprising, then, that the White House—in a rare moment of lucidity and with the advantage of hindsight—should note in 1961 that conditions in prerevolutionary Cuba "constituted an open invitation to revolution."[11]

In 1959 Cuba embarked on a radical new direction as it attempted to right these many wrongs and build a new, independent, and free society. The dream of Fidel Castro and the other *barbudos* ("bearded ones") in 1959 probably closely resembled what José Martí wanted in 1891. The famous "Resolutions Taken by the Cuban Immigrants in Tampa on November 27, 1891," drawn up by Martí, called for Cubans "to build a just, open Republic, united in its territory, law, work, and cordiality, in short a Republic created with the help of all and for the good of all."[12] Our readers are invited to study the following chapters, which reflect various levels of praise and criticism of the Cuban process, and then decide to what extent this has been realized.

THE ANTHOLOGY PROPER: SOME BROADER QUESTIONS AND CONTEXTS

The most profound and exciting transformations wrought by the Cuban Revolution in the past 25 years have been social ones, changes in the lives and propects of its citizenry. These changes are detailed in Section II. It is significant to note the link between these changes and one of the significant issues implicated in efforts at economic development and social transformations. Is the historic phenomenon of growing internal disparities in numbers, power, wealth, services, and the like within a nation—between regions, urban and rural populations, and classes—the inevitable outcome of development; or is it the result of one particular form of change, that is, development derived from capitalist processes and models?

One of the major concerns of Cuban policy has been to reduce inequalities and secure balanced population and equitable social and economic growth between regions, communities, and social sectors. A major aspect of such policy has been to diminish the inequalities between urban and country areas, particularly the dominance of the primate city of Havana. Cuba's policy has been succinctly stated by Fidel Castro as "a minimum of urbanism and a maximum of ruralism." While the evidence is not all in, the Cuban experience provides strong evidence that internal inequalities need not be an inherent outcome of development. Nationwide accomplishments in the areas of health, education, food distribution, and improved living standards support such a conclusion, as do the strides made in the decentralization of industry, in economic development, and in the notable achievement of curbing the spiraling growth of Havana.

The achievements in the field of education reveal most strongly the Cuban ability to both carry out an economic development program while bridging the gulf between rural and urban, between Havana and the remainder of the country, and between social classes. The 1961 literacy campaign provided an elementary level of literacy to those lacking such a skill, a population disproportionately poor and rural. More importantly, it brought the urban and rural populations into intimate contact and symbolized the commitment of the nation to a nonexploitative integration with all disadvantaged social sectors and regions of the society. Since 1970 rural areas have received a disproportionate amount of funds. This is exhibited in a number of programs, most notably the schools in the country program. The location of the schools and the joining of education with farm labor seeks to bridge the gap between manual and nonmanual work, countryside and urban, and the invidious attitudes toward the former.

Health care achievements include the reduction of the regional and countryside imbalance in the availability of medical facilities and personnel. Disparities were also lessened by nationwide public health measures, immunization campaigns, and the like. Other policies and programs—the early agrarian reform, the continued application of resources to agriculture, controlled prices and very low rents, free or low cost services, full employment—serve to diminish disparities in the standard of living, as a rise in the social wage and related programs diminish the real differences in wage levels between Havana and elsewhere and between regions. The culture revitalization of the last 25 years has also had a nationwide character.

To significantly reduce regional and class inequalities, and urban-rural imbalance, additional policies were required. The programs put into effect were various. They included the expansion of the infrastructure (railroads, highways, irrigation, etc.), especially in the eastern portions of the country, development of light industry variously in the nation, development of the mineral resources of Oriente province, diversification and decentralization of the economy and an effort for greater regional self-reliance, and the development of an imaginative "new town" program that has created hundreds of communities throughout the country and, in an important sense, an urbanization of the countryside. Joined with the other steps taken the combined effects of such programs are various, the most important being they create conditions of greater equity, and they remove the major impetus for migration out of these areas and into Havana by meeting the economic, social, and housing needs of more disadvantaged regions and the countryside. Thus the common Third World phenomenon of transplanting rural and regional inequalities and problems into the increasingly crowded and fetid primate city is directly and successfully confronted by a set of policies in Cuba that deal with the roots of existing inequalities and population migration. Thus, in comparison with the doubling of population common in many major Latin American cities within a space of 15 years or so, Havana's population growth in the 1970s was only 7.7 percent, scarcely more than half of the rate of national population growth (and its percentage of the total national population has actually declined from 1971 to 1981). The most rapid provincial growth from 1971 to 1981 occurred in the eastern and central provinces.

What the Cuban experience suggests is that a growing imbalance between communities, regions, and classes in not an inevitable consequence of either economic change or development. What is of particular interest is that the measures which stem and even reverse growing social, economic, and population disparities are ones unlikely to be initiated by nonrevolutionary/nonsocialist states. Carrying out a Cuban-style development program means, in effect, shifting power, resources, symbolic merit, and other valued resources away from those with power in such societies—generally urban and primate-based political elites, middle-class and professional elements, and business interests profiting from available migrant or cheap labor. It means various professional personnel working other than in the primary urban center(s) of the country. It involves the urban youth going to the countryside, performing manual labor, and the like. It requires putting societal or collective aims above individual and material purposes. Thus, on all these grounds it will be opposed. The programs pursued in Cuba require a political leadership committed to societal transformation and greater equity, oriented to the countryside, and powerful enough to implement its policies. These are conditions lacking in other Third World nonsocialist societies.

While there are some significant similarities between part of the analysis offered here and Claes Brundenius's treatment of growth with equity (in Chapter 10), the present discussion develops the central issue somewhat differently, by introducing its spatial or regional component.

The topics covered in the first three chapters of Section II on Cuba's social revolution include education (Marvin Leiner), medicine (Ross Danielson), and nutrition (Joseph Collins and Medea Benjamin). The broad range of social change in Cuba is examined in the two final contributions. Chapter 4 by Alfred Padula and Lois Smith details both the advances Cuban women have made and their existing struggles, and in Chapter 5 John Kirk offers an analysis of how a conservative church overtaken by revolutionary change seeks to come to terms with it.

* * *

Dramatic cultural change is understandably a major component of any revolutionary movement, and the Cuban case is no exception. As in economic matters, Cuba's cultural activities in prerevolutionary times clearly depended on North American models and, as is so often the case in Latin America, indigenous cultural values were frequently downplayed—

if not totally ignored. That has changed drastically, although popular U.S. music and the existence of dozens of Florida radio stations less than 100 miles away still have a magnetic effect, particularly among Cuban youth.

However, it is clear that Cuba has conscientiously and carefully developed independent cultural expressions and despite an occasionally heavy-handed approach, has been remarkably successful in this campaign. In North America, too, the influence of this cultural boom has been felt. Film festivals featuring recent Cuban movies have taken place in several U.S. and Canadian cities; concerts featuring a variety of musicians, such as classical guitarist Leo Brouwer, the traditional "Orquesta Aragón" or the modern jazz-rock group "Los Irakere" have been well received. Cuban posters and paintings have been exhibited in various art centers; and the legendary Alicia Alonso and other members of Cuban ballet companies have danced to rave reviews in North America. Given the nature of prerevolutionary Cuban cultural expression, this movement has been phenomenal.

Section III includes recent pieces on a variety of cultural matters. The essay by Judith Weiss sets the scene for a discussion of cultural reform, providing an introduction to cultural advances in a variety of activities, from an outline of the development of cultural policy to a study of the local *casas de cultura*, the emergence of the "revolutionary pop-folk" music by the *Nueva Trova* movement, and regional theater groups. Julianne Burton details the impressive development of the film industry, studying both the documentary and feature film production and analyzing the role played by the national film institute (ICAIC). The final piece in this section is Roberto Gonzáles Echevarría's thoughtful summary of the emergence of literature and academic criticism over the past 25 years. The final section of this essay—in essence a criticism of Cuban cultural policy—provides an opinion contrary to the generally positive interpretations of Professors Burton and Weiss. All three agree, however, that the revolutionary process has had a major impact upon the cultural awareness of Cubans, who engage in such pursuits to an astonishing degree. Reasons for such awareness include the decentralization of cultural administration, the dramatic educational reforms implemented, and extensive subsidies of books and artistic activities.

* * *

The Cuban effort to develop and reorganize their economy can be better understood if it is placed within a broader context. Cuba is in an unenviable position, as are the other twentieth century societies that have initiated or maintained a revolution under the banner of socialism. It confronts both the need to transform social relations and the task of developing the productive forces of society. Marxist theory assumed that in the course of capitalist evolution the development of the economy would be carried through by the bourgeoisie, with revolution arising from the contradictions appearing within the fully developed capitalist economy. However, it is not within the industrial nations but within the Third World that successful revolutions have taken place. The reality has been that socialist regimes confront an underdeveloped economy, not an industrial one, and become principally involved in the task of its transformation.

Cuba and other socialist states have found that Marxist theory, the ideological basis for the transformation of Cuban society, offers few substantial guidelines for the achievement of either a developed economy or the transformation of social or political relationships. Nor has it shed much light on the more specific question of the structure and process of production relations in a socialized economy, that is of relationships at the level of the workplace. The importance of the latter concern is both ideological and moral, as well as being relevant to the narrower issue of successful economic development. New attitudes and values toward work and the collectivity do not arise merely with the destruction of prerevolutionary social and political structures. They have to be nourished and supported by appropriate organizational forms and conditions of responsiveness. And new attitudes may also mean increased labor productivity. Contributors in both Sections IV and V on economic and political reform discuss the efforts and policy fluctuation directed toward attaining both economic development and a transformation of class relations and, somewhat less successfully, participatory forms of production relationships and nonmaterial labor incentives. Many of the dilemmas, achievements, and qualified success attained in these diversions of revolutionary change are illustrated in these essays.

A number of factors has shaped or characterized development policy. One such factor was Cuba's dependence on the U.S. as a market for raw materials and source of goods, machine parts, and the like, and the costly readjustments that the American embargo entailed. More general is Cuba's partial dependence on the world capitalist economy. Reliance on world economic market conditions has at times created severe problems, although significantly mitigated by Soviet assistance. However, the ties to COMECON—another of the external involvements—

may carry other less significant consequences for Cuban economic growth. In contrast to traditional forms of socialist development, Cuba has given agriculture a leading role. The reasons are a mix of ideological commitment to the farmer and rural sector, the need for foreign exchange, and the assured market and price provided by the Soviet bloc for a portion of the sugar harvest.

Apparent in many of the following essays is the relationship between economic policy and other spheres of Cuban society and policy. Every nation, of course, exhibits a relationship between economy and society. In Cuba it assumes its own distinctive form, as transcending capitalism requires change in all spheres of the society. Thus, for instance, an intimate link exists between economic policy structure and the transformation of class relations, the redistribution of resources, increased equity, decentralization, the reorganization of labor, forms of motivation, sources of political support and regime legitimacy, and the like.

Many changes are occurring in economic development strategy and organization. The reasons for this include the far-ranging and in many ways experimental nature of some efforts, the less institutionalized character of earlier decision making, the consequences of the voluntaristic element in Cuban revolutionary thought and behavior, the Cuban revolutionary movement's pragmatic spirit and openness to innovation, and crucial elements in Cuba's relations to the two superpowers, the United States and the Soviet Union. In view of the extensive development efforts and the extensive support provided by the Soviet Union, the still considerable distance to be covered suggests how great are the barriers to development for the small Third World nations heavily dependent on primary production.

The particulars of economic strategy and organization, its link to other purposes and goals, and the accomplishments and difficulties experienced in the Cuban effort at economic reform are detailed in the contributions by Joel Edelstein (Chapter 9) and Andrew Zimbalist (Chapter 11). Claes Brundenius provides a broadly focused account of the accomplishments of the Cuban economy in terms of economic growth, the satisfaction of basic needs, and increased equity in Chapter 10. Other selections also consider concerns relevant to economic reform, such as, the Collins and Benjamin contribution on the food distribution system and Marifeli Pérez-Stable's discussion of workplace organization.

* * *

The dominant and guiding role of the state in societies undergoing revolutionary change, including Cuba, is important to remember when examining the political structure and process of such societies. The centrality of the state is vital in defending and advancing revolutionary transformation. At the same time it makes more precarious the possible range of freedom permitted and heightens the importance of access to and control over the state. The dominance of the state lends special importance to the question of the character of democratic forms and practices. Consideration of such a question, however, requires taking account of the circumstances and dilemmas faced by the revolutionary society. While application of abstract standards or criteria of democratic functioning are useful, both in regard to capitalist and socialist states, attention to the situation faced by revolutionary states is essential if abstractions are to be translated into terms both meaningful and responsive to the realities of socialist societies. This need not mean total acceptance of Cuban practices, of course, but it may suggest a more realistic and even-handed assessment than would otherwise be attained.

A number of factors are relevant. For one, revolutionary states experience a much higher degree of threat, internally and externally, than established democratic societies. Obviously, the threat goes far beyond that of armed action. With the overthrow of the previous government there may be many groups disadvantaged by, and adverse to, revolutionary reforms and hostile to the rural and working class population upon which the new regime is based. They are a potential threat to the revolution. Another factor is that the transformation of institutions and political culture and the development of political capacity and consciousness within the population is a long-term process.

While large sectors of a population may be supportive of the new revolutionary regime, the greater part of this population probably will have played little role in the victory of the revolution, had few links with the revolutionary militants, or had little organizational experience in revolutionary struggle. Revolutionary consciousness and awareness may be modest, in terms of an understanding of changes required and associated policies, the position and purposes of diverse social groups, the limitations of what can be achieved in the short-term, and the willingness—or better, the understanding—of the degree of sacrifice needed. Expectations may exceed the reality. The years that follow a revolution are difficult ones, especially since revolutions arise in societies already beset by problems for which no rapid solution is possible. In addition, there is likely to be the need for economic reconstruction, the rebuilding of treasuries and physical plant, the problem of severed trade links, the absence of spare parts for factories, and so forth. Similar problems were faced by Cuba.

In such circumstances an erosion of the revolutionary consensus may occur in the years that follow the revolution. Similarly, groups seeking to derail or weaken socialist transformation (although at times their programs may not be explicit on this point) may gain acceptance. Without first developing organization and consciousness among the popular base of the new government, including an understanding of what successful revolutionary change implies and requires in terms of sacrifice, commitment, and priorities, an informed comprehension of local and national problems and their linkage, and a sense of the play of different interests and purposes, too precipitous an initiation of large scale electoral democratic forms could destabilize the revolution.

Nonetheless, if the revolution is not to blight the human spirit, as well as its own goals of equity and opportunity, it must be responsive to many of the freedoms and democratic forms slowly secured, even if rather imperfectly elaborated, in the western bourgeois societies. The concentration of power in the hands of the regime runs the risk that without a more open and representative electoral political system power and position may coalesce, probably within a political and bureaucratic elite joined to managerial and professional social sectors. The resulting isolation of the government and growth of a new class would seriously jeopardize some of the major purposes of the revolution. Yet, in light of the circumstances noted, democratic forms cannot necessarily be wholly transplanted upon the assumption of power by a revolutionary regime.

From the perspective suggested here the crucial question that requires consideration is how to secure the representation, participation, and effective voice of the population and, analogously, the accountability of political and organizational leaders, while maintaining the security of the revolution and a modicum of cohesiveness. It is a difficult question for which there are no simple or ready answers. All we would suggest are a range of forms and practices useful in achieving a democratic order in substance and responsiveness, not merely in form. As such they go beyond those currently existing in many of the older democracies. Some useful elements might be a forum or mode of representation of diverse social sectors, opportunities for more direct control over services by the relevant population, closer and more responsive relationships between electorate and representatives, stronger organization and representation of mass-based interest collectivities, more effective means of citizen information networks and communication, and a wider political agenda, among other conditions.

The Cuban political structure and process has offered a flawed response to a question for which no ready answer is available. Yet, it has made some significant beginnings. One senses that in the arena of local-based concerns—those in one's immediate environment—the Cuban citizen secures greater input, greater responsiveness, and a greater sense of efficacy than appears to be the case in Western democratic societies, where a sense of powerlessness and estrangement on local, as well as national affairs, is considerable. This and other efforts are examined in Section V.

However, even acknowledging the circumstances discussed previously and faced by Cuba and other similar societies, significant reservations can be raised in regard to a number of the properties of the Cuban political system. The introduction of political forms of representation and responsiveness in organizations and the broader community were long delayed. Constraints and party dominance in these spheres are unreasonably great. Organized opposition is prohibited. Constraints on civil liberties exceed the requirements of the system. Serious as such conditions are, judgment can be tempered by the very real and considerable limitations and apprehensions that the Cuban revolutionaries faced. In addition, it is important to recognize the increased democratic strengths of the Cuban system and the real and important arenas within which citizens and their representatives can exercise a vigorous role (e.g., the local Organs for Popular Power, local health districts, and the provision of basic services). However, the ground still to be covered is considerable.

The contributions in Section V, "Political Process and Change," offer a fuller discussion and assessment of a number of the issues raised here. The structural and processional elements of the political system generally, with particular attention to the role and character of the Communist Party as a vanguard party is considered by Rhoda Pearl Rapkin in Chapter 13. The Organs of Popular Power and the question of democratic participation is detailed by Archibald R.M. Ritter in Chapter 14. Marifeli Pérez-Stable examines the changing organization and authority of the trade unions in Chapter 15, and in Chapter 16 Max Azicri discusses the evolution of the legal and justice system. Very different in its concerns and style, Chapter 12 by C. Fred Judson reveals the important role assigned to national symbols and myths in the process of developing the strong commitment and motivation necessary for a revolutionary transformation of self and society.

* * *

Few subjects in the international arena are as charged with emotion and contention as Cuba, in terms of its own internal characteristics and development, as well as in regard to its relations with other nations. The reasons are not hard to find. They involve questions of national prestige, hegemony, and independence, a great deal of which is situated in the vortex of the U.S.-Soviet rivalry. Cuba's revolution and survival, especially after an exceedingly close and dominant U.S. presence of 60 years and in the face of the abortive Bay of Pigs invasion in 1961 and the U.S. embargo, signalled a significant crack in the American hegemony in the Caribbean and Latin America. The impotence exhibited by America's failed effort at rape in 1961 may have had still other consequences for the American psyche. And all this but 90 miles off the southern shore of Florida! Clearly, the situation is immeasurably compounded by Cuba's alliance with the Soviet Union and the support it provides at the international level. In a different although related direction, concern over Cuba reflects apprehensions over the possibility of her serving as a model for independent and revolutionary change for other Third World societies. Concern also arises from the ability of Cuba to project power on a worldwide scale, as in Africa. In addition, the properties of independence and the social accomplishments of the revolution, aided by the charismatic and purposive role of Fidel Castro, have permitted Cuba to play an active role as a spokesman for Third World concerns. The response to Cuba and its international role is also heightened by an elaborate set of contractual and other aid relationships that it maintains with many Third World nations.

Many questions can be raised concerning Cuba's international presence and nation-to-nation relationships. For instance, what are the circumstances of its break with the United States? Has Cuba avoided improvement of relationships with the United States? To what extent is Cuba a surrogate for the Soviet Union? What has been Cuba's role in Africa? What is the nature of its role among other Third World nations? What are the characteristics, advantages, and costs of Cuba's foreign aid programs? The three essays in Section VI "Foreign Policy Developments," span a broad range of concerns and shed light not only on these queries but on other matters as well. In Chapter 17 Wayne Smith brings his many years of first-hand diplomatic experience with Cuba to an analysis of U.S.-Cuban relations. In Chapter 18 Marjorie Woodford and Donald Bray offer a thorough and sensitive analysis of Cuba's political role among the Third World nations, while Susan Eckstein provides a comprehensive analysis of the character and benefits of Cuba's considerable overseas programs in Chapter 19.

* * *

Each of the contributions in Section VII is a response to or overview of the Cuban experience. Louis Pérez, Jr. provides a sense of the scholarly ferment aroused by the Cuban Revolution and the changing concerns of such scholarship and he offers an excellent guide to much of the literature. The remaining four brief essays are of a more personal nature, especially Chapters 21, 24, and 25 by André Gunder Frank, Philip Foner, and Margaret Randall, respectively. Frank's comments of November 1960 have a special poignancy as they catch the tone of the Cuban experience in the opening heady days of the revolution, while Foner's and Randall's reflections in April and May of 1984 trace the evolving nature of the Cuban revolution as experienced over the years by two sympathetic observers. The other contributions offer two different responses to the Cuban Revolution, but responses that share a concern with explaining those circumstances, internal and external, during and prior to the revolution, that have significantly shaped part of the trajectory of the revolution. In an historically sensitive analysis, Arthur MacEwan explains why Cuban society is more open than other socialist states such as the Soviet Union. In Chapter 23 James Petras's and Morris Morley's analysis offers the reader an understanding of the particularities in the Cuban situation that have shaped the evolution of the Cuban Revolution. While both essays appear in the concluding section of personal responses to the revolution, they also offer the reader a basis for understanding some of the discussions that have appeared earlier in the volume.

NOTES

1. José Martí, *Obras Completas* (La Habana: Editorial Nacional de Cuba, 1963–66), vol. 5, pp. 368–69.
2. Robert Scheer and Maurice Zeitlin, *Cuba, an American Tragedy* (Harmondsworth, England: Penguin Books, 1964), p. 18.
3. Cited in Jan Knippers Black et al., eds., *Area Handbook for Cuba*

(Washington, D.C.: American University, Foreign Area Studies, 1976), pp. 201-02.

4. See Susan Schroeder, *Cuba: A Handbook of Historical Statistics* (Boston: G.K. Hall and Co., 1982), p. 75, (Table III.8, "Five Principal Causes of Death in Children 1-4 Years of Age").

5. "Further, the proportion of illiterates in 1953 was even officially higher—23.5 percent instead of 22 percent—than in 1943." Hugh Thomas, *The Cuban Revolution* (New York: Harper and Row, 1971), p. 349.

6. Ibid., p. 350.

7. Ibid., p. 353.

8. Black, *Area Handbook for Cuba*, p. 195.

9. Schroeder, *A Handbook of Historical Statistics*, p. 199.

10. Herbert L. Matthews, in his readable study, *Revolution in Cuba: An Essay in Understanding* (New York: Charles Scribner's Sons, 1975), p. 31, cites former U.S. Ambassador Philip Bonsal diplomatically noting, "I know of no country among those committed to the Western ethic where the diversion of public treasure for private profit reached the proportions that it attained in the Cuban Republic."

11. Ibid., p. 35.

12. Martí, *Obras Completas*, vol. 1, p. 272.

Fidel Castro: 25 Years of the Cuban Revolution

The following is a speech given by Fidel Castro Ruz, first secretary of the Central Committee of the Communist Party of Cuba and president of the Councils of State and of Ministers, at the solemn ceremony to mark the twenty-fifth anniversary of the victory of the Revolution and the presentation of the honorary title of Hero of the Republic of Cuba and the Antonio Maceo Order to the city of Santiago de Cuba. The ceremony was held in the old City Hall on January 1, 1984, Year of the twenty-fifth anniversary of the triumph of the Revolution.

"We have finally reached Santiago! The road has been long and hard but here we are!

"The Revolution starts now; the Revolution will not be an easy task; the Revolution will be a difficult and hazardous undertaking!

"The Revolution cannot be made overnight, but you can rest assured that we will make the Revolution; you can rest assured that for the first time, truly, the Republic will be totally free and the people will have what they deserve.

"We do not think that all the problems will be solved easily; we know that the road is plagued with obstacles; but we are men of faith who always face great difficulties head on. The people can rest assured of one thing, and that is that we may make mistakes once and many times; but the only thing that they will never be able to say about us is that we embezzled...that we made shady deals, that we betrayed....

"Fortunately, the task of the guns is over. The guns will be kept where the men whose duty it will be to defend out sovereignty and our rights can reach them; but when out people are threatened, not just the thirty or forty thousand members of our armed forces will fight; three hundred thousand, four hundred thousand, five hundred thousand Cubans, men and women alike, who can wield a weapon, will fight....

"The Republic was not free in 1895 and the dream of the *mambises* was frustrated at the last moment. The Revolution was not carried through in 1933 and was foiled by its enemies. This time the Revolution has all the people behind it, all the revolutionaries...its power is so great and so boundless that this time its triumph is assured! We may joyfully say that for the first time in four centuries...we will be entirely free and the work of the *mambises* will be completed....

"The men who fell during out three wars for independence today join their efforts with the men who fell in this war, and we can tell all those who died in our struggles for liberty that the hour has finally come for their dreams to be fulfilled; the time has finally come for you, our people, our fine and noble people...to have what you need."

These words were said twenty-five years ago.

That speech was improvised in the heat of the emotion and amid the whirlwind of events that day. The language has changed. Today we have other goals, objectives and problems, ones that seemed so distant then. It is not necessary to express what has already been demonstrated these 25 years, but the basic ideas of that day, the very ideas that inspired us years before, on the 26th of July 1953, have remained immutable. They are and will continue to be indefeasible.

No mention was made then of the Marxist-Leninist Party, of socialism and of internationalism; capitalism was not even mentioned by name. Indeed, very few would have understood its true meaning at the time. But everything that has happened since then in out homeland, the advancement of our political process to unbelievable heights, the historic place that our people hold today in the world, our ideas and our national experience, all this is the direct result of that sacred revolutionary commitment we made to the people.

* * *

This time frustration was not for the people, but rather for imperialism, the big landowners, the oligarchs, the bourgeois and other reactionaries who were always certain that any revolutionary program in Cuba or Latin America would only remain on paper and wind up in corruption or in the trash can.

If the road that began in Yara on October 10, 1868 to arrive at January 1, 1959 was long, the road that has led us to this twenty-fifth anniversary of the victorious Revolution has been long and hard, glorious and heroic.

* * *

The Revolution did not tremble or waver before the colossal task of doing away with unemployment, illiteracy, ignorance and the calamitous state of public health in our country, creating work centers; child care centers; primary, secondary and high schools; technical schools; universities; special schools for handicapped children; rural hospitals; pediatric, maternal-infant, and clinical-surgical hospitals; polyclinics; dozens of specialized research and medical care centers; and numerous cultural and sports facilities for the mental and physical development of our youth and our people.

It did not tremble or waver in resolutely undertaking the long and difficult road of economic and social development, starting with a backward, deformed and dependent economy, inherited from colonialism, and in the midst of a brutal economic blockade by those who had been our suppliers of equipment, technology, plans and raw materials. A long and difficult road was begun demanding countless efforts, perserverance and sacrifice: the drawing up of five-year and annual plans; the creation of construction, industrial assembly and design enterprises, the building of a solid infrastructure of roads, highways, railways and ports; the creation and development of the merchant and fishing fleets; the mechanization of the sugar harvest and all agricultural activities; the electrification of the countryside; the building of dams and irrigation and drainage canals; the introduction of fertilization and chemicals in general, cattle improvement, artificial insemination and numerous other techniques in our backward agriculture; the beginning of the industrialization of the country; the training of hundreds of thousands of workers, middle-level technicians and university graduates; the founding of dozens of scientific research centers and the development of solid economic relations with the socialist camp; a thoroughly new road in which at the beginning we had no experience whatsoever.

Along this road we have built thousands of industrial, agricultural and social projects over the years. As a result of this, the profile of our countryside and cities has changed drastically. Work in all the basic spheres of production has been humanized through technology and machines. Many highly important works are under construction or near commissioning in the sphere of energy, including the first nuclear power plant, a new oil refinery, large nickel processing industries, important textile factories and spinning mills, the geological survey of the country, oil prospecting and extraction, big iron and steel works and plants pertaining to basic industry and the light and food industries. New sugar mills are being built with 100 percent of the design and over 60 percent of the components produced in Cuba. Intensive and methodical work is being done on future plans and economic and social development lines until the year 2000.

Proof of the way work productivity has been increased is that whereas only 12 years ago 350,000 canecutters were employed in the harvest, today fewer than 100,000 are used in producing much more sugar without entailing any unemployment. The same has happened in other branches of agriculture, industry, construction and transportation, while increasing the quality and quantity of jobs in the various branches of production and services. Can any other country in Latin America say the same?

Today the whole world—including our enemies—acknowledges that our public health and education are impressive achievements, never before attained by any other country of the so-called Third World, or even by several of the countries listed as industrialized. Our enemies, nevertheless, dare to question the success of our economic development. The truth is that our economy, in spite of the brutal Yankee economic blockade, has grown at an annual rate of approximately 4.7 percent—higher or lower in given years—since the triumph of the Revolution, one of the highest growth rates in Latin America for this period. Otherwise, how could we afford an educational system that costs more than 1,500 million pesos per year and a health system whose cost surpasses 500 million pesos, which is dozens of times more than what was spend in these areas during capitalism? How could we have become a country without unemployment, with an advanced social security system that benefits all workers without exception? How could we be—after Argentina, with its huge expanses of agricultural land and herds of cattle—the second best-fed country in Latin America, with almost 3,000 calories and almost 80 grams of protein per capita a day, as was recently acknowledged by an institution that is an enemy and a detractor of the Cuban Revolution? How could we hold an outstanding place in sports, culture and scientific research? How could we be a country without destitute children, without beggars, without prostitution, gambling or drugs? Are not many of these activities the bleak livelihood for countless individuals, not only in underdeveloped countries, but in almost all the industrialized capitalist countries? How could we take on and technically train more than 20,000 young people from Asia, Africa and Latin America and cooperate with more than 30 Third World countries?

This is all possible, of course, not only because our economy has grown, but also because our trade with the socialist countries, which today accounts for more than 80 percent of Cuba's foreign trade, is not subjected to the growing unequal and arbitrary prices the Third World faces in its economic relations with the developed capitalist countries; it is possible because our wealth is better distributed, because the fruits of our economy do not go into the hands of the monopolies or the pockets of the rulers; because there is no capital drain, and because we have a hard-working, enthusiastic, generous people, full of solidarity, who are equal to any task, any mission, at home and abroad. That is, we have a priceless treasure, unknown in capitalist societies: a new man with new values and a new conception of life, for whom there is no difficult or impossible task. Speaking of our internationalist spirit, we recently said to some foreign journalists that when teachers were requested for Nicaragua, almost 30,000 volunteered; when some months later, some Cuban teachers were murdered in Nicaragua, 100,000 volunteered. The United States has its Peace Corps; the churches have their missionaries; Cuba alone has more citizens ready to fulfill these tasks voluntarily anywhere in the world than the United States and all the churches put together. This spirit is reflected in our work, both at home and abroad.

Further proof of the soundness of our development may be added. In spite of the huge resources we are forced to invest in the defense of our country, the budgets for education, health, culture, sports, science and technology are growing every year; every year we invest more resources in the maintenance and construction of housing; every year we invest a greater amount in industry, agriculture and in the economic infrastructure. This year, 1984, the budget for science and technology will grow by 15.6 percent; public health by 14.3 percent; housing and community services by 14.1 percent; sports by 10.8 percent; culture and art by 9.1 percent; education by 5.1 percent; and social security and welfare by 4.2 percent. In spite of this, our budget income and outlays will be balanced. In the rest of the countries of this hemisphere, one only hears news of increased unemployment and decreased budgets for education, health and other social expenditures.

In the midst of a world economic crisis, while the Latin American economy as a whole decreased by 1 percent in 1982 and by 3.3 percent in 1983, the Cuban economy grew by 2.5 percent in 1982 and 5 percent in 1983. A similar growth to that of the past year is forecast for 1984.

I recently explained how the Revolution had begun its successful health program with only 3,000 doctors, that now we had almost 20,000, and that in the next 16 years, 50,000 more would graduate. In just 15 or 20 years, the selection, previous training and work of these doctors, their adequate use and our health system will make Cuba rank first in the world in this field.

* * *

We have said that production and defense are our main slogans today. They are not in the least contradictory, they complement each other. The greater the fighting spirit of a people, the more they are aware and ready to fight for their homeland, all the more will they work, all the more will they devote themselves to the work of the Revolution and the development of their country; the more production and services are developed, the more we struggle for the well-being, future and happiness of our countrymen, the better we care for children in the schools and the sick in the polyclinics and hospitals, the better will be our attention in all other services in the country; the more brilliant our writers, artists and scientists, more outstanding our athletes, more efficient and vigorous our Party and our State, all the more determinedly and heroically will our people defend our homeland and our Revolution.

If in the beginning, at Girón and during the October Crisis, when we had nothing but ideas for which to fight, our people did not hesitate for a moment to take up arms or to be ready to fight until the final consequences, think what would happen now when, along with the dignity, sovereignty, freedom and independence of our homeland and the right to make the Revolution, we have all the achievements of the Revolution and a wonderful future to defend.

All Party and State cadres, all members of the Central Committee, and all the leaders of the Revolution, together with the people and the armed forces, would fight with dignity and be prepared to die and to win.

Santiago de Cuba: We have come before you again on the 25th anniversary with a Revolution that is a reality and with all promises kept.

* * *

May your heroism, your patriotism and your revolutionary spirit forever be an example to all Cubans. May the heroic watchword of our people forever be what we learned here: Patria o Muerte! May what we found here that glorious January 1st always await us: Victory!

Section II
Social Revolution

1   Cuba's Schools: 25 Years Later

Marvin Leiner

After my first visit to Cuba in 1968–69, I reported that "throughout Cuba, in the city streets and alongside rural roads, banners proclaim education as one of the most important themes of the Revolution." I recognized that slogans like "The path up from underdevelopment is education" or "The school plan is your responsibility" were not simply propagandistic platitudes but rather reflected the high priority given to education there.[1]

Now 25 years after its revolution, Cuba's highest flag is still the banner of education. More than one-third of the people—3.5 million—including nearly all children between the ages of 6 and 12, are enrolled in school. The number of teachers committed to the educational enterprise is a source of national pride. During the 1982–83 school year Cuba had approximately 250,000 teachers and professors, more than 83,000 in the primary schools, more than 94,000 in the secondary schools, almost 8,600 in special education, approximately 25,000 in adult education, and nearly 12,500 in university centers. The present teaching population is approximately 11 times higher than before the Revolution with 130,000 having been added to the teaching force since the early 1970s.[2]

EDUCATION IN PREREVOLUTIONARY CUBA

During the 1950s, just before the Revolution, only about one-half of the island's primary-school age children were enrolled in school. In poor communities, especially in rural areas, enrollment was even lower. Lowry Nelson, in his study of rural Cuba, noted: "In some places there are school buildings, but no teachers; in other places there are teachers, but no school buildings. There has been no systematic plan of school-building construction for rural areas...." He concluded that "little if any progress has been made since 1907 in providing school opportunities for the nation's children."[3]

A 1951 World Bank report documenting administrative waste, inefficiency, and corruption in the schools explains that historically "A teacher in Cuba was a government official, with life tenure on full salary, whether teaching or not." It found that outright purchases of appointments occurred and quoted a former education minister, who characterized his Ministry as "an opprobrium," "a shame," and "a dangerous menace to the Cuban nation." The report recognized the decline in "the quality and morale of the teaching and supervisory force" and noted the public's lack of confidence in its public schools.[4]

Whether the decline in prerevolutionary education can be closely correlated to sugar fluctuations, as suggested by some observers, or whether the chaos can be attributed to corruption and graft at the time of the Revolution,

> The Cuban school system provided strikingly unequal educational opportunities to students according to their socioeconomic status and place of residence. The system intensified rural-urban divisions and inculcated upper-class values and fostered aspirations that were simply unrealistic for the vast majority of Cuban children and largely dysfunctional for national development.[5]

NATIONAL GOALS AND EDUCATIONAL CHANGE

Once the revolutionary leadership assumed power, Cuba's education was set on an altogether different path. The new objectives sought to halt stagnation and give education highest priority—not merely in state planning but also in practice—by providing large budgets for school construction, program development, teacher training, and the national mobilization to eliminate illiteracy.

At the end of the new Cuban road, schooling was to be made available to all, especially the poor living in rural areas. In addition, education was reoriented to help achieve national goals: "to replace the rigid class structure of capitalist Cuba with a classless and egalitarian society; to eliminate sexism and racism; to end the city's economic and cultural domination over the countryside."[6]

What's more, education came to be regarded as a tool for promoting development through the training of a skilled and technically proficient population and for drastically altering the traditionally hostile attitudes toward science, technology, and modern agricultural methods. With education of the masses as one of its top priorities, Cuba nationalized all schools, reorganized its school system, and embarked on its extraordinary Literacy Campaign. The changes initiated in 1959—which continue even today—are unique in the history of world education.

The Literacy Campaign is considered by a number of scholars to be a major achievement of the early stages of the Cuban Revolution, representing a "large-scale government effort to advance the level of education and break down the psychological barriers to participation by adults in efforts to educate them."[7]

Literacy is a word with various definitions—both historically and currently. It is important, therefore, to note the achieved literacy level in 1961: "from a technical point of view, the campaign was one of providing a first grade level of reading and writing."[8] The achievement of a first grade level for 96.1 percent of the population was the highest in Latin America and among the highest in the world. For the next decade, adult education classes throughout the island followed up the literacy campaign to win the "Battle for the Sixth Grade." From 1962-63 through 1973-74 more than one half million adults completed sixth grade adult education programs.[9]

Commenting on recent Cuban history, Erwin Epstein, president of the Comparative and International Education Society, observed, "By any measure, the last 20 years of Cuban education have been remarkable.... Illiteracy has been virtually eliminated, and about one-third of the entire population is enrolled in some type of formal education." Epstein lauds the Cubans' "heroic effort to raise their standard of education and make learning a natural part of their everyday lives. Few, if any other nations can claim the use of schools to achieve such a pervasive transformation of social, political, and economic life."[10]

QUANTITATIVE ACHIEVEMENTS

Jorge I. Domínguez, noted scholar on contemporary Cuba, suggests that "because the middle third of the twentieth century witnessed educational stagnation in literacy and school enrollment, the quantitative

TABLE 1.1. Enrollment, Schools, and teachers in Cuba 1958-59 and 1982-83

Type of Education	1958-59			1982-83		
	Number of Students	Number of Schools	Number of Teachers	Number of Students	Number of Schools	Number of Teachers
Day care				80,575	839	17,688
Kindergarten and day care centers	91,700			118,072 (13,358)*		5,258 (651)*
Elementary	625,717	7,567	17,355	1,363,078	11,215	83,358
Secondary	88,135	80	4,571	1,116,930	1,915	94,193
Special				37,058	352	8,576
Adult				392,945	1,418	25,376
Youth				19,663	143	2,165
Higher education	2,063	6		200,000	40	12,433
Others	3,730	28	669	2,303		393
TOTAL	811,345		22,595	3,330,624		249,440

*These figures are included in total kindergarten numbers. Note that Kindergarten programs are offered in elementary schools and day care centers.

Blank spaces indicate that data were not available. "Youth" includes special programs for 13-16 year olds who are behind normal grade level. "Others" include foreigners taking special courses.

Sources: *Suplemento al Resumen del Trabajo del MINED* (Ministerio de Educatión), 1982-1983 Ministry of Education, 1983; Ministry of Education, 1983, Office of the Vice-Minister.

achievements of the revolutionary government are truly impressive."[11] Some of these quantitative changes, that is, the numbers of students, schools, and teachers, are illustrated in Table 1.1. These would not have been possible without a huge investment in education—the budget increasing steadily from 12 pesos per person in 1959 to 137 pesos per person in 1980.[12]

A major indicator of social and educational change is the percentage of children in school. Whereas a little over one-half of Cuba's children were enrolled in school in 1956, virtually all children aged 6 to 12 go to school today. The secondary school population has also increased dramatically. Today, more than 84 percent of the 13-16 year olds are enrolled in secondary schools, a figure 13 times higher than that for 1958-59.

The impact of the Revolution on the content and accessibility to education is shown in Table 1.2. In 1959 there were only three university

TABLE 1.2. Enrollment in Cuban Higher Education, 1956–57 and 1975–76

Specialization	1956–57		1975–76	
	Number of Students	Percent of Total	Number of Students*	Percent of Total
Humanities	3,600	23.1	10,200	12.2
Economics	4,500	28.8	9,300	11.1
Science	1,200	7.7	5,000	6.0
Technology	1,700	11.0	19,800	23.6
Medicine	300	1.9	6,800	8.1
Agriculture and fishing	600	3.8	9,200	11.0
Education	3,700	23.7	23,500	28.0
Total	15,600	100.0	83,800	100.0

*Data from 1975–76 are the most recent data compiled using this classification system. Total university enrollment was 222,200 in 1983–1984.

Sources: Junta Central de Planificación, 1976, p. 204; Castro, 1980; Ministry of Education, 1984.

centers in the country, and all were located in provincial capitals. Humanities (23 percent) and economics (29 percent) were the dominant disciplines. Few students came from the working class or peasant families.

In contrast, there are now 40 university centers with a student population 14 times greater, a curriculum embracing 150 different specialties and a large number of blacks and women in all specializations, ranging from medicine to the agricultural sciences. Women are 46 percent of the total university population. In 1983 Cuba ranked twentieth of 142 countries in the world—ahead of major Latin American countries such as Argentina, Brazil, Chile, Mexico, Colombia, and Venezuela—in percentage of women enlisted in university programs.[13] About 50 percent of the current student body works, and higher education is not only tuition-free, but students also receive support in the form of lodging, board, and stipends.

Even while recognizing Cuba's giant steps in higher education, the real drama has been elsewhere—in day care, primary, and secondary education, and adult education. Day care centers, known as *círculos infantiles,* are open to children from 45 days old up to age 6 (through kindergarten), although many of the nurseries I visited had few children less than one year old. From extensive interviews with day care leaders and staff, I learned that their goal was to educate the "whole child."

Specifically, they wanted to provide a strong basis for later growth in reading, mathematics, and science. At the same time these centers insist upon three nutritionally balanced meals a day, emphasize health care, and are much concerned with cleanliness.

These *Círculos*, under the direction of the Federation of Cuban Women, permit mothers to enter the country's work force and provide them with their first real opportunity to further their education. In 1983, 839 day care centers existed with an enrollment of 93,200 and a staff of almost 17,000.[14]

THE "PERFECCIONAMIENTO"—A PLAN FOR IMPROVING SCHOOLING IN CUBA (1976-1981)

In 1976, after 17 years of experience under the new policies, Cubans started to restructure their school system. The "Plan for Improving Schooling" had its roots in the National Congress of Education and Culture held in Havana, April 23-30, 1971. Among the 3,106 recommendations proposed by teacher delegates were suggestions for changes in curriculum, more efficient organization of the school system and use of time, improvement of teacher training, and development of new textbooks and materials. According to a five-year *Perfeccionamiento* (1976-1981) plan, the educational system would offer 12 instead of 13 years of schooling for all children. More classroom hours would be demanded, however. Under the new plan, the nation guaranteed to all its children one year of kindergarten. There were 107,700 enrolled kindergarten students in 1983-1984, although the universalization of kindergarten education has not yet been realized.

The revamped elementary school program now offers two stages— grades 1-4 in self-contained classrooms (cycle 1), grades 5-6 (cycle 2) offering "special subjects." In the first cycle, children stay with the same teacher for all four years. Cycle 2, more conventional in nature, is followed by three years of junior high and three of senior high school.[15] Compulsory education through grade 9 has been discussed but has not yet been put into effect. Currently, a sixth grade education is compulsory.

The first elementary school cycle is expected to provide "solid training in the mother tongue and mathematics." Schools at that level aim at helping children develop "skills and habits necessary for independent work." What's more, they hope to "inculcate a love for study and to contribute to the ideological and integral formation of the pupils."[16]

Cuban educators argue that the self-contained, same-teacher organization of cycle 1 enables the teacher to support and know the young child. They claim that the resulting continuity of instruction and the strong, supportive base better equip the children for the more demanding and specialized studies to follow.

Cuban educators have placed strong emphasis on mathematical proficiency and on mathematics/science foundations in the curriculum. Consequently, in elementary school and high school all children are required to study biology, physics, chemistry, and mathematics. In a recent interview (1983) José R. Fernández, minister of education, told me that "There is no doubt that mathematics, physics, chemistry, and biology form the basis for development in today's world."

Table 1.3 shows that mathematics far outranks any other subject in the curriculum (grades 1–12) in total number of hours of instruction; the combined sciences come next, and Spanish and physical education follow in third and fourth places.

Except for offering students two hours per week in senior high school, Cuban educational leadership does not advocate "electives" in the curriculum. They reason that curriculum designs and "requirements" are determined by consideration of "quality education" and the nation's modern developmental needs.

Cuba is beginning to reap the benefits of their 25 years of educational strategy, and has become one giant school through heavy budget commitments and public and social will. In an article titled "Cuba's Great Leap," in the English science journal, *Nature*, a member of a 1983 U. S. science delegation to Cuba reports that "Cuba's leap into twentieth-century science and engineering in only one generation has hurtled the island in most fields far beyond its Latin American neighbors." This is not restricted to such areas as health care, cattle breeding, and world leadership in sugarcane by-product research. Cubans have now pushed "into more sophisticated terrain—computers, interferon, tissue culture and biotechnology."[17]

Cuba has also become a "medical power," "creating large armies of young doctors." In 1959 there were 6,300 doctors in Cuba; half of them left the island by 1964. In 25 years Cuba has trained 16,000 physicians. There are presently over 17,000 medical students enrolled in 17 medical schools and 4 medical colleges. "Last year alone, Cuba produced just under 1100 doctors. Sergio del Valle, the minister of public health, reports that this year Cuba expects to add over 2,500 more as part of a new policy aimed at training large numbers of physicians in the next decades. By 1985, we expect to graduate 3,000

TABLE 1.3. Curriculum I: Cuban Schools Grades 1–12—Number of 45 Minute Classes per Week in Each Subject Area

	Primary						Basic secondary			Preuniversity		
	Cycle 1				Cycle 2							
Subject	1	2	3	4	5	6	7	8	9	10	11	12
Spanish	5	5	5	4	3	3	3	2	2	1	1	1
Reading	5	5	5	4								
Reading literature					3	3						
Literature							3	2	2	2	2	2
Mathematics	5	5	5	5	5	5	5	5	5	5	4	5
History				2	2	2	2	2	2	2	2	2
Social sciences				1					2			2
Geography					2	2	2	2	2	2	2	
Natural sciences			2	2								
Biology					2	2	2	2	2	2	2	2
Physics							2	2	2	3	3	3
Chemistry								2	2	3	3	3
Technical drawing							2	2	1			
Shop education	2	2	2	2	2	2	2	2	2			
Bases of production										2	2	2
Astronomy												2/0
Plastic arts	1	1	1	1	1	1						
Music/dance education	1	1	1	1								
Foreign language					3	3	3	3	2	2	2	2
Physical education	3	3	3	3	2	2	2	2	2	2	2	2
Technical/military preparation											1	0/2
Elective classes										2	2	2
TOTAL	22	22	24	25	25	25	25	28	28	28	28	28

Source: Victor Martuza."Recent Changes in Cuban Education." Presented at the Middle Atlantic Council on Latin American Studies annual meeting, Temple University, Philadelphia, Pa., 1981.

and then increase continuously. Between 1983 and the year 2000, we expect to train 50,000 doctors, del Valle predicted."[18]

On various trips, when I asked adolescents in different parts of Cuba to tell me about their future vocational aspirations, I learned that they heavily favor scientific and technical specializations.[19] In 1983 and 1984 students also volunteered interest in nuclear energy careers.

Curiously, Cuba's intense focus on science and technical subjects has not come from some master plan devised to steer the work force in predictable directions. Rather, it "flows from a general conviction that scientific and technical knowledge will provide solutions to Cuba's economic problems."[20] Cubans feel that a scientific, technically literate population is the only way "up from underdevelopment."

RURAL FOCUS: LA ESCUELA-EN-EL-CAMPO

For prerevolutionary Cuba, no less than for the rest of Latin America, the rural sector was the most economically depressed and the most educationally neglected. Consequently, the Cubans have attempted to change the educational landscape in the countryside. Flying in an airplane over rural areas, one sees many instances of a Cuban educational innovation dotting the rural fields and hills, *la escuela-en-el-campo* ("the school-in-the-countryside"). This uniquely Cuban adventure grows out of a major investment of its national resources and its efforts in education.

The first school in the countryside was built in 1971. Today, there are 384 junior high and 183 senior high schools of this type. They are seen as "the model of the future school."[21] Each *escuela-en-el-campo* costs approximately $1.7 million to build and houses 500 to 600 students with equal numbers of boys and girls. Each new rural school offers not only classrooms, laboratories, library, and recreational areas for students and teachers but also has its own dormitories, a dining room, and a kitchen.

A large fraction of Cuba's youth are now educated in these countryside schools—37 percent in junior high and 47 percent in senior high. The annual cost of maintaining each school is reported to be approximately $572,000. From 1975 to 1980, enrollment in junior high countryside schools increased from 277,000 to 478,000, an extraordinary jump. José R. Fernández, minister of education, summarized the admission policy as follows: "These schools are for all students, but those who pass the sixth grade and don't have a secondary school near where they live are given priority."[22]

The schools set aside one-half of the day for academics and one-half for work. The early evening, from 5:30 to 7:30 P.M., is devoted to individual and group study time. The students attending a school of this type work on the school farm (citrus, tobacco, or other cash crops) and, in this way, contribute about 600,000 pesos per year to support school development and maintenance. All schools-in-the-countryside are boarding schools: both students and faculty sleep in dormitories.

Transportation to and from home on weekends and for summer vacation is provided by the school.[23]

Although work/study programs exist in other socialist and capitalist countries, the Cuban boarding school, which is located in rural areas and offered as *the* national mode for secondary school education is unique. The Cubans see this model as consistent both with Cuban historic roots and Marxist philosophy. Fidel Castro has said that the *escuela-en-el-campo* "unites fundamental ideas from two great thinkers: Marx and Martí. Both conceived of a school tied to work, a center where youth are educated for life... this school responds to conceptions about pedagogy, realities, necessities... consistent with the development of man—connected to productive and creative work."[24]

For developing nations, and advanced countries as well, Cuba's *campo* program raises a number of significant issues. The boarding school, designed to accommodate adolescents, must be considered in the light of what we know about development during these years when children are filled with energy and idealism. What effect do these adult-supervised, away-from-home environments have on them? What are the consequences of a peer-group living arrangement for both self-help and collective aims? What opportunities are available for extended study, cooperation, health, hygiene, and nutrition?

SOME PROBLEMS AND DILEMMAS

Even while the record of educational progress is impressive in many ways, particularly in view of Cuba's developmental status, certain problems persist: a shortage of fully trained teachers, an emphasis on achievement testing as the gauge of progress, the problem of dropouts and holdovers, the emergence of special schools for scientifically and technically gifted students in a society dedicated to egalitarianism, and an apparent overemphasis on political considerations in the selection of educational leaders. I will discuss these briefly.

Teacher Quality

The rapid expansion of opportunity after the revolution and the consequent explosion in student enrollment caused an enormous demand for teachers. The commitment to expansion combined with the exodus of middle-class professionals resulted in a shortage of trained personnel.

But since the Revolution had promised to push ahead, the new government felt it had no choice; it was forced to make concessions. The quality of Cuba's new teachers would be modest, but at least there would be teachers.

For example, when *Círculos Infantiles* were first opened, they were led by *asistentes*, that is, teachers having at least a sixth-grade education. In 1971, the *Instituto de Infancia* established the *Escuela de Educadoras* to prepare day care teachers with a minimum ninth-grade education and training in the arts, physical and social sciences, and language skills important for preschool children.[25]

I first visited the national elementary school teacher-training facility, located in the mountains of Oriente Province, during the 1960s. This was a time when Cuban policy proclaimed that if the revolution in education was to occur, teacher training should take place in rugged, isolated, rural conditions. Students would then be prepared for the toughest assignments.

In the 1970s, I interviewed both leaders and classroom teachers about this policy and found many critical of it, claiming that it had adversely affected teacher recruitment and the quality of teacher training. Fidel Castro, in his report to the First Congress of the Communist Party, acknowledged that the regime had made "a major mistake in education during the 1960s" by adopting this policy. "We were slow in realizing that the system was unrealistic," Castro said, "and that for a time it affected the availability of graduate teachers."[26]

In the early 1970s, teacher training was decentralized, and teacher training centers began to emerge all over the island. In 1983 there were 21 teacher-training facilities with an approximate enrollment of 48,025 students. The five-year program consists of academic subjects, psychology, pedagogy, and intensive field practice.

The dramatic increase in secondary school enrollment generated opportunities for staffing classrooms using a variety of creative approaches. I personally observed classes taught by veteran teachers as well as by paraprofessionals and "monitors," that is, outstanding students who taught selected classes under the guidance of an experienced teacher. Other untrained classroom aides came from the "pedagogical detachment," a group of dedicated 18 and 19 year olds. Still others were trainees, enrolled in pedagogical institutes, who taught during the day and attended teacher-training classes in the evening. In one school-in-the-countryside which I visited in 1979, 40 out of 60 teachers were licensed, and the remaining 20 were still in training.

Recognizing that certain dislocations would result from using an unevenly trained teaching force, the country chose nonetheless to expand education. In visits to classes, I found many teachers who dynamically and effectively used a variety of materials and children's experiences in their work. In other cases, I observed boring lessons in which the inservice teacher or trainee rigidly held to the text in dull question/response style. Too often a "blue book syndrome," the copying of teacher-dictated notes in little blue notebooks, dominated the student/teacher interaction.

Aware of these problems, educators organized a massive inservice training program which operates during the academic year and for one month in the summer. While all students are on holiday during July and August, the teachers attend workshops during one-half of this period, giving them one month for vacation.

Elite Schools in an Egalitarian Society

A persistent dilemma is raised in Cuba by the existence of special or elite high schools, designed to develop scientific and technical talent, in the midst of the call for equality. In 1969, there was only one such school; now there are similar schools in each of the provinces. Students are chosen on the basis of scholastic achievement.

In 1980–81 a new elite school, The School for Exact Sciences, opened to develop talented students in mathematics, chemistry, and physics. Students are selected by a national competitive examination on which they demonstrate their ability in mathematics and chemistry or mathematics and physics. There are currently 150 students enrolled in the school, 50 in each of the three major areas. While the students are expected to carry out the usual maintenance and cleanup responsibilities, they do not participate in the countryside program. This school structure is an exception to the countryside model in Cuban secondary education.

Intelligence testing and ability grouping are *not* used in Cuba's elementary and secondary schools. One teacher explained that such "segregation within the school would contradict socialist principles of our society." Exceptions are the special scientific high schools just mentioned. According to the Cubans, these special enclaves in each province are dictated by national necessity, the need for a scientific cadre. On a visit to the Lenin School I discovered through interviews with students and faculty that textbooks in use there were the same as those used elsewhere in the nation, but the quality of teaching and equipment were superior. This contradiction persists into the 1980s.

Curriculum Change

Shortages of textbooks, poor quality of old texts when available, and lack of supplementary aids and materials plagued a school system which was expending rapidly in every city and rural community. Serious and important changes in curriculum and materials have been made to improve the quality of instruction. For example, Cuba now produces its own modern audiovisual materials. These include large, "come apart" models of cows and human bodies for primary school science lessons and a variety of concrete materials for modern mathematics. With the help of East German consultants, Cuba has introduced a high quality, well organized modern mathematics program for grades 1-12.

Over the past decade I have witnessed a carefully orchestrated curriculum change. There has been a tremendous investment in the production and distribution of new textbooks at every grade level. Teams of gifted Cuban teachers, in consultation with experts from abroad, have prepared new materials and courses of study appropriate for the country's needs.

Testing Emphasis

In the "battle for quality" in Cuban education, the focus is now on how well the schools are doing on their exams (on a quarterly basis and especially on the final) and the "percentage of promotion," starting especially in grade 5. Students, faculty, principals, and parents cite examination and promotion data as evidence of achievement. For senior high school graduates, entrance to the university is determined by one's scholastic average.

The pressure on students to succeed on exams has caused some unfortunate disruptions. Evidence of fraud and cheating has been acknowledged publicly by Fidel Castro on a number of occasions.[27] In my own opinion, the heavy emphasis on tests as a measure of student and teacher worth often leads to stultification of both teacher and student, with critical thinking and creativity supplanted by rote learning.

Educational Leadership

While selection of school principals is governed by various criteria, it appears that the principal's "political history," that is, dedication to the Revolution, is still a crucial factor. While this might pay off in terms of conscientiousness and long hours of service, it does not of itself ensure educational leaders who stimulate instructional improvements.

The problems of Cuban schools, especially the issues of the quality of instruction and the implementation of curriculum change, have been publicly acknowledged and discussed by teachers and educational leaders. Minister Fernández recently noted that "a whole driving force of new ideas" has of necessity come up against traditional teaching ideas. Beyond the difficulties in providing textbooks, workshops, and laboratories, there have been

> difficulties of a subjective nature, such as breaking with the ingrained mentality of some teachers who have not been able to put into practice the principles of current socialist, Marxist-Leninist pedagogy....
> It should be realized that the improved system entails a profound change in the content of curricula and that this in turn demands greater teaching qualifications.... Moreover, there was the well-known explosion in enrollment in intermediate education, which forced us to open hundreds of schools almost simultaneously. Problems that have had to be tackled on the way were finding new teachers, new school principals and administrators, and seeing that they further improve their qualifications.[28]

When asked what Cuban educational priorities for 1981-1985 would be, Fernández replied that the main task is to continue to improve the quality of teaching and education, primarily through staff training. Overall, he reported,

> We will struggle to improve schooling for students between the ages of 13 and 16; to introduce morning and afternoon sessions in primary schools; to improve our work in vocational training and professional guidance; to give added impetus to physical education, sports and cultural activities; to expand and improve special education; to apply the principles of contemporary educational concepts; to see to it that all intermediate education teachers get their diploma and primary school teachers improve their education level.[29]

CUBA'S SCHOOLS AND LATIN AMERICA

To appreciate Cuba's dilemmas and achievements, we must keep in mind the status of children in the rest of Latin America. A recent study reported that "most young children in Latin America are profoundly affected by poverty, both physically and emotionally. More than 50 percent suffer from the effects of protein deficiency. Nutritional anemia affects 10 to 20 percent of them directly. Malnourished children exhibit apathy and reduced responsiveness in the environment, irritability, withdrawal, and an inability to carry out tasks."[30] But even if these children were offered early childhood education, two additional conditions must be met: "secondary education must be available to those who finish primary school and jobs must become available."[31] Obviously political and economic realities make it unlikely that this will happen in the near future in much of Latin America.

In the case of Cuba, we have the one Latin American country that has overcome the lockstep of school failure, the absence of educational opportunity, and poverty. Cuba has gone a long way toward fulfilling the educational needs of children at all school levels and has adopted broad measures to provide sound health care and proper nutrition, indispensable ingredients in a comprehensive effort to achieve victory over a history of neglect.

I have briefly cited the persistence of several problems in Cuban education. Nevertheless, given the nation's earlier educational stagnation, there have been significant, remarkable educational accomplishments in the last 25 years. These include:

- A daring national commitment to a revolution in education, unparalleled in developing countries. Cuba has devoted about one-fifth of her total productive capacity to formal schooling, "a figure unsurpassed among the major countries of the world, rich or poor.[32]
- A major offensive in mass education of the day care, primary, and secondary levels. This included almost doubling the number of elementary schools, more than 1,000 new junior high schools, and 9 times more senior high schools than in 1958-59.
- The training of thousands of new teachers and the introduction of a national staff development program employing a variety of strategies: university expansion of teacher training, inservice seminars, television, summer workshops, correspondence courses—all in an effort to improve teacher quality and introduce major curriculum changes.
- A strong attack on adult illiteracy, beginning with the historic Literacy Campaign of 1961 and institution of follow-through

programs throughout the island. A symbol of this commitment was the designation of a Vice Minister of Adult Education as one of the key leaders in educational administration, with a major investment of budget and resources. By 1968 one-third of a million adults received their primary school diploma. Cubans now talk about the need for universal secondary education, including education for adults.

- The adaptation of a two-fold dynamic strategy for educational change which (a) did not hesitate to borrow or learn from basic research and development from developed countries and (b) introduced their own Cuban innovation such as the *escuela-en-el-campo* model, boarding schools, work/study programs for adolescents and adults, parental and community involvement, and nonformal programs such as *círculos de interés*.
- A national effort to bridge the large gap between rural and urban educational opportunity. This emphasis has reversed the historical Latin American legacy by giving top priority to rural schools—resources, scholarships, teachers, new buildings, and medical and dental benefits.

In conclusion, Cuba has been in the process of a major transformation of education in both formal and nonformal structures and programs. This Cuban revolution in education, with its staggering support for a universal, free system and its impressive achievements over 25 years, merits the careful attention of others—especially in developing nations—concerned with the herculean task of bringing about viable, radical, nationwide changes in education.

NOTES

1. Marvin Leiner, "Cuba's Schools, Ten Years Later," *Saturday Review*, October 17, 1970, p. 59.
2. Office of the Vice-Minister of Education, Ministry of Education, Cuba, 1984.
3. Nelson Lowry, *Rural Cuba* (New York: Octagon Books, 1970), pp. 236, 239.
4. International Bank for Reconstruction and Development, *Report on Cuba* (Baltimore: Johns Hopkins Press, 1951), pp. 404, 425, 434.

5. Rolland G. Paulston, "Education," Carmelo Mesa-Lago, ed., in *Revolutionary Change in Cuba* (Pittsburgh: University of Pittsburgh Press, 1971), p. 385.

6. Samuel Bowles, "Cuban Education and the Revolutionary Ideology," *Harvard Educational Review*, vol. 41 (November 1971), pp. 41, 474.

7. Jorge I. Domínguez, *Cuba: Order and Revolution* (Cambridge: Harvard University Press, 1978), p. 165. See also Richard Jolly, "Education," in Dudley Seers, Andrés Bianchi, Richard Jolly, and Max Nolff, *Cuba: The Economic and Social Revolution* (Chapel Hill, N.C.: University of North Carolina Press, 1964).

8. Anna Lorenzetto and Karel Neys, *Methods and Means Utilized in Cuba to Eliminate Illiteracy*, UNESCO Report (Havana: Ministry of Education, 1965), p. 72.

9. Azucena Plasencia, "Montaña Adentro: La Batalla del Sexto Grado," *Bohemia* vol. 67 (7 March 1975), p. 35. See also the February 1981 special issue of the *Harvard Educational Review*, *Education as Transformation: Identity, Change, and Development* for articles by Abel Prieto Morales on the 1961 Cuban Literacy Campaign, Fernando Cardenal and Valerie Miller on the 1980 Nicaraguan Literacy Crusade, and Paulo Freire on the São Tomé and Prîncipe Campaigns. Although facing different national, cultural, and literacy conditions, all three programs advocate that the first steps in a massive attack of literacy are (1) recognition of the importance of the relationship between "reading and context" and (2) the need to undertake a "major effort to mobilize and organize the people to become genuine participants." (Paulo Freire, "The People Speak Their Word: Learning to Read and Write in São Tomé and Prîncipe," *Harvard Educational Review*, February 1981, p. 29.

10. Erwin H. Epstein, review of *Children of the Revolution* by Jonathan Kozol, *Comparative Education Review*, October 1979, p. 456.

11. Domínguez, *Order and Revolution*, p. 167.

12. Fidel Castro, *Granma Weekly Review*, 21 September 1980, p. 3.

13. Ruth Leger Sivard, *World Military and Social Expenditures, 1983: An Annual Report on World Priorities* (Washington, D.C.: World Priorities, 1983), p. 36.

14. For further discussion of day care in Cuba (history, goals, organization and curriculum) see Marvin Leiner, *Children Are the Revolution: Day Care in Cuba* (New York: Penguin Books, 1978). See also *Educación en Cuba: Regional Conference of Ministers and Education December 4–13, Mexico*, UNESCO (Havana: Empresa Impresoras Gráficas, MINED, 1979), pp. 12–18, and *Suplemento Al Resumen del Trabajo Anual del MINED, 1982–1983* (Havana: Ministry of Education, 1983).

15. Max Figueroa, "Improvement of the Educational System: On a Thesis of the First Congress of the Party," *Granma Weekly Review*, 29 June 1975, p. 4

16. Cuba, Ministry of Education, *Cuba: Organización de la Educación. Report of the Republic of Cuba to the 26th International Conference on Public Education* (Havana: Empresa Impresoras Gráficas, MINED, 1977), p. 122.

17. Robert Ubell, "Cuba's Great Leap," *Nature*, April 28, 1983, p. 745.

18. Robert Ubell, "Special Report: High-Tech Medicine in the Caribbean: 25 Years of Cuban Health Care," *New England Journal of Medicine*, Dec. 8, 1983, pp. 1471-72. See also Helen Smith, "Castro's Medicine: An On-the-scene Report," *M.D.*, May 1983, pp. 144-63.

19. Marvin Leiner, "Cuba: Combining Formal Schooling with Practical Experience," Manzoor Ahmed and Philip Coombs, ed., in *Education for Rural Development: Case Studies for Planners*, (New York: Praeger, 1975), pp. 95-96.

20. Bowles, "Cuba Education and the Revolutionary Ideology," p. 493.

21. *Suplemento Al Resumen del Trabajo Anual del MINED, 1982-83* (Havana: Ministry of Education, 1983).

22. Jesús Abascal López, interview with José R. Fernández, Vice President of the Council of Ministers and Minister of Education, *Weekly Granma*, 16 November 1980, p. 2.

23. See Marvin Leiner, "Cuba: Combining Formal Schooling with Practical Experience;" Arthur Gillette, *Cuba's Educational Revolution* (London: Fabian Society, 1972); Jonathan Kozol, *Children of the Revolution* (New York: Delacorte Press, 1978); Rolland G. Paulston, "Cuban Rural Education: A Strategy for Rural Development" in the *World Year Book of Education*, 1974, pp. 249-50.

24. Fidel Castro, "La Escuela en el Campo," *Educación*, Año 1, April/June 1971, p. 13.

25. See Marvin Leiner, *Children Are the Revolution*, Chapter 2, "The Paraprofessional Solution," pp. 33-50, and introduction to Penguin edition, p. 1.

26. Fidel Castro, *Report of the Central Committee of the CPC to the First Congress* (Havana: Department of the Revolutionary Orientation of the Central Committee of the Communist Party of Cuba, 1977), p. 173.

27. Fidel Castro, "Speech delivered on 4 September 1978 for opening of the 1978-79 School Year," *Weekly Granma*, 17 September 1978, pp. 2, 4.

28. López, interview with Fernández, p. 2.

29. López, p. 4.

30. Robert Halpern, "Early Childhood Program in Latin America," *Harvard Educational Review*, vol. 50 (November 1980), pp. 484-85.

31. Ibid., p. 485.

32. See Bowles, "Cuban Education and Revolutionary Ideology," *Harvard Educational Review*, p. 486, for an analysis of the 1968-69 labor force. He further states that 20 percent is "really an underestimate of Cuba's resources devoted to education."

2 Medicine in the Community

Ross Danielson

INTRODUCTION

Medicine in the community is the name given to the dominant model of health services organization in contemporary Cuba. An analysis of the development of this concept and a description of its essential elements is intended to communicate the salient features of the overall health system and the dynamics of twenty-five years of health care revolution.

It may be useful to begin by having in mind three periods within the Cuban health care revolution—early transition in 1959–1964, consolidation in 1965–1973, and the remaining years as the period of medicine in the community. Early transition pitted the medical-political imagination against the prerevolutionary system and signaled the directions which were eventually consolidated in a unitary national health system. Medicine in the community evolved in turn from the critique of the consolidated socialist system itself.

Perhaps we are now entering yet a new period, the emergence of Cuba as a "medical power."[1] Cuba has achieved remarkable health statistics (see addendum at the end of this chapter), a large and growing cadre of health professionals (one physician per 600 people), impressive institutions of technical training and research (with 453 scholarship medical students from 71 countries and 99 others in residency training), proven dedication to sharing health resources with other developing countries (with 3,044 health personnel—1,675 of them physicians—helping in 30 nations), and a model of services which appears to provide access, continuity, and integration of preventive-curative activities in social, environmental, and personal health services.[2]

HEGEMONY OF SOCIAL MEDICINE

In the history of Western medicine, the concept of social medicine is of special interest. Social medicine may be defined as the pursuit of an integrated and implemented understanding of both health needs and health services, giving attention to physical environment and human biology, but emphasizing (1) optimal consideration of social, organizational, and economic factors insofar as they relate to health needs and effective services; (2) attention to and measurement of health status and health services within defined social and geographical categories; and (3) achievement of social equity in health.

Contemporary Cuban health ideology holds that the entire enterprise of health care in Cuba is social medicine, an identity which derives from the social transformation and from the ideological hegemony of social medicine that was achieved early in the revolutionary years. To evaluate this point of view, it is important to appreciate the degree and speed to which the Cuban revolution virtually ended private interest medical care and introduced a new ideology of health.

The perspectives of social medicine were present in prerevolutionary Cuba as enclaves in the medical profession, private prepaid medical care, public health, and medical education. High aspirations for public health were formalized early this century in the legislation which created the Secretariat of Health and Social Assistance.[3] But lack of funding, redundant hierarchical programs, and persistent graft constantly frustrated public health aspirations in prerevolutionary Cuba. Prepaid medical care programs flourished after the mid-nineteenth century in Cuba, and in 1959 some one-half of Havana's metropolitan population was covered under some kind of nongovernmental prepaid program. Less dominant in other major cities, these programs were regarded as a form of social medicine.[4]

Finally, the major association of physicians, the Cuban Medical Federation, embraced a range of social medical perspectives which were editorialized in its official organ, the *Tribuna Médica*. This range of social medical philosophy—support for public health programs and critique of maldistribution of medical resources—was often compromised, however, by the federation's defense of disparate and often conflicting interests within the profession.[5] A dominant sector of the medical profession was formed by physicians employed in mutualist and public medical programs and nurtured in university and political activism. Without exclusionary limits on medical education but also without effective public means of achieving optimal employment and distribution of medical resources, the medical profession (one physician per 1,000 population in 1959) included many marginal practitioners who were crowded into Havana and larger provincial capitals. From this base within the physician class, as it was called in Cuba, the Medical Federation came to be dominated after 1945 by progressives and socialists. It was precisely these sectors of physicians who were recruited to direct the new government health endeavors after 1959.

By 1963, social medicine had passed from its roots in minority medical perspectives to the status of official ideology. This ideology was affirmed in its implementation in the following:

- rural health programs
- regionalization of public health and hospitals
- regionalization of private prepaid medical care programs
- creation and expansion of preventive medical care programs (including the dramatic eradication of polio)
- free medical care in all public institutions
- cost reductions, standardization, and regionalization of pharmacy services
- expansion of epidemiology, biostatistics, administrative medicine, family medicine, and medical psychology
- popular involvement in health work and health education
- comprehensive authority by the Ministry of Public Health over all health matters
- recruitment of rural, poor, and nonwhite youth into the medical profession
- required rural service by medical graduates
- formalization and expansion of nursing education
- formalization and expansion of allied health occupations
- improved employment opportunities for physicians and other health workers.

The period of system consolidation, 1965-1973, integrated four somewhat competitive processes that had been set in motion in 1959-1964: (1) extension of the primary care base and periphery of the health system, notably the development of small, rural hospitals and health centers; (2) extension and regionalization of the hospital system, notably administrative integration and construction or expansion of services outside of Havana and the closure of small, redundant facilities; (3) integration/regionalization of the small private sector and the large metropolitan mutualist sector, wholly incorporating them within the public sector by 1970; and (4) development of national public health campaigns involving a range of health resources and community/"mass" organizations.

In the consolidated system, freestanding community health centers, called area polyclinics, were emphasized as the first point of access to physician services. Area polyclinics housed an increasing range of health services, including curative and preventive, personal and social, and clinical and environmental programs. Addressing the health needs of specified geographical areas, the area polyclinics became the conceptual focus of regionalized health care planning and administration. Area polyclinics were also used as teaching settings for medical education, preparing students for the practice of primary medical care in the community setting. After 1965, medical students not only trained in anticipation of postgraduate rural service but also, necessarily, in anticipation of public employment.

The consolidation by 1970 of the Cuban health system could be summarized in the virtual extinction of medical practice outside the authority of the Ministry of Public Health. Comprehensive planning was effected in yearly and multi-yearly planning cycles. Institutes of research, postgraduate education, programs of nonuniversity training, and traditional public health and sanitation matters were directed and planned within the ministry. A comprehensive model guided the organization of health services everywhere; and the ambiguity and multiplicity of entry to the medical services system was significantly ended by making the area polyclinic the focal unit of the system.

COMMUNITY MEDICINE: SOCIALISM VERSUS CAPITALISM

Thus, in 1974, when officials of the Cuban Ministry of Public Health began to prepare for an Inter-American conference on community medicine, they were struck by the contrast between Cuba and other American states. In Cuba the perspective of social medicine pervaded the dominant ideology of the entire health system, but in other countries community medicine was a minor perspective within the larger medical system. While the Cuban Ministry of Public Health, guided by its social medical ideology, enjoyed comprehensive authority in all health matters, in other societies the role of community medicine was restricted to secondary tasks which seemed to derive from the failure of the dominant medical system to serve the entire population. Community medicine did not address the entire community in nonsocialist countries, but only a part of the community; operationally, community medicine was poor people's medicine.

The very word "community" had different meanings in different contexts; from one viewpoint it was argued that the profound class antagonisms of labor and capital meant that a true community could not exist in capitalist nations. Community medicine thus appeared to be an obfuscating misnomer. By contrast, the contradictions of labor and capital were considered resolved in Cuba by the process of socialist transformation.[6]

Given these differences of social context, Cuban medical leaders rejected the idea of developing a departmentalized, specialized role for community medicine, in the fashion of other countries. Cuban medicine sought to serve all the people, all the community. Therefore, Cuban medicine could proclaim itself to be community medicine.

CRITIQUE OF CUBAN HEALTH ORGANIZATION

Despite its somewhat self-congratulatory tone, the critique of community medicine under capitalism coincided with an intense period of critique and experimentation in the health and other sectors of Cuban society. After the first decade of profound social change new conditions had emerged which were analyzed in terms of a newly evolving ideology. The new directions of the health sector were embodied in the concept of medicine in the community, while the new directions of the political sphere were embodied in the Socialist Constitution of 1975.

After 1970, the following system-level characteristics presented themselves as potential tensions or antagonisms for change:

 1. In administration and planning, a continuing interaction between the national centralization of normative responsibilities and the decentralized concentration of administrative, operative responsibilities in the provinces, regions, and areas;

2. In medical services, a tension between the centralizing tendencies of inpatient services and the decentralizing direction of outpatient services;

3. In the area polyclinic, a tension between its relation to the community and its relation to the hospital system;

4. In medical education, a tension between the community service philosophy of medical care and the dominant role of hospital-based learning experiences and specialty training;

5. In the community of medical workers, a difference in perspective between physicians and nonphysicians; and

6. In the evaluation of health work, the continuing experience of service deficiencies and consumer complaints, notwithstanding the many well-intentioned efforts at resolving them.

The tensions of the health system particularly affected the area polyclinic, which was soon to become the primary focus of medicine in the community.

The polyclinic was also becoming the primary focus of actual medical visits. While the combined total of medical visits to all medical facilities doubled in the period 1964-1969, the relative proportion of all Cuban medical visits which were recorded for polyclinics increased from 32.3 percent in 1964 to 63.3 percent in 1969. This represented an increase from 3,666,000 polyclinic visits in 1964 to 13,818,000 visits in 1979.[7] (A portion of this increase may be attributed to conversion of facilities—small hospitals, mutualist clinics—to polyclinic function, but there remains a very substantial real increase in the polyclinic role.)

The community relationship in the area polyclinic (circa 1970) emphasized the following key elements: (1) an area health commission, chaired by the polyclinic director, with representatives of health-relevant, program-relevant community bodies; (2) a defined role for lay institutions; and (3) interaction between lay health workers and professionals at the level of the sector. (The sector is a neighborhood category of regionalization.)

The polyclinic was designed to provide, integrate, or otherwise be responsible for the provision of clinical services, environmental services, community health services, and related social services to a specifically defined area and population. Under the leadership of a physician-director, these functions were served by four health teams. With an average population of 25,000 (ranging from 60,000 in one urban area to as few as 7,500 in some rural areas), the health areas were intended to be small enough to be accessible and large enough to efficiently provide a substantial range of primary services. These primary services included the typical "public health" tasks of sanitary control and community health work, organized and directed from the same organization that provided clinical and social services. Thus, the goal, predominant in all socialist societies, of integrating curative-preventative and clinical-social-environmental dimensions was served in Cuba by the central role of the polyclinic. Polyclinic personnel were responsible for nine programs: women's health, child health, adult medical care, dentistry, control of infectious diseases, environmental services, food control, school health services, and occupational and labor medicine.[8]

As the principal point of entry to the health system, it became the task of the polyclinic to define, orient, and protect the relationship of the health area population to the system of hospital and specialist services. To foster such a relationship, Cuban health leaders determined that the polyclinic should enjoy administrative independence from the hospital. Unlike similar institutions in other countries, including Czechoslovakia, the most directly relevant socialist prototype, the Cuban polyclinic was not to be an administrative extension of a regional hospital but was, like the regional hospital, an administrative unit under the purview of the regional office of the Ministry of Public Health.

Administrative autonomy of the polyclinic vis-à-vis the hospital was an extremely critical structural development, for it provided favorable conditions for the area polyclinic to develop its unique perspective and for health workers in polyclinics to evolve a sense of constituency interests and mission. Independence from the hospital protected the polyclinic leadership from the tendencies of hospital technocracy while giving the Ministry of Public Health more direct influence over an important community-level institution.

Independence, however, was not to imply isolation. The polyclinic director was a member, alongside other health officials, of the regional technical committee which elaborated the primary operative component of national health planning. Hospitals and other health organizations, laboratories, and epidemiological services were charged with specific obligations to the polyclinic. While each polyclinic employed a core of full-time staff, hospital physicians were required to work part-time in nearby polyclinics, providing primary services and specialist consultation. This measure was intended to encourage a community focus by hospital-based specialists. On the polyclinic side, staff physicians were required, whenever possible, to serve for short periods in the regional or provincial hospitals. This requirement was facilitated by the policy of training primary care specialists rather than comprehensive generalists.

Thus, the clinical team of the polyclinic included physicians and nurses working in internal medicine, pediatrics, obstetrics-gynecology, and dentistry, with primary and secondary care specialists who were available, on a part-time basis, from the staffs of nearby hospitals. In addition, many general practitioners moved from their solo office to the polyclinic, where they continued to provide traditional general services. Nurses, it seems, under this arrangement of organized primary services, began to assume greater clinical responsibilities. The polyclinic, then, in Cuba replaced the general practitioner (and comparable roles in private and mutualist clinics), but the core staff of the polyclinic consisted of primary care specialists, nurses, and auxiliary personnel.

The direct neighborhood work of the polyclinic was organized geographically into neighborhood health sectors, with a growing national average in 1970 of 8.3 sectors per area. To each sector the polyclinic sought to assign a field nurse, a sanitarian, and sometimes, a social worker. In addition to the unsurprising tasks of such personnel, it was partly through them that technical support was given and collaboration was maintained with the extensive health-related functions of lay neighborhood organizations. Depending on geographical conditions, first-aid posts could also be found in the sector, staffed by volunteers, auxiliary nurses, and, especially in rural areas, by teachers.

Interestingly, in 1968, Cuban public health officials considered the development of the sector as a kind of final stage in the process of achieving regionalization. However, it is unlikely that there was yet an idea of the full importance of this development or of the exact form that it would later take.

Notwithstanding the conceptual harmony and achievements attributed to the area polyclinic by 1970, attention to user complaints and official studies of the polyclinic[9] began to reveal persistent shortcomings. The increased use of polyclinics in medical education not only increased the visibility of problems but also intensified the search for models which would more closely approximate an ideal community-polyclinic relationship (and thus provide an appropriate teaching setting for new health workers).

A very important experiment was begun in 1972, in the new "Plaza Polyclinic," adjacent to a new housing project in central Havana. Designed to serve an expanding population of prerevolutionary poor who were now occupying new housing in the area, the polyclinic was also intended as a teaching center which could serve as a model of health care with a community focus. It was here that many of the features and roles of the contemporary model of medicine in the community were first introduced.

ASSESSMENT COMMISSION FOR MEDICINE IN THE COMMUNITY

In 1974, the Ministry of Public Health designated an interdisciplinary commission to "elaborate the conceptualization of community medicine within the Marxist-Leninist and socialist ideology and character of the health system."[10] The commission began its work by first considering the different meanings of community medicine under capitalism and socialism. This analysis, already summarized in a previous section of this chapter, concluded that the community aspect of medicine in Cuba was primarily a consequence of socialism. But while the need to invent a separate community medicine disappears, another question, both technical and political, gains primacy: how is medicine to be integrated into the community? This question the commission then considered to be its area of concern—medicine in the community.

The commission vigorously pursued its evaluation and issued its assessment and recommendations. Coming from another quarter, the assessment might easily have been interpreted as an exaggerated attack on Cuban medicine. Reviewing user complaints, the commission noted: "insufficient appointments; inadequate facilities; physicians frequently in bad humor, hurried, and multi-referring; cancellation or substitution of consultations...; waiting lists; and pilgrimage through different hospitals in search of technological support (complementary tests)." A "tremendous" pressure was felt by the regional and provincial hospitals and institutes, and, the same report continued, "particularly worrisome is the overload to which emergency services are subjected, overutilized to treat problems which are not in themselves urgent."[11]

But how could such a situation exist in a country that had focused its attention on the area polyclinic? Precisely, the Commission on Medicine in the Community answered, because the conceptual focus of the system was not adequately matched by substantive focus. There was, in the words of the commission, "a noncorrespondence between the conceptual and the structural framework of the polyclinic" that was evidenced in the polyclinic's relative poverty of human and material resources. Idealistic staffing methods (somewhat similar to the mobilization methods in the "productive" sectors) made it difficult for a patient to be seen by the same person. The opposite was true as well. Physicians had trouble following a single patient through the various stages of treatment. Due to the movement of personnel and a somewhat diffuse concept of teamwork, exactly who had responsibility for a given patient at a given time was sometimes unclear and easily overlooked. The tug-of-war between hospital and polyclinic had not gone easily for the latter, and meanwhile, the patient, in the middle, was suffering.

Performing polyclinic duties only one or two days a week, physicians easily overrelied on referrals. And teaching physicians, who worked under the same conditions, were also pressured to work in the same fashion, removed from the community and its problems. Although the political interests of students were often successfully directed toward the community, this interest was soon frustrated by the noncorrespondence between concept and structure. Technical training and interests continued to be hospital-bound—even when they were developed in the polyclinic. Insufficient training to understand the concerted activities of community health promotion contributed to a technical disinterest in primary care, and the hospital's dominance of training continued the tendency to underrate the social, psychological, and ecological aspects of health. The orientation toward prevention was similarly weakened, favoring in practice, if not in theory, the cure of disease over the promotion of health. The physician was in the polyclinic, but his mind was in the hospital.

The commission also criticized the mediocre and passive community involvement of physicians: "Instead of serving, the physician tends to be served by the community and its people, in conformity with a medicine of consumption."[12]

Leaving none of the exalted concepts of Cuban socialist health organization untouched, the commission also castigated the polyclinic for deficient teamwork and the health system in general for incomplete lay participation. The polyclinic director was the only person who could be counted on with any certainty to have a view of the whole task of the health area, and this limited distribution of organizational consciousness served along with other factors to stifle teamwork.[13] At the primary level of attention, there were thus few real health teams, and the feeble teamwork which existed had insufficient ties with the community, where the leadership capacity of lay volunteers remained underdeveloped. The latter shortcoming was declared unacceptable, not only in light of the objective of community-medical integration, but also from the view of the dominant ideology of Cuban socialism: "In our country mobilization of the people is significant in its own right, for it makes possible the construction of socialism and foments, with this social practice, the development toward a new revolutionary consciousness—community consciousness."[14] The community, declared the commission, should pass from object to subject of health programs, participating in planning, execution, and control, while the health team should adopt an advisory role, sharing its technical understanding and letting itself be transformed by this practice.

In order to avoid undue emphasis on the problems of the polyclinic as a source of agitation for reform, it should be noted that problems of discontinuity in hospital care also pointed toward reform. For example, an analysis in 1970 of pediatric hospital readmissions led to a program of discharging high-risk children not to their parents alone but to the parents *and* the area health facility, designating a specific health worker personally responsible for the subsequent recuperation of the child. It was not merely the polyclinic, but also the hospital which stood to gain from an improvement of medicine in the community. But the thrust for new development, nonetheless, came primarily from the polyclinic, or perhaps one should say from the tension between the hospital and polyclinic. In this sense, the outcome of the work of the Advisory Commission on Medicine in the Community could be considered the ideology of a "polyclinic movement" which sought hegemony over the entire health system.

A NEW MODEL FOR THE AREA POLYCLINIC

The changes proposed by the Advisory Commission and adopted by the Ministry of Public Health were expressed in a new model of work for the area polyclinic. Many of its features were already present in the Plaza experiment and were soon applied in a second teaching polyclinic in the new town of Alamar, a few miles east of Havana. By March 1976, there were five model polyclinics in Cuba and at least 20 were targeted for 1980. Meanwhile, all area polyclinics were mandated to develop plans to incorporate elements of the new model in accord with local conditions. (The national plan now calls for 100 percent conformity with the model of medicine in the community by 1985.[15]) This transformation of Cuban polyclinics was to be expedited by the use of new polyclinics as teaching settings.

The new polyclinic defined by the model of medicine in the community differs from the previous model chiefly by its method of work. The polyclinic's responsibility for the health of the people in its area is entrusted to full-time physician-nurse teams and the work of these teams is "sectorized" in the fashion of a geographically-bound capitation system. That is, just like the community work of the sanitarian, whose work was already sectorized in the 1968 model, the work of each team is directed almost exclusively toward a specified geographical segment of the polyclinic's area. A pediatrician-and-nurse team, for example, is thus responsible for the health promotion of all children in a specified sector. Such teams are called primary horizontal teams.

Two kinds of activities replace the former requirement of hospital work. On the one hand, the physician-nurse teams are expected to spend a relatively large amount of time (about 12 hours per week) making home visits or doing related community work such as health education or liaison with community groups. On the other hand, the physician dedicates time to "intra-consultation." That is, instead of referring patients away to specialists, the primary care physician participates directly as a third party in consultations between patient and specialists. Although the patient may consequently follow a course of treatment with the specialist or in the hospital, the primary team follows the case and continues to schedule appropriate intra-consultations. But following the case does not include, except in special circumstances, the direct participation in hospital care by polyclinic staff physicians.

A number of consequences follow from the new approach to care. The patient no longer has to wait for a centralized clinic record room to draw his chart. Instead, she or he goes directly to the team office where all records of the catchment area are located. Although the care providers may not be specifically trained in "family practice," the new organization of health care delivery is expected to promote a family and social approach, since the primary horizontal team is likely to deal with several persons in a dwelling and neighborhood. Health activities of lay organizations are also expected to be improved by the direct involvement of physicians and nurses. The staff of the polyclinic holds regular meetings with the citizens of each sector in order to ensure continuing community participation in the protection and promotion of health. Finally, an important consequence is that preferential, systematic, and aggressive attention is given to persons of high risk. On a visit to a primary health team, one therefore sees not only the actual patient charts, but also the card files of patients with appropriate flags indicating risk categories. For each category, the team follows a specific protocol of case review. Thus, the obstetrics-gynecology team will routinely request to see the mother of a high birthweight newborn to be certain that the mother is not diabetic. And the hypertensive adult will be examined regularly by the adult medicine team (internist-and-nurse).

The polyclinic physician, then, is responsible not only for the patients who appear in the polyclinic but also for those who do not. The methodology for aggressively serving the community according to a prioritization by risk is called, after the Soviet fashion, dispensarization, but could be simply called, I think, active medicine. In the first six months of the Alamar experiment in 1975, targets for dispensarized adult medicine included adolescents, the aged, heart disease, hypertension, diabetes, stroke, asthma, tuberculosis, and cytological exams for cervical and uterine cancer.[16]

Teamwork, which was considered deficient in the critique of the "old" polyclinic, is subject to increasingly sophisticated analysis. Primary horizontal teams form the base of polyclinic work and are composed of physicians (internist, pediatrician, or obstetrician-gynecologist) and corresponding nursing staff. At the same time, these personnel are part of secondary horizontal teams, defined by the overlapping work of primary teams in a particular sector. Finally, the complete team of the sector also includes a sanitarian, perhaps a field nurse, and lay health activists.

In addition to having the usual characteristics of teamwork (practical understanding of interrelated, well-defined roles in the light of common objectives), these teams are expected to accept new members from time to time, according to specific task requirements, and even to let the lines of authority within the team shift according to the same requirements.

Departing from the nucleus of primary and secondary horizontal teams, the structure of the new polyclinic resembles the old. The polyclinic as a whole comprises the "basic team" and is guided by a director, an administrative council, and the service assembly. The latter is the institution, common to all enterprise management in Cuba, of regular assemblies of the entire workforce. The administrative council includes the leaders of secondary vertical teams: clinical, laboratory, environmental, and statistics, along with labor union representation. "Primary vertical teams" include social work, psychology, stomatology (dentistry), pediatrics, facility maintenance, statistics, and so on.

The new model for the polyclinic has a number of implications which may not be obvious. First of all, it requires the training of even more physicians than the number implied by the previous model. In this regard Cuba seems well equipped, challenging conventional wisdom with continuing plans for an increasing abundance of physicians, and anticipating a time when physicians will be found in schools, factories, and farms.[17] These tendencies increase the need for general physicians, and experimentation is currently taking place in generalist training.

By creating a clear vocational role for a physician exclusively dedicated to primary care service in the community, the new model resolves an ambiguity which was always expressed in previous years between the goal of training the "integral" physician and achieving coverage by hospital-based and primary care specialists, between the goal of community service and the goal of integration between service levels. The previous strategy of vertical integration (via academic specialties and program categories) has been modified by the prioritized strategy of horizontal integration at the base. The replacement of hospital-polyclinic rotation by the mechanism of intra-consultation, together with the definition of horizontal teamwork, creates conditions for a new set of community-bound affective relationships for the integral physician. The same process favors the advancement and integrated roles of other health workers, whose numbers and scope of training and responsibility were greatly enlarged in 1972, prior to the implementation of the new model of work. Although hardly for the first time, physician dominance is being concretely if not loudly challenged, modified by a criterion of teamwork which specifies situations where the physician is to yield team leadership to nonphysicians.

To a degree that cannot yet be specified, the turn toward medicine in the community seems to break a trend which maintained and even increased (by improving) the influence and prestige of clinical specialization. The clinical specialists, powerful on the technical committees of the ministry, exerted a dominant budgetary claim, even when the social medical perspectives determined the overall philosophy and structure. The trend in the flow of resources to the parts of the structure seemed to favor the former, and with the always expansive appetite of hospital and specialist technology for greater shares of public funds, it seems inevitable that the polyclinic perspective would be constantly threatened, particularly if it did not assert and expand its role and particularly after the Cuban budgetary generosity of the sixties was tempered by the pragmatism of the seventies.

In 1983, Cuba's commitment to health drew upon 7.8 percent of the national budget,[18] an expenditure of resources which underscores the Cuban technological optimism, believing in the ultimate value of such levels of investment.

Clearly there are parallels between the developments in the health arena and developments in the larger society, some perhaps circumstantial and others less so. Just as the economic sector suffered at the point of production in 1970 from insufficient decentralization, so the health system suffered at the point of primary services from insufficient focus of resources in the polyclinic. Just as the large-scale mobilization approach in the economy created insufficient clarity of responsibility and accountability, so the assignment of physicians for certain hours or days to the polyclinic failed to sustain either the teamwork or the individualized accountability required for patient and community health affairs.

The conditions which pressed upon the society for criticism and experimentation in 1970 similarly affected the health system. The Plaza experiment emerged in the initial period of debate following the 1970 harvest; the Alamar project coincided with the Matanzas experiment in elected government.

The Socialist Constitution of 1975 has affected the health arena in ways that appear to be supportive of decentralizing tendencies. Public health commissions at the area and municipal level are now being influenced by the participation of elected delegates to the municipal Popular Power Assembly. After the provincial reorganization, the new thirteen provinces (created out of the previous seven) have become the new loci of tertiary-level services. Each of these provinces includes teaching hospitals and teaching polyclinics.

The model of medicine in the community has had diverse effects on other parts of the health system, especially medical education and related training. Specialized models have thus developed for the "professor in the community," "the internist in the community," "the social worker in the community," and so on. The variety of these elaborations on the theme of medicine in the community is frequently expressed in Cuba's medical press and, in particular, in the work of the new Institute for Health Development (Instituto para el Desarrollo de la Salud), which publishes the influential *Revista Cubana de Administración de Salud*. This institute, founded in 1975, and the similarly new scientific association, the Sociedad Cubana de Administración de Salud, seem to have inherited at once the accumulated ideologies of social medicine, Cuban socialism, and medicine in the community.

Considering the far-reaching structural and institutional implications of medicine in the community, the concept has become much more than a model for work in the area polyclinic. As medicine in the community has come to broadly affect the entire health system, one again begins to think of medicine in the community as Cuba's community medicine.

STATISTICAL ADDENDUM (1982 statistics unless noted)—Infant mortality 17.7 per 1,000 live births. Life expectancy 73.5 years. Maternal mortality 4.8 per 10,000 live births. Immunization coverage virtually complete for common infections of childhood. 97% primary school attendance. 90% of all dwellings with plumbing. Garbage disposal available to 92.7%. Mean yearly population growth 1.1%. Percentage of deaths attributed to infectious and parasitic diseases 13.3% in 1962, 2% in 1982. Acute diarrheal diseases leading cause of death among children under one year of age in 1962, fifth cause of death in 1982. 410 tetanus deaths in 1962, 11 in 1982. No newborn deaths from tetanus since 1973. 1,402 tuberculosis deaths in 1962, 99 in 1982. Poliomyelitis eliminated in 1965. Diphtheria eliminated in 1980.

NOTES

1. Cuba, Ministerio de Salud Pública, *Indicaciones generales del Ministerio y plan de actividades principales para el desarrollo del trabajo en el sistema nacional de salud pública, 1983*. (Havana: Ministerio de Salud Pública, 1983), p. 6.
2. Margaret Gilpin, "Health and the Right to Health in Latin America: The Cuban Experience" (Paper delivered at the November 1983 Annual Meeting of the American Public Health Association, draft copy).
3. César Rodríguez Expósito, *La primera secretaria de sanidad del mundo se creó en Cuba*, Cuadernos de Historia de Salud Pública, no. 25. (Havana: n.p., 1964).
4. Joseph F. Thorning, "Social Medicine in Cuba," *The Americas*, 1 (April 1945), pp. 440-55.
5. Augusto Fernández-Conde, *Biografía de la Federación Médica de Cuba* (Havana: Colegio Médico de La Habana, 1946).
6. José Fernández Sacasas and Julio López Benítez, "El professor en la communidad," *Revista Cubana de Administración de Salud*, 2 (January-March 1976), pp. 1-9.
7. Francisco Rojas Ochoa, "El policlínico y la asistencia a pacientes ambulatorios en Cuba," *Revista Cubana de Medicina*, 10 (January-February 1971), p. 214.
8. Vicente Navarro, "Health, Health Services, and Health Planning in Cuba," *International Journal of Health Services*, 2 (August 1972), p. 397.
9. Cuba, Ministerio de Salud Pública, Dirección Provincial Habana, *Estudio estructural y funcional de los policlínicos de La Habana metropolitana*, mimeographed (Havana: Ministerio de Salud Pública, 1974).
10. Sacasas and Benítez, "El professor en la communidad," p. 1.
11. Ibid., p. 4.

12. Guillermo Barrientos Llano, "El equipo de salud en el primer nivel de atención," *Revista Cubana de Administración de Salud*, 2 (January-March 1976), p. 12.

13. Ibid., p. 19.

14. Sacasas and Benítez, "El professor en la comunidad," p. 4.

15. Cuba, Ministerio de Salud Pública, *Indicaciones generales del Ministerio*, p. 3.

16. José Fernández Sacasas et al., "Programa integral de salud para el adulto según el modelo de medicina en la comunidad," *Revista Cubana de Administración de Salud*, 1 (1975), p. 155.

17. Fidel Castro Ruz, Address to the National Assembly, *Granma*, July 24, 1983, (quoted by Gilpin).

18. Gilpin, "Health and the Right to Health."

3 Cuba's Food Distribution System

Joseph Collins and Medea Benjamin
Institute for Food and Development Policy

ON THE EVE OF REVOLUTION

Detractors of the Cuban Revolution commonly assert that Cuba was already fairly developed before the revolution. The academically inclined are wont to refer to United Nations statistics to "prove" their point. Cuba's per capita income in the 1950s—about $500 per person—was higher than that of any other Latin American country, except oil-exporting Venezuela and industrialized Argentina. Cuba's "food availability" was outdone by few other Third World countries. Even for "meat availability"—the ultimate benchmark in the West of prosperity on the food front—the island nation could boast of 70 pounds per person annually, about twice as much as Peru.[1]

But for the 1.5 million other landless farmworkers, marginal farmers, and jobless Cubans, such per capita figures would have seemed a cruel taunt.[2] Half of rural families struggled to get by on incomes of 45 pesos per month.[3] And while 70 pounds of meat were theoretically "available" annually for every Cuban, in fact only 4 percent of farmworker families ate meat regularly, according to a 1956-57 Catholic University Association survey. Only 2 percent of the families consumed eggs on a regular basis; only 11 percent regularly drank milk. "The reality is more indicting than the numbers indicate," the survey's authors commented. "The statistics are incapable of expressing the anguish of a family sitting down day after day at the dinner table—or what serves as a table—to eat the same thing with only slight variations: rice, beans and starchy root crops."[4]

Sociologist Lowry Nelson wrote in 1950 of rural Cuba's "unsightly and unpleasant human landscape" and of the "naked children, their swollen stomachs testifying to an unbalanced diet and infection from parasitic worms."[5] Chicken with rice was the favorite dish, he noted, but "needless to say, it is not within the reach of large numbers of the rural population—or the urban, for that matter."[6] Poor folks' subsistence, according to Nitza Villapol, a longtime student of Cuban food habits, was *sopa de gallo*. Perhaps the name ("rooster soup") made it sound palatable, but it was nothing to crow about, just a mix of water and brown sugar.[7]

In 1951 the World Bank sent a team of experts to Cuba to examine the nation's ills. In the health field, the study reported: "Although we have no master statistics, it is possible to estimate that more than 30 percent or 40 percent of the city population, including Havana, suffers from hyponutrition (undernutrition).... In the rural zones that percentage is doubtless more than 60 percent."[8] A 1956 study of sixth-grade children concluded that "about a third of the public school group is not receiving sufficient nutrients to maintain normal weight."[9] This study did not even cover half of Cuba's sixth-grade population—those who did not attend school and undoubtedly had the greatest nutrition problems.

THE SINGLE GREATEST ACHIEVEMENT

By the 1970s, malnutrition appeared to be reduced to a very low level, as evidenced by the 1972 child growth study administered by the Cuban Ministry of Health—one of the most comprehensive growth studies ever undertaken in any country. It found no incidence of second-degree or third-degree malnutrition, and only three percent of the children had the milder first-degree malnutrition.[10] The study also found that younger children, who benefited from the generalized improvements in health services and nutrition since the Revolution, are growing at faster rates than older ones. A 1982 follow-up study, to be completed in late 1984, is expected to confirm that Cuban children are getting taller.

The infant mortality rate, one of the best indicators of a nation's health, has decreased steadily throughout the 1970s. By 1983, it had reached the astonishingly low figure of 16.8 per thousand.[11] By comparison, in the neighboring country of Haiti the 1975–80 estimate of infant mortality rate was 126.9 per thousand.[12] Cuba's rate is now the lowest in Latin America and on par with the most industrially developed countries in the world. In fact, it is lower than the rate for the black population in the United States, which in 1982 was 18.1 per thousand.[13]

Diseases associated with poverty, such as acute diarrhea and tuberculosis, are no longer among the top 10 causes of death. Infectious and parasitic diseases caused 13.3 percent of deaths in 1962, but only 2 percent of deaths in 1980.[14] As some Cuban officials are proud to note, the principal causes of death in Cuba today are similar to those causes in developed countries: heart disease, malignant tumors, cardiovascular disease, and accidents. As a result of these changes, the rate of life expectancy has risen from 57 years in 1958 to 73.5 years in 1983, comparable to rates in advanced industrialized nations. Cubans are dying from diseases associated with older populations. A 1982 report prepared for the Joint Economic Committee of the U.S. Congress acknowledged that Cuba had achieved a "highly egalitarian redistribution of income that has eliminated almost all malnutrition, particularly among young children."[15]

While there are still isolated cases of malnutrition—children of alcoholic or very young mothers, children not living with their mothers, families who have recently migrated from the countryside and live on the periphery of the cities—malnutrition as a social phenomenon has been eliminated. While in the United Stated this may not seem to be a startling accomplishment, let us remember that no other country in all of Latin America—including those with greater per capita food supplies—can make this claim. It is the single most unassailable achievement of the Cuban Revolution.

HOW THE POOR GOT MORE

How has Cuba, an economically underdeveloped country, achieved the elimination of malnutrition? Key factors include the provision of health care for all Cubans and the improvement of sanitary conditions, which has reduced the incidence of infectious diseases such as acute diarrhea and tuberculosis. The most important factor, however, undoubtedly has been the more equitable distribution of food.

The elimination of hunger in Cuba cannot be attributed to any spectacular gains in food production. In fact, Cuba's food production record has been rather dismal. Gains in some areas (e.g., milk, eggs, and rice) have been offset by failures in others (e.g., meat, beans, and traditional root crops), and per capita food availability today is not significantly greater than before the Revolution (although we should not overlook that the population has grown by almost 50 percent). The radical change has not been in food availability, but in its distribution.

The "first and foremost duty" of the revolutionary leadership according to Ché Guevara was to ensure that no one in Cuba went hungry. Viewing inadequate income as the fundamental reason why people were undernourished, they implemented policies designed to boost the earnings of the poorer sector and to enlarge the portion of their earnings spent on food.

Above all, the government sought to generate fuller employment. Job opportunities for farmworkers soared. On the large estates converted into "people's farms" by the first agrarian reform law, the number of workers employed year-round in August 1962 was three times greater than the less than 50,000 employed in 1959.[16] In addition, numerous sugar plantation workers previously unemployed during the long "dead season" now found steady work on the construction projects that seemed to be springing up everywhere—roads, schools, clinics, government offices, and housing.

Many poor farmers, thanks to the new government's policies, also found themselves with more money. By granting land ownership to some 100,000 tenant farmers, sharecroppers, and squatters, the first agrarian reform of 1959 freed farmers from the obligation to pay absentee landlords as much as 40 percent of the value of their crops.[17] Moreover, they could now obtain cheap credit from the government and depend on stable prices for their produce.[18] In urban areas, many workers won substantial wage increases, thanks in part to the strength of their unions. Even the earnings of the poorest workers notched upward. By one estimate, the bottom 40 percent of wage earners enlarged their slice of the national income "pie" from 6.5 percent before the revolution to 17 percent by 1962.[19]

Gains for the urban unemployed came more slowly, but by 1962 expanding state payrolls and productive investments were sharply cutting unemployment. Eighty-six percent of those workers who had found employment for less than six months a year before the revolution were finding work for ten or more months three years later, according to one survey.[20] Higher wages and reduced unemployment meant more money in the hands of poorer urban households, especially those with more than one wage earner.

The new government also sought to enable low-income households to spend more of their earnings on food. It made basic social services free for everyone, including not only schooling, medical care, medicines, and social security, but also water, burial services, sports facilities, and even public phones. The government lowered the charges for electricity, gas, and public transportation that had eaten up so much of working people's earnings. The numbers racket and other forms of gambling that preyed on the incomes of the poor were outlawed. In 1960 the government initiated its "urban reform" by decreeing bold rent reductions.

The net effect of fuller employment and expanded free or highly subsidized services was an historically unprecedented redistribution of income—the transfer of 15 percent of the national income from property owners to wage earners in the first year alone.[21] In no other society have the poor and middle classes so rapidly found themselves with "extra money" on their hands. (For further information, see Chapter 10 by Claes Brundenius, "Cuba: Redistribution and Growth with Equity.")

What did people do with so much extra money? Among the most pressing desires for the poor was to eat more and better. Peasant families, freed from landlord obligations and moneylenders, could eat more of what they produced. Those who for years had raised pigs but could never afford to eat them, now could do so. Nationwide consumption of such coveted foods as pork and milk soared: beef consumption shot up by 50 percent in just two years.[22] Even the economically advantaged consumed more locally produced goods, since it was increasingly difficult to go on shopping sprees in Miami or buy luxury imports in Cuba.

SUPPLY LAGS BEHIND DEMAND

The food supply failed to keep pace with the growing demand. Overall agricultural production was handicapped by the flight to the United States of administrative and technical personnel. The consequent lack of organizational and technical experience on the newly created people's farms and cooperatives lowered production. The Eisenhower administration's 1960 embargo on most exports to Cuba seriously disrupted the island's agriculture, which had become dependent on the United States for farm machinery, fertilizers, pesticides, seeds, and other items. In addition, the Central Intelligence Agency fostered acts of sabotage, including burning fields and slaughtering cattle. Such sabotage, as well as repeated military attacks culminating in the failed Bay of Pigs invasion in April 1961, forced Cuba to divert scarce human and material resources into defense, exacting a toll on production. As if all this were not enough, a severe drought in 1962 further aggravated food production problems.

In a reversal of the pre-1959 pattern, shortages became more chronic in the cities than in the countryside. Not only did farmers consume more of their own produce, but finding ever fewer consumer goods to buy in the countryside, especially imports from the United States, they had little need for cash and thus produced less for the market.[23]

The disruption of normal imports further aggravated supply problems. Before the revolution, Cuba was dependent on large quantities of food imports—wheat, rice, beans, lard, poultry, dairy products, and eggs, even onions and garlic. The abrupt embargo on U.S. trade with Cuba left the country in dire straits, since over 70 percent of these imports came from the United States.[24] Cuba depended not only on imports of U.S. food and agricultural inputs but also on the materials needed to package food, the machines needed to process food, the trucks needed to transport food, and so on. The U.S. trade embargo revealed the true depth of Cuba's food dependency.

The irony of the mounting food crisis was apparent by the third year of the revolution. Prime Minister Fidel Castro, in a high-level national conference on production in 1961, responded to Western reports about Cuba's food crisis: "The problem in Cuba is not one of hunger. That was the problem before, when 300,000 to 400,000 people didn't have a cent in their pockets. Our problem is precisely that now people have work and have money.... While production has gone up since the revolution, it hasn't caught up to the increase in purchasing power.... The only way to produce more is to put everyone to work, but by putting everyone to work, we find that the goods and production capacity which existed fall short of the demand created."[25]

BEYOND THE "FREE-MARKET"

Even in the revolution's first months, it was clear that the ground rules of the "free market," that is, instituting higher prices could have taken care of the shortage problem. Such a development, which would have wiped out the gains in living standards made by urban and rural workers, was unacceptable to the new government. Instead it tried price controls.

Just three months into the revolution the government set official prices for a number of state foods and placed ceilings of 10 and 20 percent respectively on wholesale and retail profit margins. Still the situation was far from under control. Price controls proved extremely difficult to enforce in a society with a multitude of small retailers and with the unwritten law that everyone looks out for his or her self. Speculation and hoarding were widespread enough for Fidel Castro to label speculators "the number one enemy of the revolution."[26]

In an attempt to stem speculation, the wholesale food business was nationalized and those retail stores accused of hoarding and profiteering were taken over by the government. By 1961, some 8,000 retail outlets had been taken over.[27] At the same time, the government's agrarian reform agency set up *tiendas del pueblo* ("people's stores") in the rural areas in an effort to improve the supply of basic consumer goods—at official prices. There were 2,000 such stores throughout the countryside by 1961.[28]

But try as the fledgling government might, speculators' prices reigned as supply problems multiplied; and it was poor Cubans who were being shortchanged. The result was a form of rationing by income which was against all that the revolutionary leadership stood for. They might have opted simply to make certain basic staples available to the poor at low prices (and thus to create different diets for the rich and the poor), but instead they decided to institute a rationing system for all Cubans covering most important food items.[29]

Rationing was initially intended as a stopgap measure, until supply caught up with demand. Many of the desired production increases still have not materialized, and rationing, as a way to equitably distribute scarce goods, continues to this day.

How Does Cuba's Ration System Work?

Ration books are distributed each year by household. Each household chooses the neighborhood store where it wants to shop, and then registers with the National Rationing Board (OFICODA) so that its rations will be sent to that store. The household must continue to buy in the same place. If for some reason the members of a household want to change stores—another shop becomes more convenient, they dislike the grocer—they can go back to the rationing board and reregister elsewhere. Household members must also reregister if they move to another neighborhood, and they must advise the rationing board of any change in the household size (through births, deaths, marriages, etc.), so that its ration may be changed accordingly.

All stores are government owned. The takeover of private businesses began early in the revolution when the government expropriated stores engaged in hoarding and speculation. Later the government nationalized all stores owned by U.S. citizens and those run by Cubans who had left the country. The expropriation of the remaining 55,600 small private businesses—which accounted for about one-third of retail sales—came in 1968 as a major part of the "revolutionary offensive."[30]

Prices for rationed foods remained frozen from the early 1960s, when rationing was introduced, until 1981 when they were modestly raised. But even the new prices are low. Prices are uniform throughout the nation, no matter the size of the store or the distance the goods were transported, so there is no point in shopping around for a better deal.

Every member of the household is entitled to a fixed monthly "food basket" consisting principally of rice, beans or other legumes, oil, lard, sugar, salt, coffee, beef, and chicken, plus a varying supply of fruits and vegetables depending on availability. Certain individuals are entitled to extras according to their special needs. All children under seven years old, for instance, receive a liter of milk daily; children under two years of age receive, in addition to their daily liter of milk, 20 jars of strained fruit a month. Those over 65 years old may buy six cans of milk a month, instead of the normal three; and workers in particularly strenuous or hazardous jobs, such as miners and canecutters and national athletes, are entitled to extra rations. (During harvest canecutters get about 5,000 calories in rationed food items, more than twice the normal allotment.) There are many special rations (called *dietas*) provided with a doctor's prescription. These allow for the sale of extra food rations for pregnant women, underweight or lactose-intolerant children, and people suffering from such diseases as ulcers, diabetes, and anemia.

During a couple of difficult periods in the first decade of the revolution, the *libreta* ("ration book") represented virtually all the food available to Cubans, and even then the amounts varied. As one top Cuban planner said, "We're not ashamed to admit it: there were years when we had to live on the ration alone, and there was practically nothing in the cafeterias and restaurants. Those were years when we really went hungry."[31] But since the early 1970s, the situation has changed radically, and the ration not only can be counted on, but for the vast majority of Cubans it supplies only a part of the basic diet.

A breakdown of the ration's caloric content is shown in Table 3.1. While it varies somewhat from month to month, the ration provides around 1,900 calories a day, on a relatively equitable basis. (Again, for almost all Cubans the ration supplies only part of diet. According to the U.N. Food and Agriculture Organization, Cuba's daily per capita caloric intake in 1980 was 2,795 calories, well above U.N. standards.)[32]

Nonrationed Sources of Food

In addition to the ration system, there are any number of other sources of food. But prices tend to be much more significant, and thus income differences can play a role. During the 1970s, the number of foods sold off the ration substantially increased.[33] The most important items "liberated" from the ration have been staples such as bread, eggs, fish, spaghetti, and butter. The supply of these staples has become sufficient to meet demand, and they are generally inexpensive.

Also there are now many goods sold both on and off the ration, the critical difference being price. A liter of milk, for example, costs 25 centavos on the ration and 80 centavos off the ration; a package of coffee sold on the ration for 30 centavos goes for three pesos—ten times more—off the ration.

The black market and what we call the "gray market" are other important channels of food distribution in Cuba. Privately exchanging goods obtained through the ration is a good example of the gray market in action. One family might trade their excess milk for their neighbor's sugar. Technically illegal, these kinds of exchanges go on everyday in Cuba and are really an unofficial way of adjusting for the fact that the ration allots a standard amount for everyone, regardless of individual tastes and needs.

Black market deals, on the other hand, often involve goods stolen from government sources and then resold. Such sales are obviously illegal, but they are only sporadically prosecuted. Butchers are notorious for shortweighing meat sold to their customers and then selling the extra meat on the black market. Not surprisingly, black market prices are high. Chicken may cost three pesos a pound, and beef may cost up to eight pesos a pound. The administrator of a snack bar can snip a little cheese from each of the sandwiches and sell it on the side for about four pesos a pound.

TABLE 3.1. Caloric Content of Ration: Average Allocation for One Month, One Person

Food	Weight	Calories/day
Beef	1 lb. 4 ozs.	84
Chicken[a]	1 lb. 11 ozs.	40
Rice	5 lbs.	275
Cornmeal[b]	4 ozs.	14
Beans	1 lb. 4ozs.	66
Oil	8 ozs.	68
Lard	1 lb.	136
Sugar	4 lbs.	242
Milk (fresh)[c]	4 qts.	86
Milk (canned)[d]	3 qts.	55
Coffee	4 ozs.	0
Bread[e]	15 lbs.	624
Tomato Sauce	8 ozs.	3
Other[f]	--	150
According to Supply[g]		
Viandas (Vegetables)	6 lbs.	35
Fruit (Orange)	1 lb.	7
Vegetable (Tomato)	3 lbs.	10
Total calories/day		1,895

[a]Figure presented is the monthly average, although meat is distributed every nine days (either 12 ozs. of meat or 1 lb. of chicken).

[b]Cornmeal is the only fixed ration item that is not always available. It seems the government is not very concerned about fulfilling this quota because people are not anxious to buy it.

[c]The 4 qt. figure was obtained by multiplying the milk ration for children under seven years old by the percentage of the population under seven.

[d]The 3 qt. figure was obtained by multiplying the milk allocations for different population groups (6 cans per month for the 7-13 age group; 3 cans per month for those 13-65 years old; 6 cans per month for those over 65 years old) by the proportion of the population in each age group.

[e]Officially part of the ration but often so readily available that it is sold off the *libreta*.

[f]Mayonnaise, sweets, cooking wine, baby food, etc.

[g]Fruits and vegetables are seasonal, and the ration varies according to supply. This is a rough estimate.

There are also restaurants and snack bars. The choices available today range from fast food pizza and fried chicken chains—excruciatingly slow by American standards—to deluxe dining with tuxedoed waiters, extensive wine lists, and prices to match any posh New York eatery. Another important source of food is school and work cafeterias. School meals are free. Workplace meals, which were free until the more cost-conscious economic policies of the mid-1970s are now subsidized.

In 1982 over two million Cubans—one-fifth of the population—ate at least one hot meal a day in cafeterias at schools, work centers, and hospitals.

Despite the growing number of additional sources of food for Cubans, demand for more and better quality foods has continued to outdistance supply. In 1980 the government attempted to further stimulate food production through the creation of farmers' markets. These markets allowed private farmers (who in 1980 still held 20 percent of the land) to sell directly to consumers once they had fulfilled their government production quotas. Prices were to be determined by supply and demand, without government interference. The concept of government-administered private markets represented a major departure from past policy, which had virtually outlawed private food sales and left private farmers little legal incentive to increase their production.

Farmers' markets blossomed throughout the island, and for the first time since the revolution Cubans had access to a more varied and higher quality diet. But the markets, which President Castro later condemned as "a capitalist way of solving socialist problems," were immediately plagued by a myriad of abuses, which soon led to their downfall.

Prices on the markets were so high that only the affluent could afford to buy there. State resources, such as tractors, fertilizer, and seeds, were being illegally diverted to the private sector. Worst of all, with an easing of restrictions on buying, selling, and transporting food, and a lack of control in the marketplace, the markets where all vendors were supposed to be producers became overrun by intermediaries. These go-betweens, President Castro charged, so skillfully manipulated the markets that "some of them would have been brilliant on the New York Stock Exchange."[34] They held back goods until supplies were scarce, illegally transported produce from the rural areas to the cities where they would fetch higher prices, and raised prices to exorbitant levels when demand outdistanced supply.

The government was obviously in a quandary. On the one hand, the markets were satisfying certain demands, and many Cubans had come to depend on them as a regular supplement to their diet. On the other hand, the government could not continue to sanction the full-fledged corruption and price gouging that had become rampant in the markets, especially in Havana. In February 1983 the police raided all 12 markets in Havana and several elsewhere on the island, arresting hundreds of vendors. It did not officially close the markets but instituted greater controls over who and what could be sold. It also levied a 20 percent tax on gross sales in an effort to make private sales less appealing to the farmer, while significantly increasing the prices at which farmers could sell their extra products to the government.

The government also moved to expand its own role as a marketer of nonrationed foods. New larger government markets were opened and existing ones expanded. The array of foods available at these new government stores—meats, coffee, export-quality rum, candies, pastries, beans, rice, sugar—is unprecedented in post-revolutionary Cuba. The prices, however, are equal to or in some cases even higher than those that had prevailed on the black market and in the farmers' market.

THE FUTURE OF CUBA'S FOOD DISTRIBUTION SYSTEM

The significance of this expansion of nonration food sales (the so-called parallel market) on the future of the ration system remains to be seen. Some policymakers believe the parallel market should sell only luxury goods with the ration continuing to provide the basics; others think it should sell both luxury and basic goods, and the ration should be eliminated.

The ration system has led to a lack of selection and of quality—take it or leave it is the rule. The result is a dearth of attractive goods on the marketplace. Thus the current policy of monetary incentives to motivate people to work more and better is undercut. Undoubtedly this consideration was a factor in the government's decisions to open the farmers' markets and to expand its own nonration market system.

In the view of some policymakers, rationing distorts the economy, for foods are sold at prices way below production costs. With prices frozen from 1962 until 1981, Cubans have been insulated from the effects of worldwide inflation, constantly rising import costs, and wild fluctuations in the price of sugar on the world market. Over the years, this protection has translated into heavy government subsidies. Meat and beans were sold at less than half the government-stated cost, and milk was sold at 29 percent below cost.[35] In 1980, the government estimated that food subsidies (taking into account both retail sales and subsidized meals at workplaces) amounted to 25 pesos a month per person.[36] The 1981 price hike substantially reduced subsidies but did not eliminate them.[37]

For these policymakers, the most troubling effect of rationing is the "mentality" they consider it to have created. Many Cubans, they argue, have come to see rationing not as an emergency response to distribute scarce goods equitably, but as a perpetual right to buy goods at prices that have nothing to do with costs. And it is true that consumers will buy this or that item on the ration simply because "it's owed them" regardless of whether they really need it.

Proponents of the expanded parallel market replacing the rationing system argue that the egalitarian basis of rationing thwarts the development of socialism.[38] The fundamental principle of socialism, as they see it, is to each according to his or her work. Those who work harder and better should earn more. (Indeed the tendency toward distribution according to need and wage equality has since the early 1970s been officially labeled an idealistic error, and a number of measures since then have tried to put this understanding of socialism into effect. For instance, wherever feasible, salaries have been made dependent on the quantity and quality of work.) But, this argument continues, rewarding greater productive effort and accomplishment is futile unless more and more desirable things are offered to the workers to buy. And that is exactly what rationing, by seeing that all receive the same, works against. Rationing, then, is not a socialist form of distribution but a communist one (to each according to his or her *need*), for which Cuba is not yet sufficiently developed.[39]

Proponents of continued rationing fear that prices would tend toward the high levels of the parallel market if rationing were stopped without a significant boost in food production. To get a sense of what this might be like, we calculated what the monthly ration would cost at November 1983 parallel market prices. Food that can be purchased for 11.82 pesos on the ration would cost 53.22 pesos—almost five times as much. Of course, the government now sets nonrationed market prices. Were rationing abolished, it could choose to set new prices somewhere between present parallel market and ration prices. But even so, an end to rationing would mean higher food prices. For those who cling to a vision of an egalitarian socialism, this is unacceptable. They would rather wait for significant production gains before ending the ration.

In response, policymakers against rationing contend that banking on increased production to end rationing is not sufficient. They think that as long as prices are kept artificially low, demand will be inordinately high. Moreover, these critics argue, low prices actually ensure the perpetuation of the ration system: they reduce the motivation to work harder, so that production declines, scarcity persists, and rationing continues.

The way to eliminate rationing, they contend, is by increased production and periodic price hikes. High prices make people work harder to earn more money. If you know, for example, that you can buy steak on the parallel market for eight pesos a pound, you might be inclined to work overtime to earn a few extra pesos. But if steak is sold only on the ration at a mere 70 centavos a pound, you might prefer to go home and watch television instead. And if people work longer and harder (and watch television less), supply could meet demand, and prices would fall. Then the rationing system, according to these critics, will be obsolete. Although prices will be higher than the ration prices, with increased worker productivity prices should be lower than they have been on the parallel market or the black market.

One approach Cuban policymakers debating the future of the food distribution system appear reluctant to consider, at least publicly, is replacing rationing with income supplements for those whose basic well-being would be threatened by an end to rationing. Such a program would appear to satisfy their concern about the fate of low-income families. At the same time, compensating the poor for increased food prices would undoubtedly be cheaper than the present policy of subsidizing everyone through artificially low prices and the maintenance of the huge rationing system. In 1980 the government estimated spending 22 million pesos on social assistance, while the whole range of food subsidies for consumers totaled almost three billion pesos.[40]

There are other ways to see that low-income households get at least the basic necessities. But in the ration system the Cuban leadership appears to have locked itself into the most expensive system, one that was developed in an emergency and quite probably has long outlived much of its usefulness.

Who is likely to win the debate on rationing—those who favor a quick frontal blow or the advocates of the long, hard pull? The ration advocates have some important advantages. One is bureaucratic inertia. The administrative apparatus needed to keep the ration system going will be very hard to dismantle. At the same time the Cuban people have become accustomed to rationing and have come to see cheap food as their right, associating rationing with the ideals of social justice upon which the revolution stakes its claim to legitimacy. The impression we get is that while Cubans constantly grumble about rationing and say they would love to see it stopped, they would feel somewhat naked without it. (Remember, more than half of the Cubans alive today were born after the start of the revolution and do not know anything else.) And they would certainly not be pleased if rationing were replaced by high food prices.

Whether because the government enjoys most people's support or because it tightly controls public activity, it is unlikely that an end to food subsidies would spark the same outbreaks of rioting that have accompanied such moves in Egypt, Tunisia, Morocco, and Poland. But the groundswell of near-universal discontent over the increase in restaurant prices in 1981 (subsequently rolled back) taught the technocratic planners a lesson they probably have not forgotten.

The ration system, with all its drawbacks, has been a useful tool in helping to eliminate hunger, but Cuba has reached a new stage of development. Its citizens will continue to demand a more satisfying diet. For the foreseeable future, government leadership will be forced to grapple with how to satisfy this demand while maintaining the original goals of creating a more equitable society.

NOTES

1. *FAO Production Yearbook, 1958* (Rome: Food and Agriculture Organization of the United Nations, 1959).
2. Robin Blackburn, "Prologue to the Cuban Revolution," *New Left Review*, October 1964, p. 83.
3. Agrupación Católica Universitaria, "¿Por qué Reforma Agraria?" mimeographed, 1956-57, p. 191.
4. The Catholic University Association survey concluded that 91 percent of farmworkers were undernourished. But a critical look at this survey reveals methodological flaws that tend to inflate the figures on malnutrition. For example, the study claims that farmworkers consumed 1,000 calories a day less than the optimal diet. When calculating caloric intake, however, they failed to include such foods as fruit and sugar. Another example is that after calculating the average height of the agricultural worker as 5 feet 4 inches, they used "commonly accepted tables" of height for weight (no reference given) to conclude that Cubans were 16 pounds underweight. However, a check of standard height/weight tables (e.g., Metropolitan Life tables) shows these workers to be within the optimal range for their heights. Therefore, we believe that the survey's conclusion that 91 percent were undernourished is exaggerated. Our misgivings about the statistics, however, in no way detract from the validity of the survey's general statements about the poverty of the farmworkers or the inadequate and monotonous diet.

5. Lowry Nelson, *Rural Cuba* (Minneapolis: University of Minnesota Press, 1950), p. 4.
6. Ibid., p. 209.
7. Personal interview with Nitza Villapol, January, 1982.
8. International Bank for Reconstruction and Development, *Report on Cuba* (Baltimore: Johns Hopkins Press, 1951), p. 442.
9. Norman Jolliffe, et al., "Nutritional Survey of the Sixth Grade School Population of Cuba," *The Journal of Nutrition* 64, (1958), p. 394.
10. José R. Jordan, *Desarrollo humano en Cuba* (Havana: Editorial Científico-Técnica, 1979). Also personal interview with Dr. Jordan, November 1983.
11. *Prensa Latina*, 4 March 1984.
12. *U.N. Demographic Yearbook*, June 1983.
13. U.S. Department of Health, *Monthly Vital Statistics Report*, vol. 31, no. 13 (Oct. 5, 1983).
14. Ministerio de Salud Pública, *Salud para todos* (Havana: Ministerio de Salud Pública, July 9, 1983), p. 23.
15. Lawrence H. Theriot, *Cuba Faces the Economic Realities of the 80s*, East-West Trade Policy Staff Paper (Washington, D.C.: U.S. Government Printing Office: 1982), p. 5.
16. Arthur MacEwan, *Revolution and Economic Development* (New York: St. Martin's Press, 1981), p. 53ff.
17. International Labour Office, *The Landless Farmer in Latin America* (Geneva: International Labour Office, 1957), p. 66ff.
18. Brian H. Pollitt, "Agrarian Reform and the 'Agricultural Proletariat' in Cuba, 1958-1966: Further Notes and Some Second Thoughts," (Glasgow: Institute of Latin American Studies, University of Glasgow, 1979), p. 10.
19. Claes Brundenius, *Economic Growth, Basic Needs and Income Distribution in Revolutionary Cuba* (Lund, Sweden: Research Policy Institute, 1981), p. 148.
20. Maurice Zeitlin, *Revolutionary Politics and the Cuban Working Class* (Princeton: Princeton University Press, 1967), Table 2.6, p. 60.
21. Eric R. Wolf and Edward C. Hansen, *The Human Condition in Latin America* (Oxford: Oxford University Press, 1972), p. 337.
22. Edward Boorstein, *The Economic Transformation of Cuba* (New York: Monthly Review Press, 1968), p. 94.
23. Andrés Bianchi, "Agriculture—The Post-Revolutionary Development," in Dudley Seers, ed., *Cuba: The Economic and Social Revolution* (Chapel Hill, N.C.: University of North Carolina Press, 1964), p. 136.
24. Dudley Seers, ed., *Cuba: The Economic and Social Revolution* (Chapel Hill, N.C.: University of North Carolina Press, 1964), p. 20.
25. *Obra Revolucionaria*, National Production Conference, August 26, 1961.

26. Ibid.

27. Archibald Ritter, *The Economic Development of Revolutionary Cuba* (New York: Praeger, 1974), p. 83.

28. Hugh Thomas, *Cuba: The Pursuit of Freedom* (New York: Harper and Row, 1971), p. 1333.

29. In this chapter we are discussing only the food ration book (*la libreta de comida*). There is a separate ration card (*la libreta de ropa*) for nonfood items such as sheets, towels, shoes, toilet articles, and fabric, as well as ration coupons for gasoline.

30. Martin Kenner and James Petras, eds., *Fidel Castro Speaks* (New York: Grove Press, 1969), p. 225.

31. Miguel Dotres, cited in Nelson P. Valdés, "Cuba: Social Rights and Basic Needs." Paper presented to the Inter-American Commission on Human Rights, Washington, D.C., 25 February 1983, p. 101 (retranslated).

32. Food and Agriculture Organization, *Food Balance Sheet, 1979–81*.

33. The Cuban Institute for Research on Internal Demand (ICIOIDI) reports that in 1970, 93 percent of basic food items were rationed and by 1980 only 41 percent were rationed.

34. Fidel Castro's speech to ANAP Congress, May 1983, available in Fidel Castro, *Speeches at Three Congresses* (Havana: Editora Política, 1983).

35. *Granma*, December 14, 1981, p. 2.

36. Brundenius, *Economic Growth*, p. 158 cites interview with Carlos Rafael Rodríguez. While not specified, we assume this figure is not just the difference between production costs and retail prices, but also includes the cost of transportation, storage, and other marketing costs.

37. The government is on record as saying that eventually subsidies will be eliminated. But as long as rationing reinforces the attitude that so much of this or that is someone's due, it seems unlikely that subsidies will be done away with. First, no spectacular gains in production are on the horizon. Second, prices of foods that are imported are likely to continue to rise, and it is doubtful that it would be acceptable to pass these increases on to the consumer regularly.

38. See, for instance, José M. Norniella Rodríguez, "El Mercado Paralelo: Una Vía del Sistema de Dirección y Planificación de la Economía para Eliminar el Racionamiento," *Cuestiones de la Economía Planificada*, vol. 3, p. 6.

39. These critics of the ration system take pains to point out that early in the Revolution rationing did help to justly distribute basic goods in scarce supply at a time when private speculation reigned. But for them, the basic circumstances have changed, and it is therefore time to do away with rationing.

40. Calculated from Carlos Rafael Rodríguez's estimate of 25 pesos per person per month cited in Brundenius, *Economic Growth*, p. 158.

4   Women in Socialist Cuba, 1959–84

Alfred Padula and Lois Smith

It was 1978. Our bus was plunging eagerly along the road toward Banes in Eastern Cuba. In front of us two young girls in proper school uniforms were alternately giggling and perusing their schoolbooks. They were learning the Cyrillic alphabet. When we inquired about this, they replied that they were training to be nurses and would soon be going to the Soviet Union for a year to continue their studies.

One could not help but be struck by the extraordinary improvement in life chances, that these schoolgirls from the country were enjoying. They were part of a revolutionary process that has had a profound effect on Cuban women. The revolution has brought women out of the home and into the "streets" of the political and economic life of the nation. It has opened new opportunities for them in the work force and provided significant educational and health benefits. It has offered new and abundant goals, values and rewards for Cuban women and has given them a new sense of dignity and worth.

But these changes have not been won without considerable costs, for both Cuban women and society as a whole. Rapid social change has shattered the traditional Cuban family. As one Cuban observer put it, the "traditional, bourgeois, and even feudal Spanish family structure does not work within a revolutionary context."[1]

The revolution has put great pressure on Cuban women, who are now called upon to excell at work, to volunteer, to study, to participate in sports and politics, and to raise families—to be super women. More than a few have been unnerved by these rapid changes. An official of the Federation of Cuban Women (Federación de Mujeres Cubanas [FMC]) noted in 1983 that housewives did not "understand" their place in society.[2] Yet it is clear that there are still more changes to come if Cuban women are to achieve the full equality with men that is guaranteed by the constitution and demanded by the Communist party.

Who would have imagined in the easygoing days of the early 1950s that this great whirlwind of social change lay just over the horizon? The Cuba of the 1950s was a loose cluster of families in an easygoing republic largely indifferent to its citizens. Women did not participate in any significant way in public life. Perhaps the best known women were the wives of presidents, such as Martha Miranda de Batista, or leaders of high society, such as the Condesa de Camargo, María Luisa Gómez Mena, who as a rich widow, played matriarch and lady bountiful with the income from her late husband's sugar mills and Havana real estate.

Beyond the canasta games and fur coats of the Havana Country Club there were also notable middle-class women such as Elena Mederos, civic leader, feminist, and president of the Lyceum Lawn and Tennis Club, and Conchita Castañeda of the Auténtico Party.[3] Employed middle-class women worked as secretaries, school teachers, bureaucrats, shop clerks and in other similar positions. Daisy Granados, a film star of the 1970s, was a part-time clerk in El Fin del Siglo department store in 1958.

There were fewer opportunities for the lower-class women, who comprised most of the female work force of some 262,000—or 17 percent of all Cuban workers.[4] Opportunities for women were diminished by the substantial levels of male unemployment and underemployment in the 1950s and complicated by low levels of education and literacy. Rural women had an even more difficult time finding employment since the major activity of the Cuban economy, sugar plantation agriculture, employed few women, and Cuba lacked the kind of handicrafts tradition that provided part-time employment for rural women elsewhere in Latin America.[5]

Domestic service—often in the homes of the urban bourgeoisie—provided the major opportunity for poor Cuban women. Perhaps as many as 200,000, or 70 percent of all working women, served as maids and domestics.[6]

Some women found work as prostitutes. Indeed, Fidel Castro once stated that he believed there were 100,000 prostitutes in the old Cuba. Castro and Cuban journalists have repeatedly blamed imperialism for this sordid situation. But as Luis Salas has noted in his study of Cuban criminality, prostitution in Havana had been a well-established routine since the 16th century when Spanish treasure fleets bound from Mexico to Spain stopped in Havana prior to braving the broad Atlantic.[7] The director of the program to rehabilitate prostitutes has estimated that there were 10,000 prostitutes in Havana and between 30,000 and 40,000 in all of Cuba.[8]

Prostitution in prerevolutionary Cuba reflected the double standards and patriarchal nature of the old society. At the onset of puberty, boys were taken by their fathers to neighborhood brothels to be initiated into the mysteries of sex.[9] Brothels were a necessary function in a society that emphasized machismo and experience for men and virginity for women—of a certain class.

For most lower-class women, life was an endless struggle of caring for large broods of children whose fathers were often absent or unemployed. Often, conjugal unions were not sanctified by marriage. The Cuban slave Esteban Montejo recalls making love to 50 women during a visit to Havana to celebrate Cuba's independence in 1898, but in his old age in the 1960s, he could not recall whether or not he had had any children.[10]

Women's participation in Castro's guerrilla rebellion against the Batista dictatorship was a limited one. Some women demonstrated against the dictator, while others aided the rebels by gathering intelligence, serving as couriers, or selling war bonds. A small number fought in the hills. A few were martyred. Others such as Celia Sánchez, Haydée Santamaría, and Melba Hernández, survived to become heroines and to hold high office in the postrevolutionary society.

Castro did not make any particular appeal or special promises to Cuban women during his rebellion. His classic exposition, "History Will Absolve Me," scarcely mentions women or their problems.[11] But once in power, he began to pay increasing attention to women. He was apparently not following any particular script, as he did in the case of blacks, but rather proceeded pragmatically, seeing in women an untapped resource of energy that he might employ to aid his revolution.

Prostitutes were among the first beneficiaries of the moral crusade that Castro launched in 1959 against the corruption of the old regime. Brothel owners fled, and pimps were arrested. A program to close the brothels began in 1961 and concluded in 1966. Prostitutes were sent to special schools to be re-educated and trained for more socially acceptable tasks, such as factory work.

The threat of counterrevolution in 1960 and 1961 led to the first systematic mobilization of women. Women were asked to join the militias and the Committees for the Defense of the Revolution. Young women, sometimes barely teenagers, were sent to the countryside to participate in the great literacy campaign. Perhaps 50,000 went. It was a dramatic moment for these young women, who, armed with a lantern, a blanket, and a primer, ventured, often for the first time, into the interior. Many young urban women became radicals as a result of this experience. They had become participants in great national events.

For their parents, it was a moment of great anxiety; the first confrontation between the Revolution and the patriarch-dominated Cuban family. Fathers did not want their daughters to go. "One goes, two come back," they said. Their role as guardian of their daughter's virtue—and as patriarch—was being challenged by the state.

The lives of middle-class women began to disintegrate. The Church, long the solace of bourgeois women, was under attack. The Virgin de Caridad de Cobre, patroness of Cuba, was scarcely mentioned in the media. The private school system was nationalized. Many commodities, from deodorants to food stuffs, were scarce, making it increasingly difficult to keep one's body and one's home looking attractive. Some mothers, alarmed by rumors of plans for the "communist indoctrination" of children and by fears that their children would be sent to Russia, sent them instead—sometimes unaccompanied—to Miami.

Other middle-class women went into exile themselves and would suffer a horrendous drop in status. Bourgeois matrons, accustomed to giving orders to their maids in Havana, ended up performing menial tasks themselves—picking tomatoes at Belle Glade or wiping tables at the University of Miami. They would find that many of the threatening social forces they had fled from in Cuba were present in the United States.

However, life was improving for rural Cuban women of the lower class. Thousands journeyed to Havana to take courses in sewing, reading, and revolution in the Ana Betancourt School. They would return to their villages with a sewing machine and a new sense of themselves. They would pass on their newly learned skills and new sense of independence to their friends and neighbors. It was the beginning of a great consciousness-raising process—a process carefully guided by the revolution.

To utilize the new energies of rural women, in August 1960, Fidel Castro created the Federation of Cuban Women (FMC) by merging prerevolutionary feminist organizations. The initial membership was less than 100,000. Eventually it would include nearly all Cuban women.

Fidel nominated his sister-in-law, the revolutionary heroine and one-time M.I.T. Student, Vilma Espín, to be chief of the FMC. Vilma declared the FMC to be a feminine organization, not a feminist one. She thought the future of Cuban women would be best served by integration into the revolution, by social communion, rather than pursuit of individual fulfillment as in Western countries. The FMC would aid in the construction of Cuban socialism.

In the early 1960s the literacy campaign merged seamlessly into a great national drive to raise educational levels. Education became a national crusade. Schools began to appear in the most remote districts of the nation. Girls who had often stayed home to aid their mothers while their brothers went to school now went to school themselves. By 1974, 73 percent of all Cuban women had reached the sixth-grade level, as opposed to 55 percent of the men.[12]

Health also became a revolutionary crusade. Health care declined at first due to the lack of medicines and the flight of doctors into exile. Thereafter it began to improve. As health care became more widespread, more women delivered their children in hospitals. Before the revolution, 80 percent of all children were delivered at home. By the 1980s more than 90 percent of all births occurred in hospitals.[13] The infant mortality rate declined substantially. The maternity law of 1974 provided women twelve weeks of paid leave before and six weeks after birth. It also guaranteed their jobs for nine months.

In the prerevolutionary era, abortion—although illegal—had been a major method of birth control The Castro regime found abortion repugnant and tried to eliminate it. When clandestine abortions continued, the regime changed their position and legalized abortion on demand. Simultaneously, birth control materials became available at the island's expanding network of neighborhood health clinics as well as local pharmacies.

Interestingly, female employment changed very little during the first decade of the revolution, growing only from 14.2 percent of the labor force in 1958 to 15.6 percent in 1968.[14] There were many reasons for this slow growth, including the great economic difficulties of the 1960s. The departure of the bourgeoisie on "freedom flights" to Miami meant unemployment for their maids and other service personnel. Eventually, substantial numbers of maids found employment, although on different terms, as maids for party officials, embassies, tourist resorts, and other government services.

The great surge in female employment began in 1968-69. The nationalization of small enterprises in 1968 meant that women who had formerly worked part-time at home—typically as seamstresses—were now obliged to join the work force full-time.[15] In 1969, women were urged to leave their homes to participate in the great national challenge of the 10 million ton harvest. They responded in record numbers, as 100,000 women joined the labor force that year.

Rapid social change placed a great strain on the Cuban family. Husbands went to work in distant provinces, to study in Eastern Europe, or, in the mid-1970s, to fight in Africa. Wives left the home to work in factories, to weed sugar cane fields on weekends, and to study at night school. These strains were increased by the new sexual freedom of women provided by easy access to birth control materials—a change difficult to accept in a nation in which machismo, patriarchy, and pregnancy were intimately linked.

The children of Cuban families increasingly spent their time away from home, first in day care centers and later in primary school. There they ate in school cafeterias, participated in government-sponsored recreational activities, such as the Young Pioneers, and, having reached their teens, went off to live in boarding high schools in the countryside. They returned home on weekends for brief visits. Boarding schools reflected a belief that the Cuban family was inadequate to the task of creating the "new man," which was a major goal of the revolution.

The Cuban home was literally crumbling. Due to a great scarcity of paint and roofing supplies, and the materials that were being used to repair public buildings and especially schools, Cuba's housing was becoming alarmingly dilapidated. In 1979 alone, 25,000 houses collapsed. Castro admitted there was a housing shortage of a least 1 million units.[16] The collapse and declining prestige of the home helped to encourage women to seek employment.

The strains imposed by revolutionary change were reflected in a soaring divorce rate, rising from 8.5 percent of marriages in 1959 to 30.2 percent in 1974.[17] Female fertility began to decline. By the late 1970s the new Cuban couple had only 1.8 children. The size of the Cuban family had been declining since the turn of the century, but 1.8 children was below replacement level.[18]

In 1969 a study by the Cuban Academy of Sciences found the Cuban family to be in a state of crisis. The findings of this report were dramatized in Pastor Vega's Film, *Portrait of Teresa*. Teresa, played by Daisy Granados, is the modern *cubana*. Educated and intelligent, Teresa works at a textile plant by day and helps organize a factory musical at night, while struggling to keep her household with three children and oafish husband afloat. She takes tranquilizers. She washes, irons, cooks, and cleans. She dresses and feeds the children. Her husband provides little assistance. He is distressed by Teresa's night-time activities. They quarrel, he begins an affair. As the film ends it appears Teresa, like so many other *cubanas*, is headed for divorce.

Portrait of Teresa gives only passing attention to the three children. The film makes clear that it is in activities outside the home that women's fulfillment is to be found. This idea is a major theme of the revolution and is widely reflected in the Cuban media.

While many women began to enter nontraditional occupations in the 1970s, most continued to find employment in the traditional and lower-paying service sector. The absence of women from the construction industry was perhaps the most salient example of the continuing sexual division of labor. Castro wanted women to work, but he wanted them to perform "jobs that cannot be accomplished with machinery, jobs which are not hard physical labor and not jobs unsuitable for women."[19] The Cuban Constitution of 1975 ratified Fidel's view by stating that women would be given employment in accordance with their physical make-up. A government document of that year specified that women would be barred from various jobs, including work in cemeteries and underwater work.

The social services required by working women remained in short supply in the 1970s. Though day care in Cuba has been lauded, as of 1980 there were only 832 day care centers, sufficient to care for 90,000 children or about 8 percent of the children six years or under.[20] As the government struggled to provide more day care services, it was learning the value of women's work at home. The government estimated that day care cost $100 per child per month. Though initially free, by 1970 the government was charging Cuban mothers $25 a month for day care services.

The lack of social services contributed to the instability of female labor. Women would go to work and then quit. Perhaps they had become pregnant; perhaps they were alienated by the kinds of work available; perhaps they decided that given the lack of consumer goods in the Cuban marketplace, there was no need for extra income. In 1969 for example, 106,258 women joined the work force, while 80,781 women quit.[21] In addition, women tended to work shorter hours than men, as they frequently had to leave work to do domestic chores, shop, and check on the children.

These factors became increasingly significant in the 1970s as Cuba began phasing in the "New Economic Calculus," which called for a more decentralized economy with a high priority on efficiency and profitability. Maternity leaves, which were paid for by the factory did not aid economic performance. This made managers reluctant to hire women.

In 1974 women suffered another setback when in the provincial elections held in Matanzas, a trial run for the national elections of 1975, only three percent of the candidates elected were women. The results were all the more frustrating given the revolutionary leadership's firm belief that sexism, chauvinism, and patriarchy were all fruits of capitalism—the capitalism that had been eliminated in Cuba more than a decade before.

Another anomaly was the failure of the revolutionary government itself to promote women to significant role model positions in society. Castro observed in 1974 that his seemed to be a "party of men and a state of men and a government of men."[22]

These problems were considered at the First Congress of the Cuban Communist Party in 1975. The result was a special report entitled "On the Full Exercise of Women's Equality." The report noted that while the revolution had brought many specific advantages and guarantees for Cuban women, problems still remained. Many of these difficulties stemmed, according to the party, from "backward ideas that we dragged with us from the past."[23]

One major problem was the double day. A survey of 251 working women undertaken in 1975 showed they spent an average of 24.5 hours per week on housework. How could this burden be eased? More *electrodomésticos*, or household appliances, was one answer. Another was obliging husbands to share in housework.

Shared housework was the centerpiece of Law 1289, the Cuban Family Code of 1975. It is significant that the code, referring to the family as the "elementary cell of society," argued for its preservation and strengthening, not its abolition as Marx had once suggested. The key article of the code, Article 26, reads: "Both partners must care for the family they have created and each must cooperate with the other in the education, upbringing and guidance of the children.... They must participate, to the extent of their capacity or possibilities, in the running of the home..."[24]

The idea of doing housework has been difficult for Cuban men to accept. It seemed a violation of the traditional separation of spheres in which women did not work outside the home, and men did not work inside it. For many Cuban men, it was easier to volunteer for Angola than to do the laundry. It simply was not masculine. No member of the revolutionary elite has even been photographed doing the laundry. Death before dishonor! One party official agreed to do the laundry, but not to hang it outside. Suppose the neighbors saw him![25] Schoolboys tried to persuade their girl friends to do it. Fidel tried to ameliorate this dilemma by promising more laundromats.

Men were not the only ones who resisted changes in old habits. Many women were reluctant to seize the new opportunities offered them. FMC Director Vilma Espín complained that the parents and boy friends of young women often discouraged them from taking jobs in fields not ordinarily thought of as women's work.[26]

Women have also been slow to participate in competitive sports. Cuban coaches complain about this. While Cuba has produced a number of able sportswomen, such as María Caridad Colón, the first Latin American woman to win a medal in the Olympics, most women have not been interested. Of the 2,622,169 participants in organized competitive sporting events in Cuba in 1980, 83 percent were men. Women did not participate at all in organized sports in 16 different fields ranging from boxing and weighlifting to more genteel sports such as horseback riding and sailing. The sports in which women were most active were horseshoes, gymnastics, fencing, volleyball, and table tennis. Women were present in the greatest numbers in track and field events, table tennis, and volleyball.[27]

These are great advances, and, as in many areas, the changes seem to be accelerating. University women must not only participate in sports, they must become proficient in them. And Cuban women are entering new fields. In 1980 women did not participate in organized jujitsu, but by spring 1983 there were 7,000 young *judokas* in Cuba, enough to begin national competitions.[28]

A sign of the new mentality is the impressive entry of women into technical training. The 1981 census indicates that women are receiving half of the degrees awarded in such fields as geology, mineralogy, and metallurgy—fields once dominated by men.[29]

The role of the FMC in this process of change is far from clear. Its infrequent national conferences (1962, 1974, and 1980), and the fact that its director, Vilma Espín, speaks only occasionally on women's issues and is only an alternate member of the inner circle of the Central

Committee have led to skepticism about the FMC's role. But others credit the FMC for the Family Code of 1975 and for pressing for more jobs for women.[30]

By 1980 women comprised 30 percent of the work force. But in March of that year, Fidel Castro announced that economic difficulties brought about by the world recession and low commodity prices might limit the increase in female employment that characterized the 1970s. Priority in employment would, he said, go to men.[31] Did full employment, a major goal of the revolution, apply only to males? What about the increasing number of divorced women and working mothers who needed jobs?

Interestingly, despite Castro's warning and a worsening economic situation from 1981 to 1984, female employment continued to climb, striking a new high in 1984 of approximately 1 million, or 36 percent of the work force. Part of this may be attributed to a discreet affirmative action program. In new factories certain numbers of jobs are set aside for women. At the new Celia Sánchez textile factory, for example, 1,785 of the 4,089 jobs or 44 percent, have gone to women.[32]

Women have also been the beneficiaries of a discreet affirmative action program in the political sphere. In the late 1970s, disturbed by the revolt of Polish workers who claimed their "proletarian" government did not represent their interests, more women were added to various levels of the party and governmental apparatus. By 1980, 22 percent of the members of the national assembly were women.[33]

By the 1980s women were scoring major advances at almost every level of the Cuban educational system. In higher education, there were as many women as men, and in some university faculties, medicine for example, there were so many more qualified women applicants that quotas to protect slots for men were created.[34]

The revolution was also making some interesting concessions to old ideas of femininity. Despite Fidel Castro's oft-expressed disdain for the fripperies of "consumer society," a socialist consumer society, impelled by women, was emerging in Cuba. Cosmetics were becoming more plentiful, and a perfume institute was launched. *Bohemia,* Cuba's leading magazine, began to feature developments in Cuban fashions. Fashion shows returned to Havana.

Another old-fashioned tradition remains as well, that is, male dominance of government and power. Whether it is the composition of a delegation to an international conference, the membership of a literary committee, or a list of the 10 best athletes for 1983, men dominate.[35] At an International Conference on "Health for All" in Havana in May 1983, Granma identified 21 Cubans who were to present papers. Only one, María Teresa Trincado, director of the national Department of Nursing, was a woman.[36] Although 21 percent of the Cuban Foreign Ministry officials are women, the head of the U.S. interest section in Havana from 1979 to 1982 could only recall dealing with one woman at the ministry.[37] With a few exceptions, the highest levels of government remain an exclusive male preserve. In the Council of State there are 27 men and 2 women. Of Cuba's 32 ministers in 1983, only 1 was a woman. Cuba has perhaps 100 ambassadors. About one-half dozen are women.[38]

Thus the situation of women in Cuba is paradoxical. Women are gaining everywhere—in social services, in education, in the labor market—but they are being barred from the ultimate expression of equality, that is shared power. The basic decisions on Cuban foreign policy, economy, and society are made by a small male elite. Why? Is it perhaps the simple tenacity of a Cuban culture with deep and patriarchal roots, at once Hispanic and Catholic, African and Arabic? Are Cubans who are so proud of being modern world leaders of social change, simultaneously reluctant to abandon a past which for all its faults is theirs—their history, their traditions? A comment by Vilma Espín exemplifies this dilemma. When asked by a visitor to a Cuban nursery why girls had pink blankets and boys had blue ones, why girls had dolls and boys had trucks, Espín replied that Cubans loved their children so much that they did not want to "experiment" on them.[39]

Does this attitude reflect the male bond of the Castro and guerrilla elites that defeated the Batista dictatorship a quarter of a century ago—a bond that largely excludes women? Or does it perhaps flow from the personality of the revolutionary chief? Some call him "Cuba's leading feminist," but to many Cubans he is *el caballo*, (the horse) Cuba's macho *extraordinaire*. Is he willing to share power with women? There is no sign of it.

One reason for this is quite simply the nature and direction of Cuban interests. Cuban life is dominated by its commitment, enshrined in the Constitution, to engage in revolutionary solidarity and proletarian internationalism. This guarantees a future of endless conflict with the international guardian of the status quo—the United States. Castro does not seem to mind that destiny; indeed he seems to enjoy it. In a way he sees this as continuing a sacred mission handed down to Cuba by the great Cuban *prócer* and patriot, José Martí.

In the short run, tension with the United States has helped to create opportunities for Cuban women. Indeed, Castro has used women as a major arm in his struggle with the United States, employing them first in local defense and later using them to replace the male workers for service in the enlarged armed forces.

But over the long run, the improvement of women's status in Cuba depends on a more fruitful economy, which in turn requires a cessation of hostilities and constant tensions with the United States. This does not mean the abandonment of socialism, but rather it means Cuba must concentrate on improving the domestic economy rather than dwelling on the moral satisfactions of foreign adventures. Such a domestic socialism, even a feminized socialism, might ultimately be far more influential abroad than the macho-military and dependent socialism currently in vogue in Havana.

A quarter century of socialist revolution has profoundly changed the lives of Cuban women. They have gained in health, education, and work, in self-confidence and self-respect. For many women the opportunities and benefits offered to their children by the revolution are highly significant. As one would anticipate in a Marxist, class-oriented revolution, these gains have gone largely to the women of the lower and lower-middle class.

The process of revolutionary change has battered and transformed the traditional Cuban family as evidenced, in part, by high divorce rates and low birth rates. Perhaps these two developments are indicative not of failure, as some have suggested, but rather of the bitter-sweet realities of progress. Indeed, Cuba's low birth rate may be one of the most significant, if unsung, achievements of the revolution.

Finally, patriarchy, that central and persistent element of Cuban culture and, indeed, of Latin American culture, has also been transformed. Men clearly have less power over their wives and daughters, but patriarchy has not disappeared. Rather, in various ways patriarchal power has been assumed by the bureaucratic state which, controlled almost exclusively by white male elites, has emerged as the new patriarch in Cuban life. While women have advanced, full female equality remains a distant and elusive goal for Cuban women under socialism.

ACKNOWLEDGMENTS

The authors would like to thank the following colleagues for their assistance on this project: Jorge Domínguez, Susan Eckstein, Sandra

Levinson, Marifeli Pérez-Stable, Doris Sommer, Nelson Valdés, and Lucia Valeska. Needless to say, the views expressed here are strictly their own.

NOTES

1. Interview with Pastor Vega in Patricia Peyton and Carlos Broullon, "Portrait of Teresa: An Interview with Pastor Vega and Daisy Granados," *Cineaste*, Winter 1979–80, p. 24.
2. Harriet Alonso, "Update on Women," *CUBATIMES*. January/- February 1984, p. 7.
3. For data on prerevolutionary women see Alfred Padula, "The Fall of the Bourgeoisie, Cuba, 1959–1961" (Ph.D. dissertation, University of New Mexico, 1974), and K. Lynn Stoner, "From the House to the Streets: Women's Movement For Legal Change in Cuba, 1898–1958" (Ph.D. dissertation, University of Indiana, 1983).
4. Eugenio R. Balari et al., *La mujer cubana: el camino hacia su emancipación* (pamphlet, Havana, 1980), p. 2. The figures on working women in prerevolutionary Cuba vary. According to Margaret Randall there were 194,000 working women. See Margaret Randall, *Women in Cuba: Twenty Years Later* (New York: Smyrna Press, 1981), p. 23.
5. Isabel Larguîa and John Dumoulin, "La mujer en el desarollo: estrategia y experiencias de la revolución cubana," (Paper presented at the XV Congreso Latino Americano de Sociologîa "Simón Bolîvar," Managua, Nicaragua, October 1983), p. 3.
6. Balari, *La mujer cubana*, p. 2.
7. Luis Salas, *Social Control and Deviance in Cuba* (New York: Praeger, 1979), pp. 98–100.
8. Oscar Lewis et al., *Four Women: Living the Revolution* (Urbana: University of Illinois Press, 1977), p. 279.
9. Mirta de la Torre Mulhare, "Sexual Ideology in pre-Castro Cuba: A Cultural Analysis" (Ph.D. dissertation, University of Pittsburgh, 1969), p. 258.
10. Esteban Montejo, *The Autobiography of a Runaway Slave* (New York: Vintage Books, 1973), p. 88.
11. Rolando E. Bonachea and Nelson P. Valdés, *Revolutionary Struggle: 1947–1958, Volume 1 of the Selected Works of Fidel Castro* (Cambridge, Mass.: The MIT Press, 1972), pp. 164–221.
12. Elizabeth Stone, ed., *Women and the Cuban Revolution* (New York: Pathfinder Press, 1981), p. 94.
13. Randall, *Women in Cuba*, p. 76.
14. Lewis, *Four Women*, p. xviii.
15. *Ibid.*, p. 406.

16. Sergio Roca, "Housing in Socialist Cuba," (paper delivered at the International Conference on Housing Problems, Florida International University, Miami, Florida, December, 1979), p. 18.
17. Stone, *Women and the Cuban Revolution*, p. 25.
18. Sergio Díaz-Briquets and Lisandro Pérez, "Fertility Decline in Cuba: A Socioeconomic Interpretation," *Population and Development Review*, vol. 8, no. 3 (September 1982), p. 514.
19. Nicola Murray, "Socialism and Feminism, Women and the Cuban Revolution," *Feminist Review*, no. 2 (1969), p. 69.
20. See Randall, *Women in Cuba*, p. 29 and *Anuario Estadístico de Cuba, 1980* (Havana: Comité Estatal de Estadísticas, 1981), pp. 213-14.
21. Stone, *Women and the Cuban Revolution*, p. 83.
22. *Ibid.*, p. 71.
23. *Ibid.*, p. 80.
24. *Ibid.*, p. 146.
25. Information from a North American visitor.
26. *Latin American Weekly Report* (WR-83), March 11, 1983, p. 3.
27. *Anuario Estadístico de Cuba, 1980*, p. 239.
28. *Granma Weekly Review*, April 3, 1983.
29. Larguía and Dumoulin, "La mujer en el desarollo," Table 3.
30. Communications with Marifeli Pérez-Stable, State University of New York, Old Westbury, and Sandra Levinson, Cuban Studies Center, New York City, 1983.
31. *Latin American Weekly Report*, March 28, 1980.
32. *Bohemia*, August 12, 1983, p. 73.
33. Jorge I. Domínguez, "Revolutionary Politics" in Jorge I. Domínguez, ed., *Cuba: Internal and International Affairs* (Beverly Hills, Cal.: Sage Publications, 1982), p. 32. Also, Larguía and Dumoulin, "La mujer en el desarollo," p. 28.
34. Jorge I. Domínguez, "Political Rights and the Cuban Political System," (Paper prepared for the Inter-American Commission on Human Rights, February 1983), pp. 24-27.
35. For an extensive review of the evidence, see Alfred Padula and Lois Smith "Women and Power in Socialist Cuba" forthcoming in *Signs*.
36. *Granma Weekly Review*, May 29, 1983.
37. Interview with Wayne Smith, Portland, Maine, October 11, 1983.
38. Padula and Smith, "Women and Power in Socialist Cuba."
39. Information from a North American visitor.

5   From Counterrevolution to *Modus Vivendi*: The Church in Cuba, 1959-84

John M. Kirk

Travelers to Cuba often remark on the highly visible time warp factor: fashions, buildings, and cars (often of North American design) seem uprooted from a 1950s Hollywood set and located in downtown Havana. Utilizing the time warp is, in some ways, a useful measuring stick for the religious factor in revolutionary Cuba, particularly if compared to advances in religious life made in other Latin American nations (most notably in Nicaragua). Indeed, at first glance, time does seem to have stood still in Cuba for a certain sector of the Church. Such an interpretation provides, however, a rather simple explanation of the complex development of religious life since the revolutionary victory on January 1, 1959.

Much has been written about the radical transformation of the Church in Latin America since the 1960s: the momentous conferences of Latin American Bishops (CELAM) in Medellín (1968) and Puebla (1979); the trail-blazing activities of Gustavo Gutiérrez and a host of articulate "teólogos de la liberación"; the foundation of Christian socialist groups in most countries; the establishment of some 200,000 Christian-based communities; the active participation of Church sectors within the Nicaraguan revolutionary process (with key positions being held by clergy such as Edgar Parrales, Ernesto and Fernando Cardenal, and Miguel d'Escoto); and the brutal repression of the Church by the security forces—most clearly seen in Central America. What impact have these many dramatic changes had on the Church in Cuba? How has the Church adapted to these different circumstances, and how has the Cuban government reacted to this evolution? Is there a notable, autonomous progression in the Church's position, or has it simply reacted to official prodding?

The media have paid little attention to the religious situation in Cuba, in part because it lacks the human drama of Church-State tension in Poland (Cardinal Glemp versus General Jaruzelski) or the Philippines (Cardinal Sin versus Ferdinand Marcos). A few excellent academic works have appeared in recent years, but in general the religious question has been neglected. This chapter presents a brief study of the notable phases of the Church's development over the past 25 years, with specific reference to the Catholic Church, and offers some thoughts on this evolution.

THE PREREVOLUTIONARY CHURCH

> It seemed to me that this was the most reactionary Church in Latin America.
>
> *Ernesto Cardenal*

Most of the academic research undertaken on the prerevolutionary Church (e.g., works by Crahan, Hageman and Wheatman, Dewart, Jover) presents a fairly uniform, and generally unflattering, picture of a Catholic Church that had little popular support. Historically there had been general indifference to Catholicism: the leaders of the movement for Cuban independence were defiantly rejected by the pro-Spanish Church, and this conservative trend continued throughout the twentieth century. The Spanish nature of the Cuban Church was a major factor in the declining favor of the Church: Cubans simply found little with which to identify. The vast majority of the clergy were foreign (including a preponderance of Spanish priests and nuns), trained in Franco's Spain, and of the few seminarians, many went to Spain for their religious training. In 1959 two of the six dioceses were administered by Spanish bishops.[1] Later, when tension arose between the government of Fidel Castro and Church leaders, the "Spanish connection" was again emphasized, as masses were prominently celebrated, it is claimed, on the anniversary of major Franco victories.

If the Catholic Church tried to establish its credibility by clinging to Spanish tradition, to a large extent the Protestant churches can be seen to have gained much of their support from the North American "parent." In 1907 Methodist Bishop Candler eloquently illustrated the careful targeting of Cuba as an area for extensive mission and political development:

> It is a matter of our interest as well as our duty to bring the gospel to the Cuban people. The world knows from the history of the French Revolution what happens to a nation that throws off a monarchical government and Christianity at the same time.... Unbelief and disorder now prevail among them and will continue to do so unless Protestantism rescues them from the abyss of doubt that is opening before them. And disorder in Cuba is harmful to us here in the USA. Our country is committed to maintain order there.[2]

As a result of missionary expansion in Cuba, there were 609 evangelical pastors as compared with 723 Catholic priests by the time of the revolution, although they ministered to between only 150,000 and 250,000 people.[3] Once again the Protestant Churches, accidentally or by design, inculcated North American values into their followers.[4]

This heavy dependence on Spain and the United States can be seen as an indication of the lack of autonomous Cuban development, as well as the generally unhealthy condition of the Cuban Church. Commenting on the stagnation of the prerevolutionary Church, Professor Leslie Dewart noted the general disinterest in religion, lack of respect for the clergy, purposelessness within the Church leadership, as well as the limited native vocations. The Church might have been a pillar of the community in Central American at this time, but in Cuba it had long since lost all claim to being a major influence.

This general feeling of mediocrity and aimlessness is substantiated by all available statistical data. While some 90 percent of the population had been baptized, most estimates place the proportion of practicing Catholics at only 5 percent. Jover's study, citing a well-known 1954 survey undertaken by the Agrupación Católica Universitaria, points out the tremendous differences between rural and urban Catholics. Although 72.5 percent of those interviewed claimed to be Catholic, the number fell to 52 percent in rural areas, with 41 percent claiming indifference concerning religious affiliation.[5] Three years later a similar survey of some 4,000 agricultural workers revealed even more startling figures: in rural areas 53 percent maintained that they had never even *seen* a priest.[6] Clearly the Church was concentrating on urban projects, to the detriment of the rural communities. There may well have been 750 priests and 2,500 religious in 1959, but the vast majority were widely viewed as representatives of the urban middle class, with little to offer most Cubans, regardless of their religious affiliation. There is little wonder, then, that in a 1957 survey cited by Crahan, "only 3.4% of (agricultural workers) expressed any belief that the Catholic Church would be of any assistance in improving their lot."[7]

On the eve of the *fidelista* revolution the Church was in tremendous disarray. Racked by growing dissatisfaction with Church leadership and facing stiff competition from the Protestant Churches and *santería*, the Church was falling into an increasingly marginalized position. Admittedly there was both a low ratio of clergy to lay followers and a high rate of baptisms (although this dropped sharply for the percentage who took first communion, again underlining the nominal nature of Catholicism), but beneath this superficial framework there was little of substance. The Church was in an early state of crisis. As J. Lloyd Mecham pointed out, the greatest threat facing the Catholic church was the "inability of the Church to combat general apathy and indifference and thus retain a hold on its own 'nominal' communicants."[8] To solidify this faltering base it urgently needed a cause, something that would act as a catalyst to rally the faithful behind the Christian banner. That *santa causa* was the *fidelista* victory, which helped to reassert Catholic unity and develop an identity.

FROM EUPHORIA TO DESPAIR: 1959-60

> We are not ashamed to affirm—indeed, it would seem to us cowardly not to do so—that between the Americans and the Russians we would choose (the former) without the slightest hesitation.
>
> *Monsignor Pérez Serantes*

When Fidel Castro arrived in Havana, following his routing of Batista and the triumphant march from Santiago de Cuba, the Christian sector was genuinely pleased. In part this was due to an understandable revulsion at the Batista tyranny, accompanied by a respect for this young, idealistic, and articulate lawyer, well known in Havana since his student days and the Moncada attack of 1953. The support among Catholic groups was also based, to a certain extent, on a feeling that "one of their own" (almost) was heading this revolutionary force. After all, Castro had been educated at the prestigious Jesuit College, Belén, in Havana, and in 1953 had had his life saved by the direct intervention of

Santiago Archbishop (and former parish priest) Pérez Serantes. The opposition of various Catholic Action groups to Batista (many of which had been victims of Batista's brutality), as well as the role of guerrilla-priest Guillermo Sardiñas in the Sierra Maestra, spoke well for a major Church role in the liberated Cuba. Castro recognized this contribution noting that "The Catholics of Cuba have lent their most decided cooperation to the cause of liberty."[9] He thereby fanned the flames of expectation.

Unfortunately, the honeymoon was short-lived, and the heady days of ebullient optimism were quickly replaced by gloomy despair, and presentiments of an impending clash. There were two fundamental reasons for this rapid alienation: (1) a somewhat tardy reaction to the radical social changes that quickly occurred and (2) the fear of a communist takeover, which played an increasingly important role as further reforms were introduced. The early agrarian reform and the Urban Reform Law dealt a major blow to the Catholic land-holding bourgeoisie. The planned educational reforms were also seen as a threat to this wealthy and powerful sector. Opposition to the government grew, and to a large extent it mobilized behind the Catholic Church. At the end of November 1959, this opposition crystallized at the National Catholic Congress, attended by almost one million people—a figure far in excess of the actual number of practicing Catholics. The stage was being prepared for a major confrontation.

While this broad frustration was taking shape within the Church, the second essential element of this explosive situation was evolving in the increasingly tense U.S.-Cuban relationship. Since the United States had always played the role of "godfather" in Cuba (given its geographical proximity, controlling economic interest, manifest political influence and cultural dominance), it seemed normal for many Cubans, particularly the bourgeoisie, to accept the American way of life as the norm to which one aspired. Therefore, there was shock in these sectors when Castro clearly refused to buckle under to U.S. pressure following his radical reforms, preferring instead to justify Cuban actions in outspoken fashion. This apparent cockiness and the rejection of traditional subservience were greeted with much consternation, particularly as tensions escalated between the United States and Cuba, with the United States cutting off the sugar quota, the Cuban government nationalizing U.S. property, and the war of words increasing between both countries.

An indication of the impending Church-State showdown came in the spring of 1960, first in February, with the visit to Cuba of Soviet

Foreign Minister Anastas Mikoyan, and then in May as diplomatic relations with the Soviet Union were formally restored. Large sectors of the Protestant and Catholic churches reacted with outrage: Church demonstrations were arranged to condemn these diplomatic initiatives, and religious leaders denounced what the Catholic hierarchy referred to in its collective pastoral letter as "the growing advance of communism in our country."[10] A flurry of pastorals followed, all inspired by rabid anticommunism. The collective pastoral of December 4, calling on Castro to reject communism outright, clearly set the tone for the ensuing confrontation.

The social and political polarization taking place in Cuba, accentuated, of course, by the rising international tension, had an unfortunate reaction on the Church-State problem. By December 1960, the hierarchy clearly interpreted the recently enacted social reforms as positive proof that the Castro government had decided to opt for a communist solution. Accordingly they opted for the "Christian" alternative, namely supporting the option afforded by the example of the United States and the "free world." For the Church hierarchy it became increasingly clear that they had to state their case vociferously, openly taking sides against the socializing *fidelista* trend. In the grip of the Cold War, they were understandably wary of anything that could be interpreted as closer Cuban ties with the Soviet Union. Moreover, with pressure and increasing support from the disgruntled bourgeoisie, the stagnating Catholic Church saw the possibility of regaining some of its earlier grandeur and so decided to take a stand. In doing so, however, Church leaders openly aligned themselves with official U.S. policy. (Later Castro would, with some justification, accuse them of being loyal to the Church of Washington.) While this helped to attract many Castro opponents to support the beleaguered "Christian cause," it also alienated many Christians who believed in the needed social reforms. By stating their case so unequivocally, the Church hierarchy acted as a catalyst in separating these two interpretations of the Church's social role. The stage was set for the Bay of Pigs invasion of April 17, 1961.

CONFRONTATION: 1961–62

> Everything came to a head when many well-off individuals who were feeling the pinch of the Revolution tried to use the Church as the standard-bearer of their anti-Communism.
>
> *Carlos Manuel de Céspedes, ex-rector, San Carlos Seminary*

The C.I.A.-sponsored Bay of Pigs invasion was a major factor in the consolidation of Fidel Castro's power, as he skillfully underlined the David versus Goliath nature of the struggle. The invasion was also important in separating the *fidelistas* from their opponents. Unfortunately the Church too was drawn into this societal bloodletting and emerged much the worse for wear. To a large extent, the Church did so because its base of supporters—the urban bourgeoisie—encouraged it to take a stand, thereby protecting their own interests. There were other reasons, however, such as its anticommunist "crusade," its understandable fear of being further neutered, and its general desire to return to the good old days—essentially to the Batista days, without Batista. Unfortunately they miscalculated, not realizing that Castro's plan was that rarity in Latin American politics—a true social revolution.

The April 17, 1961 invasion and its aftermath resulted in the Church being stripped of its temporal power. Not only did tens of thousands of Cubans (many of whom were active in Church circles) leave for Miami, they were also followed by many clergy—Catholic and Protestant alike—who decided to flee the continuing social radicalization. That the invasion force itself contained three Spanish priests and a Methodist clergyman did not help the *santa causa*, particularly in view of the cross on the emblem worn by the invaders and of their proclamation, composed by Father Ismael de Lugo, "in the name of God, Justice and Democracy" to liberate Cuba: "Our struggle is that of those who believe in God against the struggle of spiritual values against materialism, the struggle of democracy against communism."[11]

For the government, this all confirmed what they had already suspected about the conspiracies being hatched in Church circles. They arrested dozens of priests (Cardinal Arteaga sought refuge in the Argentinian embassy), and on May 1 Castro announced that the Catholic university as well as all private schools—particularly those in which the "falangist priests" had conspired—were to be nationalized, providing free public education without religious instruction to all Cubans. The loss of more than 300 Catholic schools broke the back of Church resistance to Castro, and hundreds of Protestant missionaries as well as priests and nuns hurriedly left the country, their teaching jobs no longer possible under the new lay system. This humbling of the Church authority and the physical expulsion in September of some 135 priests (estimated at about one-half of Cuba's remaining clergy) following a "religious" procession that deteriorated into a political riot also meant that anti-Castro rallies, held under a religious pretext, were no longer possible. Church-State relations plunged to an all-time low.

Examining this troubled period of church-state tension from a post-Vatican II perspective causes one to wonder why this religious problem ever arrived at such a disastrous level. In part this can be attributed to what is politely termed revolutionary zeal, as the formerly underprivileged sought to fulfill what they saw as the revolution's mandate. On the other hand, the Church can also be faulted for ignoring (with the notable exceptions of Catholic Action and like Protestant programs, introduced in the 1930s) the glaring need for social reform and for turning a political struggle into a religious one. The resulting conflict was "not between the Revolution and religious beliefs (but rather) was between the Revolution and a social class that tried to use the Church as a weapon to oppose the Revolution."[12] It was a struggle that the Church, living in the past, with a weak popular base and without the benefit of the teachings of Vatican II or Medellín, was bound to lose.

SILENCE: 1962–69

> The existing relations between the government and the Church are very cordial.... I believe that the Church is aware of the change in system that has taken place in this country; it is an incontrovertible fact that will not turn back. The Church must therefore adapt itself to the changes, as it has done in Europe.
>
> *Monsignor Zacchi, papal nuncio*

Many Church observers agree that it was essentially through the intelligent intervention of Msgr. Zacchi that the icy Church-State relations did not freeze over completely, particularly as Cold War rhetoric escalated following the October 1962 Missile Crisis. Monsignor Zacchi's decade in Cuba was of indisputable value in formulating a reassessment, both on the part of the government (in particular, on the part of Fidel Castro, with whom he enjoyed an unusually frank and cooperative relationship), and on the part of the Church, clearly in a disastrously weak situation following the expulsion of so many religious and the voluntary exile of most of their followers. It is to Zacchi's credit that the trend of manifest confrontation and mutual hostility was ameliorated during his tenure as papal nuncio. In this context, then, the silence that existed for the next seven years represents a diplomatic triumph.

Symbolic gestures and visits by both government leaders and Church representatives played an important role in preparing the way for the dialogue that followed. A period of fence-mending was needed in the wake of the earlier hostility, and the Church responded intelligently. Pedro Arrupe, then Superior General of the Jesuit order, and the powerful diplomatic representative of the Vatican, Monsignor Agostino Casaroli visited Cuba and met with Castro. In his attempt to contribute to an easing of this tension, Castro made official visits to the Nunciate in 1963, for a Vatican celebration, and in 1967 when Monsignor Zacchi was appointed bishop. The well-publicized chess games between Castro and Zacchi and the nuncio's frequent attendance at State functions also contributed to better relations.

While it may seem trite to reduce the dynamics of this Church-State relationship to the social conduct of two representatives of these groups, such a thesis is in fact quite tenable. Given the official opposition to the nuncio's position, it is astonishing that he was successful in silencing these criticisms. To a large extent he was successful because, following his earlier experiences in Yugoslavia, he was aware that (1) the Church in Cuba was painfully "behind the times" and (2) that in view of this retrograde, and at times, counterrevolutionary role, "the Castro government has been very tolerant."[13] The Church was clearly in need of an *aggiornamiento* (witness the Second Vatican Council in Rome of 1962–65), and nowhere in Latin America was this more true than in Cuba.

The papal nuncio went out of his way to seek dialogue with the government, commending government reforms, encouraging young Catholics to join the militia, in short, to use the words of former External Affairs Minister Raúl Roa, he went "beyond the demands of diplomacy."[14] Cuban Catholics were urged by Monsignor Zacchi to participate in voluntary work and join cultural organizations and unions—in other words, to emerge from their silence and recognize the new revolutionary situation. Zacchi advised young Catholics to participate in political life as members of the Juventud Comunista (since this was the only major political organization), and he noted that there was a need for a greater liberalization by all the Church. All of these actions understandably shocked conservative Church sectors. The Cuban hierarchy even refused to publish the encyclical *Mater et Magistra*, considering it too radical, and as a result "the Nuncio himself published it, and the government distributed it."[15]

Castro responded expansively to these initiatives of the nuncio. He had already shown, in several speeches made between 1959 and 1961, that the government would respect freedom of religious choice and was opposed, not to Church people as such, but only those who were counterrevolutionaries. On March 13, 1962, at a ceremony to commemorate the anniversary of the death of Christian student leader, José Antonio Echevarría, Castro reacted angrily when the master of ceremonies, reading aloud José Antonio's political will, omitted references to God. After reading them aloud himself, Castro referred to "cowards" and "moral cripples" who would ignore the student leader's Christian beliefs. He then continued: "A revolutionary can hold a religious belief.... In the struggle for national liberation, in the struggle against imperialism, all progressive elements, all patriots, ought to unite, and in this front ought to be the sincere Catholic who has nothing in common with imperialism, as well as the militant marxist."[16]

Of course there were problems and inevitable friction during this period, most notably in the treatment meted out to Christians in the infamous UMAP penal centers and the purging of Christian faculty members from universities. Yet, progress was made in overcoming the earlier hostility that had plagued Church-State relations. To understand this development one must also keep in mind the historical context of the Church. Vatican II concluded in 1965, its revolutionary message sending shock waves through conservative sectors throughout the world. It was followed by the Latin American Bishops' meeting in Medellín, Colombia in 1968. The resulting espousal of the theology of liberation, criticism of capitalism and Marxism alike, the acceptance of the preferential option for the poor clearly influenced Church teaching—even in Cuba. Combined with the skillful political conduct of the papal nuncio and Castro's response, this made for a reversal of the earlier trend of doubt and uncertainty. This is not to say that the Church's activities were welcomed with open arms, for with the lack of respect for the Church in prerevolutionary times, as well as the confrontational role adopted in 1959-60, such a welcome was simply not feasible. However, since the Cuban government felt more secure and less threatened by potential opposition, a greater tolerance of religious activity resulted. New missionaries were allowed into Cuba, and several priests who earlier had been deported returned. Clergy and seminarians were excluded from compulsory military service, duty-free imports of some 40 church vehicles were allowed in 1967, and special rations were provided for the Jewish community. A visiting rabbi commented on these changes in 1969: "The practicing denominations are at the least tolerated, perhaps respected, and always treated with consideration by the government."[17] The confrontational period was finally over.

BACK TO THE TABLE: 1969-79

> When faced with such grave tests, our Christians have grown in their faith. It's no longer a case of simply organizing religious processions, or bingo to raise funds for our schools. Now we have to sow the Good Word, and try to live it out.
>
> Sr. Gisèle Piché, Canadian missionary

Following eight years of self-imposed silence, the Cuban bishops released their first pastoral letter in April 1969. While many radical Christians unrealistically criticized the mild tone of the document, many others interpreted it as a positive omen for future Church activities. The collective pastoral, clearly influenced by the 1968 meeting of Latin American Bishops in Medellín, Colombia, was a major step for the conservative Cuban Church. Some priests even refused to read the letter, while at some services people angrily stomped out of the church. The pastoral quoted from the pope's recent address in Bogotá and from the Medellín documents and emphasized the need for a revitalized, socially conscious Church. In the contemporary Cuban context, continued the pastoral, one way that the Episcopal conference could help was by condemning the U.S. economic blockade: "In seeking the common good of our people and of our faithful, in serving the poorer among them, according to the command of Jesus and the commitment of Medellín, we denounce the unjust conditions of the blockade, which is contributing to unnecessary sufferings, and to making all efforts at development more difficult."[18]

In September 1969 the Episcopal conference issued a second collective pastoral, "On Contemporary Atheism." The document called upon Catholics to live out their faith and to treat their atheist neighbors as their brothers since, it claimed, "We have to approach the atheistic man with all the respect and fraternal charity which the human person deserves by the mere fact of being a human."[19] Fifteen years later these policies are certainly progressive, although they can hardly be viewed as revolutionary in nature. However, in the Cuba of 1969 they created a tremendous furor among Catholics who, following the earlier conservative stance of their Church, were "unprepared, intellectually and emotionally, to hear such a document."[20]

In the 1970s internal divisions grew within the Church as the "traditional" sector—realizing that its influence was waning in the wake of Church modernization, as well as with the impact of Vatican II and

Medellín—sought to retrench. This group ignored all "political" pronouncements, preferring instead to follow the pursuit of "spiritual" goals. Examples of this conservative tendency can be found in both Catholic and Protestant Churches—particularly among older Christians.[21] Yet the "progressive" sector continued to make significant advances, in part through symbolic gestures, such as the activities of the staff and student body of the Matanzas Protestant seminary who in 1969 cut sugar cane as part of their voluntary labor contribution, and through theological reform and dialogue with government authorities.

Major Church developments occurred throughout this decade. Summer camps for theological reflection were instituted: in the summer of 1982 more than 300 people from 18 to 23 years old attended one such Catholic camp. The Presbyterian-Reformed Church of Cuba, which had become an autonomous, national Church in 1967, adopted a new "Confession of Faith." Other developments include the following: in 1975 the Cuban government normalized relations with the Vatican; in 1979 the first Cuban Theological Encounter took place in Matanzas between Cuban Christians from the island and from abroad; and between 1970 and 1980 approximately 100 young Cubans were ordained priests.[22] The spirit behind these developments—unthinkable a few years earlier—is best summarized by Canadian nun Gisèle Piché:

> A remarkable evolution has taken place, both in our mentality and in our way of working.... In essence we've rediscovered the evangelical spirit of Yahweh's poor. Enlightened by the Word and by events here, we've learned to lose our fear in communism and communists, now seeing in man—even in atheists—our brother, and in the Cuban system, the positive values of work, as well as a definite humanism.[23]

This decrease in mistrust and hostility was due to several factors, including Monsignor Zacchi's continuing diplomacy, the exodus of many Cubans opposed to the system, the influence of Vatican II and Medellín, the ability of some sectors of the Church to come to grips with the irreversible nature of the revolutionary process, the young hierarchy (appointed to replace several retiring bishops), and improved relations between the hierarchy and the government. On several occasions Castro mentioned the changing nature of the post-Vatican II Church in Latin America, noting to leftist priests in Chile in 1971 that this factor was virtually unknown at the time of the revolution:

There was no effort to understand the other's position. It was impossible, since no precedents existed for such a development. Instead the precedents came from the movement of leftist priests in Latin America. It's curious, but you are the ones who are going to help us to develop a policy and search for a rapprochement.[24]

He emphasized the need for a "strategic alliance" between Church and State, noting that this had proved its worth elsewhere in Latin America. He added, "We need to take the initiative so that these developments can also occur in Cuba."[25] Six years later, speaking with Church leaders in Jamaica, Castro again emphasized these ideas, concluding, "There are no contradictions between the aims of religion and the aims of socialism."[26]

For their part, the Catholic hierarchy has continued to seek dialogue with government leaders, and on several occasions has adopted progressive positions. In August 1976, for instance, the Church released "Toward Community Renewal: Evangelized and Evangelizing," essentially a call for Church renewal and social participation, while in November—in the wake of the brutal destruction of a Cuban airliner and its 73 passengers by an exile group—the bishops condemned such barbarous acts of terrorism. However, the most obvious illustration of their renewed social awareness came in 1978, one year before the Latin American Bishops' meeting in Puebla, Mexico. Prior to the meeting, a draft of proposals to be presented at the forthcoming CELAM meeting was sent out to the Episcopal conferences throughout Latin America. Since it was seen by the old guard of CELAM that the meetings held in Medellín had pursued an overly radical line, the Puebla meeting was seen as a way to establish a more conservative position. Accordingly, a preparatory document denouncing atheism was circulated; however, the Cuban bishops, who 15 years earlier had been among the conservative, rejected it. Monsignor Carlos Manuel de Céspedes, secretary of the Permanent Council of Cuban Bishops, saw the draft as aggressively simplistic:

> In all six dioceses there was agreement in their critique of the document's position towards atheism. The view of atheism in that document was very negative. We insist on having a more positive view of atheism in general and the possibilities of collaboration with different kinds of atheism. The document doesn't speak much about Marxism; some, but not much. We think in the development of our country we must take into account these people (Marxists) without this narrow view.[27]

A spirit of reconciliation and modernization was apparent within key circles of Cuban society and widely encouraged by the young Church hierarchy. This trend was influenced by an active Christian-Marxist participation in the 1979 Sandinista Revolution, and with certain limitations it is still in effect today. The main thrust of the churches has been, as Archbishop Oves announced in 1971, "to help Christians to assume positively their commitment to help construct this new society, recognising those human and evangelical values where Christianity and socialism converge, but without ignoring the influence of the fundamental rights emanating from our firm religious conscience."[28]

DIALOGUE AND MODUS VIVENDI: 1979-84

> In a revolutionary process you can't separate the religious from the political.
>
> Father Rutilio Sánchez

This quotation, taken from the January 1, 1984, full-page article in *Granma* on the Church in El Salvador, illustrates eloquently the extent to which a compromise arrangement, tempered by fairly frequent dialogue, has resulted in recent years. To critics abroad this is seen as a mixture of mere government toleration, of coopting "red" clergy and manipulating them to provide a "human face" for the revolution, and of maintaining respectability with Christian guerrilla forces in post-Medellín Latin America. By comparison, supporters of the Cuban government will view these changes as a sign of progress and maturation—for Church and State alike—during a 25-year period when extraordinary changes have taken place. Both interpretations will be partially correct.

It can be claimed with some justification that the government (many of whose leaders were educated almost 50 years ago in Catholic schools) is not convinced that the post-Vatican II Church is here to stay, particularly in view of the firmly anti-Soviet, and pro-West, stance of John Paul II. They view the changes, particularly in the Latin American Church, as being extremely positive and important, but it is feared that conservative sectors in important positions within CELAM are trying to subvert this process (witness the behind-the-scenes wrangling prior to and during the 1979 meeting at Puebla). This deeply rooted suspicion, supported by the experiences of 1959-61, and current attempts by conservative sectors in Nicaragua and the United States to manipulate tension within the Church in Central America, have understandably created a filter through which all facets of this rapprochement are viewed. To expect anything else would be naïve.

From the government's perspective, the Church represents a variety of people with many socio-political views and with different levels of *compromiso* toward the revolutionary process. Although there have been outspoken supporters from the Church sector who have become visibly integrated into the process, they do not necessarily represent the majority of practicing Christians. The Church's earlier role as a counterrevolutionary refuge has clearly ended—both because its middle-class adherents have left the country and because the Church itself has changed dramatically—but understandably the suspicion still exists that the Church may well revert to its earlier role, something the security-conscious State is not prepared to tolerate. A dialogue has been established then, and both sides have engaged in a cordial spirit of compromise (from which both benefit), yet problems clearly remain, from exclusion of Christian participation in political activities to the banning of Christian journals.

It is often claimed, with some justification, that practicing Christians are discriminated against when seeking membership in the Young Communist organization and in the Communist party and when pursuing advancement to the upper levels of government ministries. Indeed, the 1976 "Plataforma Programática" of the Cuban Communist Party, while emphasizing the right enjoyed by all citizens to practice freely the religion of their choice, demands that all members hold "an ideological formation in agreement with basic Marxist theory."[29] Within the last five years, little has happened to develop Church-State ties, claim critics, who indicate that the Castro government simply manipulates religious activities for their public relations value: "Catholics are not persecuted in Cuba: they are simply tolerated. An inevitable problem. They are viewed with a certain ironic scorn—much like the way arrogant whites consider the kaffirs."[30]

Such an overview, with its thesis of "tokenism" exhibited by the government, would appear to be somewhat simplistic, failing to take into account major changes of the last five years. This is not to deny, however, the overly dogmatic view of religion shown by state functionaries, many of whom quite simply "have neglected to update their views of the changing Church."[31] Nevertheless, important developments have taken place in the last five years, to a large extent due to the revolutionary struggle in Central America, where the teachings of Archbishop Oscar

Romero, the continuing torture and murder of practicing Christians, and the popular victory in Nicaragua have shown that some Christian, Marxist, and nationalistic currents can work successfully side by side.

In this period major changes of great symbolic significance have occurred. In 1979, for instance, the installation of the new bishop of Pinar del Río was accompanied by a religious procession, the first in nearly two decades. Also in 1979, Dr. Carneado, a member of the Central Committee and the government representative responsible for religious matters, accepted an invitation to address the annual assembly of the Cuban Ecumenical Council. Finally, since 1981 there has been a noticeable increase in Cuban media coverage of Church matters, particularly in publications intended for distribution abroad. Even five years ago this attention to Church matters in the mass media would have been unthinkable.

Within the Protestant church one can also see an impressive theological development, in an attempt to define clearly the role and responsibilities held by Christians in a revolutionary society. Influenced by the Presbyterian-Reformed Church and the energetic activities of its theologians, Adolfo Ham Reyes and Sergio Arce Martínez, both of whom teach at the Protestant Seminary in Matanzas, the Church has developed an extremely progressive stance on social matters in recent years, as exemplified by the superb series of theological reflections, *Cristo vivo en Cuba*.[32] The close ecumenical ties and the outspoken support for government programs that have developed can be seen in *Cristianos contra invasión militar norteamericana a Granada*, a condemnation of the U.S. invasion by, among other Church groups, the Ecumenical Council of Cuba, the Christian Council for Peace, the Cuban Student Christian Movement, the Worker-Student Baptist Council of Cuba, the Cuban Coordinator of the Caribbean Conference of Churches, the Methodist Church of Cuba, the Presbyterian-Reformed Church of Cuba, the Pentecostal Christian Church, and the Salvation Army.

It is clear that the earlier Church reforms have continued within the last five years and that the Church has slowly embarked on a progressive path, both in regard to domestic and international policy. The dynamic Protestant leadership and the young Catholic hierarchy have attempted to realign the Church on post-Vatican II lines. However, this has not been without much criticism and foot-dragging on the part of the mainstream of Christian congregations. As a result, the numbers of practicing Christians might have dropped substantially since the early days of the revolution (when the Church was clearly manipulated, with or without its knowledge), yet as Canadian missionary Yvon Bastarache pointed out in 1983: "But what really counts are not just the figures: the Church revolves around the quality of believers, and the quality of their lives. From that viewpoint, I believe that the Cuban Church is more beautiful than it has ever been."[33]

CONCLUSION

> The Church is progressively passing from the ghetto to dialogue: from evasion to commitment; from forced coexistence to shared living together; from the psychosis of escape to the loyal acceptance of remaining on the island; from global condemnation to recognition of the values that nourish and promote the revolutionary phenomenon.
>
> Aldo J. Büntig

In August 1983 at a Managua taping of a remarkable Nicaraguan community show, "De cara el pueblo," junta coordinator Daniel Ortega was asked about the role of the Church in the Nicaraguan Revolution, specifically why the Cuban Revolution had proved so different in this regard. The Sandinista spokesman's answer was direct and concrete. If we had undertaken our revolution in 1959, he noted, the Church, which now exercises such a major role in Nicaragua, would have probably been our enemy. Cuba's revolution and its thorny relations with the Church were, he concluded, simply the result of bad timing. Ortega oversimplified the situation, ignoring the Spanish *franquista* influence, the urban-based nature of the Cuban church, and the tremendously vibrant Afro-Cuban folk religion, yet his central point does hold a certain validity. The radical reforms of Vatican II (1962–65) and of Medellín (1968) plunged the Church into a whirlwind, seeking to change centuries of superstition, privilege, and oppression. The retrograde Cuban church, already dramatically behind the times in 1959, was caught hopelessly off guard and has been playing catch-up ever since.

An examination of the past 25 years, shows that major achievements have followed a disastrous beginning. Relations with the State have improved dramatically, due initially to the intelligent and sensitive role played by papal nuncio Zacchi and later expanded by the young Cuban hierarchy. The Castro government, within the rather rigid limits of its Marxist position, has proved sympathetic to Church initiatives and has been warmly praised by most religious sectors. The resulting moral agreement between Church and State has been in effect since the mid-1960s and would appear to consist of a fairly appreciative understanding of the other's position.

The "Cubanization" of the clergy, generally viewed as a welcome change from the early days of the Revolution when the confrontationist policy of the Spanish "falangist priests" (to quote Fidel Castro) created a profound abyss between Church and State, is a welcome improvement and a yardstick for measuring the health of the Church. The remarkable number and quality of religious vocations, their openness to the Vatican II spirit, and the resulting theological reflections, augur well for the development of a dynamic, responsible Church.

These changes are all the more remarkable, because they have been realized against a background of latent State suspicion, and with a vast majority of the faithful leaving for the allegedly greener pastures of Miami. The result of the exodus, the fact that approximately one-half of one percent of the population are practicing Catholics (similar proportions are probably true for other faiths), obviously could have meant the death of organized religion. Yet a remarkable evolution has taken place, as the Church has recognized the error of her earlier ways. "All that has happened to us has been providential. We loved our schools more than Jesus Christ," Archbishop Pérez Serantes is reported to have said on his deathbed.[34] Since 1969 the Church has made a conscious effort, particularly at the level of the hierarchy, to alter earlier dubious conduct. The Church of Cuba has realized, although belatedly, what its mission is supposed to be. Addressing the Caribbean Conference of Churches in September 1983, Adolfo Ham, chairman of the Cuban Ecumenical Council, expressed this eloquently:

> We are not a martyred or suppressed Church, but we have lost all the privileges and comforts of the Churches who were part of and responsible for the Establishment.... We have learned the hard lesson that only when the Church is a servant—when the Church can be fully identified with the needs and spirit of the people, is when she can be the Church.[35]

ACKNOWLEDGMENTS

This project has been funded by the Canadian Association for Latin American and Caribbean Studies and by the Social Sciences and

Humanities Research Council of Canada. The author would also like to thank Roland Laneuville, director of the Canadian Missions Étrangères (and a priest in Cuba from 1965 to 1979), for his generous assistance and support and Margaret E. Crahan of Occidental College in Los Angeles for her perceptive remarks on the paper. All quotations from Spanish and French have been translated by the author, who assumes responsibility for the accuracy of the translation as well as for all views expressed here.

NOTES

1. Celso Montero Rodríguez, *Cristianos en la revolucion cubana* (Estella, Spain: Editorial Verbo Divino, 1975), pp. 287–88.
2. Quoted in Adolfo Ham, "Evangelism in the Socialist Society of Cuba," *International Review of Mission*, vol. 66 (January 1977), p. 280.
3. J. Lloyd Mecham, *Church and State in Latin America: A History of Politico-Ecclesiastical Relations* (Chapel Hill, N.C.: University of North Carolina Press, 1966), p. 304.
4. An American observer noted in 1971 the strength of this influence: "Many of the Presbyterians and other Protestants who had left Cuba had done so because to remain in an 'anti-Yanqui' communist land seemed to them an act of disloyalty to the stateside 'mother church,' the church that had brought them the gospel—indication indeed of colonialist mentality!" See Dean Peerman, "Church-Hopping in Havana," *The Christian Century*, vol. 88, no. 49 (December 8, 1971), p. 1435.
5. Mateo Jover Marimón, "The Church," in Carmelo Meso-Lago, ed., *Revolutionary Change in Cuba* (Pittsburgh: University of Pittsburgh Press, 1974), p. 400.
6. Cited in Margaret Crahan, "Salvation Through Christ or Marx: Religion in Revolutionary Cuba," *Journal of Interamerican Studies and World Affairs*, vol. 21, no. 1 (February 1979), p. 162.
7. Ibid., p. 171.
8. Mecham, *Church and State in Latin America*, p. 304.
9. Cited in Leslie Dewart, *Christianity and Revolution: The Lesson of Cuba* (New York: Herder and Herder, 1963), p. 115.
10. Ibid., p. 160.
11. Ibid., p. 166.
12. Fidel Castro, "Christianity and the Revolution," *New Blackfriars*, vol. 59, no. 695 (April 1978), p. 154.
13. This is from a 1966 interview with Monsignor Zacchi, quoted by Beverly Swaren in her article, "The Church in Today's Cuba," *America*, vol. 119, no. 8 (September 21, 1968), p. 212.

14. Cited in Ernesto Cardenal, *In Cuba* (New York: New Directions, 1974), p. 231.
15. Ibid., p. 231.
16. Aldo J. Büntig, "The Church in Cuba: Toward a New Frontier," in Alice L. Hageman and Philip E. Wheaton, eds., *Religion in Cuba Today: A New Church in a New Society* (New York: Association Press, 1971), p. 116.
17. Everett E. Gendler, "Cuba and Religion: Challenge and Response," *The Christian Century*, vol. 86, no. 31 (July 30, 1969), p. 1013.
18. See "Cuban Bishops Call of End to Trade Blockade," Hageman and Wheaton, *op. cit.*, p. 293.
19. See Hageman and Wheaton, *op. cit.*, p. 301.
20. "Can one still be a Christian in Cuba?" *LADOC*, vol. 2, no. 50, (September 1976), p. 17.
21. See Gendler, "Cuba and Religion," p. 1015. See also Peerman, "Church-Hopping in Havana," where the priests of one of the churches visited even saw ecumenical activities as proof of communism: "The revelation that ours was an 'interfaith' group—four Protestants, three Catholics—brought a frown to the priest's face and the incredible comment that 'ecumenism leads to confusion—and to communism,'" (p. 1436).
22. See Michel, "Une terre sans Dieu?," *Missions Étrangères*, vol. 21, no. 7 (February 1984), p. 8.
23. See Sister Gisèle Piché, s.b.c., "Heureuses en pays socialiste," *Missions Étrangères*, vol. 15, no. 12 (November/December 1972), pp. 18–19.
24. Cited in Álvaro Argüello H., S.J., ed., *Fidel Castro y los cristianos revolucionarios* (Managua: Institute Histórico Centroamericano, 1979(?), p. 13.
25. Ibid., p. 13.
26. Castro, "Christianity and the Revolution," p. 158.
27. Cited in Dow Kirkpatrick, "Cuban Church at Puebla," *Cuba Review*, vol. 9, no. 1 (February 1979), p. 19. As part of this radically different perspective, one can also cite the words of Archbishop Francisco Oves of Havana in his opening address to representatives at the 11th Youth Festival held in Havana in August 1978. He noted, for example: "It is our objective, based on our Christian identity, to develop our actions, directing them to encourage a responsible, sincere participation in this, our socialist society." See "Intervención de Francisco Oves, Arzobispo de La Habana," *Encuentro de los Jóvenes Creyentes por la Solidaridad Antimperialista, le Paz y la Amistad* (Havana, n.p., n.d.) p. 9.
28. Cited by Rodríguez, *Cristianos en la revolución Cubana*, p. 300.
29. Rosa Alfonso, ed., "Plataforma Programática del Partido Comunista de Cuba," *Acerca de la religión, la iglesia y los creyentes* (La Habana: Editora Política, 1982), p. 2.
30. Carlos Alberto Montaner, *Fidel Castro y la Revolución Cubana* (Madrid: Editorial Playor, 1983), p. 125.

31. Kenneth A. Briggs, "In Atheist Cuba, Soft Spot for Church," *New York Times*, April 20, 1981, p. 3.

32. *Cristo vivo en Cuba: Reflexiones Teológicas Cubanas* (San José, Costa Rica: Departamento Ecuménico de Investigaciones, 1978).

33. Havé Caron, "Ministère à Varadero," *Missions Étrangéres*, vol. 21, no. 4 (August 1983), p. 18.

34. Cited in Hageman and Wheaton, p. 30.

35. See "A View from Cuba," *Caribbean Contact*, November 1983, p. 16.

Section III
Cultural Change

6 The Emergence of Popular Culture

Judith A. Weiss

The term "popular culture" is a problematic catch-all that embraces both those forms of cultural expression and creation that involve a strong native, mass-based participation and those created *for* mass consumption. The speed with which elements of mass culture are integrated into popular culture (i.e., one which involves the people as agents rather than as passive recipients) might have been a contributing factor to this confusion, but the fundamental distinction should remain.

Cuba has been engaged in the struggle to maintain this distinction, both with regard to the "truly national" versus "neocolonial" contradiction and with regard to the "popular" versus "elite" sources of creation. What has resulted since 1959, has been a rich, if somewhat uneven, combination of foreign and native elements, of elite and traditional-popular culture. State policy has, on the whole, been substantively inclusive, guarding only against penetration by "cultural imperialism," that is, what is seen as the use of media and cultural symbols as a Trojan horse of capitalist North American values. Some discretion is always in effect; therefore, in determining which Hollywood films will be shown in Cuba and which books will be translated.

Critical vigilance is exercised with varying degrees of rigidity through internal discussion (in production units, seminars, congresses, and assemblies) and through self-censorship (i.e., a prudent navigation through the politics of an insular society).

In reviewing the emergence of popular culture in Cuba since 1959, we are faced with the need to comprehend the structural mechanism of the administration of cultural policy and with a need for a definition of the term that is both broad and yet concrete. Are we to focus primarily on traditional culture as it is being revived? Or are we not better advised to examine new forms that traditional cultural creation has taken in the new society?

Considerations of space lead me to opt for the latter, which is where a culture *of* the Revolution is emerging. It is, increasingly, a hybrid kind of culture, fed by traditional forms and by elite sources (be these national, as with writers and artists formed in a more academic tradition, or international, as with foreign music, theater, and even institutional development).

A survey of the relations between popular forms of expression and an elite-based culture shows that there has always been an uneasy interaction between the two. Progressive intellectuals, writers, and artists have resorted periodically to the people's voice and language to affirm national identity (in the nineteenth century independence struggle) or to oppose a corrupt *comprador* elite (in the 1920s and 1930s, particularly). Academic circles in which such progressive elements had some influence would acknowledge the significance of traditional culture, and the work of Fernando Ortiz, Alejo Carpentier, and other leading intellectuals validated the importance of a popular culture rooted in the Afro-Cuban tradition.

The triumph of the revolution affirmed this tendency and placed the institutions of the State at the service of the effort to retrieve and publicize cultural elements that had often survived quite marginally. The mainstreaming of traditional culture (and its vindication as "popular") paralleled the educational drive, which grew and broadened to bring elite forms to the masses (with the intention of popularizing culture). Both streams appear to have equal importance in Cuban cultural policy, and one by-product of this effort has been the emergence of a hybrid popular culture, the offspring of national tradition and relevant foreign and elite influences.

THE INFRASTRUCTURE OF CULTURAL PRODUCTION IN CUBA

The thrust toward government sponsorship of culture was not a creation of the revolutionary government. Like many of the efforts that the Revolution supported, the principle of government involvement along with the ministerial structures existed in Cuba prior to 1959. The main difference lay in (1) the *continuity* of cultural policy that Fidel Castro's regime allowed, (2) the *extent* of government initiative and responsiveness, and (3) the *geographic scope* of ministerial activities.

The Revolution did not break radically with past practice. Instead, it built on precedents established by the well-intentioned and enlightened elements of previous governments. The first significant recognition of the importance of Cuban culture had been the establishment of the Dirección de Cultura (Cultural Division) of the Ministry of Education in 1934.[1] This active commitment to culture became possible under the progressive government that followed the overthrow of Machado and had the support of a strong, educated elite.[2]

The degree of the Ministry's cultural involvement appears to coincide with the periods of greatest involvement by socialists in government. The main problems lay in the inconsistent allocation of funds (which fluctuated with the regimes and the state of the economy), in the geographic distribution of government assistance (which did little to break the virtual monopoly of Havana,[3] and in the impossibility of long-range or even medium-range planning and coordination.

In this scheme, popular culture suffered the added disadvantage of having to compete—often with no advocates nor even the most basic response—against the favored elite modes and against class and racial prejudice. The poor and the geographically marginal sectors had little or no access to mainstream culture, and popular culture had to fend for itself, often under siege by an overwhelming mass culture.

The uneven accomplishments of the previous 25 years were precedents for the new regime. With the allocation of funds to the Ministry of Education, culture began to benefit. As a working class and nationalist ideology took root and spread, the scientific preservation of popular and traditional culture ranked as high as the support of elite forms.

Parallel with the literacy campaign of 1961, Cuba saw the mushrooming of amateur and professional activities, and the materialization of the dreams of those artists and intellectuals who had for decades been in the vanguard, exploring national culture and defending its traditional values. These same cultural leaders now were the cultural establishment.[4]

Several factors accelerated the development of new audiences and the galvanization of the masses as agents, rather than mere consumers, of cultural creation:

> 1. The success of the literacy campaign in creating a *de facto* literate population and in making urban youth more aware of the needs of the less developed regions;

2. Closely monitored compulsory education and the promotion of continuing education, with the concomitant exposure of greater numbers of students to cultural activity in educational centers;

3. The involvement of mass organizations[5] and unions in cultural activities that range from folksong festivals and art contests to the promotion of amateur writing circles and theater groups;

4. The involvement of professionals as advisors to amateur groups and to newly formed professional groups throughout the country, in a centrifugal pattern out of Havana and the other main urban centers;

5. Coverage, by publications such as *Bohemia* and the newspapers, of new cultural developments, and promotion by radio and television of popular and elite culture as a matter of policy;

6. A ten-fold increase in the university student population,[6] many of whom become involved in cultural research and preservation or community-based cultural activities; and

7. Increased book production, from less than one million copies annually before 1959, to about 50 million in the early 1980s.

In 1960, the Division of Culture of the Ministry of Education became the Consejo Nacional de Cultura (CNC). This followed the nationalization of printing shops and the founding of the Cuban Film Institute (ICAIC) and of the National Publishing House headed by Alejo Carpentier. It also coincided with the founding of the Casa de las Américas, an autonomous institution that promotes exchanges with other Latin American nations.

The CNC became the Ministry of Culture in 1976, because of the "need to create a higher body to coordinate, guide and serve as a link between the state and other agencies."[7] The present minister of culture, Armando Hart, has been in charge almost uninterruptedly since 1959, when he was appointed minister of education, and his humane vision has guided the development of an inclusive national policy of cultural development.[8]

The cultural agencies of the state had to keep pace with the changing conditions "through which culture can penetrate all aspects of life,"[9] and a pattern of collaboration has been established among mass organizations and government agencies. Since the institutionalization of People's Power (1976–78), for instance, the ministry has been sharing responsibilities for local activities with the Popular Councils of Culture (an arm of the People's Power structure).

Official statistics indicate steady and substantial growth in the area of cultural production and mass participation in Cuba. The first National Congress of Culture, held in 1962, brought together seventeen agencies and 85 delegates. The *responsables de cultura* ("coordinators and administrators") at the national, provincial, and municipal levels totaled no more than 270.[10] By 1975, the CNC employed 19,540 workers, including artists, technicians, administrative personnel, laborers, service personnel, and directors.[11]

The council projected 2,140 more activities in 1963 than in 1962, with one million more spectators, for a total of more than five million.[12] The figures released fourteen years later list 587,369 activities for 1975, with an attendance of over 62 million. If museum and library use are included, total participation exceeds 67 million, for an average of 7.3 percent activities and/or services per inhabitant. This does not include the services of radio and television (ICR) or of the tourist industry (INIT), whose combined total exceeds 300,000. During this 14-year period, activities and/or services increased by 65 percent and public participation increased by 50 percent.[13] The increase can be attributed in large measure to the greater number of museums, libraries, and cultural centers.[14]

The Five Year Plan (1976–80) called for a rationalization of existing resources (a tacit acknowledgment of financial restraint, perhaps), but it did not forecast a retrenchment or curtailing of services and activities. A greater emphasis was to be placed on the quality of cultural production and "on higher ideological principles...in a direct struggle against the expressions of ideological diversionism."[15] Art education would gain a fresh impetus through the long-established National School of Art (ENA), through the new Higher Institute of Art (ISA), which functions largely as an extension program for training specialists, and through mass organizations, particularly the structure of People's Power.

CULTURAL POLICY

The cornerstone of official cultural policy in Cuba is the 1961 statement by President Castro to the First Conference of Writers and Artists, the famous "*Dentro de la Revolución, todo. Fuera de la Revolución, nada*" ("Within the Revolution, everything. Outside the Revolution, nothing").[16] Virtually every official and semi-official statement since then has echoed that general principle, and subsequent documents of cultural policy do little more than expand on it and analyze it.

One inference that can be made from this statement is that there really is no need to censor cultural creation as long as its authors are actively involved in the revolutionary process. The guiding example of José Martí, for whom the intellectual/creator and the socially responsible human being were inseparable, echoes Castro's words. The statement also takes into account any subconscious dissent or counterrevolutionary values that might emerge from even the most involved revolutionary, by suggesting that the creation itself must conform to the needs and values of the revolution.

Major policy declarations of the past two decades have made those two aspects much clearer, reaffirming the need to train cultural workers who are able to contribute to the building of socialism (i.e., furthering the ideology of the revolution).[17] The specific role of this cultural vanguard is clearly outlined and analyzed in an article published shortly after the 1968 Cultural Congress of Havana. The authors maintain that the cultural vanguard must "establish a critical opposition to tradition while at the same maintaining a sense of its essential continuity, until it, too, becomes a living tradition as it consolidates its achievements."[18]

That "critical opposition" includes several factors, such as the ability to distinguish between the authentic culture of the people and a mass culture "produced to serve the system," a "reworking" of folklore and tradition in general, and an openness to international influences that are not "imperialist concoctions."[19] One is an anti-imperialist perspective, the other, a struggle against "populism, ultra-nationalism and traditionalism."[20]

Most of the members of the cultural vanguard of Cuba who are not working at the ICAIC or Casa de las Américas, or in the universities are in the Ministry of Culture. According to Armando Hart, the ministry is responsible for responding to the cultural demands of the population. It functions as a complex hierarchy of administrators and creative individuals (not mutually exclusive categories). Its responsibility now lies principally in the area of professional activity, with amateur activities left largely to the mass organizations. It does, however, continue to provide advisors and training personnel and to coordinate cultural policy.

The two main steams of activity involving national culture and ministerial initiative in Cuba are the retrieval and preservation of traditional values of culture and the offering of "elite" culture to the masses. The latter is not the focus of this chapter, but it is important to note that both currents are fed by a common axiology (nationalism + anti-imperialism + internationalism), and both have developed with a common infrastructure of education and communications. Academics and intellectuals have played key roles in both currents,[21] and a Marxist-Leninist line is reflected in the ministry's promotion of the two streams. According to Armando Hart, "We have to look at it (culture) from the point of view of... the masses, including the creators, the artists, and specialists. The popular roots of our culture lie in the people, in its past, in its present."[22]

REVOLUTIONARY INSTITUTIONS AND THE EMERGENCE OF POPULAR CULTURE

The double thrust of cultural policy in Cuba enables the two currents to meet, and it encourages a synthesis, wherever possible. The following examples demonstrate the method of Cuba's cultural policy and its accomplishments: two serve as extensions of the Ministry of Culture, as part of the infrastructure for the implementation of cultural policy, and two have developed as representative and internationally acclaimed expressions of national cultural creation in the revolution.

Revolución y Cultura: The Medium and the Messenger

Revolución y Cultura is the principal informational tool of the Ministry of Culture. It superseded *Pueblo y Cultura*, the organ of the cultural division of the Ministry of Education and of the CNC. Its contributors are ministry staff or foreign guests, and articles range from texts of speeches to interviews with writers and artists. Illustrations include drawings, photographs, color plates of posters, and examples of the plastic arts in Cuba.

The magazine is aimed at a broad population. Unlike publications of prerevolutionary regimes (e.g., *Anuario Cultural*), it is clearly a mass publication. It serves to profile official policy statements and outline ministerial initiative (and occasionally to present position papers on issues in the arts). It chronicles cultural development, from the life's work of individual artists or groups, to the efforts of scholars and researchers to reexamine classics of Cuban art, architecture, literature, and traditional culture.

Most of the magazine is devoted to professional artists, although the work of professionals with amateurs is also detailed. The journalistic reporting (i.e., profiles and interviews) is skillfully conducted. The overall quality of the magazine is uneven, however. Much of the analysis does not rank with the best of the cultural reports of *Juventud Rebelde* and *Granma* or *Bohemia*, and its contents rarely match the quality of *Caimán Barbudo*. Still, the variety of its contents and its value as a gazette of cultural life are undeniable. It is a useful central source of information, which is retrievable through carefully compiled indexes.[23]

Its significance as a vehicle for cultural policy is obvious. Reports, interviews, and speeches offer an historical continuum. The picture remains more or less constant, through periodic restatements of the basic goals and tenets of the cultural programs of the revolution.

Culture in the Neighborhood: The *Casa de Cultura*

The concept, and indeed the first designs, were imported from the Soviet Union,[24] and in some respects the structured nature of these local cultural centers may seem to be somewhat alien to the Cuban spirit. To many people the *casas de cultura* smack of organized fun, and they certainly have to rely on structuring leisure time, if only because of the demands on the building which result from the wide range of activities that they sponsor.

Jointly administered by the Ministry of Culture and the municipalities/People's Power, the *casa de cultura* is housed usually in a mansion that passed into government hands. Optimally, its facilities will include a library, a museum and/or art gallery, a small amphitheater, and where possible, an auditorium, conference rooms, and music rooms or studios. Children's programming is normally scheduled at different times from the adults' activities.

The *casa* offers individual and group classes in art, ballet, music, and photography. It serves as a center for community theater (professional groups for children and adults, as well as amateur groups) and for performances by visiting troupes or musicians.[25]

Each community puts its own seal on its *casa de cultura*. In a place where traditional popular culture is strong, as in a neighborhood of Santiago, or the small town of Remedios in the north, or in the Havana suburb of Guanabacoa, arts and crafts exhibits, musical performances, and the general spirit of the center reflect the particular influences at work on the local culture.

In the Vedado section of Havana, a high-powered program usually mirrors the demographics of that municipality. In that *casa de cultura*, the *crème* of the Ministry might be present on a more regular basis at openings, mingling with local intellectuals, artists, and remaining members of the bourgeoisie.

There is an element of forced decorum in some of the *casas*—sometimes a kind of formality that sits strangely with a visitor and almost makes the *casa* ring false. But it is here that a young girl can come for free ballet or piano lessons, or the local papier mâché artists display their colorful sculptures, or a touring exhibition of prints or paintings will stop, or the region's main theater company will perform. The *casa* is the way station of highbrow culture and a showcase for popular culture, a place where new talent can be tapped, and the physical space for implementing the two-stream policy of the revolution.

Revolutionary Pop-Folk: The *Nueva Trova*

They echo popular Cuban balladeers of the early part of the century (sentimental minstrels), but, more especially, the new song movement of Spain and Latin America. They are wildly successful at home and popular ambassadors abroad. The handful of musicians known collectively as the *Nueva Trova* (roughly translated, "the New Minstrels") began, in the late 1960s as the "Grupo de Experimentación Sonora del ICAIC," the ensemble that provided music for the Film Institute's productions. The founding nucleus still studies musicology and holds seminars, in addition to touring, and over the years it has attracted new talent from around the country. These musicians now constitute a network or, as the official title prefers it, a movement.[26]

Each of the singer-songwriters has a unique sound and style, although often the styles do blend into a few characteristic patterns. The best-known members are still the founders—Pablo Milanés, Silvio Rodríguez, Noël Nicola, Eduardo Ramos, and Amaury Pérez. Others joined later and gained a strong reputation, including Sara González, Alejandro García (Virulo), and many others. The members of the founding group are about 40 years old now, and their style has matured accordingly, but the intention is the same.

Songs such as "Ho Ch Minh," "Fusil contra fusil," a lasting eulogy to Ché Guevara, and "Playa Girón" praise revolutionary heroism quite unabashedly and get away with it because of their skillful engineering of imagery or symbolism and the beauty of the music—its passionate tones and harmony. The singers may satirize bureaucrats or, in their quasi-underground songs, may criticize repressive parenting (in such lyrics as "¿Quién te está dando el desayuno para cobrártelo mañana?" "Who's giving you breakfast, only to charge you for it tomorrow?"). They produce love songs that blend tenderness and a mature awareness of the stuff of relationships—a subject that other generations of Latin musicians would never touch. Sara González is well known for her sharp defense of women's rights ("¿Qué dice Usted, que una mujer no es capaz de construir, de analizar y de luchar por la vida?" "What do you say, that a woman isn't capable of building, analyzing, struggling for life?").

A more complete integration of traditional styles with contemporary music is heard in the works of Virulo, whose two comic operas take jabs at convention and clichés in ideology and art. They are a rough composite, in Nueva Trova sounds, of musical comedy and traditional music, such as the *son* and the *rumba*. His lyrics mock almost everything, from blind acceptance of literal readings of the Bible, to laziness and corruption on the job. Occasionally, Virulo flirts with the boundaries of good taste and political orthodoxy, but he is tolerated as a mildly outrageous genius, partly because his humor and his language are so genuinely Cuban. He has become one of Cuba's cultural representatives abroad. Virulo and Sara González, his main interpreter, are often featured on the same bill with an established poet such as Eliseo Diego—once again reflecting the double thrust of revolutionary policy.

The Nueva Trova movement includes a different wing, represented by the Grupo Moncada (social scientists who research and perform Latin American music) and the group Manguaré. This wing is more inclined toward performing the traditional styles of folk music from different Latin American countries. Irakere, the well-known jazz group, is sometimes included in this movement. The inclusion of such groups makes it difficult to determine the precise parameters of the Nueva Trova. The name usually applies mainly to the individual artists and to Grupo Moncada, who combine folk (both rural and urban) with popular music from Cuban dance halls and North American and European new folk music currents.

The Nueva Trova has brought together a diversity of artists and groups through concerts, festivals, workshops, and informal jam sessions. It is the acknowledged expression of a new musical synthesis—a quasi-academic appreciation and use of traditional forms (from the *son* and the *guajira* to the work of the old *trova* singers like Sindo Garay, to the *guaguancó*) and the most contemporary styles and techniques of composition, arrangement, accompaniment, and sound mixing and engineering. It is also the nerve that links Cuba's musical youth to their counterparts abroad and a cultural lifeline across the blockade.

A Renewal of Sociocultural Creation: The New Theater

Cuba's theater has a rich and varied history, and its Workers' Theatre of the 1930s was acknowledged as an important contribution to Latin American theater; both the mainstream tradition and the experiments in political theater have influenced the theater that has emerged since 1959.

With the triumph of the revolution and the shift from commercialism in the arts, which had limited the possibilities of serious theater companies, these groups became competitive with low-brow or medium-brow forms (musical comedy and melodrama). Repertory theater was actively promoted, and the theater people, in turn, looked for ways to make their art more relevant and accessible.

Social drama was the mainstay, especially if it had a political message (usually an indictment of prerevolutionary society), but some experiments in the Absurd or in the theater of cruelty were attempted. Still, audiences remained limited, and few people outside the main urban centers had access to the theater. By the mid-1960s, the crisis was being felt throughout Latin America, particularly by left-wing artists alienated from commercial mainstream creation that they considered stagnant and useless for conveying a new message.

The work of Enrique Buenaventura and his Teatro Experimental de Cali (TEC) became known outside their native Colombia as the first genuine departure from theatrical tradition in years. It coincided with the work of the San Francisco Mime Troupe and the experiments of Augusto Boal in Brazil and Peru. Like these, it took its cue from Bertolt Brecht's propositions for a radical political theater.[27]

The TEC and other groups were involved in collective creation of original works or elaborations of classics, nondramatic texts, or material to suit a contemporary concern. They were usually based in specific communities, out of which material was obtained and for which the productions were staged. Their work was always in process, evolving through dialogues with their audience/constituency and through internal discussions. Their main objective was *concientización*, a raising of consciousness that had implications for the aesthetic as well as the sociopolitical development of their audiences. A new aesthetic had to be developed to project the new message/intent, and the forms adopted or devised were to be based, wherever possible, on forms familiar to their constituency. Just as the content was an airing of their constituency's concerns, the forms would tie in with that audience's own tradition of cultural expression. The masks, the puppets, the costumes, the dances, and the music of the *Nuevo Teatro* tend, therefore, to be those of the region where each group's main activity is concentrated.

And so in Cuba, too, between 1966 and 1969, discontent with a serious theater that attracted few new spectators outside an intellectual elite, and an uneasiness about the political effectiveness of their work as a cultural vanguard, led some Havana-based and Santiago-based professionals searching for an alternative in the type of theater that Boal and Buenaventura were postulating.

In 1966 the Conjunto Dramático de Oriente set out to study the tradition of street theater known as *relaciones*—a form that used a narrator, masks, dance, and music and went in search of audiences. The group began to work with historical legends and Afro-Cuban myths, and brought their new versions to the neighborhoods of Santiago—neighborhoods with a large, low-income, black population—stopping to perform in plazas and on the steps of the city. The group became the Cabildo Teatral in 1971, adopting its name from two colonial institutions: the town hall (assembly of civic leaders) and the cultural-national grouping of blacks, both known as *cabildo*.

The masks and stock characters of Italian comedy are congruous with colonial themes. Other stock characters are classics of Golden Age Spanish drama and Cuban popular tradition. Costumes and dances are carefully recreated. African myths are reconstructed with attention to the detail of the story, the figures, and the social context of their creation. The method (lines of musicians and players dancing through the town) is also truly classical, suggestive both of medieval, renaissance, and colonial festive pageants and of Afro-Cuban street dancing (from colonial festivities), which might have its roots in African itinerant theater.[28]

Every play has a message, be it a moral about social responsibility to the revolutionary work ethic or a Marxist rereading of an African death myth. The other groups that have arisen independently of the Cabildo Teatral or derived from it have stressed a similar concern with the relevance of form as well as of content. Thus, in areas with different demographics, groups have adopted different forms—the *décima*, the *guajira*, the *son*—even though they operate on the same principles of *concientización*, research into local history and problems, issues and traditions, and aesthetic education of their constituency.

The representative of the majority stream of the New Theater movement is the Grupo Teatro Escambray, begun in 1969 by about 10 professionals of the Havana theater with the help of a social science research team that surveyed the target region, identifying the main concerns of the population of this highly underdeveloped region of the country.

The Grupo Escambray developed its repertoire around a number of issues, including the social impact of the collectivization of dairy farming, the struggle against counterrevolutionaries (1960-65), the proselytizing activities of Jehovah's Witnesses, and the condition of women. They also set up a children's theater group. Like the Cabildo Teatral, they have represented Cuba at festivals abroad.[29]

These groups of the New Theater movement, now numbering 20 or more, work in consultation with the local party and mass organizations in developing their schedules and materials. The main objective of the Grupo Escambray and other groups is to involve the audiences in the production. This may be accomplished through discussions or sometimes by structuring a play to turn the audience into an assembly (*El juicio, Ramona*). The narrator figure will sometimes sing his narrative in a traditional folk song form, and performances often culminate, as early Cuban drama had, with a *guateque* ("a dance party") involving the spectators.

Offshoots of the Grupo Escambray, the Grupo La Yaya and the Teatro de Participación Popular (TPP) actually included trained amateurs from the communities in which they were based. The Grupo La Yaya, from the new township in the Escambray region, included dairy workers (almost all female); and the TPP included men and women from the defense committees of a poor central neighborhood of Havana, from the longshoremen's union, and from the Lenin School. With this shift from an all-professional cast to an amateur group under professional directors, community theater moved one step closer to the ideal of a popular form of cultural creation, a people's theater, a forum in which the community itself, with little mediation, could work through its issues and concerns and develop its aesthetic expression.

The genuinely popular nature of this movement is sometimes questioned by critics of the Castro regime who perceive it purely as an ideological arm of the government and another tool of social control.

Yet its popularity persists because it does provide good entertainment, it speaks a familiar language, and it can be a forum for the community's concerns. How much coercion or official initiative is involved, even in getting professionals out to the communities to start these groups, is very difficult to determine.

CONCLUSIONS

Officially, the cultural policy of the Cuban Revolution has been relatively open, inclusive of valuable foreign, elite, and traditional popular elements. The Ministry of Culture has been systematically developing both the personnel (cultural workers) and the audiences and making available, on an increasingly large scale, a variety of cultural activities that involve the masses as spectators and as active participants. The ministry encouraged the diffusion of elite or academic forms of culture among a broader base of the Cuban population, through educational programs and cultural outreach involving professionals, touring groups, and shows, and through substantial use of the media. It has been actively involved in the gathering and preservation of traditional forms of popular culture and has encouraged the creative expression of traditional artists through festivals, workshops, and exhibitions.

The ministry collaborates with the mass organizations and with other cultural institutions (the Radio and Television Institute and the Film Institute) in promoting programs and special activities. It has, independently and in cooperation with other agencies, developed an efficient infrastructure that includes publications and buildings (e.g., museums, libraries, *casas de cultura*, and theaters). The ministry has also increased the number of training programs for professional artists and other cultural workers and broadened the educational offerings to include every municipality in the country.

Through ministry sponsorship, several new forms of cultural creation have developed in Cuba since 1959—chiefly the new music and theater movements. The groups of individuals who initiated these innovative forms of expression in the late 1960s have been joined by amateurs and professionals all over the country who, taking their cue from the founding group, work to integrate traditional and modern styles and forms.

The question of what constitutes popular culture in Cuba is a complex one. Traditional values have been popular in certain sectors of the population and since the colonial period have occasionally filtered into the elite culture. Mass culture (from musical comedy to North American pop music of the 1960s) has had an impact on national culture, and some of *its* values are now part of popular culture. The culture being made by the people in Cuba is influenced by academic or elite forms and concepts, as in the case of classically trained musicians and writers who teach amateur groups and are involved in the creation of new, hybrid forms of expression (e.g., the Nueva Trova).

A highly politicized culture that relies on a revolutionary content and on the notion of a socially responsible artist also requires, in order that the product be aesthetically superior or even acceptable, that certain critical criteria be developed by the artist and the audience. These criteria are being developed as part of the educational policy of the Ministry of Culture, although it is not clear how rigorous the training and follow-up (e.g., evaluation or testing) are.

Cuban cultural policy favors a nationalism that does not glorify tradition as a pure ideal. A revisionist approach is at work in the study of myths, legends, and history as well as in the updating of traditional artistic forms by integrating them with newer ones. The result is often a type of art or cultural expression in which Cuban identity comes across as the main value (equated with the Revolution) and that takes into account the syncretic nature of contemporary popular culture.

NOTES

1. Bill 283, June 6, 1934.
2. Its first director was José María Chacón y Calvo. Félix Lizaso was appointed head of the General Culture section, Caridad Benítez of the Fine Arts section. The division was in charge of educational extension, cultural relations, information, and copyrights. It published a cultural annual and a journal, organized book fairs, art exhibitions and contests, sent out bookmobiles and traveling theater companies, and developed the José Martí Archives.
3. Santiago and, to a lesser extent, Santa Clara were aided largely by the strong cultural presence of their universities.
4. Nicolás Guillén, Alejo Carpentier, José Antonio Portuondo, Juan Marinello, Fernando Portuondo, Cintio Vitier, and other leading progressive writers and scholars were appointed to head important cultural institutions, including the Union of Writers and Artists, the Academy of Sciences, and the José Martí Studies Centre.

5. The Committees for the Defense of the Revolution (CDR), the Federation of Cuban Women (FMC), the National Association of Small Farmers (ANAP), and the Young Pioneers are the main organizations.

6. The population increased from 17,000 in the late 1950s to 200,000 in the early 1980s. Armando Hart in an interview by Luis Báez in *Changing the Rules of the Game* (Havana: Letras Cubanas, 1983), p. 24.

7. Báez, *Changing the Rules*, p. 12.

8. The influence of its director on an institution is widely acknowledged, as in the cases of the late Haydée Santamaría, head of the Casa de las Américas, and the director of ICAIC.

9. Báez, *Changing the Rules*, p. 18.

10. Report of Vicentina Antuña, chairperson of the CNC, in "Segunda Plenaria Nacional de Cultura," *Pueblo y cultura*, no. 19 (January 1964), p. 3.

11. Luis Pavón Tamayo, chairperson of the CNC, "Informe a la VII Plenaria," *Revolución y Cultura*, no. 44 (April 1976), p. 5.

12. Antuña, "Segunda Plenaria Nacional de Cultura."

13. Pavón Tamayo, "Informe a la VII Plenaria."

14. Belarmino Castilla Mas (of the Central Committee of the Party and Deputy Prime Minister in charge of Education, Science and Culture,) "Discurso," *Revolución y Cultura*, no. 44 (April 1976), p. 7.

15. Ibid., p. 9.

16. Fidel Castro Ruz, *Palabras a los intelectuales* (La Habana, 1961).

17. Edith García Buchaca, executive secretary of the CNC, told the II Plenary of the Council in December 1963 that "the cultural cadres are political cadres...on this ideological front (that is the Cuban Revolution)." (*Pueblo y cultura*, no. 19 (January 1964): 5). See also *The Paths of Culture in Cuba* (a document of the 1st National Congress on Education and Culture, Havana, 1971), which restates this position in no uncertain terms. The Party Congresses of 1975 and 1980 and the Cuban Constitution of 1976 declare their support for cultural activity as a priority for the Cuban nation and, of course, for a political definition of culture.

18. Jesús Díaz and Juan Valdés-Paz, "Vanguardia, tradición y subdesarrollo," in Mario Benedetti et al., eds. *Literatura y arte nuevo en Cuba* (Barcelona: Editorial Estela, 1971), p. 67.

19. Ibid.

20. Ibid., p. 79. This echoes the debate engaged by Armando Mattelart in *La cultura como empresa multinacional* (México: ERA, 1974).

21. Rogelio Martínez Furé, ethnologist and folklorist, was a founder and advisor of the Conjunto Folklórico Nacional, one of Cuba's leading cultural institutions founded since 1959. Odilio Urfé and Argeliers León are well-respected musicologists whose work on popular (i.e., dance-hall) and rural folk music has been vital to the positive reevaluation of nonmainstream culture. Samuel Feijóo has published several valuable collections of Cuban

folk tales and *décimas* (the most characteristic Cuban poetic form), as well as studies of folk culture. These are representative of a solidly established movement of scholars who have made valuable contributions to the preservation of national culture.

22. Armando Hart, "El pueblo es el gran creador," *Revolución y Cultura*, no. 61 (1977), p. 6.

23. Published in issue no. 50 (October 1976, pp. 50–84) and no. 76 (December 1978, pp. 76–84).

24. See Mirta de Armas, "Casas de cultura," *Revolución y Cultura*, no. 61 (1977), p. 27.

25. Information on this and for the other sections are gathered firsthand, by observation and in conversations, and from articles in the popular Cuban press.

26. Leonardo Acosta, "La nueva trova: un movimiento masivo," *Revolución y Cultura*, no. 63 (1977), pp. 80–83.

27. See Gerardo Luzuriaga, ed., *Popular Theatre for Social Change in Latin America* (Los Angeles: Latin American Center Publications, 1978).

28. On the beginnings of the Cabildo Teatral and its method, see Carlos Padrón, "Conjunto Dramático de Oriente," *Revolución y Cultura*, no. 64 (1977), pp. 64–72. Some basis to my theory of the continuity of African popular theater in the Americas through the Cabildo might be found in Oyin Ogunba, "Traditional African Festival Drama," in Oyin Ogumba and Abiola Irele, eds., *Theatre in Africa* (Ibadan: Ibadan University Press, 1978), pp. 3–51.

29. Graziella Pogolotti, introduction, *Teatro Escambray* (Havana: Instituto Cubano del libro, 1978), Laurette Sejourné, *Teatro Escambray: Una experiencia* (Havana: Instituto Cubano del libro, 1978), and my own unpublished manuscript on the group, which focuses on the relation between the dramatic texts and their socio-historical sources.

7   Film and Revolution in Cuba: The First Twenty-Five Years

Julianne Burton

In the initial moments of Tomás Gutiérrez Alea's *La Muerte de un Burócrata* (*The Death of a Bureaucrat*, 1966) there is an audacious and brilliantly comic sequence. The deceased worker around whose disinterred remains the plot will revolve is seen in semi-animated flashback at his workplace. An "exemplary" proletarian artist, he has reduced art to a science, having devised a machine which produces busts of Cuban national poet and patriot José Martí with the monotonous regularity of cogs emerging from a press. In a moment of carelessness, the worker falls prey to his own invention. The last bust to emerge is his own; he has been martyred to his misguided concept of art.

The sequence imaginatively conveys the Cuban film industry's rejection of mechanical concepts mechanically imposed on the creative process. In 1973, to their surprise, American audiences discovered the delightful unpredictability which characterized many Cuban films of the 1960s and 1970s with the theatrical release of *Memories of Underdevelopment* (Tomás Gutiérrez Alea, 1968). Disarmed by its complexity and inventiveness, by its sophisticated wit and sympathetic portrayal of its bourgeois protagonist, U.S. critics greeted the film with ringing praise. *The New York Times* listed it among the year's ten best films. The National Society of Film Critics offered its director a special award, though the State Department's refusal to grant him a visa prevented him from attending the ceremony. However regrettable, such a response was not unexpected given how the Treasury Department had shut down the First New York Festival of Cuban Cinema the previous year, confiscating all prints on the second day of the week-long program and eventually driving American Documentary Films, co-sponsors of the festival, into bankruptcy.[1]

For a quarter century, the U.S. has sought to isolate Cuba from the rest of the world by imposing an economic and cultural blockade on the island. During this period, Cuban cinema and the related arts of music and poster design have continued to break through the cultural blockade to assert the creative energy of this struggling socialist society.

CINEMA AND CULTURAL PRIORITIES

The leaders of the guerrilla struggle were quick to perceive the artistic and educational supremacy of the film medium. In early 1959, soon after Fidel became head of the new revolutionary government, he ranked cinema and television, in that order, as the most important forms of artistic expression. A decade later, the First National Congress on Education and Culture pointed to radio, television, the cinema, and the press as "powerful instruments of ideological education, molders of the collective consciousness whose use and development must not be left to improvisation or spontaneity." The congress singled out film as "the art *par excellence* in our century."

Histories of postrevolutionary Cuban cinema customarily begin by observing that the decree which founded the Cuban Institute of Cinematographic Art and Industry (ICAIC) on March 24, 1959, was the first cultural act of the revolutionary government, coming less than three months after the overthrow of Batista. In fact, another revolutionary film organization preceded ICAIC. Cine Rebelde, part of the Rebel Army's National Board of Culture, was founded as soon as the rebels took power. After producing two documentary shorts, Tomás Gutiérrez Alea's *Esta Tierra Nuestra* (*This is Our Land*) and Julio García Espinosa's *La Vivienda* (*Housing*), Cine Rebelde became part of the newly founded film Institute. Alfredo Guevara, founding Director of ICAIC, insists that film was in fact the second priority of the new government, preceding but subordinate in importance and in impact to the national literacy campaign of 1960–61.

PREREVOLUTIONARY HISTORY

Cubans frequently stress the absence of a cinematic tradition in prerevolutionary Cuba, as Fidel did in his Report to the First Party

Congress (1975) when he commended the achievements of "a new art form, without a history or a tradition in our country." Leading filmmaker and theorist Julio García Espinosa concurs regarding the dearth of constructive models but emphasizes the potential impact of what was in fact a powerful negative heritage.

Cuban film historians emphasize the parallel historical development of the film medium, the U.S. drive toward extraterritorial expansion, and the history of Cuba as a nation. Cubans were exposed to the moving image as early as citizens of any country on the continent when the first Lumière films made their debut there in 1897. By 1898, Cuban audiences were already being treated to the cinema as a vehicle for historical falsification imposed upon them by their neighbors to the north. *Fighting With Our Boys in Cuba, Raising Old Glory Over Moro Castle, The Battle of San Juan Hill,* and the like alternated authentic footage with blatant simulations filmed not in Cuba but in the U.S. Their purpose was less to relay an accurate picture of the Cuban War for Independence from Spain than to rouse patriotic Yankee sentiment in favor of U.S. intervention in that war.

In the early years of the American movie industry, independents fleeing the watchful and monopolizing eye of Edison's Motion Picture Patents Company took refuge on Cuban shores before eventually setting up shop in southern California. Sporadic attempts to establish a national Cuban film industry capable of competing with entrenched foreign concerns seemed doomed to perennial failure and were virtually abandoned after the advent of sound. Film production, distribution, and exhibition in Cuba became the province of American and Mexican companies. From the thirties through the fifties, Cuba's major cinematic role was to furnish exotic sets, sultry sex queens, and a tropical beat for Hollywood and Mexican productions. Cuba offered an audience as well. In proportion to its population, the Cuban movie market was the most lucrative in Latin America. A population of less than seven million produced the astonishing number of one and a half million movie-goers per week despite the fact that large segments of the rural population had never seen a single film.

Escapist tropical musicals, melodramas, and detective flicks characterized national film production during the twenty years preceding Batista's overthrow. The 8,000 workers in the industry were primarily employed in the production of advertising shorts for theaters and television, newsreels for local consumption, and technical or scientific films for specialized audiences. One other specialty of the prerevolutionary film industry deserves mention: Cuba had more than its share of enterprising pornographers.[2]

During the fifties, most serious film activity was centered in film societies, in particular the *Nuestro Tiempo* (Our Times) and *Visión* groups. In 1954, two members of the former, Julio García Espinosa and Tomás Gutiérrez Alea, fresh from two years of film study at the Centro Sperimentale in Rome, collaborated with several other Cubans on a short dramatic feature in the style of the Italian Neorealists, called *El Mégano* (The Charcoal Worker). This denunciation of the hardships of charcoal production on the island's southern coast was confiscated by Batista. Though its style and formulation now seem embarrassingly naive, the film still enjoys the special distinction of being the only recognized antecedent of postrevolutionary cinema. All who collaborated on it have gone on to become leading figures in ICAIC: screenwriter Alfredo Guevara was head of the Film Institute from its founding until 1982; production assistant Jorge Fraga, now a director in his own right, has also served as Head of Film Production since 1978; cameraman Jorge Haydu is a leading cinematographer; Gutiérrez Alea is ICAIC's foremost director, and Julio García Espinosa—filmmaker, script consultant, theoretician—was appointed to succeed Guevara as Head of ICAIC in 1982.

Despite the remarkable size of the national film audience, the most reliable estimates conclude that the Cuban film industry produced no more than 150 features in its six decades of prerevolutionary history. Aside from newsreels, noncommercial documentaries were virtually unheard of. In the succeeding 24 years, ICAIC produced 112 full-length films (feature and documentary), some 900 documentary shorts—educational, scientific, and technical as well as animated and fictional films—and more than 1,300 weekly newsreels.[3]

EMPHASIZING DOCUMENTARY

As these production statistics demonstrate, ICAIC has given priority to documentary over fictional subjects. Both economic and ideological factors motivate the preference. The economic motivations are obvious: when funds and equipment are limited, professional actors, elaborate scripts, costuming, and studio sets can be regarded as nonessentials. In a society which subscribes to the principles of Marxism-Leninism, it is believed fitting that creative activity be based on the confrontation with material reality. The impulse to document the euphoria of the rebel victory and popular response to the resulting social transformations brought aspiring filmmakers out into the streets. What had previously been an impossible dream—making serious cinema in Cuba—was now an immediate possibility for scores of young cinemaphiles. This attempt to record the first convulsive moments of revolutionary victory had a profound effect on artists who had previously conceived of filmmaking as above all a vehicle for personal expression. In their documentary apprenticeship, Cuban filmmakers came face to face with unimagined aspects of national life. Their newly found growth in awareness and social sensitivity is largely responsible for the intense dialectic between historical circumstance and individual response which informs fictional as well as documentary production in postrevolutionary Cuban cinema.

The newsreels, produced under the direction of Santiago Álvarez and aimed not just at Cuban audiences but toward all of Latin America, are exceptional examples of the genre. Álvarez explains that his concern

> has not been to make each news item independent of the others, but to connect them in such a way that they pass before the spectator as a unified whole, according to a single discursive line. This accounts for the deliberate structuration which we use to achieve this thematic unity. For this reason, many classify our newsreels as genuine and autonomous documentaries.[4]

Initially restricted by the shortage of funds, material, and resources, Álvarez was one of many Cuban filmmakers to successfully turn practical handicaps into expressive assets. Obliged to draw from existing film archives and such "second-hand" sources as news photos and television footage, he developed a methodology which circumvented the need for on-the-spot footage and elevated the film-collage to a high level of political and artistic quality.

The innovative display of secondary footage, rhythmic editing with dramatic variations in pace, graphically innovative titles and eclectic musical selections (in preference to any spoken narration), superimposition and other experimental montage techniques characterize his early films. Material and political circumstances encouraged Álvarez, like his spiritual ancestor Dziga Vertov, to create the essence of his art on the editing table. As circumstances changed and more resources were put at his disposal, he shifted from black and white to color and began making longer films in which primary footage predominates. More recent films are characterized by more traditional cinematography, longer takes and less experimental editing, and the frequent use of voice-over narration.

In general, we can loosely divide Cuban documentary production into five thematic categories. Films which deal with *domestic politics* promote governmental policies and encourage popular participation and mass mobilization. *Historical* films chart various aspects of the formation of national identity through the five centuries of the island's recorded history. Documentaries of a *cultural* nature may be either national or international in their focus. Films which take *international relations* for their theme might focus on Cuba's role in international affairs, analyze the developed sector, or express solidarity with other Third World nations. Finally, *"didactic"* documentaries, highly technical or scientific in nature, are generally produced by specific agencies rather than ICAIC.

PROJECT AND PROCESS

Two central themes run through all of Cuban cinema, fictional and documentary production alike—history and underdevelopment. Cubans interpret each of these terms in a broad and fluid way: underdevelopment as the economic and technological heritage of colonial dependency which has its more stubborn manifestations in individual and collective psychology, ideology, and culture; history as a complex of formative influences which elucidates the present and informs the future. Both themes have had an impact on the form as well as the content of revolutionary Cuban cinema. The dialectical tension between practical limitations and artistic aspirations has encouraged innovation and spontaneity. The filming of *Memories of Underdevelopment*, for example, became itself a "memory of underdevelopment" as Gutiérrez Alea describes it: "At each step we felt the touch of underdevelopment. It limited us.... It conditioned the language with which we expressed ourselves." "I have to say," he concludes, "that this is the film in which I have felt most free...in spite of the everpresent limitations imposed by underdevelopment. Perhaps I felt free precisely because of those limitations."[5] After his visit to the island in 1975, Francis Ford Coppola attempted to compare the situation of Cuban filmmakers with their U.S. counterparts. Having perceived the kind of creative freedom which comes from overcoming practical constraints, he observed, "We don't have the advantage of their disadvantages."[6]

At an early stage in the development of ICAIC, founder Alfredo Guevara expressed the organization's determination to lay bare the form and technique of the filmmaker's craft, formulating the purpose of the Cuban film project as follows: "to demystify cinema for the entire population; to work, in a way, against our own power; to reveal all the tricks, all the recourses of language; to dismantle all the mechanisms of cinematic hypnosis."[7] In part, this determination grows out of the conviction that all forms of artistic expression carry an ideological dimension. If this ideological bias is veiled in the vast majority of art works produced in capitalist societies, Cuban filmmakers reason, it should be made explicit in the artistic production of a revolutionary socialist regime. Thus the eclecticism of Cuban film style is in part the result of the effort to appropriate forms of cinematic expression from the developed capitalist sector in order to dismantle them and expose their inner workings. Cubans call this operation "decolonization" and consider it the first priority of their film effort.

Cuban filmmakers have used many formal devices in their attempt to convert the audience from passive consumer into active participant. The Bazinian realism of the first postrevolutionary feature, Tomás Gutiérrez Alea's *Historias de la Revolución* (*Stories from the Revolution*, 1960), soon gave way to more self-reflexive forms, exploring the paradoxical Brechtian contention that dislocation and distancing, rather than unbroken identification, increase the conscious and critical participation of the spectator. Formal self-consciousness, initially apparent in the allusions to leading world filmmakers in the early feature *The Death of a Bureaucrat* (1966) and in García Espinosa's picaresque farce, *The Adventures of Juan Quin Quin* (1967), has subsequently found expression in multiple self-reflexive devices. García Espinosa's feature-length documentary *Third World, Third World War* (1970) incorporates the actual filmmaking process into the finished picture, as do the subsequent feature-length documentary *Bay of Pigs* (Manuel Herrera, 1972) and the historical biography *Mella* (Enrique Piñea Barnet, 1975). Established film genres are often parodied and subverted: the Hollywood war movie in *Bay of Pigs*; the ahistorical Latin melodrama in *The Other Francisco* (Sergio Giral, 1974). Octavio Cortázar's poignant account of one mountain community's first exposure to moving pictures—*For the First Time* (1967)—is an early example of the film-within-a-film device. *With the Cuban Women* (1974), by the same director, opens with startling disjunction between aural and visual information. Films like *Memories of Underdevelopment* (1968), *Lucía* (1968), and *The Other*

Francisco (1974) are characterized by a marked shift between lyricized and naturalistic visual styles. Experimentation with film stock, laboratory techniques, lighting, and camera lenses accounts for the visual expressionism of films like Manuel Octavio Gómez's *The First Charge of the Machete* (1969), Part I of Solas's *Lucía* (1968), and the same director's first color film, *Simparele* (1964), as well as many of the Álvarez documentaries. Other self-reflexive devices include the experimentation with musical and nonmusical sound and the print medium which also characterizes Álvarez's work and that of several other directors and, finally, the dramatization of the documentary form through the appropriation of narrative techniques traditionally associated with fictional filmmaking as in shorts like Alejandro Saderman's *Hombres de Mal Tiempo (Men from Mal Tiempo,* 1968), Oscar Valdés's *Muerte y Vida en El Morrillo (Death and Life in El Morrillo,* 1971) and Miguel Torres's *Historia de una Infamia (History of an Infamy,* 1983). The reverse of this operation informs films like *Memories of Underdevelopment* (1968), *The Other Francisco* (1974), *Bay of Pigs* (1972), *One Way or Another* (1974/1977), and Gutiérrez Alea's latest feature, *Hasta Cierto Punto (Up to a Certain Point,* 1983).

But formal self-reflexiveness is not a *sine qua non* of Cuban film production. As Jorge Fraga, head of artistic production at ICAIC, puts it in our first interview, "We are not in favor of firing merely for the pleasure of hearing the shot. We shoot in order to hit the target." Many recent films seem to have subordinated issues of formal candor to other considerations and other goals. Gutiérrez Alea's *The Last Supper* (1977) and Pastor Vega's *Portrait of Teresa* (1979) are but two examples of recent films which opt for classical over modernist form. The power of Hollywood's "transparent" style continues to fascinate the Cubans, whose goal is to use that capacity to galvanize an audience for less ideologically veiled and alienating ends. In a society which purports to derive its vitality from a constant process of reexamination and renewal, even apparently conventional strategies can be used in innovative ways, and what was once innovative can become constrictive.

ICAIC's leadership stresses each film's potential for "communicability" (*comunicabilidad*) as the crucial determinant of its worth but continues to recognize multiple strategies for achieving this end. In Julio García Espinosa's words, the greatest responsibility of Cuban filmmakers is to create a kind of cinema "where the human factor, imagination and talent are more important than technical considerations; where artistic conception is completely in tune with actual existing resources."[8]

However impressive the quantity and quality of film production in a country which had no national film industry prior to 1959, this is but one aspect of a comprehensive national film program whose primary goals are universal film literacy and universal access to the medium. Consistent with the priority placed on human development over technical acquisition in the production sector, scarce financial resources channeled into exhibition in the early years were concentrated on providing the largest number of uninitiated viewers with access to film. Faced with the dire shortage of movie theaters in rural areas, and the financial and temporal obstacles to constructing the number needed, the Cubans devised the famous "mobile cinemas." Trucks, mule teams, even small boats, fitted out with projection equipment and stocked with an eclectic repertoire of film titles, were sent to the most remote sections of the island. In more densely populated regions, topical film "cycles" are continually presented at eleven theaters throughout the island. This program, run by the Cinemateca de Cuba, a division of ICAIC, provides films for 100,000 spectators per week—presumably a world record for an institution of its kind.[9] Two national television programs provide ongoing education in film history, language and technique.[10]

Though the prevalence of praxis (filmmaking and active organizational work) over theoretical deliberation in written form has been characteristic of the Film Institute to date, ICAIC's contribution to film theory has been far from negligible. Alfredo Guevara, founder and director of ICAIC, has continually given ideological direction and theoretical orientation through speeches and essays. His leadership has been a guiding force not only within Cuba but for politically-committed filmmakers throughout Latin America who have been invited to Havana to use ICAIC's facilities or to participate in the International Festivals of the New Latin American Cinema held annually since 1979.

Efforts to define in writing the nature and role of film in a revolutionary society began in 1960 with the first issues of the Cuban film magazine *Cine Cubano*, and related deliberations continue to appear in its pages. The first theoretical formulation to generate broad impact outside the island was Julio García Espinosa's "For an Imperfect Cinema" (1970). García Espinosa has subsequently written several other essays which attempt to build a bridge between practice and theory. In 1979, these were collected under the title *Una imagen recorre el mundo* (Havana: Letras Cubanos). Tomás Gutiérrez Alea has also recently turned to parallel pursuits. His *Dialéctica del espectador* (Havana: Cuadernos de la Revista Unión, 1982) was named one of the ten best books of the year.[11]

THE EVOLUTION OF ICAIC: A CHRONOLOGY

My research suggests a tentative chronological division into four periods: 1959-1960, 1960-1969, 1970-1974, 1975-1983. The initial period, from 1959 to 1960, was characterized by explosive optimism and a great sense of release, by the jubilant return of many exiled artists, the influx of foreign talent, and the artistic debut of many young and untried nationals. Enthusiastic organizational activity included the founding of ICAIC and the nationalization of all film-related holdings in foreign hands. The attitude of the government and the population at large was one of uncritical enthusiasm for artistic and intellectual activity of all sorts. Among the artists themselves, united-front politics predominated. The first film efforts were generally celebrative works in an epic or journalistic style which focused on the trajectory and triumph of the insurrection and on the corruption and injustice of the former regime.

In the second period, 1960 to 1969, the concept of revolutionary art and of the revolutionary artist became gradually more defined through a series of debates and polemics as well as the lived experience of the Revolution. Ideological maturation and intensified class conflict began to curb the "anything goes" atmosphere in the artistic sector. The concept of art as praxis and of the artist as militant participant rather than detached observer began to dominate. The broad and initially uncritical assimilation of foreign models, the virtually unlimited hospitality to visiting artists and intellectuals, and the attentive quest for their approval gave way to a more critical stance and to the growing influence of artistic inspiration from national sources and other Third World countries—particularly other Latin American nations—in preference to the developed sector.

At the beginning of this period, the prevalence of visiting foreign filmmakers at ICAIC and the organization's involvement in a number of co-productions with various countries contributed to a rather superficial and exotic interpretation of Cuban culture. The celebration of "One Hundred Years of Struggle" in 1968 to commemorate the fight for national autonomy which began a century before sparked a much richer and more penetrating analysis of national history and identity. The pervasive influence of Italian Neorealism in the early sixties and the fascination with the French New Wave in mid-decade had, by the end of this period, given way to broad-based stylistic experimentation and characteristically Cuban eclecticism. By 1964, the Cuban documentary was beginning to gain international attention through the work of

Santiago Álvarez. Fictional production came into its own four years later with the release of *Memories of Underdevelopment* and *Lucía*. This period also saw signs of diminishing tolerance for a liberal interpretation of artistic freedom and responsibility. For numerous reasons, the process of defining the role of art in a revolutionary socialist society met with more difficulties in the realm of letters, with its centuries-long tradition of isolated individual production, than in the film sector or the other more cooperative and social arts. The tensions between individual ambition and the needs of the collectivity were played out between the years 1967 and 1971 in the life and career of one particular poet, Heberto Padilla, who became an international *cause célèbre* upon his imprisonment in 1971.[16]

The failure of the projected ten-million-ton sugar harvest in 1970 brought about a critical reappraisal of policies and priorities in all sectors of society, beginning with Fidel himself and including ICAIC and other cultural agencies. The period between 1970 and 1974 saw an increased emphasis on mass participation and the search for more indigenous cultural forms. Elitism and manifestations of artistic privilege were rejected in favor of an attempt to define and produce a genuine people's culture. At ICAIC there was a consequent decline—by no means absolute—in formal experimentation, which had reached a peak of virtuosity in the late sixties. The emphasis on documentary production extended during these years to the realm of feature-length films, where for the first time nonfictional subjects outnumbered fictional ones.

Nineteen hundred and seventy-five, the year of the first National Congress of the Cuban Communist Party, marks the inception of a period of sweeping reorganization within ICAIC, a process which may or may not have culminated with the naming in 1983 of Julio García Espinosa to succeed Alfredo Guevara as head of the Institute. In 1976, the process of "institutionalization of the Revolution" which began in 1970[13] reached the cultural sector. The formation of a national Ministry of Culture which incorporated ICAIC under Guevara's continuing direction as one of its five vice-ministers, marked the symbolic loss of the privileged autonomy the Institute had enjoyed since its founding. Lest the motivations for the economic reorganization and redefinition of ICAIC appear to have come largely from outside the agency, it is important to note that these directives coincided with internal concerns to lower costs and increase productivity which date from the beginning of the decade. As Jorge Fraga, Head of Artistic Programming, explained in a personal interview in 1977:

Filmmaking is a living contradiction, because as an industry, it would have its optimal technical-economic efficiency if it were producing standardized products. But as an art form, it cannot be governed by standardized norms. This contradiction lies within the nature of film itself because film cannot cease to be an industry nor can it cease to be an art. The only possible answer is to seek out the organizational mechanisms that will prevent these two factors from entering into conflicts which might be harmful to the development of either component.

Predictably, ICAIC's structure has grown progressively more complex during the successive stages of this reorganization process (see Figures 7.1, 7.2, and 7.3).

Alfredo Guevara has stated that the greatest innovations of the Cuban film industry have been in the social relations of the labor process, and other leaders within ICAIC have seconded this claim. The Cubans have tried to balance the needs of the collectivity with those of personal creative expression through their commitment to workers' control and the collective evaluation of each other's work, as well as through the high degree of initiative granted to the director. *Conciencia* (sociopolitical awareness and sense of responsibility) and *subjetividad* (personal artistic judgment) are regarded as the dual components of the creative process.

The reorganization process has included a revision of the salary system (under discussion since 1979) and the introduction of a system of bonuses (*primas*) to encourage directors to finish their films within the time and budget allotted to them. Differential pay has been instituted as a means of rewarding those who perform their job particularly well, as judged by a blue-ribbon committee of their peers. Whether such changes will eventually have a positive or negative impact upon the social relations of production at ICAIC remains to be seen.

FIGURE 7.1. Phase I: Before 1975

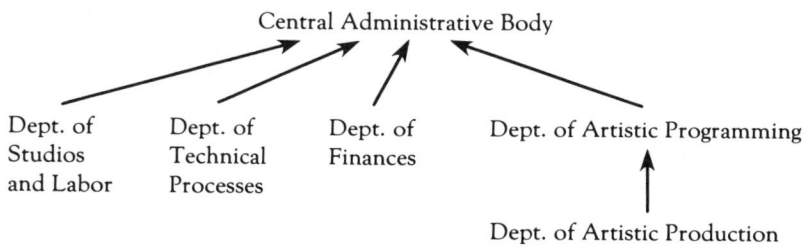

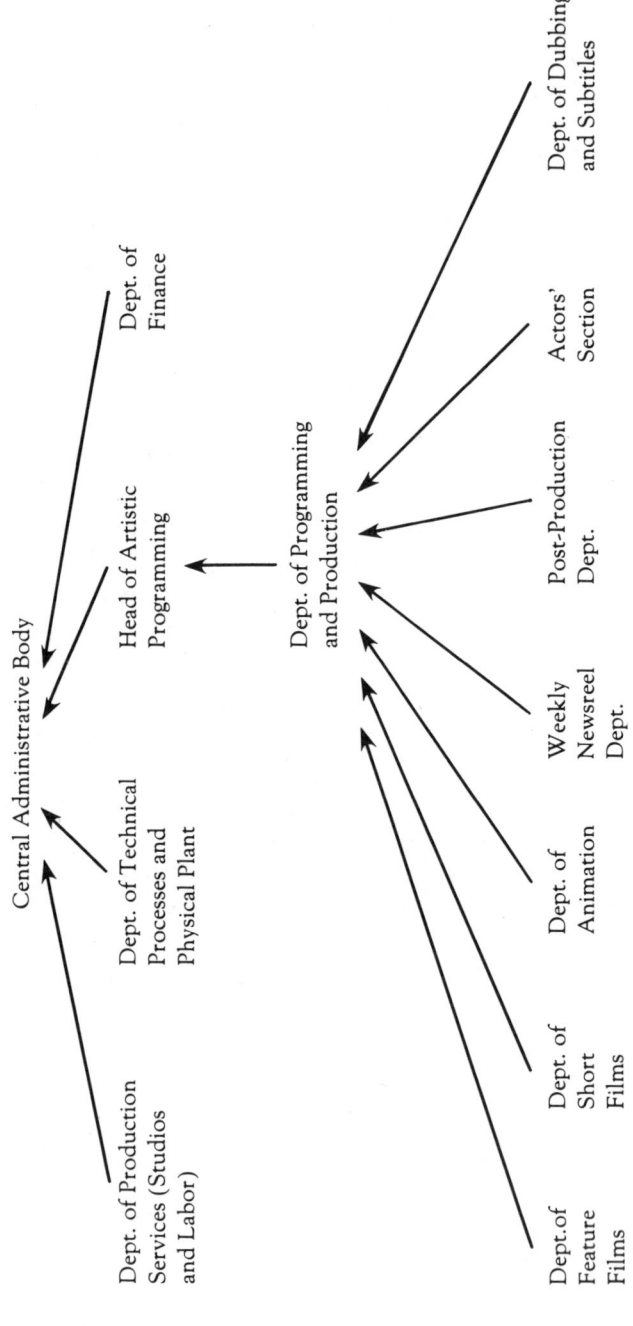

FIGURE 7.2 Phase II: Interim Structure

FIGURE 7.3 Phase III: After 1981

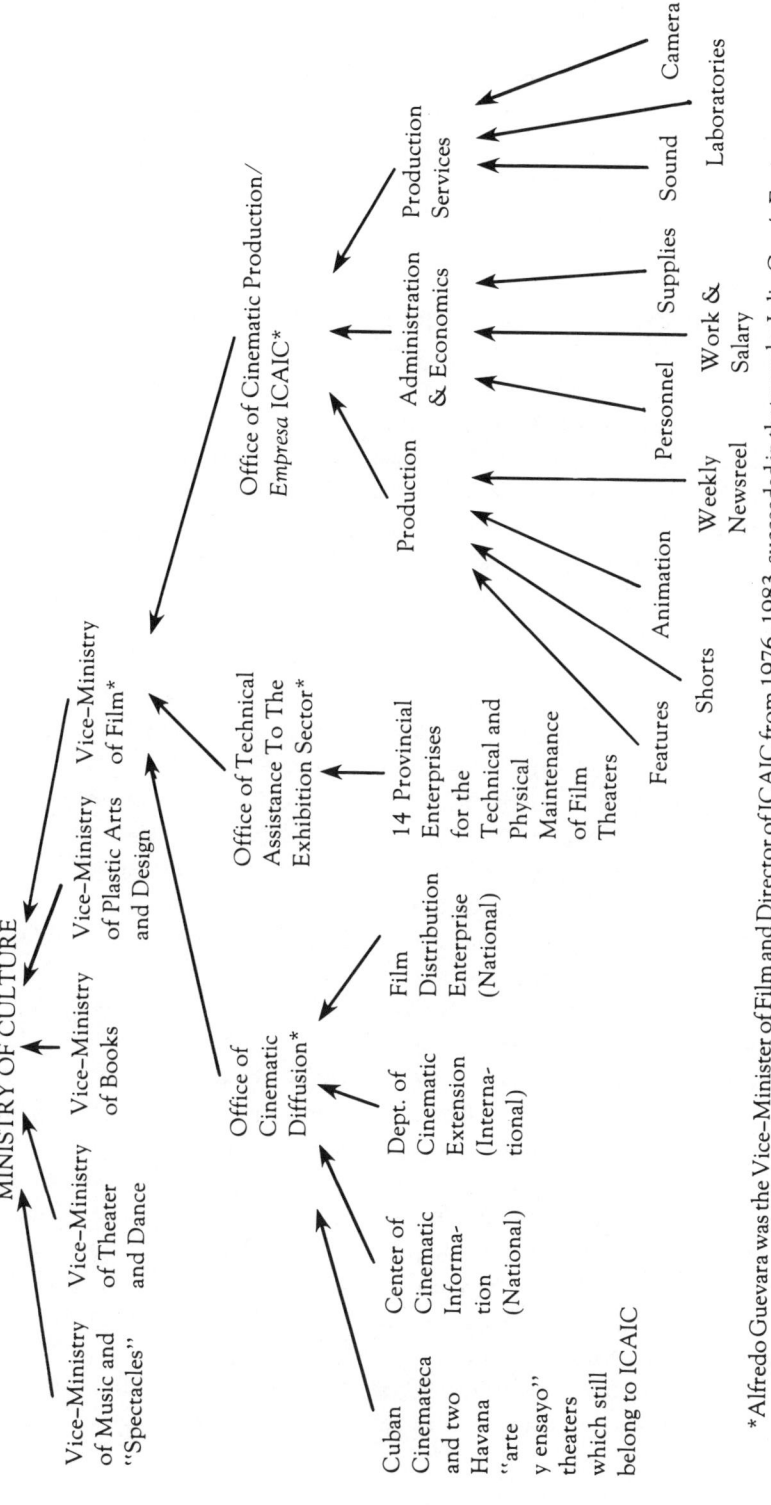

*Alfredo Guevara was the Vice-Minister of Film and Director of ICAIC from 1976–1983, succeeded in that year by Julio García Espinosa, who was the Vice-Minister of Music and Spectacles during the same years, after having served as Head of Artistic Programming at ICAIC. The Heads of the three "Enterprises" which now make up ICAIC are: Diffusion, Benigno Iglesias; Technical Assistance to the Exhibition Sector, José Manuel Pardo; Cinematic Production, Jorge Fraga.

The prolonged and time-consuming efforts to restructure the film sector constitute a tentative response to a number of ongoing problems within ICAIC and within the larger society. These include: limited financial and technical resources; a demand for film products which exceeds existing production capacities; lack of procedures and resources to develop and incorporate new talent; a tendency to rely excessively, for both artistic and organizational leadership, on a limited number of recognized figures without adequate mechanisms for distributing responsibility; the persistent separation and subordination of documentary to fictional filmmaking in practice if not in theory.

ICAIC's entire annual budget is only 7,000,000 pesos ($7,000,000). According to Jorge Fraga, this allocation must cover not only production expenses but salaries for all of ICAIC's 1,100 employees.[14] Current production levels stand at approximately 40 documentaries, 5–10 animated cartoons, 4–6 features, and 52 weekly newsreels. Though documentary production has remained fairly steady over the past decade (1972–1983), with high points of 47 in 1976–77 and 1980–81, it declined to below 40 in 1979 and 1983. Production levels for feature films have remained chronically lower than projected targets. The projected goal for 1985 is 12 features annually, or one per month, though to date feature output has never exceeded eight, and has in fact only risen about five if one includes feature-length documentaries in the tally. The decade of the 1960s saw only two feature-length documentaries; nearly twenty times this number were produced between 1970 and 1983, closely rivaling the number of fictional features.

As Julio García Espinosa and a number of others have pointed out, though nationalization gave Cubans ownership of the movie theaters in the early sixties, they have still not been able to claim full ownership of the screens. Of the 130–140 feature films annually premiered in Cuba to supply the 510 theaters on the island, only about 3 percent are national products; the vast majority are imported from abroad. Cuban audiences' potential demand for Cuban features far exceeds current ICAIC production levels. The institution of positive and negative material incentives to increase efficiency and productivity is one strategy to make greater use of existing resources. International coproductions are another. Whether or not one views these methods as constructive and consistent with ICAIC's ideology and goals, they do not seem fully proportionate to the dimensions of the problem.

Despite the ideological importance conferred upon the documentary, fictional filmmaking continues to be regarded as the highest expression of the cinematic vocation, at least as much by the members of ICAIC as by the filmgoing public. With a single exception (Humberto Solas) all of ICAIC's filmmakers have begun as documentarists. The opportunity to make feature-length fiction films is a "promotion" earned through a long process of "documentary apprenticeship." Rather than increasing over time, the number of documentarists who "graduate" to fiction has declined. Since 1977, only three directors have been awarded this distinction: Pastor Vega made his first fictional feature *Retrato de Teresa (Portrait of Teresa)* in 1979; Manuel Herrera made *No Hay Sábado Sin Sol (There's No Saturday Without Sunshine)* the same year; and Jesús Díaz's fictional debut came in 1981 with *Polvo Rojo (Red Dust)*. (All three had previously made at least one full-length documentary.) Between 1974 and 1976, as a response to the need to inject "new blood" into the institution, ICAIC took on a score of university graduates (the vast majority women) for training as *"analistas,"* using them as apprentices in all sectors of the production process from script research to assistant direction. These aspiring filmmakers face an additional hurdle, the jump from assistant or apprentice to documentarist. Here, too, the process of ascent seems deplorably slow.

North American visitors to ICAIC continue to question the dearth of women directors and the limited number of blacks. Sara Gómez, who belonged to both the above categories, died in 1974 of acute asthma on the verge of completing her first feature, *One Way or Another*. Sergio Giral, the only black feature director, made his third feature (*Maluala*) in 1979. Among the documentarists, there is one black (Rigoberto López) and three women (Marisol Trujillo, Belkis Vega and Rebeca Chávez). In response to this criticism, the Cubans reply that they reject any notion of quotas as inherently discriminatory, and that they have had only twenty-five years to try to reverse centuries-old legacies of discrimination. Mayra Vilaris, assistant director, stated in a recent interview, "I would feel personally offended if I were told to start working on a film as the director because we need more women directors."[15] Her position is representative of many women at ICAIC. In a 1977 interview, Sergio Giral stated, "...not even I, as a black man, can conceive of a 'black' filmmaker or a 'black' film.... We have to retain the concept of race as an historical, social category."[16] Their primary identification, these Cuban cineasts declare, is as Cubans, not as women, or blacks, or Chinese, and it is as Cubans that they feel they can best work together to create a society that, in Jorge Fraga's words, "permits everyone the possibility to develop fully."[17]

As an island, Cuba has always been very aware of how much a vigorous national culture depends upon the quantity and quality of visits to and visitors from abroad and what baggage they bring ashore. Under Minister of Culture Armando Hart, Cuban artists and intellectuals have enjoyed increased opportunities for foreign travel, but even more important to the people and the project of ICAIC has been the influx since 1979 of filmmakers and critics from all over the world to attend the International Festival of the New Latin American Cinema held annually under its auspices. This remarkable forum for cultural exchange and discussion also testifies to the support and leadership role which ICAIC continues to play in the evolution and development of oppositional cinema in Latin America. In order to increase the worldwide diffusion of Latin American films, the Latin American Film Market (MECLA) was launched at the Second International Festival in 1980. The Fifth International Festival (December 1983) expanded its exhibition scope northward to include more than a decade of American independent filmmaking in a program called "The Other Face: Independent Films in the United States."

Cuban poet and patriot José Martí said that the only way to do away with the need for soldiers is to become one. Leery of professional critics, Cuban filmmakers decided early on to assume the critic's task in *Cine Cubano* themselves rather than cede it to specialists. Twenty-five years later, ICAIC has only two full-time critics: Carlos Galiano, who also writes reviews for the national daily *Granma*, and hosts a weekly TV show called "History of the Cinema," and Enrique Colina, whose prime-time program "Twenty-four Frames a Second" has been one of the most popular in Cuba for over a decade. If the televised film history and criticism is remarkably sophisticated, its print counterpart is deplorably limited—both a legacy and a confirmation of the general view of the critical act as arbitrary, intrusive, superfluous. As García Espinosa wrote in 1970, "...imperfect cinema rejects whatever services criticism has to offer and considers the function of mediators and intermediaries anachronistic."[18]

García Espinosa's assumption of the directorship of ICAIC has been greeted with general approval and optimism. More than for his experience as a filmmaker or theorist, this founding member of ICAIC is valued for his ability to unleash the creative energies of others. He has served as adviser on scores of Cuban films and a list of his screenplay collaborations contain some of ICAIC's most outstanding and experimental films: Humberto Solás' *Lucía*, Manuel Octavio Gómez' *First*

Charge of the Machete, and the feature-length documentaries *Bay of Pigs* (Manuel Herrera), *¡Viva la República!* (Pastor Vega) and *The Battle of Chile* (Patricio Guzmán).

Throughout his career, García Espinosa has been concerned with reconciling artistic practice and mass society. His goal has been to displace elitist cultural forms in favor of genuinely popular ones created with the participation of broad sectors of society. His longstanding interest in problems of genre stems from his perception of both the mass appeal and transformative potential of conventional narrative formulae. In a recent interview he recalled.

> Through the experience of filming *The Adventures of Juan Quin Quin* (1967), it became clear to me for the first time that it is in fact impossible to question a given reality without questioning the particular genre you select or inherit to depict that reality. Normally the artist's critique of the genre is done independently, and only the results of the process are shared with the viewer. The challenge I faced was to discover how this critical process itself, rather than simply the results of that process, could be integrated into the film.[19]

In an earlier essay, he maintained:

> Until now, we have viewed the cinema as a means of reflecting reality, without realizing that cinema in itself is a reality, with its own history, conventions, and traditions. Cinema can only be constructed on the ashes of what already exists. Moreover, to make a new cinema is, in fact, to reveal the process of destruction of the one that came before.... We have to make a spectacle out of the destruction of the spectacle. This process cannot be individual.... What is needed is to perform this process jointly with the viewer.[20]

García Espinosa envisions a Tarzan film in which the hero takes part in contemporary political conflicts, marries an African woman, and is assimilated into African culture. He believes that the musical is a "natural" genre for Cuba, and his own *Son O No Son* (an untranslatable pun on Hamlet's "to be or not to be" and the Cuban musical form, *son*), which obtained a belated and limited release in 1980, is a delightfully comic imitation of the genre, both subversive and self-critical without ceasing to be enormously entertaining. Manuel Octavio Gómez' *Patakin,* billed as "the first Cuban musical," which premiered at the 1983 Festival to mixed reviews, testifies to García Espinosa's continued encouragement of such efforts. His previous experience with documentary suggests that this area, site of so much extraordinary creativity over the last decade, will not be neglected.

Beyond the production sector, García Espinosa envisions differentiated viewing environments (workplace-associated or workplace-disassociated depending upon the nature of the films screened) and a future time when Cuba will have the technological resources to make filmmaking a genuinely mass activity: "Short of this, we have only made it halfway as filmmakers." He believes that as the electronic media invade the home and make conventional movie theaters obsolete, people will seek out cultural products which offer a more direct, less vicarious, interaction, and that this *reto de masividad* (challenge of mass society), the greatest challenge facing cultural workers today, must not be ceded to purely commercial interests. As he wrote in 1970, in the closing lines of his famous essay "For an Imperfect Cinema," whose ideas still reverberate through ICAIC, "the future lies with folk art but then there will be no need to call it that [since there will be no need to connote the limits of popular creativity]: Art will not disappear into nothingness, it will disappear into everything."[21]

NOTES

1. See Gary Crowdus, "The Spring 1972 Cuban Film Festival Bust," *Film Society Review*, vol. 7, nos. 7-9 (March/April/May 1972), pp. 23-26.

2. Regarding this last point, see Peter Brook, "The Cuban Enterprise," *Sight and Sound*, vol. 30, no. 2 (spring 1961), pp. 78-79. The principal source for prerevolutionary film history is Arturo Agramonte, *Cronología del cine cubano* (Havana: Ediciones ICAIC, 1966). See also Julio Matas, "Theater and Cinematography" in Carmelo Mesa-Lago, ed., *Revolutionary Change in Cuba* (Pittsburgh: University of Pittsburgh Press, 1971), pp. 436-42.

3. My own updating of original figures from *Granma Weekly Review*, January 1977, based on *Filmografía del cine cubano*, 1959-1981, and Supplement: January 1982-November 1983 (Havana: Producción ICAIC 1982, 1983).

4. "Santiago Álvarez habla de su cine," *Hablemos de cine*, 54 (July-August 1970), p. 30.

5. Tomás Gutiérrez Alea, "*Memorias del subdesarrollo: Notas de trabajo*," *Cine Cubano*, 45/46 (1968), pp. 24-25.

6. Francis Ford Coppola, "Robert Scheer Interviews Francis Ford Coppola on Cuba, Castro, Communism and the Mafia," *City of San Francisco*, vol. 9, no. 21 (December 2, 1975), p. 22.

7. Cited in Marjorie Rosen, "The Great Cuban Fiasco," *Saturday Review*, June 17, 1972, p. 53.

8. Julio García Espinosa, "Cinco preguntas a ICAIC," *Cine al día*, 12 (March 1971), p. 22.

9. See José Manuel Pardo, "El Cine-movil ICAIC," *Cine Cubano*, 73/74/75 (1971), pp. 93–104.

10. On the most successful of these programs, see Jorge Silva, "Film Criticism in Cuba: An Interview with Enrique Colina," *Jump/Cut: A Review of Contemporary Cinema*, 22 (May 1980), pp. 32–33.

11. See *Jump/Cut: A Review of Contemporary Cinema*, nos. 29 and 30 (spring 1984 and forthcoming) for Julia Lesage's translation of this text under the title "The Viewer's Dialectic."

12. For full documentation of this famous case, see Lourdes Casal, *El caso Padilla: Literatura y revolución en Cuba: Documentos* (Miami: Nueva Atlatida, 1971). Padilla's poetry of the period appeared in Heberto Padilla, *Fuera del juego* (Buenos Aires: Aditor, 1969) and in J.M. Cohen, trans., *Sent off the Field: A Selection of the Poetry of Heberto Padilla* (London: Deutsch, 1972).

13. See Nelson P. Valdés, "Revolution and Institutionalization in Cuba," *Cuban Studies/Estudios Cubanos*, vol. 6, no. 1 (January 1976), pp. 1–37.

14. Susan Fanshel, "The Cuban Film Institute: Past and Present: An Interview with Jorge Fraga," in Fanshel, *A Decade of Cuban Documentary Film: 1972–1982* (New York: Young Filmmakers Foundation, 1982), p. 10.

15. Susan Fanshel, "Three Women in ICAIC: An Interview with Gloria Argüelles, Mayra Vilasis, and Marisol Trujillo," in *A Decade of Cuban Documentary Film*, p. 27.

16. Julianne Burton and Gary Crowdus, "Cuban Cinema and the Afro-Cuban Heritage: An Interview with Sergio Giral," *The Black Scholar*, vol. 8, nos. 8–10 (Summer 1977), p. 65.

17. Fanshel, *An Interview with Jorge Fraga*, p. 13.

18. Julio García Espinosa, "For an Imperfect Cinema," trans. Julianne Burton, in Michael Chanan, ed., *Twenty-Five Years of the New Latin American Cinema* (London: British Film Institute and Channel Four Books, 1983), p. 32.

19. Julianne Burton, "Theory and Practice of Film and Popular Culture in Cuba: A Conversation with Julio García Espinosa," *Quarterly Review of Film Studies*, vol. 7, no. 4 (Fall 1982), p. 345.

20. Julio García Espinosa, "Carta a la revista chilena *Primer Plano*," *Una imagen recorre el mundo* (Havana: Letras Cubanas, 1979), pp. 26–27.

21. García Espinosa, "For an Imperfect Cinema," p. 33.

8 Criticism and Literature in Revolutionary Cuba

Roberto González Echevarría

When the history of twentieth-century Latin American literature is written, much attention will have to be paid to the role of the Cuban Revolution in its development. The Cuban Revolution is the dividing line in contemporary Latin American literature, a literature of before the revolution and one of after the revolution. This can be verified by looking at the careers of major contemporary authors, such as Carlos Fuentes. Fuentes's first important novel after 1959, *La muerte de Artemio Cruz*, reevaluates the Mexican Revolution from the perspective of the Cuban (the novel was partially written in Havana). Aside from individual cases, the whole tenor and tempo of cultural activity changes after 1959, not only because of what Cuba does, but also because of what is done elsewhere in reaction to Cuba.

Only after 1959 did the United States begin to invest aggressively in the area of Latin American culture. The creation of many Latin American studies centers in U.S. universities came as a response to Cuban cultural activity, and large-scale projects—including the financing of literary journals—channeled resources into the cultural area in a way that had a crucial bearing on the creation of the new Latin American literature of the sixties. It would take too long to recall the names of Latin American authors who took advantage of U.S.-sponsored grants and invitations from American institutions. Beginning with the early sixties, Cuba offered Latin American writers incentives such as literary prizes and opportunities to work in Cuba, as well as magazines and publishing houses. The list of authors who profited from visits to Cuba, Cuban editions of their works, prizes, and the like is also very long.

Without this background it is difficult to conceive of the Boom of the Latin American novel, or even fully account for the level of notoriety that poets such as Octavio Paz or even Borges attained. Borges spent some time at the University of Texas in the early sixties, and Octavio Paz spent several months at Cornell in 1965. Opportunities such as these were not common before 1959.

Cuba has been at the center of cultural activity in the Hispanic world for the past 20 years, so much so that when we study Cuban literature or criticism we are dealing with the most urgent problematics within the Hispanic field. I say "Hispanic" because we should not forget that Spanish writers such as Blas de Otero, the Goytisolo brothers, and Alfonso Sastre also profited from their relation with Cuba. In the case of Juan Goytisolo, his works too can be divided into periods before and after his Cuban experience (at one point in his career he even identified himself as an Hispano-Cuban writer because a grandfather of his had once lived in Cuba). The same can be easily said of Cortázar or García Márquez (who is a frequent visitor to Cuba). Cuba has created a pan-Hispanic identity for artists, and in this it has repeated—with differences—a phenomenon that had occurred twice before in the Hispanic world.

There have been three major historical upheavals in the Spanish-speaking world in the twentieth century, and all three have left a lasting imprint on Hispanic culture and beyond: the Mexican Revolution, the Spanish Civil War, and the Cuban Revolution. All three have furnished a peculiar thematic to literature that was strong enough to cross national and linguistic barriers. It has been argued that the novel of the Mexican Revolution is the first truly modern Latin American novel, and the poetry of the Spanish Civil War marked the careers of many important poets. The question that ought to be asked, therefore, is not whether Cuba has had an impact on Hispanic culture, but what kind of impact it has had. Has the revolution brought a new and distinctive form of literature to Latin America? By which I mean, has the Cuban revolution changed, and in what way, the current literary production in general? The remainder of this chapter will focus on two aspects of literary development in revolutionary Cuba—the field of literary criticism, and of literature per se.

One cannot speak of literary criticism in any given period or country without first refining the concept and breaking it down into the various kinds of activities it designates. In the broadest sense literary criticism can include the commentary on a work contained within the work itself, be it in the form of a prologue, a note at the end of a book, or in the case of a novel, what a character says about the very book in which it is contained or about another novel. Every reader of *Don Quijote* knows how much literary criticism is contained in that book; the same is true of Desnoes's *Memorias del subdesarrollo*, in which there are commentaries about Carpentier, about Edmundo Desnoes himself, and even about the fictional writer of the novel. There is literary criticism in poetry too, and if one is to take my friend Harold Bloom's views to their ultimate consequences, there is nothing but literary criticism in lyric poetry. There are also essays in which commentary on literature is part of a larger meditation. But when we say "literary criticism" we usually refer to the social institution, dating from the eighteenth century, whose products are printed in newspapers, literary supplements, and the like; or the kind practiced within academic institutions, published in scholarly journals and subdivided into many activities that range from evaluation, to edition of texts and research into the biography of authors, to reviews. Since the first kind of criticism mentioned—the one contained within works of literature—cannot be readily distinguished from literature itself, I will not deal with it specifically, but rather assume that it is part of my general assessment of Cuban literature in the revolutionary period. In order to avoid confusion I will break down the more conventional criticism into the traditional categories of journalistic and academic, though I am aware that the distinction varies from culture to culture.

By "journalistic criticism" I refer not only to reviews or to light pieces on current literature, but to any work dealing with ongoing literature or criticism, or any work that proposes or glosses a new literary theory. Under this category, for instance, I would include the kind of piece that Ortega y Gasset wrote on literature, or the commentary that a Borges might have written for a newspaper or a journal. By "academic criticism," on the other hand, I mean almost exclusively literary history: the edition of texts, the compiling of bibliographies, and the accumulation of facts. I would also include in this category theoretical work if it takes up the writings of figures other than contemporary thinkers. In brief, what distinguishes one form of criticism from the other is that one deals with past literature and involves some sort of research, while the other is concerned with contemporary literature and does not normally involve research.

In terms of journalistic criticism the situation was dismal in Cuba before 1959. Whereas the River Plate area, Mexico, Santiago de Chile, and other cultural centers in Latin America have enjoyed a long and uninterrupted tradition of journalistic criticism, Cuba suffered a dramatic reduction in the forties and fifties. In the nineteenth and early twentieth centuries, Cuba had enjoyed a thriving critical tradition. Anyone who looks at critical activity in the Cuba of the twenties, for instance, is astounded by the quantity and quality of production and wonders where it all went later. Newspapers such as *Discusión* and *Diario de la Marina* and popular magazines such as *Carteles* or *Social* were actively involved in the literary currents of the times, not to mention the more conventionally literary *Revista de Avance,* or the academically oriented *Revista Cubana.* All this withered. This does not mean that there were no great literary journals in Cuba in the thirties, forties, and fifties, but they were the exception rather than the rule, and they were not usually engaged in dialogue with other publications contemporary to them in any significant way; neither did they have the broad impact of a *Sur,* for instance. One could trace the history of Cuban literature from *Revista de Avance* to *Orígenes* to *Ciclón.* But these magazines—with the possible exception of *Revista de Avance*—flourished on their own, without a broad base of literary activity at other levels. They were magazines read by a tiny majority at home and abroad.

What Cuba lacked in the forties and fifties was journalistic criticism of the kind practiced regularly in newspapers and popular journals or literary supplements. I do not mean that there was none at all. Magazines like *Carteles* and *Bohemia* sporadically dealt with cultural and literary matters, as did *Diario de la Marina,* but they could not compare with Buenos Aires's *La Nación,* or Caracas's *El Nacional,* or with early Cuban publications such as *Diario de la Marina* itself, *Discusión, Social* and *Carteles* in the twenties; in the latter one could feel the pulse of current literature, be aware of its contemporary relevance. The reasons for this impoverishment are clear. On the one hand, it is obvious that journalistic criticism is the most blatantly ideological, therefore the most feared by authorities. By the end of the Batista era very few publications destined for the mass market were not on the government payroll. But there is a deeper reason. Cuba was the beachhead of postwar American expansionism in the mass media. A mass-media culture was created which corrupted the old values that supported cultural activity. In the United States, with institutions solidly financed and charged with the preservation of culture, the assault of the mass media on the arts has changed the arts significantly. In Cuba, with no such buffers, they were nearly destroyed.

Academic criticism was not in much better shape in 1959. In fact there was really no academic criticism to speak of, other than that produced in journals such as *Universidad de La Habana* and *Islas*. But these were not thriving journals. As far as I can tell, academic criticism languished in the stupor of positivism, or worse yet was a mere rhetorical exercise. As part of the general debasement of culture mentioned before, the art of teaching literature was for the most part bankrupt in the Cuba of the forties and fifties. It was not taken very seriously by intellectuals and had little if any impact on literary production (which was sparse anyway). Two exceptions must be noted: the books by Roberto Fernández Retamar and Cintio Vitier on Cuban poetry; but even their narrow focus is a measure of the reduction mentioned before. Whereas it cannot be denied that there was some prosperity in the Cuba of the fifties, evident in the number of television sets per capita, this very prosperity meant the impoverishment of cultural activity.

Except for the existence of the *Ciclón* group, literary criticism was pretty much nonexistent in Cuba when the revolution took over. We may marvel at the courage and tenacity of the *Nuestro Tiempo* group, but they were nevertheless insignificant in their time. This absence is what produced a great deal of confusion in the early sixties, and it explains why one of the first things to happen in the cultural area was the foundation, first of a literary page in the newspaper *Revolución*, and later in the supplement *Lunes de Revolución* (March 30, 1959). *Lunes* became, in rather spasmodic fashion, the kind of journal that Cuba lacked in the fifties—a literary supplement that could serve as an outlet for journalistic literary criticism, in the fashion of *Marcha* in Montevideo, the *Papel Literario de El Nacional* in Caracas, or *Siempre!* in Mexico. But *Lunes* had no tradition in Cuba to fall back upon. Its contributors were, in the main, those who had gathered around *Ciclón*, but soon it included everybody. *Lunes* belonged to the fifties: it had no position; it represented no literary school; it had no cohesion; and it was therefore vulnerable. As the revolution became more radical, it collapsed. *Lunes*, with no compelling figure heading it (Guillermo Cabrera Infante was not well known then), with no political or literary ideology, was curiously an emblem of the Cuba of the fifties, when there were no powerful journals, very few dominating figures, and certainly no recent tradition of critical exchange. José Lezama Lima, after the demise of *Orígenes*, did not have a magazine and his group dispersed. Alejo Carpentier was in Caracas; Nicolás Guillén was in exile or in jail;

Marinello the same. Of the younger group, Roberto Fernández Retamar was at Yale, Lisandro Otero in Paris, Edmundo Desnoes in New York; many others, like César Leante, were in Havana writing for radio or television.

In the area of literary criticism there was very little to build on in 1959, or even to build against. While in other areas this may have been a blessing, in this case it was not. Literary criticism thrives on dialogue, a dialogue that takes place in the present, between living critics and writers, but that involves the immediate past as a repository of values with, and against, which to operate. Without this foundation, fruitless confusion reigns; all work has to begin from scratch; there is no shared language and no sense of values; as a result misunderstandings reign supreme. This is very much what happened in Cuba during the first years of the revolution until the first Padilla affair in 1968, which was triggered by a critical debate about two novels by young Cuban writers: Lisandro Otero's *La Pasión de Urbino* and Guillermo Cabrera Infante's *Tres tristes tigres*. Though there are many other factors involved, in my opinion a great deal of the acrimony was due to the lack of experience with this sort of polemic.

As we move to the postrevolutionary period it is wise to remember that the effort in Cuba to integrate all activities is difficult for us to understand from our perspective in American universities. In Cuba, as in all socialist societies, there is an effort to make all aware of how their individual activities mesh in a grand design that includes, presumably, education, national defense, and the achievement of a classless society. We are well aware of the dangers that such a totalizing and totalitarian view of culture and society can engender in its implementation, and it would be naïve to expect some of these dangers not to have become menacing realities in today's Cuba. At the same time, it is only through such broad-based collective efforts that achievements, even in the cultural area, are realized. The argument of bureaucrats in charge of culture would be that the latter are bought at the cost of the former; but this is a specious argument, as history has shown in a number of cases.

Achievements in the area of academic criticism are remarkable. Now, in addition to *Universidad de La Habana* and *Islas*, published by the Universities of Havana and Las Villas respectively, the Universidad de Oriente publishes its journal, *Santiago*. There is also *Casa de las Américas*, which publishes both kinds of criticism, journalistic and academic, though it prefers the former, and *Unión*, more like a conventional literary journal, but with occasional contributions of an academic nature. There is also the Instituto de Lingüística y Literatura, which publishes its own journal, *L/L*. Casa also puts out a journal devoted to theater called *Conjunto,* and the writers' union publishes, in addition to *Unión, La Gaceta de Cuba,* nominally directed by Nicoláas Guillén but really in the hands of young critics. To this list we must add the very erudite and elegant journal published by the Biblioteca Nacional José Martí. It would be difficult to exaggerate the progress made in these journals in terms of what we generally call academic criticism. One might quarrel with pieces published in them, but on the whole the level of bibliographical information and analysis is high.

There has been a massive effort to edit forgotten Cuban texts as well as many of Latin America's most important books, not to mention the publication of translations of the classics of European and North American literature. But the most significant part of the effort is related to Cuban literature. Let me give three examples. Three books by Miguel de Carrión, a belated naturalist with a specific interest in the role of women in society (he wrote in the early years of this century) have been reissued. Carrión is as powerful a novelist as there was at the turn of the century in Latin America, but he was practically unknown in Cuba. The new editions of his novels are first editions for all practical purposes. But novels such as *Las impuras* or *Las honradas,* delving into the way of the decadent society of his times seen through sexual exploitation and bizarre sexual practices, are as hard and incisive as Robert Arlt's would be in Argentina a few years later. Carrión is now available in editions that cost about sixty cents. A second example is the edition of the correspondence between two important Cuban poets of the Republican era, Regino Boti and José Manuel Poveda. This volume is a careful and thorough scholarly effort by Sergio Chaple, who has put in the hands of the general public significant texts about poetic activity in Cuba. The book reads like a novel. Boti and Poveda, particularly the former, are poets who deserve more recognition, and Chaple's edition of their letters is an excellent example of academic criticism in the postrevolutionary period. The last example deserving mention is Cintio Vitier's three-volume anthology entitled *La crítica literaria y estética en el siglo XIX cubano.* This book is part of a substantial effort to detail literary activity in nineteenth-century Cuba, an effort that includes the publication of novelists, poets, collections of anonymous ballads, and *artículos de costumbres,* dealing with local customs, not to mention a monumental new edition of the complete works of José Martí. Vitier's book rescues from oblivion a host of critics who can provide an historical foundation for today's critical activity. I know of no other Latin American country where there is a comparable degree and quality of activity in academic criticism.

The kind of criticism that predominates is positivistic with emphasis on research. But the context—social and economic—is analyzed in Marxist terms, which has led to a fruitful rewriting of nineteenth-century Cuban history. Hollingsworth is right when he notes that the more serious attempts at Marxist criticism are to be found in literary history. But it is not polemical or militant Marxism, nor does it take into account recent work on Marxist theory. It is not jargony and tends to be thorough and even-handed in approach. Research predominates over theory or methodology, surely because methodology is more ideologically dangerous. Also, given that so much of the preliminary work has been neglected before, attention had to be devoted to it immediately; there can be no criticism until there are texts. The lack of a more recent critical tradition precluded the existence of very advanced critics in the academy. Revolutionary Cuba has tended to be conservative in areas where there were no young people at the beginning of the revolution, and there were no young Marxist critics in Cuba in 1959. Academic criticism has been benevolently ruled by a gerontocracy. The Instituto de Lingüística y Literatura was initially under the direction of José Antonio Portuondo, a Marxist critic formed in the thirties, and now is under the direction of Mirta Aguirre, another competent but rather traditional critic. As a result, the Instituto's main function has been the production of a dictionary of Cuban literature. Academic criticism has achieved a great deal in postrevolutionary Cuba, but it has not been innovative in approach, rather the opposite.

However, one cannot minimize its achievements in terms of its impact on society at large, and in this sense it has been very innovative. It is teams of *investigadores* who make possible the editions of Cuban authors mentioned before. This is a great achievement that is influencing today's Cuban literary production, as we shall see later. Today's Cuban people know who Carrión and Boti were, whereas before they did not even recognize Carpentier or Lezama. Cuban literature of the nineteenth and twentieth centuries is finally being read by Cubans in large numbers thanks to efforts by these academic critics.

Nearly all the work in this academic area has a Marxist imprint, but it is certainly not militant to the point of excluding areas of reality. As we scan journalistic criticism a pattern begins to emerge: the less academic and more popular a work, the more militant it is. Articles in *Universidad de La Habana, Islas,* and *Oriente* are written mostly for an audience of specialists and hold to the general premises of academic criticism—the whole field is taken into account; no matter how ideologically "regressive" an author or critic is considered to be, his work is cited and discussed with equanimity. Works intended for a larger audience are a different matter. For instance, a recent anthology of the short story, *Cuentos cubanos del siglo XX* edited by Salvador Bueno, excludes all mention of Lino Novás Calvo and Guillermo Cabrera Infante (two exiled authors); yet Novás Calvo was a very influential short-story writer in the thirties and forties, and Cabrera Infante's *Así en la paz como en la guerra* was the first best-seller after the triumph of the revolution.

This sort of cropped version of reality occurs with greater frequency in journalistic criticism of the sort published in *Casa de la Américas*, *Unión*, *Caimán Barbudo*, and *La Gaceta de Cuba*, which tends to be less reliable in terms of information. The formula is clear: if the author is alive and has engaged in some sort of aggression (real or at times imaginary) against the revolution, he will not be mentioned. The justification for this phenomenon, which disturbs many people not otherwise unduly concerned with truth, is simple: while in theory the works of a man and the man may be distinct entities, in the world of real politics, authors employ the positions that society accords them because of their works for political purposes. Given that the revolution has been under constant threat and under constant attack on many fronts, the priorities are clear. The revolution cannot contribute to the accumulation of prestige by individuals who are out to destroy the revolution. As one moves back into the scholarly journals, this militancy diminishes as the dangers also diminish. These limitations no doubt have had a deleterious effect on Cuban criticism and literature.

Journalistic criticism is a much more polemical and debatable field. I shall subdivide journalistic criticism into two kinds. The first is the popular kind printed in magazines devoted to a mass market. The second is the type printed in journals such as *Casa de las Américas*, *Unión*, *La Gaceta de Cuba*, *El Caimán Barbudo*, *Conjunto*, and also in the more academically oriented *Universidad de La Habana*, *Santiago*, *Islas*, *Signos* or *Revista de la Biblioteca Nacional José Martí*. I include in this category not only commentary on current literature, but also theory and essays dealing with problems in contemporary Latin American literature. This area of criticism is the most ideologically tense, the one responding more readily to political conflicts. All of the debates have taken place at this level, and consequently it is the only critical activity known by nonspecialists outside of Cuba. The results, in my view, are very mixed in this area, and whereas I believe that the accomplishments of academic criticism, taken collectively, are indeed very substantial, I could not say the same in the case of journalistic criticism.

Popular journalistic criticism in Cuba has not attained a level comparable to that of Mexico or Argentina, but it has improved considerably. A quick glance at journals such as *Bohemia*, *Revolución y Cultura*, *Cuba Internacional*, the newspaper *Granma*, and many others will convince the most skeptical that literature is an important component of Cuban culture today. There are interviews with authors, light pieces on nineteenth-century literature, reviews of current books, short stories, commentaries on literary competitions, poems by established poets and poems sent by readers, fables, popular tales—indeed, the whole gamut. Any critic working on a Cuban author has to go through these journals, for in them he is bound to find a great amount of relevant material.

More serious literary criticism is a different matter altogether; all who have written on Cuban criticism agree that this is a very weak area. Marinello, Portuondo, Feijóo, Arias, all writing from within Cuba, have decried the poverty of this kind of criticism. Samuel Feijóo has a drawing that depicts "El común kakafuako seudo-crítico del subdesarrollo cultural, en plena sonriencia (autoprovechosa) halagomerongótica." This could be translated as "The common shitty pseudo-critic of cultural underdevelopment in full smile (self-profiting) praisesweetypieing." Marinello spoke in 1969 of a "cierta indigencia," a certain poverty of criticism, and in 1977 Portuondo pontificated about the sudden change in values that only left "plumas maduras" (oh, *rara avis*) with the necessary "concepto firme de la realidad," or firm concept of reality, needed for the critical task.

In relation to theory, the same principle applies here as to the Instituto de Lingüística y Literatura: the more powerful voices have been, with few exceptions, those of old critics such as Bueno and Portuondo. This gerontocracy has viewed with alarm recent literary theory; it has tended to reject the new Latin American literature of the sixties and seventies and has proceeded as if Borges and Octavio Paz did not exist. In this they do not differ from older critics in the rest of the world who have found themselves obsolete almost overnight, but in Cuba they have been entrusted with an institutional power that allowed them to stifle innovation. Until he was sent as ambassador to the Vatican, José Antonio Portuondo was the leading ideologue of serious Cuban journalistic criticism. His brand of elementary Marxism mixed with a simplistic view of Latin American reality was prominent in many debates, and one can see his hand in documents such as the disclaimer appended to Padilla's and Arrufat's books in 1968. A critic of Carpentier, totally impervious to Lezama's poetic allure, Portuondo advocated a politicized form of *novela de la tierra*, oblivious to the fact that such a novel had been created by the bourgeoisie in the twenties and thirties in a fit of populism and could not therefore be recreated *in vitro*. Portuondo's critical ideology led to the writing and promotion of Cofiño López's lamentable novel, *La última mujer y el próximo combate*, which was hailed in some circles as the true novel of the Cuban Revolution. Portuondo, much like a colonial critic, established a false connection between underdevelopment and the quality of cultural production:

> Since they represent an expression by developing nations, these national literatures of Iberoamerica still suffer, speaking in general terms, from a certain formal poverty which impedes their striving to equal those literary expressions which are based on old, refined cultures. On the other hand, they are overflowing with fresh, barely harnessed vigor and vitality which are the harbinger of immediate, promising creations.... We have available to us a proven, fitting instrument, yet we are lacking the spirit capable of deriving from it lasting influence (translation of editors).

Portuondo wrote this in 1962, at a time when, to mention only a few, Guimarães Rosa had published *Grande Sertão Veredas*, Neruda his *Canto General*, Carpentier his *Los pasos perdidos*. Portuondo was in 1959, with the exception of Juan Marinello (who was exceptional in every sense) and Mirta Aguirre, the only Cuban critic with Marxist credentials, which explains why he was entrusted with the mission of voicing the Cuban position on literary developments. Portuondo's Marxism, however, was not only very simplistic but contaminated with conflicting ideologies. A close reading of the above quotations or of the whole prologue from which they are taken will no doubt reveal an uncritical mélange of Orteguian *vitalismo* and *kulturgeschichte*, not to mention a very intoxicating dose of Sartrean existentialism.

Some may argue that I am giving undue importance to Portuondo, but the fact is that the younger group of critics who attained power in the sixties pay homage to him at every turn. Roberto Fernández Retamar's *Para una teoría de la literatura hispanoamericana y otras aproximaciones*, the most ambitious attempt to produce literary theory in revolutionary Cuba, pivots on an essay on Portuondo that ends with a panegyric elevating Portuondo to dizzying heights and offering him as an example for future generations of critics. More disturbing and revealing is Fernández Retamar's recent essay, "La contribución de las literaturas de la América Latina a la literatura universal" ("The contribution made by the literatures of Latin America to universal literature"), collected in a new edition of *Para una teoría*. Although he claims that there is no necessary connection between underdevelopment and underdeveloped literature, Fernández Retamar speaks of Latin American literature as "being *now* a major literature" (meaning in the sixties), which betrays the same outlook of Portuondo in 1962. It is true that the premises of the essay were furnished by the theme of a symposium, but I am surprised by Fernández Retamar's acquiescence. Does Latin American literature make contributions to an abstract category called universal literature? Or is universal literature an abstraction invented in eighteenth-century Europe? Whereas in other areas the Cuban Revolution has been radical enough to demystify such pomposities, journalistic criticism has not on the whole heeded Juan Marinello's 1969 warning that "the definition of the relationship between a revolutionary change and the resulting artistic change is not something which can be resolved in two fervent sentences" (translation of editors).

Portuondo was challenged by other younger critics on various occasions but never with as much verve as in a 1964 polemic with Ambrosio Fornet in *La Gaceta de Cuba*. Fornet went so far as to say that each generation needs its own critics, and added that "being over fifty is a serious obstacle to interpret certain things, fly a MIG or make love." Portuondo was not amused, charged Fornet with being a revisionist, and continued to urge literature to deal directly with the battles that the revolution was waging on various fronts. Fornet refused to allow for such a simplistic, negative view of literature and argued for a literature that would incorporate the avant-garde, which Portuondo was insisting could not be relevant to revolutionary writers. Manuel Díaz Martínez, a young poet, joined the polemic against Portuondo, referring to him mockingly as "The Professor," but it was The Professor who closed the debate with yet another appeal to have literature reflect the present.

In my view the shortcomings of serious journalistic criticism have been significant. For instance, very little work on major Cuban writers has been published in *Unión*, *Casa*, or any of the other journals. It is curious that hardly anything was published up to 1969 in *Casa* about Carpentier (his own contributions were meager too); there is little on Lezama and nearly nothing on Guillén beyond a certain hagiography. Since then the situation has improved somewhat with regard to Carpentier, but nothing powerful on any of those writers has appeared. It is true that there have been volumes devoted to Lezama and Carpentier in the "Valoración Múltiple" series published by Casa, but a glance at those volumes and their bibliographies reveals the scarcity of pieces published in Cuba. In my view, the failure of journalistic criticism has been in not drawing from such powerful Cuban authors a theory of literature and consequently of criticism. Up to now this has been a wasted opportunity: the works of Lezama, Carpentier, and Guillén can provide—and have provided—such a basis, but journalistic criticism has been unable or unwilling to profit from it, preferring more often to import from Europe well-worn Marxist formulas.

A similar failure in my view is the way in which Latin American authors not in favor of the revolution have been omitted from Cuban cultural life. The most glaring absences are Borges and Octavio Paz, though there are others, such as Pablo Neruda, whose relations with the Cuban intelligentsia were rather strained, as his acerbic comments on Fernández Retamar and Guillén in his memoirs make clear. The defensive attitude that these omissions reveal is witness to a general intellectual poverty that has no counterpart in literature itself and that is the opposite of what exists in other areas of intellectual activity such as history.

Whether a cause or a symptom of these failures, journalistic criticism has remained unaffected by recent trends in critical theory, though there have been efforts in the opposite direction. Portuondo fumed against Lévi-Strauss, Foucault, and Lacan in an essay entitled "Crítica marxista de la estética burguesa contemporánea," ("A marxist critique of contemporary bourgeois aesthetics"), published in *Casa de las Américas* in 1972. More recently Mario Benedetti, the notable Uruguayan writer living and working in Cuba, voices alarm because structuralism nearly destroyed French literature and could do the same to Latin American literature, a rather odd perception of the workings of literary history. Benedetti's understanding of "structuralism" is no better informed than Portuondo's, though it is certainly more colorful. Roberto Fernández Retamar has a more balanced view of some of the new critical tendencies, and occasionally even quotes Barthes. He has also published Julia Kristeva and Gérard Genette in *Casa de las Américas*. A younger group of critics, some trained in Eastern Europe, have been doing interesting work in *La Gaceta de Cuba* (an issue devoted to criticism including a great deal of structuralism). But up to now the views of Portuondo and Benedetti have prevailed, and the promising young critics of *La Gaceta de Cuba* (Sergio Chaple, Desiderio Navarro) do not publish their work in *Casa de las Américas*, the most powerful journal. In short, the failure to draw useful lessons from new criticism and apply them fearlessly to major Cuban authors has prevented serious journalistic criticism from going beyond a primary level of ideological analysis.

It is not too difficult to explain why these failures have occurred. In the first place there is the lack of a recent critical tradition mentioned at the beginning. Secondly, journalistic criticism is more subject to general ideological shifts and to bureaucratic control (a control exercised silently by the mechanisms of the bureaucracy itself, not necessarily by political commissars or repressive forces). Thirdly, there was no Marxist criticial foundation in Cuba, the influence of the militant anti-communism of the fifties in the United States precluding such a foundation (whereas in other Latin American countries the situation is quite different). Other than Portuondo and Aguirre, the only serious Marxist critic was Juan Marinello, who was above all a writer.

Cuban literary criticism in the revolutionary era has made great accomplishments in the academic area, but not in that of journalistic criticism. Even so, no book of the quality of Manual Moreno Fraginals's *El ingenio* has emerged. No Cuban critic has sifted evidence with the clarity of mind and the sense of drama that Moreno Fraginals displayed in studying economic transactions in nineteenth-century Cuba. But the collective effort of those who have edited Cuban literary works from the past and made them available to the general public may be of comparable value. The work of Robert Fernández Retamar in attempting to define Latin American literature is a worthy, though polemical, successor to a long tradition on the Continent. Besides, by keeping an ideologically aggressive stance, his criticism has had a visible impact on Latin American literature in general; Latin American writers of the left have been influenced by the way Cuban criticism sees them. Such a stance has often been taken at a great cost to the enduring values of their work, but this is the price Cuba has been forced to pay by historical circumstances.

But historical circumstances change, and the 1975 pronouncements by the new Minister of Culture, Armando Hart, are encouraging. There is a liberalization that appears to be due to a feeling of security in the revolution. The harsh statement on literature and art issued by the First Congress of Education and Culture spoke from what is called a *plaza sitiada*, or "besieged center." The more recent proclamations do not speak in such terms. This new openness is already making possible a reaction on the part of young writers and critics. A good example both of the liberalization and of the malaise besetting Cuban critics is the following excerpt from a review of Alejo Carpentier's *La consagración de la primavera*, published by the promising young writer Manuel Pereira in *Bohemia*:

> (Carpentier's) novel is one that is difficult both in its undertaking and scope—as well as in its organization and the manner in which it unfolds. So, people want novels that are easy to read? They shout aloud that they demand less complexity, less learned references, less wordplay, and associations, in short less intellectual references? Any work which tries to penetrate, reveal, interpret, and be fully acquainted with a given reality simply has to be complex, and that complexity makes an occasional dosage of obscurity inevitable (translation of editors).

A few lines before this appeal, Pereira had quoted the Delphic injunction to the effect that only that which is difficult can be stimulating, an allusion to the opening line of Lezama Lima's *La expresión americana*: "Only *lo difícil*, the difficult element, is stimulating; only that resistance which truly challenges us is capable of awakening, provoking and maintaining our power to acquire knowledge" (translation of editors). I am encouraged by Pereira's appeal, by the fact that *Bohemia* published it, and above all by the reinscription of Lezama, even if surreptitiously, into the debate on literature.

Given the strides made in academic criticism, such an attitude, provided that political conditions prevail, could produce a powerful criticism that will really fulfill the aim of creating out of Latin American literature a theory of its own production and the values with which to judge it. But, as in other areas of Cuban reality, the potential may exist at the level of the masses and in the higher echelons of institutions. It is another picture altogether that emerges from organisms where the bureaucracy, entrenched in the sixties and early seventies, is fighting for its survival. Some of the publications celebrating the twentieth anniversary of the revolution are good examples of this entrenchment in that they become not so much a celebration of the historical event as a self-celebration on the part of critics, cultural directors, and the like.

How has literary criticism contributed to revolutionary literature and what is distinctive about that literature?

As opposed to the Mexican Revolution and the Spanish Civil War, the "armed phase" of the Cuban Revolution was swift and comparatively devoid of violence. In spite of the combative spirit of Ché Guevara, in spite of a certain amount of propaganda, there was little action in Cuba to compare with the paroxystic violence of both the Mexican Revolution and the Spanish Civil War. There were no international brigades, no stirring gathering of artists at the front. As a result, no significant literature of the war remains, except for passages in Ché's diaries. Because cultural establishments tend to be mimetic, journalistic criticism made a fruitless effort to create an epic literature, encouraging writers to portray operations against invaders at the Bay of Pigs and elsewhere. The best books to come out of this effort were Norberto Fuentes's *Condenados de Condado* and *Cazabandido*, but even they follow too closely formulas used by writers of the Spanish Civil War, particularly Hemingway. There was a tiresome collection of books bent on capturing the mindless speed of battle through a supposedly immediate, terse style. None of them, including Fuentes's, were really successful.

For all of its saber-rattling and adventurism in the recent past, in spite of all the violence in Cuban history, the Cuban Revolution has been a civil revolution: a revolution won by amateurs in the hills whose most important battles have been won in civil tasks such as the literacy campaign. None of the majors in the Cuban army really knew anything about war; none had had any formal military training; none think like military men. To ask, then, that revolutionary literature be epic, or martial, or that it reflect the horrors of war was a delusion on the part of critics with little sense of history. More than urgings of these critics, more than the countless activities organized to raise the level of commitment in literature, the criticism that was aiding in the creating of the new Cuban literature was academic criticism, the one tied to education—the really major commitment Cuba has made.

The literature of the revolution has not been, as the ideologues (and bureaucrats) have wished, one that portrayed the process of social change, or one dealing with military campaigns. The literature of the Cuban Revolution has been the one created by the sense of self-questioning made possible by the countless Cuban texts put in the hands of the new writers; the literature that has delved into the opened archives of Cuban memory in search of records to assemble them for the first time; the literature that has read and reread that record relentlessly, constructing a literary past to make it available to this generation of Cuban readers and writers. The enduring products of Cuban literature of the revolution bare *Biografía de un cimarrón, Canción de Rachel, El recurso del método, El ingenio, El mundo alucinante,* and the brilliant new book by Reynaldo González, *La fiesta de los tiburones.*

Some of these books are histories, like *El ingenio*; others, like *Biografía de un cimarrón* are anthropological documents; still others, like *La fiesta de los tiburones* or *El mundo alucinante* are varieties of the historical novel. The genre does not matter. The distinguishing characteristics cut across the fields within which these books were produced. And these distinguishing characteristics are: (1) all these books involve historical research in the most tangible sense of collecting documents; (2) all assemble those texts in such a way that a political history of Cuban culture emerges, meaning one that emphasizes socioeconomic and political relations other than ethnic; (3) all assemble the historical texts in such a way that the reader reads them directly, as if he were the researcher, not through an account that blends them all into a final form (In many cases the texts are not only written ones, but visual: *El ingenio* has not only statistical charts, but also marvelous drawings of old sugar-mill machinery; *Biografía de un cimarró*n has pictures; *La fiesta de los tiburones,* newspaper clippings that include advertisements as well as articles and editorials.); (4) all these books consequently demystify the figure of the author, who is a compiler, a researcher, an investigator who gives his place to the reader, who shares with him his wonder and self-recognition before the texts; (5) all of the books mentioned, then, focus on the very activity of reading as social and political activity, not only as a subjectively creative one; (6) all of these books have been produced by writers who are marginal in relation to the centers of ideological dissemination where journalistic criticism is produced, in the same way that the *investigadores* mentioned before are marginal. For all of his well-deserved prominence, Moreno Fraginals is not one of the featured writers of any important Cuban publication; Carpentier used to spend most of his time in Paris; and Barnet, González, and Arenas are not exactly powerful in the Cuban cultural establishment. Significant modern literature tends to be unorthodox in relation to the avowed (though not necessarily true, as Marx taught) ideology of any given society, even when that ideology cloaks itself in revolutionary rhetoric.

The relationship between these books and those produced by the academic critics discussed before is evident, and in the case of *La fiesta de los tiburones* an unsuspecting reader may take that book for an edition of texts dealing with the early Menocal period. These books are the literature of the revolution, on a par and sharing many characteristics with the best Latin American literature today.

Within the last three years, though, a disturbing trend has occurred—one that has somewhat dampened this earlier enthusiasm for Cuban literature. It is evident now that Cuban culture has become bureaucratized and controlled to such a degree that very few important writers have chosen to remain on the island. Since I wrote this piece, the following writers have left Cuba (to my knowledge): Heberto Padilla, Belkis Cuza Malé, Reinaldo Arenas, José Triana, Antonio Benítez Rojo, César Leante and Armando Valladares. Edmundo Desnoes has been living in the United States for the past three years, though it is not clear whether he is staying or going back. The defections of Leante and Benítez Rojo were the most damaging to the regime, for these were writers who had been actively committed to the revolution. The testimony of these writers concerning repression and favoritism in Cuba's intellectual establishment is very depressing indeed.

Roberto Fernández Retamar, Heberto Padilla, César Leante, José Triana, Edmundo Desnoes, Pablo Armando Fernández, Antonio Benítez Rojo and Guillermo Cabrera Infante were all born around 1930, and came of age with the revolution. Only one work of world-class level has emerged from this group: *Tres tristes tigres*. There are some excellent stories by Benítez Rojo, a poem or two by Padilla and Fernández Retamar, but nothing first-rate; *La noche de los asesinos* is a good play, but not competitive with the best theater of the century, and Leante has given us some moving pages in *Capitán de cimarrones*. Most of these writers are now in exile, and it remains to be seen if they will be able to produce after the ordeal of leaving their homeland and forsaking a regime to which they had given their all. Fernández Retamar and Pablo Armando Fernández remain in Cuba, but have not published lately anything even of the level of their best previous work, which although good was not enough to make them major poets by a long shot.

With the deaths of Lezama Lima, Carpentier and Marinello added to the list of exiles, the situation in Cuban letters is anything but good. Nicolás Guillén published his important poetry before the revolution. Cintio Vitier, Eliseo Diego, and José Rodríguez Feo made their contribution in the years of *Orígenes*. Fina García Marruz occasionally publishes still a fine poem, but, together with Vitier's, their works will always be a reflection of Lezama's.

Of course, it would be rash to attribute this situation exclusively to the fact that the revolution has grown old and bureaucratized, and that in many ways it is literally becoming a revolution, a return to the same old ways. If the revolution could produce a great writer, then we would have to hold the worst years of the Republic responsible for Carpentier and Lezama. After all is said and done, the fact remains that writers cannot be generated through social policy, at least not great writers. At the same time, we simply don't know if a great writer is clandestinely working in Cuba, a Kafka of the tropics who is writing a great novel that will only be known fifty years from now.

In my view, the great works sparked by the revolutionary process came out of the critical revision of Cuban and Latin American tradition that such a process made possible. As the revolution increasingly becomes not an agent for criticism, but one for devout, uncritical acceptance of stale doctrine, the possibility of further gains in literature is dimmed.

BIBLIOGRAPHY

Arenas, Reynaldo. *El mundo alucniante*. México: Diógenes, 1969.
Casa de las Américas, no. 113 (1979). Articles by Salvador Arias, Adelaida de Juan, and Adolfo Cruz-Luis on literature, the plastic arts and theater.
Chaple, Sergio, compilador, prólogo y notas de. *Epistolario Boti-Poveda*. La Habana: Editorial Arte y Literatura, 1977.
Fejióo, Samuel. "Por una superación de nuestra crítica literaria y artística." *Signos* (1978), pp. 63-67. Originally published in *Caimán Barbudo* as part of a discussion on criticism.
Fernández Retamar, Roberto. *Para una teoría de la literatura hispanoamericana y otras aproximaciones*. La Habana: Cuadernos Casa no. 16, 1975; 2nd ed. México: Nuestro Tiempo, 1977.
Fornet, Ambrosio. "La crítica literaria, aquí y ahora," in his *En tres y dos*. La Habana: Ediciones R, 1964, pp. 13-31.
―――. "De provinciano a provinciano." *La Gaceta de Cuba*, no. 39 (1964), pp. 9-11.
―――. "Hablando en serio." *La Gaceta de Cuba*, no. 41 (1964), pp. 12-16.
González, Reynaldo. *La fiesta de los tiburones*. La Habana: Editorial de Ciencias Sociales, 1978.
González Echevarría, Roberto. "Roberto Fernández Retamar: An Introduction." *Diacritics*, 8 (1978), pp. 70-75.
Hart-Dávalos, Armando. *Encuentro con los escritores*. La Habana: UNEAC, 1977.
―――. *Discurso de Clausura del Segundo Congreso de la Unión de Escritores y Artistas de Cuba*. La Habana: UNEAC, 1977.

Hollingsworth, Charles. "*The Development of Literary Theory in Cuba, 1959–1969.*" Ph.D. dissertation, University of California, Berkeley, 1972.
Marinello, Juan. "Sobre nuestra crítica literatura [sic]," in his *Creación y Revolución*. La Habana: UNEAC-Contemporáneos, 1973.
Navarro, Desiderio, ed. "Problemas de la crítica y de la ciencia literarias." Special issue of *La Gaceta de Cuba*, no. 100 (1972).
──────, selección, presentación y traducción de. *Cultura, Ideología y Sociedad. Antología de estudios marxistas sobre la cultura*. La Habana: Editorial Arte y Literatura, 1975.
Otero, Lisandro, with the assistance of Francisco Martínez Hinojosa. *Cultural Policy in Cuba*. Paris: UNESCO, 1972.
Pereira, Manuel. "Consagración y primavera de Alejo Carpentier." *Bohemia*, 71 (March 9, 1979), pp. 28–29.
Política cultural de la Revolución Cubana. La Habana: Editorial de Ciencias Sociales, 1977.
Portuondo, José Antonio. "Respuesta a Fornet." *La Gaceta de Cuba*, no. 40 (1964), pp. 6–7.
──────. "Contrarréplica a Fornet." *La Gaceta de Cuba*, no. 42 (1965), pp. 31–35.
──────. "Crítica marxista de la estética burguesa contemporánea." *Casa de las Américas*, no. 71 (1972), pp. 5–13. Issue devoted to semiotics.
Vitier, Cintio, prólogo, selección y notas de. *La crítica literaria y estética en el siglo XIX Cubano*, 3 vols. La Habana: Biblioteca Nacional José Martí—Colección Cubana, 1974.

Section IV
Economic Reform

9
Economic Policy and Development Models

Joel C. Edelstein

The revolutionary government in Cuba has evolved a succession of approaches to the task of fostering independent national development with remarkable speed. In 1959 the anti-Batista movement came to power under the leadership of Fidel Castro with a reformist program. Castro's 26th of July Movement (M26J) dominated a broad coalition of forces. Since its emergence in the unsuccessful attack on the Moncada military barracks in 1953, M26J had been distinguished from other political forces solely by its call for unity among opposition forces and its insistence that armed struggle rather than negotiation was the only effective means of achieving change, i.e., was the only road to reform.

Once Castro was in power and the promised reforms had been introduced, internal polarization and an escalating pattern of foreign threats and attacks resulted. The government responded by taking over the holdings of its opponents, both foreign and domestic. The biggest wave of nationalizations occurred in the summer of 1960. Thus in order to secure the reformist regime, the revolution became socialist. In the midst of the April 1961 invasion of Playa Girón, Castro used the term *socialist* openly for the first time, calling upon Cubans to defend their socialist revolution. Seven and one-half months later, he declared himself a Marxist-Leninist. Despite this rapid ideological transformation, the central goals of the revolution had not changed. The petit-bourgeois humanism of M26J had become Marxist humanism.

INDEPENDENT SOCIALIST DEVELOPMENT (1962–1965)

During the first three years of the revolution, political survival was the near-exclusive preoccupation of the government as it implemented the initial reforms, engaged both foreign and domestic enemies, and organized and mobilized its supporters. Mobilization was both political and military, and included the anti-illiteracy campaign of 1961. Other steps were taken to meet commitments to the peasants, such as construction of rural housing and provision of new health, educational, and cultural services to the countryside. While nationalizations had changed the role of the state in the economy, development planning was still focused on diversification of the economy and import-substitution industrialization. Sugar was a hated symbol of colonial oppression, and in 1960 and 1961 up to 20 percent of it was plowed under to plant crops that had formerly been imported.

Because the revolution had succeeded in large measure due to previous economic stagnation, it was not surprising that the first year or so of the new government saw a satisfying prosperity. Redistribution programs provided a market that stimulated the economy. Underutilized land and capital came into production. Moreover, stores and warehouses held sizeable quantities of goods for which demand had been absent. The boom brought a wave of optimism to Cuban economists, who projected an incredible growth rate of approximately 15 percent per annum. Foreign visitors were only slightly less bullish. It appeared that the Cuban economy could simultaneously provide expanded incomes and services, invest for accelerated growth, and cope with the costs of diversification.

Concerned with avoiding debt that would threaten the country's newly won independence, the government was conservative in its use of foreign exchange, at least to the extent permitted by its disorganization and weak controls. Only when the threat of economic blockade appeared were enterprises encouraged to go on a buying spree for imports regardless of cost.

In late 1961 and 1962 economic difficulties began to emerge. Shortages appeared and rationing was adopted to assure that commodities in short supply would be shared equally. An apparent preoccupation with quantity to the detriment of quality in production led to a major economic conference in August 1962. Economic planning, organization, and administration became priority issues. Moreover, it became clear that import-substitution industrialization would initially be import-intensive. The purchase of capital plant for new industries required a huge amount of foreign exchange, and Cuba was going into debt at a rapid rate. In May of 1963 Castro announced that increasing debt could not be tolerated and that Cuba would expand sugar production to pay for its industrialization.

The significance of the reemphasis on sugar and even the origin of the decision to expand its production are not clear. In part it reflected knowledge gained in the first three years: that the upswing of the first year could not be projected into the future because it was based on the existence of unutilized capacity and an abundance of goods; that importation of capital plant was then beyond Cuba's means; that the infrastructure required by industrialization was lacking (e.g., the change of the primary trading partners from the United States to one six thousand miles away required the development of warehouses to hold imports for distribution, since in the past goods had been ordered in the quantities needed and had been available on short notice due to the proximity of ports in Florida and the U.S. Gulf Coast); that the flight of most of those who had experience in management had left the nation without a pool of personnel with the requisite skills to operate an industrial economy; and that replacement of sugar by other crops had resulted in a net loss of foreign exchange, because savings on foreign exchange earnings gained through reduction of agricultural imports had been less than the losses in sugar export earnings.

The expansion of sugar production made sense in terms of what has been called a turnpike strategy.[1] Diversification and industrialization remained the goals, but it would be necessary to travel to this desired destination via the mechanization of agriculture and the expansion of sugar production—a longer route, but a faster and safer one. Sugar exports could pay for imports and avoid or reduce the growth of foreign debt. The emphasis would include not only sugar, but the modernization of all agriculture as part of a rural development project. Thus, diversification would be achieved in the entire agricultural sector, reducing the need for importation of food products (e.g., before the revolution, Cuba had consumed most of the lard output of Chicago's stockyards) while ensuring that the people would not lack food. Rural development would minimize, if not eliminate, the alienation of the rural population that was so dominant a part of the history of the Soviet emphasis on industrialization. Moreover, the concentration of national resources in the cities while the countryside was impoverished had been identified as a distorted pattern of development created by neocolonialism. The mechanization of agriculture would develop the industrial techniques and the management skills needed for the expansion of manufacturing in Cuba. Thus, the turnpike strategy appeared to be a way to guard Cuban economic independence while establishing the human and the financial bases for industrialization.

Between 1962 and 1965, a debate took place over what kind of socialism Cuba would attempt to develop.[2] The more conservative position advocated *auto-financiamiento* (self-finance), a more decentralized form of administration that permitted each state enterprise to finance its own investment plans through retention of earnings. This position argued that the greater autonomy of the firm that self-finance implied was a more efficient way of organizing production. Managers would be in direct control and would be able to deal more effectively with day-to-day operating problems. Moreover, prices would be established in relation to the cost of production and managerial behavior with respect to cost and quality control would be under the discipline of the market. Self-finance was also associated with the use of wage differentials, relating wages to actual contributions to production in order to motivate workers and maintain work discipline. It was argued that greater centralization was beyond Cuba's present capacity to plan and administer the economy, while reliance on the consciousness of managers and workers to stimulate optimal work performance was a naïve hope beyond the level of development of the forces of production.

The opposing point of view, led by Ché Guevara, advocated *el sistema presupuestario de financiamiento* (central budgeting). Central budgeting was considered superior because it gave planners the capacity to mobilize resources for the transformation of the economy and the achievement of social justice. Self-finance, in this view, would allocate investment to the enterprises and sectors that were already strong, thus perpetuating the economic structure and the production mix established in the neocolonial period. Maintaining a close relation between prices and production costs would make production unresponsive to the needs of those with low incomes. Central budgeting advocated pricing based on social values rather than on costs. While recognizing serious problems that had already arisen in planning and administration, this position held that the difficulties were flaws in the new system that could be ironed out with experience and with efforts at raising the levels of consciousness of those in responsible positions. It was further argued that consciousness was not tied to the level of development of any single nation, but was a worldwide phenomenon, and that an advanced level of consciousness, in Cuba as in the rest of the world, had arisen in reaction to an advanced level of U.S. imperialism on a world scale. The feasibility of introducing collective incentives, basing wages not on individual contributions to production but relying on consciousness to stimulate work behavior, was said to have been demonstrated during the October crisis. In that instance production had risen despite the withdrawal from the work force of thousands of workers who had taken up positions to defend the nation. Moreover, use of market mechanisms and individual material work incentives were held to be destructive of the further development of socialist consciousness and progress toward communism.

As Bertram Silverman has pointed out,[3] the components of each position—degree of centralization of investment planning, pricing policies, and work incentives—did not necessarily have to be put together as they were. For example, it is possible to set pricing policies to conform or depart from costs in either system of finance. Moreover, the Cuban version of *auto-financiamiento* was itself rather centralized. However, while the debate was ostensibly about economic organization, in reality it concerned distinct visions of the transition to socialism, one emphasizing efficiency and growth, the other popular mobilization and radical egalitarianism.

Fidel Castro expressed no opinion about the debate until 1966, although he advocated a fiscal conservatism that coincided more closely with self-finance. During this period, both systems were used in various sectors of the economy. At the end of 1965, the debate ended and the journals in which it had been aired were closed. Cuba embarked on communist construction.

COMMUNIST CONSTRUCTION (1966–1970)

In the 1962–1965 period, advanced socialism or communism was seen in rather conventional terms as a distant goal. First, it would be necessary to pass through a lengthy stage of socialist development in which both the level of the forces of production and social consciousness would be advanced. In 1966, however, communism became an immediate consideration in day-to-day decision making.

Communism was defined nationally as an economy operating without exchange relationships. "From each according to his ability" meant that people would work as a social duty; "to each according to need" meant that goods and services would be distributed without charge. A great mobilization campaign was undertaken in which people participated in agricultural work on a voluntary basis. Thousands went to farms near their homes after completing full workdays in their regular jobs and on weekends. They also worked on farms for periods of a month or more, particularly during the *zafra* (sugar harvest), while their co-workers who remained behind put in "guerilla workdays" of up to fourteen hours to make up for the absence of the volunteers.

The volunteers did not receive extra pay for their extra work. However, workplaces that by their performance in both normal production and voluntary work contributions had earned the designation of advanced workplaces paid a full wage for sick pay and pensions, and absenteeism was not disciplined by a reduction in pay. Instead, it was hoped that the example of the volunteers' enthusiasm would affect the slackers' consciousness.

An effort was also made to expand the free goods sector. No fees were charged for education, health services, some utilities, sports events, and local bus rides and telephone calls. Rents were set at a portion of income, with a 10 percent maximum. Rent was no longer collected on some housing units, and it was proposed that in 1970 all rents would be eliminated. Volunteer work camps on the Isla de Juventud (Isle of Youth, formerly the Isle of Pines off the south coast) functioned essentially without money.

Work without monetary remuneration and the distribution of goods without charge were considered "islands of communist practice"— communist areas within socialist society. The path to communism would be through quantitative growth of these islands until they became dominant, representing a qualitative transformation of society. Thus, communism was not a completely separate stage of development following a lengthy period of socialist development. While Cuba was not yet a communist society, communism existed with socialism. Development meant the simultaneous construction of communism and socialism with the goal of ultimate qualitative change. Indications of progress were to be found in further cutting the tie between individual contributions to production and individual consumption: more voluntary work and expansion of the free goods sector with the ultimate aim of the extinction of exchange relationships and the significance of money.

In fact, money did lose much of its power to influence behavior. During this period, the rate of investment rose to over 30 percent of

GNP. Only essential commodities were available, and virtually all of them were distributed through a rationing system at low prices. Consumption was allocated and limited by rationing as it had been previously by money (though, of course, with greater equality). The only items in the state sector for which money served as an allocative mechanism were meals in restaurants. Most people who did not trade on the black or gray (legal, but discouraged) markets could not spend their incomes. A sizeable portion of the population had dresser drawers full of excess cash.

When asked about their future career plans, militant young Cubans enthusiastically responded that they would go wherever the revolution sent them to do whatever Cuba needed to be done. As Robert Bernardo has pointed out, the allocation of labor was no longer performed by the market.[4] Moreover, the entire economic structure was centralized along the lines of the central budgeting position that Ché Guevara had advocated in the earlier debate. Administrative allocation of resources became still more dominant when in 1968 bars and other small private businesses, said to be undermining egalitarian distribution in the state sector through black market activities, were nationalized.

The use of moral incentives to construct socialism and communism simultaneously was explained as the use of consciousness to create wealth. Throughout the history of the Soviet Union, emphasis has been placed on development of the forces of production to a level at which more advanced relations of production would be possible. The Cuban leadership proclaimed its rejection of this strategy of creating wealth to build consciousness. Hardly disguising its references to the U.S.S.R., the Cuban leadership insisted that the use of individual material incentives as the basic stimulus in the economic development effort resulted in "selfishness amidst abundance." Instead, it was proposed that appeals to a consciousness of social duty would bring about the effort needed to raise the level of productive forces. The fruits of this labor would make it possible to expand the free goods sector and provide for greater social welfare for those unable to work. Experiencing the benefits of the collective effort would reinforce and advance consciousness still further. In this fashion socialism would be developed, while communist practice would expand until the realm of exchange relations was limited to a number of shrinking islands in the midst of a communist society.

While romantics and those familiar only with Marx's early work were exhilarated at Cuba's daring experiment, most foreign economists, Marxist and bourgeois alike, shook their heads. Reliance on collective incentives contradicted equally the concept of economic man on which bourgeois economics has been based and the Marxian understanding that the social relations of production cannot transcend the level of development of the forces of production. The Cuban leadership had a history of over-optimism, setting unrealistic goals, and wasting resources in the effort to fulfill them.

Given the risks involved in such a heretical violation of accepted economic truths, it seems unlikely that the moral incentives strategy was chosen exclusively because it appeared to avoid the possibility of achieving economic development while failing to develop socialist consciousness. An alternative explanation, proposed in part by Bertram Silverman,[5] focuses on the need to expand the agricultural workforce. Sugar cane is a perennial grass, yielding cane for several harvests. Weeding the cane fields had previously required large amounts of labor, but the use of herbicides applied by aerial crop-dusters had drastically reduced the size of the workforce needed for this phase of cane culture. Thus, the harvesting of cane, traditionally done throughout the Caribbean by the arduous and monotonous wielding of the machete, presented the greatest problem in expanding sugar production. As noted earlier, the goal of a ten-million-ton harvest in 1970, more than twice Cuba's average annual output, was announced by Castro upon returning from a visit to the Soviet Union. During that visit, the Soviet Union made a commitment to provide Cuba with cane-cutting machines. Early on, it was made clear that the mechanization of the harvest was regarded as essential. The problem of labor for the *zafra* was due not only to the size of the harvest; there was a shortage of *macheteros* because many had taken advantage of new opportunities to enter more desirable kinds of work. In 1965, Castro remarked that it would continue to be difficult to obtain labor for the harvest, though the situation was expected to improve with the arrival of cane-cutting machines by 1967. At this time Castro still endorsed a conservative fiscal policy, suggesting that he was not about to advocate full acceptance of central budgeting and moral incentives.

A few months later the moral incentives strategy—constructing communism and socialism at the same time—was implemented. It may be that the deciding factor was information that the mechanical harvesters would not be forthcoming. Just why the Soviet Union failed to deliver is not certain. Design of a machine was not easy. A harvester must cut the cane very close to the ground so that the cane will grow properly the following year; it must cut the tops and strip leaves that grow on the stalks; often it must perform these tasks while moving across hilly ground; and it must deal with a plant that does not grow in neat rows and that often lies at an angle rather than perpendicular. Machines were developed that could perform some of these functions, but it was clear that the expansion of sugar production would require a massive increase in the agricultural workforce, since most of the crop would still be harvested by hand.

Raising the needed workforce might have been accomplished through individual material incentives. However, given the physical hardship that cane-cutting entails, substantial wage incentives would have been required to induce workers to leave offices or even factory jobs for the cane fields. Such incentives would have increased costs considerably, and the productivity of cane-cutting is relatively low. The cost would have greatly reduced the net earnings derived from the industry. As it was, the late 1960s was a period of severe austerity for the entire Cuban population. The use of material incentives would have meant concentrating the austerity among those not participating in the workforce. In concrete terms, it would have meant starvation for the old and ignoring the needs of children and those too ill to work. This would have violated a longstanding central value of the revolution. Moreover, strong material incentives to attract labor to the harvest would have rewarded unskilled labor at a higher rate than some other activities requiring greater skill or education. This would have undermined major efforts being made to prepare the workforce to develop the capacity to handle industrial operations, which remained an essential goal of Cuban development.

Aside from the moral incentives strategy with the unknown it contained and the use of material incentives, two other options were available to the Cuban leadership to bring about the needed increase in agricultural labor. One was forced labor. This could have been accomplished by levying an extra work requirement upon all able-bodied citizens, to be enforced by severe punitive sanctions for those who did not comply. Or, a portion of the population could have been isolated from the rest, based on some real or invented characteristic, and that group interned in labor camps. During the moral incentives periods, hierarchy in the workplace was increased, including the use of a military style of organization of the harvest. However, there is no evidence that the use of forced labor was even considered.

Finally, there was the option of giving up the economic goals of the revolution or accepting a very slow rate of growth. There is no indication that this option was considered. On the contrary, the moral incentive period was imbued with an attitude of aggressive optimism that identified the stage as one of austerity and sacrifice but expected extraordinarily rapid gains. The leadership appeared to believe that a few years of effort would bring a permanent solution to Cuba's problems. Developing the sugar industry would provide export earnings sufficient to finance industrialization without increasing indebtedness, and the program was to include much more than sugar. Throughout the period, Castro insisted that the effort in sugar was not intended to draw resources away from other sectors. Agricultural diversification and modernization were to continue and accelerate as well. In crops from garlic to rice and in dairy animals the plan was to hold down consumption in order to use most of the present yield for reproduction until the expanded production fulfilled domestic needs and even provided a surplus for export. There was a feeling that the need to import agricultural products as well as the problem of export earnings insufficient to finance industrial development could be brought to an end "once and for all." Cuba would emerge from the years of sacrifice with an economic base that could provide for independence and industrial development. Moreover, successful economic growth would enable the free goods sector to expand, reinforcing a growing communist consciousness and expanding the sector of communist practice.

On July 26, 1970, before more than a million people gathered in the Plaza of the Revolution, Castro offered his resignation. He blamed the leadership, including himself, for failing to effectively manage the industrial side of sugar production. Although production had exceeded the previous record harvest (of 1952) by about 20 percent, it was one and a half million tons below the goal of ten million tons, and the cost inflicted on the rest of the economy had been severe. In many areas of production output was only half what it had been. Castro praised the Cuban people, who had harvested enough sugar cane to exceed the goal by 10 to 20 percent, if the ratio of raw cane to processed sugar had been maintained at normal levels. Instead, the schedule for the modernization and expansion of grinding capacities in the mills had lagged. In some cases the work had not been completed until the big harvest was well underway. Breakdowns occurred due to problems in the newly installed capacity, which should have been solved before the cutting began, and because of inadequate maintenance of many of the old *centrales* (sugar mills). The cut cane lost much of its sugar content when breakdowns resulted in delays in milling. A massive operation had been required to transport cut cane to operating *centrales* at greater-than-normal distances from the fields because closer ones had failed. The sometimes desperate effort had left much of the economy without transportation. Although production of steel rods to reinforce concrete had continued, the finished rods lay in the yards because they couldn't be moved to the cement plants. Breweries capable of their normal output lacked trucks to transport the finished product. Part of the problem was attributed to a failure to maintain the quality of the industrial workforce and to management systems that did not operate efficiently. He criticized technical and administrative personnel in the sugar sector for taking advantage of the priority that sugar had been given, drawing from other sectors resources that were not needed for sugar and that, in some instances, had not even been used.

DEPENDENT SOCIALIST DEVELOPMENT (1970-PRESENT)

Whether the moral incentives strategy was adopted as a new road to communism or as the acceptable means of increasing the agricultural workforce, it was rejected for its failings. A significant portion of the workforce was not stimulated to work solely by a desire to develop society; workers benefited not in relation to individual contributions, but as members of the collectivity without regard to individual work performance. Absenteeism was high and work productivity was low. Some jobs involving night work or other hardship (e.g., nursing) went unfilled. Some commodities whose consumption was not restricted by price or ration were wasted. For example, no charge was made for water, regardless of usage; as a result, leaks were not fixed. Managerial attention to conservation of resources was no higher than that of the general population. Without the discipline of either the market or effective central cost controls, emphasis was placed on meeting output goals. Workers were hired when they were not needed. Voluntary labor was evaluated by some managers at its cost to the enterprise and was employed in marginal ways as if it had no value.

Centralization caused a number of problems. The consequences of errors in planning and administration became more serious as centralization increased. As administration of many services became more distant from those who were served, a bureaucratic isolation grew. If stores and restaurants were poorly maintained, those who frequented them had no recourse. Conditions of mobilization and austerity led to greater hierarchy in the workplace. Unions declined, and the most able party cadres were drawn away from political tasks into administrative positions. As a result workers were unable to take the initiative when their instructions were inadequate or wrong. When management acted without concern for efficiency in the use of resources or for the welfare of the workforce, the workers could do little to correct the situation.

By 1970 discontent was considerable. Some of the causes were the years of austerity and shortages during 1970 caused by disorganization of production outside the sugar sector. There was frustration on the part of some of those who had contributed extra effort in voluntary work, only to find their product consumed by slackers or wasted by inefficiency. Others were alienated by their inability to affect conditions in stores and restaurants.

The leadership responded to the deficiencies of the moral incentives strategy with measures which signal more acceptance of economic inequality. At the same time this post-1970 strategy has been aimed toward greater political equality, creating new structures for political participation and strengthening democracy within existing institutions.

Mobilization under moral incentives had generated an atmosphere of equality through its emphasis on recognition of voluntary effort in largely unskilled labor and through equality in distribution, a result of shared austerity. In this context, the post-1970 economic strategy appears as a move toward a more conservative direction. First, an increased proportion of national income was allocated for current consumption, and individual material incentives were instituted. The resultant increase in inequality in consumption was accepted as necessary to stimulate work performance. Second, rationalization of the economy for greater efficiency carries with it the acceptance of some unemployment and consequently, some loss of job security. Finally, in the new economic strategy the social wage has been de-emphasized, with a turn away from expansion of the free goods sector and from the pensions at full pay which earlier had been awarded to workers in vanguard factories.

While the new strategy accepts greater economic inequality, it favors political equality through increased participation. Despite the mood of equality generated by the moral incentives strategy, hierarchy actually increased in the second half of the 1960s. Mass organizations were pressed into service as structures of command in the economic battle. Their role as channels for input from below and as agencies to protect the rights of individual workers lost priority to the demands of production. The post-1970 strengthening of the mass organizations and the creation of the Organs of Popular Power offer the population expanded opportunities for participation, providing experience in governance and increasing the level of political efficacy. While the economic policy represents a conservative path, the post-1970 strategy is a shift in the opposite direction.

ECONOMIC DEPENDENCE AND SOCIALIST DEVELOPMENT

The moral incentives strategy appears to have viewed the project of socialist development as a great leap over a deep chasm, requiring a brief period of strenuous exertion to gain the momentum necessary for the flight to advanced socialism or communism. A mobilized population would exert great effort under conditions of severe austerity for a few years. But the result would be a nation self-sufficient in food and able to pay for its industrialization with expanded sugar exports. Economic growth would provide for an increase in the free goods sector, bringing "communist practice" to the level of a qualitative transformation of society. The period of hardship was to be short so that political distortions caused by its stresses would not be serious.

This vision clearly underestimated the period of time required. Socialist development now appears as a long climb up a tall mountain. The period in which Cuba will be faced with hard choices between current consumption and investment is one measured in decades, not years. This is true as well of the period in which the country will necessarily remain dependent on traditional exports and in which trade will continue to be characterized by an over-concentration among a limited number of partners. Thus, political distortions arising from economic stress are understood to be more dangerous to the goal of independent socialism. For the security of the long-term project of socialist development, the enhanced political capacity of the Cuban people, engendered by the post-1970 strategy, will likely be far more important than the income differentials which result from its economic policies.

The U.S.S.R. continues to be Cuba's major market for sugar at a price far above the capitalist market price and a principal source of petroleum at a price far below that of the capitalist market. The U.S.S.R. also remains the major source of economic and military assistance.

Since 1970, Cuban concepts of economic organization and Cuban foreign policy have coincided substantially with those of the Soviet Union. Observers often assume that policies coincide because the Soviet Union has used its influence to dictate to Cuba. However, changes in policy by the Cuban leadership may well have been made on their own merits.

The U.S.S.R. had never favored the moral incentives strategy rejected in 1970. Disorganization of the economy and significant discontent among the people placed Cuba in a weak position. An ultimatum to conform to Soviet policies or be cast adrift as China had been ten years earlier would have threatened the Cuban leadership. On the other hand, the decision could well have been one of abandoning an approach whose failures had led to this vulnerability. Moreover, by 1970 Cuba no longer had to rely on mobilization. Progress had been made in the mechanization of the harvest. Through irrigation and the development of new varieties of cane, the harvest season could be extended, reducing the peak need for labor. Also, in the late 1960s, an institutional net was created that ensures that Cuban youth will participate in agricultural tasks when needed. Such work is part of the school curriculum, particularly in the schools-in-the-countryside in which older children attend boarding schools where they work for a portion of each day in addition to their studies. The armed forces were given a larger role in the harvest (a tendency that was reversed when Cuba moved toward a military force based on smaller numbers and more sophisticated weaponry). Idle youth who were not attending school, in the armed forces, or employed elsewhere were conscripted into the Army of Working Youth, which performs agricultural labor. Before the need for labor had been reduced and before the institutional net to provide labor had been established, there seemed no alternative to policies of mobilization. By the early 1970s, new options had been created. In some degree, an alternative to centralization was also developed as progress in turning out more people with managerial and technical training provided personnel to effectively manage a larger number of smaller enterprises. And in a broader sense, with completion of the task of setting the country's workforce and productive resources in motion, it is not surprising that the priorities shifted toward efficiency. In summary, while Cuba was and continues to be vulnerable to Soviet pressure, the rejection of the moral incentives strategy could well have been simply the outcome of the domestic situation, a reappraisal of the experience gained in the second half of the 1960s, and progress that reduced the need for mobilization and in other ways opened up new options and new priorities.

Of course, Cuba is vulnerable to Soviet influence because a withdrawal of favorable trade agreements and aid would be disastrous to the Cuban economy. Since 1970, the Cuban leadership appears to have accepted the reality that this economic dependence results from an inherited neocolonial economic structure whose contradictions allowed the revolution to come to power in 1959; that economic diversification to end dependence will require still more time; and that until this transformation is accomplished, there is no alternative to dependence and consequent vulnerability to Soviet influence.

In light of this vulnerability, an over-riding priority for the future of socialist development in Cuba is the avoidance of the political dependence characteristic of dependent capitalism. In the imperialist-dominated countries, the ruling classes are in charge of a system of exploitation. They rely on support of the imperial center to maintain their rule. Within this structure, conflicts exist between these comprador classes and the interests of the center. Efforts of dependent ruling classes to press their interests are necessarily constrained because they can't mobilize on their behalf the workers and peasants over whom they rule.

While it is possible for this condition of political dependence to prevail in relations among countries with state- or otherwise collectively owned and planned economies, economic dependence such as that to which Cuba is subject need not lead to political dependence. Many of the instruments of domination present in dependent capitalism, such as direct foreign ownership and ideological and cultural penetration can be controlled by a socialist leadership. Most important is the maintenance of national solidarity based on an identity of interests between the leadership strata and the population. If a gap were to arise, the interests of the leadership strata could become aligned with the country with which the relation of economic dependence prevails, rather than with the people. The result would be a comprador party or state apparatus. On the contrary, the maintenance of solidarity enables the leadership to rely upon mass support to accept great sacrifices, should they become necessary to defy a country which seeks to use economic dependence to impose policies that fundamentally distort the process of socialist development.

In this light, the continuing development of political participation and political equality is the fundamental element of Cuba's post-1970 strategy. There are other problems inherent in the process of socialist development which cannot be discussed in this brief article. To date, no fundamental distortions have arisen. While Cuba's future is necessarily uncertain, remarkable progress has been achieved in the economy, in education, in health and social welfare, and in the political capacity of the Cuban people.

NOTES

1. David Barkin, "Cuban Agriculture: A Strategy of Economic Development," David Barkin and Nita Manitzas, eds. *Cuba: The Logic of the Revolution* (Andover, Mass.: Warner Modular Publications, 1973), reprint 261, pp. 1-21.
2. See Bertram Silverman, *Man and Socialism in Cuba: The Great Debate* (New York: Atheneum, 1971).
3. Ibid.
4. See Robert Bernardo, *The Theory of Moral Incentives in Cuba* (Tuscaloosa, Ala.: University of Alabama Press, 1971).
5. Bertram Silverman, "Economic Organization and Social Consciousness: Some Dilemmas of Cuban Socialism," J. Ann Zammit, ed. *The Chilean Road to Socialism* (Sussex: Institute of Development Studies, 1973).

10

Cuba: Redistribution and Growth with Equity

Claes Brundenius

In the 1970s some attention in development economics was, at last, given to the importance of equity, redistribution and satisfying basic needs of the poor majorities in the Third World. A case in point is the publication *Redistribution with Growth*,[1] published by the World Bank and the Sussex Institute of Development Studies. In that report, and in many other subsequent studies by international agencies, Cuba was given considerable attention as a case of basic needs-oriented growth strategies although, it was argued, the price might have been economic growth foregone, at least in the short run, or the so-called trade-off dilemma of growth strategies focusing on equity.[2]

The Cuban achievements in the field of redistribution of income and basic needs satisfaction were recently even recognized by a report on the Cuban economy prepared for the Joint Economic Committee of the United States Congress. This study begins with the following acknowledgment:

> The genuine socio-economic and political accomplishments of the Cuban revolution have attracted international attention. These accomplishments include:
>
> > A highly egalitarian redistribution of income that has eliminated almost all malnutrition, particularly among children;

Establishment of a national health care program that is superior in the Third World and rivals that of numerous developed countries;

Near total elimination of illiteracy and a highly developed multi-level educational system; and

Development of a relatively well-disciplined and motivated population with a strong sense of national identification.[3]

What is not mentioned in this report, however, is that this Cuban success story of meeting basic needs of the population has since the early 1970s been accompanied by a relatively high rate of sustained economic growth. But this road towards equity with sustained growth has been both bumpy and difficult as I shall discuss briefly in this chapter.

THE REDUCTION OF OPEN UNEMPLOYMENT

Perhaps the most serious problem haunting many underdeveloped countries, including those in Latin America, is that of high rates of open unemployment coupled with perhaps half the population of working age being underemployed in subsistence agriculture and in the service sector in exploding cities. The eradication of mass unemployment had been one of the priorities outlined in the Program Manifesto of the 26th of July Movement where it was stated: "there cannot be democracy or social justice if man does not have the means to satisfy in an honourable way his material needs...[and] the state is obliged to provide those means, principally in the form of adequate production instruments and well-paid opportunities to work."[4] On the eve of the revolution over half of the rural labor force of 900,000 workers were employed in the cane fields, and during the "dead season" it has been estimated that more than 400,000 workers were unemployed, the majority of them sugar workers.[5] These numbers represented about 20 percent of the total labor force, but even during the *zafra* (November through April) open unemployment was as high as 9–11 percent.[6]

In spite of the determined efforts by the government to tackle the problems of those deprived of adequate work, open unemployment was as high as 9 percent as late as 1962 (see Table 10.1). But then,

TABLE 10.1. Labor Force Absorption Indicators for Cuba, 1958–81

Year	Total Labor Force (000)	Female Labor Force (000)	Female Participation (%)	Open Unemployment (000)	Open Unemployment (%)
1958	2,218	290	13.1	262	11.8
1962	2,481	n.a.	n.a.	215	9.0
1968	2,579	407	15.8	110	4.3
1970	2,633	482	18.3	34	1.3
1972	2,787	576	20.7	78	2.8
1974	2,947	688	23.3	116	3.9
1976	3,117	823	26.4	151	4.8
1978	3,339	983	29.4	178	5.3
1980	3,527	1,108	31.4	146	4.1
1981	3,703	1,219	32.9	126	3.4

Source: Brundenius, *Economic Growth, Basic Needs and Income Distribution in Revolutionary Cuba* (Lund: Research Policy Institute, 1981), Table 8.1, and Brundenius, *Revolutionary Cuba: The Challenge of Economic Growth with Equity* (Boulder, Colo.: Westview Press, 1984), Table 3.5.

during the following six years, the unemployment rate went down to 4.3 percent thanks to mass mobilization, the expansion of the educational system (which meant young people spent more years in school), and, not least, the effects of massive emigration particularly during the first five years of the revolution. By 1970—the year of the 10-million-ton *zafra*—the unemployment rate was as low as 1.3 percent (see Table 10.1). It is probable that at least some portion of the 1.3 percent belongs to what is sometimes called "frictional" unemployed in the industrial countries in the capitalist world. At any rate, the problem by the end of the 1960s was no longer eradication of open unemployment so much as getting enough skilled people to do a particular job at a particular time.

Women have always constituted a large labor reserve in Cuba, as in most other parts of Latin America, but they have seldom been motivated to join the labor force. This is partly due to attitudes and partly a reflection of already high unemployment and underemployment rates. Since the revolution, considerable efforts have gone into changing these attitudes, and with the expansion of the educational system it has been natural for girls to look for jobs after finishing school. When this new generation of girls, with at least six years of primary education, started leaving school at the beginning of the 1970s, female participation rates also increased dramatically (see Table 10.1).

As a matter of fact, the female labor force more than doubled between 1970 and 1981. Of the more than a million new jobs created in this period, almost 70 percent were occupied by women. Ironically, however, this explosion of the female labor force took place when the government was pleading for increased productivity in all fields and making commitments to link wages to productivity. These contradictory trends no doubt help to explain the temporary increase in unemployment rates in the late 1970s. In fact, female unemployment explains the major part of the unemployment levels in those years.[7]

SATISFACTION OF BASIC NEEDS

When the Programme of Action, adopted by the World Employment Conference in 1976, declared that "strategies and national development plans should include explicitly as a priority objective the promotion of employment and the satisfaction of the basic needs of each country's population,"[8] the Cuban delegation probably could not have agreed more. Even if these priorities have not always been specifically spelled out, they have been self-evident goals in all Cuban development plans since 1959. But how successful have these basic needs-oriented strategies been? In order to get some quantitative indicator of the Cuban performance in satisfying the basic needs of its population, I have tried to construct indices of the availability of basic goods and services per capita in Cuba since the revolution. The index is based on quantity data for the following broad basic-needs categories: food and beverages, clothing, housing, education, and health. The quantity data have then been weighted with constant shadow prices.[9]

The indices in Table 10.2 show that Cuba has done fairly well with respect to food and beverages, very well in health, and extremely well in education (that was expected), but has a rather poor record in regard to clothing and housing. The food situation remained critical during the first decade, primarily due to inefficient planning, and the textile industry suffered heavily from the embargo policies adopted by the countries that were enemies of the revolution, notably the United States.[10] Quite a lot of raw material for the textile industry, which had formerly been imported, had to be produced with local inputs, a structural transformation that has been long and difficult.

TABLE 10.2. Availability of Basic Goods and Services per Capita in Cuba, 1958-1978 (1958 = 100)

Year	Food and Beverages	Clothing	Housing	Education	Health
1958	100	100	100	100	100
1962	94	88	107	167	103
1968	107	81	105	180	113
1972	122	96	103	242	113
1974	123	87	103	338	139
1976	126	104	103	528	163
1978	127	98	104	595	187
1982	153	117	119	623	213

Source: Brundenius (1984), Table 4 and 1982 estimates based on *Boletín Estadístico Mensual de Cuba*, October 1983.

Housing construction boomed during the first years of the revolution when some 17,000 dwelling units, on the average, were built annually.[11] Then, during the hard years after 1963 and through 1970, annual housing construction dwindled drastically when priority in the construction industry was given to building infrastructures (roads, dams, etc.), schools, and industrial plans. By the end of the 1970s housing construction had again reached an annual level of 17,000 to 20,000 units but was far from the goal of 70,000 to 80,000 new homes to be built annually, beginning in 1975, and was just about enough to make up for the population growth and the annual demolition of old houses.[12]

However, with the rapid increase in output of construction materials at the end of the 1970s and early 1980s, housing construction is now booming. In 1983 state enterprises built more than 30,000 new homes, and according to a recent census, individuals had built a further 70,000 homes on their own.[13] The reason for this upsurge in building homes on individual initiative is that since the beginning of the 1980s Cubans can, through the Committees for the Defense of the Revolution, purchase construction materials directly and also hire construction workers to help in building new homes. According to a special census taken in 1983, people built 180,000 new homes between January 1981 and November 1983.[14]

The Cuban health record is impressive, especially considering that more than one-third of all doctors left the country during the first three

TABLE 10.3. Medical Services in Cuba, 1958-82

	1958	1962	1968	1972	1974	1976	1978	1982
Physicians								
Number	6,257	6,570	6,000	6,549	8,190	10,671	14,388	17,231
Per 1,000 inhabitants	0.93	0.91	0.72	0.74	0.89	1.13	1.48	1.75
Dentists								
Number	2,100	1,054	1,100	1,346	2,029	2,425	3,356	4,774
Per 1,000 inhabitants	0.31	0.15	0.13	0.15	0.22	0.26	0.34	0.49
Nurses								
Number	5,000	6,724	13,000	13,871	19,131	23,725	26,457	31,702
Per 1,000 inhabitants	0.74	0.93	1.57	1.57	2.08	2.51	2.72	3.22
Hospital beds								
Number	28,536	36,487	41,027	40,313	44,739	42,940	42,988	48,186
Per 1,000 inhabitants	4.22	5.03	4.95	4.55	4.83	4.53	4.45	4.90

Source: Brundenius (1984), Table 4.7 and 1982 estimates based on *Cuba en 1982* (Havana, 1983).

years after the revolution. Medical services suffered again during the first decade (1960s) when the Ministry of Education and the universities, in order to compensate for this brain drain, reduced the requirements for medical professions.[15]

The health situation also deteriorated in those years. For example, the infant mortality rate rose slightly in the 1960s, but since then has gradually fallen and in 1983 was as low as 16.1 per thousand, one of the lowest rates recorded in the Third World.[16] During the second decade many diseases were completely eradicated in Cuba (malaria and poliomyelitis), and mortality rates from diseases such as tuberculosis, diphtheria, and intestinal parasitism were sharply reduced.[17] This is, no doubt, the result of the rapid expansion of medical facilities in the 1970s, especially as regards the number of physicians, dentists, and nurses (see Table 10.3). The success is particularly due to the extension of medical services to the rural areas. Medical treatment is totally free and newly graduated doctors have an obligatory service for at least two years in the countryside. While the administration of health has been centralized, the actual service has been very much decentralized. Free medical care has been provided in conjunction with the mobilization of the population to be immunized, give blood donations, clear garbage dumps, and similar activities, usually organized by the numerous committees for the defense of the revolution.[18]

The educational expansion is perhaps the most spectacular accomplishment of the Cuban Revolution. Chapter 1 by Marvin Leiner provides a discussion of these accomplishments, including among other considerations the historic literacy campaign, increasing levels of schooling, adult education, the upsurge in the rural areas and the *escuelas en el campo* program, and the expansion of higher education.

REDISTRIBUTION OF INCOMES AND ASSETS

Although little quantitative information has been supplied by the Cuban government to support the claim that a radical redistribution of incomes and assets has taken place in the country since the revolution, few observers of the Cuban Revolution seem to doubt it. As a matter of fact, Dudley Seers thinks that "the degree of equality in Cuba is now probably unique,"[19] and Robert Bernardo even argues that Cuba "is the first [country] to institutionalize the communist or egalitarian rule of production and distribution."[20] Although those claims may be somewhat exaggerated, they nevertheless reflect the large number of redistributive reforms and laws enacted following the revolution, especially during the first ten years.

The most important reform was the Agrarian Reform Law of May 1959. To summarize, it allowed for:

1. a maximum limit of 400 hectares on land ownership,
2. the transfer of land to those who farm it but do not own it,
3. the establishment of People's Farms and Sugar Cooperatives in place of the large expropriated sugar estates,
4. the nationalization of 40 percent of all rural property, and
5. compensation to owners of expropriated land in the form of Agrarian Bonds, redeemable within a period of 20 years and with a 4.5 percent interest rate.[21]

The Agrarian Reform Law had, of course, a tremendous effect on income distribution in the rural areas, not only because the large *latifundistas* were deprived of much of their land, but also because the small farmer could get land very cheaply. As a matter of fact, the first 27 hectares of land were given him free, along with the right to purchase an additional 40 hectares. It has been estimated that some 100,000 *campesinos* benefited from this reform.[22] In October 1963, a second and final Agrarian Reform Law was passed, limiting private land ownership to 67 hectares.[23]

In the urban sector, the most effective redistributive reform was the Rent Reform of March 1959, forcing reductions of 50 percent in rents of less than 100 pesos per month and of 30 or 40 percent for rents in the higher brackets. The wealthy were shocked by this drastic measure, denounced it as virtual confiscation of their private property, and considered it Castro's first "betrayal" of the bourgeois supporters of the revolution.[24] However, there were many other reforms and laws that meant de facto redistribution of income and wealth. For instance, the minimum salary was raised; prices on medicine, electricity, and gas were lowered; gambling and prostitution were suppressed; back payments of salaries and retirement pensions of people fired during the Batista regime were made; and the establishment of "people's stores" (especially in the rural areas) guaranteed the supply of basic goods at low prices.[25]

The redistribution of income during 1959 and 1960 was impressive indeed. Exactly how much was redistributed is not known, but it has been calculated that more than 500 million pesos annually, or 20 percent of the average national income for 1959–1960, was redistributed in those years.[26] According to one official source, the proportion of the labor force earning more than 75 pesos monthly rose from 51.5 to 60.8 percent (and in the rural areas from 27.2 to 34.2 percent) between January 1958 and January 1961.[27] It has been estimated that in the same period, as a result of the negotiation of new labor contracts, wages and salaries increased between 15 and 30 percent.[28]

Although there are no official statistics on distribution of income in Cuba, either before the revolution or after, I have ventured to make some estimates for the years 1953, 1962, and 1973, of which the summary findings are presented in Table 10.4. The methodology I employed has been explained elsewhere,[29] and will not be repeated here, although it should be pointed out that the 1962 figures are slightly revised, since they did not, in the earlier version, include estimates for the private sector (which was still important at the time, especially in agriculture).

The figures in Table 10.4 suggest that an important redistribution of income took place just after the revolution, principally benefiting the poorest 40 percent of the population, although the middle deciles also appear to have gained. Between 1962 and 1973 a further redistribution of income took place, but at a much slower pace than before. This is somewhat surprising, considering that a new, more profound Agrarian Reform was decreed in October 1963, and that moral incentives were to take priority over material incentives in accordance with resolutions adopted at the Twelfth Workers' Congress in 1966.[30] Of these events, perhaps the second Agrarian Reform had the deepest effect on income distribution. In retrospect it seems that moral incentives produce increased inequalities rather than the reverse. The reason, it is argued, is that income increases went to the wrong people. Those who wanted to work more did not get any more money out of it, while those who did not want to work more for the same rate could still earn money by holding extra jobs.[31]

In the period 1962–1973, there was no doubt a drive toward narrowing income differentials, especially after the victory of moral over material incentives was proclaimed at the Twelfth Workers' Congress in 1966, but this is not the same as saying that existing wage scales actually changed. In fact, the same wage scales that were introduced in 1962–1963 were still being applied at the end of the 1970s, and they were not replaced until July 1980 (see Table 10.4). Egalitarianism in the 1960s was advanced instead through the elimination of bonuses, the

TABLE 10.4. Estimated Income Distribution in Cuba in 1953, 1962, 1973, and 1978

(IS = income shares % CS = cumulative shares %)

Deciles	1953 IS	1953 CS	1962 IS	1962 CS	1973 IS	1973 CS	1978 IS	1978 CS
0–10	0.6	0.6	2.5	2.5	2.9	2.9	5.1	5.1
10–20	1.5	2.1	3.7	6.2	4.9	7.8	5.9	11.0
20–30	1.9	4.0	4.8	11.0	5.4	13.2	6.5	17.5
30–40	2.2	6.2	6.2	17.2	7.1	20.3	7.3	24.8
40–50	4.6	10.8	6.8	24.0	8.7	29.0	8.0	32.8
50–60	6.4	17.2	9.5	33.5	10.5	39.5	8.5	41.3
60–70	10.8	28.0	12.0	45.5	12.5	52.0	9.9	51.2
70–80	12.0	40.0	13.1	58.6	13.5	65.5	12.8	64.0
80–90	21.5	61.5	18.4	77.0	15.1	80.6	14.9	78.9
90–100	38.5	100.0	23.0	100.0	19.4	100.0	21.1	100.0
(Top 5 percent)	(28.0)		(12.7)		(9.5)		(11.0)	
TOTAL	100.0		100.0		100.0			
Gini coefficients		0.56		0.35		0.28		0.25

Source: Brundenius (1984), Tables 5.2, 5.3, and 5.6.

renouncement of overtime pay, and voluntary, unpaid mobilization campaigns.[32] How much these actions really meant in egalitarian terms is difficult to evaluate, but an estimate of income distribution in 1983 (the year of the Thirteenth Workers' Congress when material incentives were reinstated), based on the same methods as the 1962 estimate except for the exclusion of the private sector,[33] shows that a rather insignificant redistribution took place, at least in relation to the 1959–1961 period. The major group to benefit in the later period was again the agricultural workers as their average annual income (in the state sector) increased from 954 pesos in 1962 to 1,416 in 1973, compared to a decrease in the industrial average from 1,941 to 1,603 pesos during the same period.[34] One explanation could be that agricultural workers were promoted to higher grades on the applicable wage scale at the same time as new industrial workers were being placed in lower grades.

Looking at the trend during the latter half of the 1970s, one would perhaps expect a regressive redistribution of income as a result of the new policy of encouraging productivity increases through material incentives. However, an estimate of the income distribution in 1978 (based on the same method as before but including the private sector) shows that the income differentials remained almost the same as in 1973, although they increased slightly for the bottom decile, but the assumption of a constant four-to-one wage span in each of the sectors over time is probably unrealistic. Since the wage scales did not change between 1963 and 1979, it would seem that the only redistribution that took place in this period was as a result of movements of workers up or down the existing wage scale (and in most cases up, one has to assume).

I thus decided to make an alternative estimate for 1978 based on the distribution of the state civilian labor force affected by the various wage scales (information not available for 1973). The result of this alternative estimate of income distribution in 1978 shows, perhaps surprisingly, a more egalitarian distribution than when one applies the other assumption (a four-to-one differential in each sector). One reason may be that the wage scales do not include bonuses and overtime pay (which were virtually abolished between 1966 and 1973), and the conclusion could be that the real income distribution in 1978 lies somewhere in between the two 1978 estimates.

An interesting question is how the new wage scales being introduced in Cuba are likely to affect the existing distribution of income. One would perhaps expect a widening of the differentials in line with the new policy (after 1973) of reward according to work accomplished. The new wage scales as such, however, do not point in this direction. There generally is a narrowing of the gap between the highest and the lowest wage paid in each category, and in the case of the highest paid categories—technical personnel and executives—the gap has narrowed considerably as there is a ceiling of 450 pesos in each. What is important, however, is that these are the basic wages applied. They do not include bonuses, overtime pay, and other fringe benefits. But even if those extras were included, it is not at all certain that there would be a regressive income redistribution since the material incentives apply to the lowest paid people at least as much as to those at the top of the wage scale. Another fact is that the so-called historical wage (applicable to those people who had higher wages before the introduction of the new wage scales in 1962) had gradually lost its importance.[35] In 1962, no less than 79.9 percent had the right to such compensation, but by 1972, this share had fallen to 18.9 percent, and by the end of the 1970s, the share was probably less than 10 percent.[36]

Table 10.5. Levels of Growth of Per Capita Income by Strata—Brazil, Cuba, and Peru (Equivalent of US $ 1980).

	GDP/Capita Dollars	Per Capita Income of Poorest 40%		Per Capita Income of Richest 5%	
		Dollars	Share of Total Inc.	Dollars	Share of Total Inc.
Brazil					
1960	651	197	11.5%	3,788	27.7%
1970	924	233	10.1%	6,450	34.9%
1980	1,652	401	9.9%	11,298	34.2%
Annual rate of growth					
1960–1970	3.5%	1.7%		5.3%	
1970–1980	5.9%	5.4%		5.6%	
Cuba					
1958*	866	182	6.5%	5,947	26.5%
1962	882	379	17.2%	2,237	12.7%
1973	996	506	20.3%	1,892	9.5%
1978	1,395	865	24.8%	3,068	11.0%
Annual rate of growth					
1958–1962	0.5%	18.3%		−24.4%	
1962–1973	1.1%	2.6%		−1.5%	
1973–1978	6.7%	10.7%		9.7%	
Peru					
1961	925	232	10.0%	4,810	26.0%
1972	1,163	234	9.0%	6,578	33.0%
1979	1,245	197	8.2%	7,255	37.3%
Annual rate of growth					
1961–1972	2.1%	0.1%		2.8%	
1972–1979	1.0%	−2.4%		1.4%	

*based on the assumption that there was no change in income distribution between 1953 and 1958.

Source: Brundenius (1984), Table 6.3.

The income redistribution for the benefit of the poor that has taken place in Cuba since 1959, although not unique in the world, is certainly unique in Latin America. In most Latin American countries the total income share of the poorest 40 percent of the population seldom reaches 10 percent,[37] and in many countries the share has even been decreasing during the last two decades. That is the case, for instance, in Brazil and Peru. Brazil was chosen because it is the country that experienced the most rapid growth in Latin America after 1960, and Peru was included because of the structural reforms introduced by the Velasco government between 1968 and 1975—reforms that aimed at radically transforming the economy of the country, including income distribution. In Brazil, the poorest 40 percent received only 9.9 percent of the income in 1980, compared to 10.1 percent in 1970, and 11.5 percent in 1960 (see Table 10.5).[38] In Peru the trend has been even worse. While in 1961 the poorest 40 percent got 10 percent of the income, by 1972 this share had decreased to 9 percent and by 1979 to 8.2 percent.

The result of this exercise is rather striking. Brazil is a good example of the limited effects of the so-called trickle-down policies. In spite of unprecedented growth in Brazil after 1960, the per capita income of the poorest 40 percent only doubled (from $197 to $401) in twenty years. In Cuba on the other hand, per capita income of the same income group increased by almost five times (from $182 to $865) in the same period of time. Peru has experienced slow growth, and its income disparities have increased, with the poorest 40 percent receiving not only relatively smaller shares of income but also living poorer in absolute terms (with income levels falling from $232 to $197 between 1961 and 1979). A tentative conclusion then seems to be that rapid growth as such does not necessarily increase the income levels of the poorer people dramatically, but the Cuban case also shows that income redistribution alone does not solve the situation of the poor unless the redistribution is accompanied by sustained economic growth of the country in the long run.

EQUITY VERSUS GROWTH: IS THERE A TRADE-OFF?

Critics of an equity or basic needs-oriented growth strategy often complain that such an approach would sacrifice productive investment, and incentives to work, for the sake of current consumption and welfare, or that there is a so-called trade-off between equity and growth.[39] Cuba has even been cited by one author as a case in point.[40] Dudley Seers, however, finds the controversy misleading and says that "the important question to pose about a country's performance is not, how much did the nation's income grow? But rather, whose income grew? And what sort of production increased?"[41] Furthermore, Norman Hicks has tried to estimate, through regression analysis, the relationship between growth performance and basic needs-oriented strategies among the developing countries in the 1960-1973 period and found "first, it would appear that countries making substantial progress in meeting basic needs do *not* have substantially lower GNP growth rates; and second, the attainment of higher levels of basic-needs satisfaction appears to lead to higher growth rates in the future."[42]

Few countries could illustrate this finding better than Cuba. Firstly, the relatively slow growth rates of the 1960s were not slow compared to the prerevolutionary rates. Secondly, the relatively slow growth certainly is not the result of lower investment levels. On the contrary, while the economy before the revolution had been highly consumption-oriented (for the upper-middle classes), with many imported consumer items, it encountered difficulties soon after the revolution when the income redistribution to the bottom half of the population led to a drastic increase in the demand for basic goods. Since there was not enough installed capacity to satisfy demand, and since there was little chance of getting these goods on the world market due to the embargo by the United States and its allies, a good many resources had to be devoted to investment in new plants and equipment, most of which had to be imported from the socialist countries.

The figures in Table 10.6 strongly indicate that there have indeed been profound economic changes in Cuba since the revolution—the changes were rather modest during the first decade, but they then took place at an accelerated pace in the 1970s. Thus, in spite of a stabilized sugar output by the end of the second decade of about 8 million tons of crude sugar, the share of sugar (both agricultural and industrial activities) fell from 14 to 7.9 percent of GDP between 1970 and 1981, and the agricultural contribution to GDP fell from 18.1 to 12.9 percent during the same period. The simple explanation is that there was a vigorous growth of virtually all industrial activities in the 1970s, with the manufacturing industry as a whole growing at a rate of 7 percent per year and the capital goods industry growing at 15.5 percent per year. Most

TABLE 10.6. **Structural Changes in the Cuban Economy 1961–1981**

	Sector Contribution to GDP (%)			Average Annual Rate of Growth		
	1961	1970	1981	1961–1970	1970–1981	1961–1981
Agriculture[1]	18.2	18.1	12.9	1.5	3.6	2.7
Sugarcane	(7.9)	(9.2)	(4.9)	3.2	1.0	2.0
Other	(10.3)	(8.9)	(8.0)	0.0	5.8	3.1
Industry	31.8	38.4	46.4	3.6	8.4	6.2
Manufacturing	(24.4)	(29.7)	(30.7)	3.6	7.0	5.5
Capital goods	(1.6)	(2.5)	(6.6)	6.5	15.5	11.5
Sugar and derivatives	(4.7)	(4.8)	(3.0)	1.8	2.2	2.0
Construction	(5.2)	(5.7)	(13.0)	2.4	14.2	8.9
Total Sugar[2]	12.6	14.0	7.9	2.7	1.4	2.0
TMP = Total Material Production	50.0	56.5	59.4	2.8	7.1	5.2
GMP = Gross Material Production	82.2	79.9	73.2	0.2	5.9	3.3
NMS = Non-Material Services	17.8	20.1	26.8	2.9	9.3	6.4
GDP = Gross Domestic Product	100.0	100.0	100.0	1.5	6.7	4.3

[1]Including forestry and fishing.
[2]Sugarcane and sugar refining.

Source: Brundenius (1984), Table 3.10.

spectacular was the growth of the construction industry, which increased at a rate of 14.2 percent per year during the period.

The rapid growth of the construction and capital goods industries is also reflected in the accelerated rate of capital accumulation. Gross investments increased from an average of 839 million pesos in the 1960s to an average of almost 2,000 million pesos in the 1970s, and gross investment as a percentage of GDP increased from an average of 17 percent to an average of 26 percent in the same period. Investment allocated to industrial projects increased from 480 million pesos during 1971–1975 to 1,350 million pesos during the first Five-Year Plan (1976–1980).[43]

In 1975 Cuba launched its first Five-Year Plan (1976–1980). The growth targets were, however, too optimistic, with a projected rate of growth of the global economy of 6 percent for the period. This ambitious plan was based on the impressive upsurge of the economy taking place during the first quinquennium of the 1970s when material output increased at an annual rate of 10 percent.

One of the major reasons for the disappointing performance of the economy during the first plan (total material production increased at a rate of 4 percent compared with a planned rate of 6 percent) was no doubt the sudden reverse in the behavior of the world sugar market. The price of sugar had soared in 1974 and for a brief period was as high as 70 cents per pound, an unprecedented figure, and although the price quickly went down to a more normal level, the Cubans still were optimistic that the price would stabilize around 20 cents. But the price went down the drain and during most of the plan period it was below 10 cents, at times even below production cost. This was a very serious situation indeed because the boom years had generated 3.7 billion dollars of credits from the Western World.[44] Now, as a result of disappointing price movements, many industrial projects envisaged by the plan had to be discontinued. As so many times before, the Soviet Union had to come to the rescue of the Cubans, and thanks to improving terms of trade with the Russians the trade balance with them was favorable for the first time since the early 1960s; thus, the overall trade deficit was lower than during the preceding quinquennium.[45]

But it is not only the fall in terms of trade with the West (30 percent lower during 1976-1979 than during 1971-1975[46]) that explains the sluggish growth rates during the last years of the plan. There were also significant difficulties in agricultural and livestock production at the end of the period due to plagues and pests, such as sugar rust, tobacco blue mold, and African swine fever.

* * *

In 1980 Cuba launched its second Five-Year plan (1981-1985) and the tone of the declared goals of the plan was what one might call cautiously optimistic. The plan envisaged an annual rate of growth of the economy of 5 percent, and personal consumption was expected to increase by 4 percent a year. At the same time important resources were going to be diverted to heavy industry in order to diminish the foreign dependency in the long run. One of the most determined efforts of the plan was to enter into the construction of some 200,000 housing units, more than twice the number achieved during the first plan.

TABLE 10.7. Annual Growth Rates of Material Production During the First* and Second** Five-Year Plans

	Agriculture Forestry and Fishing	Mining Manufacturing and Electricity	Construction Industry	Total Material Production
First Five-Year Plan				
1976	3.6	3.1	5.6	3.6
1977	4.2	1.1	9.9	3.1
1978	6.2	9.0	7.4	8.2
1979	2.7	1.9	0.8	1.9
1980	4.5	2.5	−0.4	2.4
Average 1976-80	4.2	3.7	4.9	4.0
Second Five-Year Plan				
1981	14.3	17.7	17.6	16.9
1982	2.4	2.1	0.8	1.9
1983	1.1	6.6	11.6	6.5

* Constant 1965 prices.
**Constant 1981 prices.

Sources: Brundenius (1981), Table 8.10 and estimates by the author (for the perio 1981–83) based on official data in *Anuario Estadístico de Cuba 1981* (Havana, 1983) and th *Anuario Estadístico de Cuba 1982* (Havana, 1984).

In contrast to the first Five-Year plan, the second plan was initiate with a real boom in the economy (see Table 10.7). In 1981 it estimated that material production increased by almost 17 percent (i constant prices), spearheaded by the manufacturing and constructic industries increasing by almost 18 percent, but with agriculture followir suit not far behind, with an impressive 14 percent. Important in th remarkable increase in agricultural output is that most of it was accounte for by the non-sugar sector.

During the last years, growth rates have slowed down (particular in 1982) but the accumulated growth rate as of 1983 indicates th Cuba is very likely to achieve most of its goals set for the target ye 1985. In 1984 the Cuban economy was estimated to increase by 4.5–5 percent, implying an accumulated increase in the first four years of t plan of not less than 33 percent, quite an achievement considering t deep recession affecting practically all other countries in Latin America in the same period.

NOTES

1. H. Chenery et al., *Redistribution with Growth* (London: Oxford University Press, 1974).

2. Dudley Seers, "The Cuban Experience," in H. Chenery et al., *Redistribution with Growth*; Oxford, 1974; Paul Streeten, "Growth, Redistribution and Basic Human Needs," in Claes Brundenius and Mats Lundahl, eds., *Developmental Strategies and Basic Needs in Latin America* (Boulder, Colo.: Westview Press, 1982).

3. Lawrence Theriot, *Cuba Faces the Economic Realities of the 1980's*, Joint Economic Committee, Congress of the United States, March 22, 1982 (Washington, D.C.: Government Printing Office, 1982), p. 5.

4. "Program Manifesto of the 26th of July Movement," in Rolando E. Bonachea and Nelson P. Valdés, eds., *Cuba in Revolution* (New York: Doubleday, 1974), p. 131.

5. James O'Connor, *The Origins of Socialism in Cuba* (Ithaca, NY: Cornell University Press, 1970), p. 182.

6. Dudley Seers et al., *Cuba—The Economic and Social Revolution* (Chapel Hill, N.C.: University of North Carolina Press, 1964), p. 84.

7. Claes Brundenius, "Some Notes on the Development of the Cuban Labor Force, 1970-1980," *Cuban Studies*, vol. 13, no. 2 (1983).

8. International Labor Office, *Employment, Growth and Basic Needs: A One-World Problem* (New York: International Labor Office, 1977), p. 191.

9. Claes Brundenius, *Revolutionary Cuba. The Challenge of Economic Growth with Equity* (Boulder, Colo.: Westview Press, 1984), chapter 4.

10. Gunnar Adler-Karlsson, *Western Economic Warfare 1947-1967* (Stockholm: Almquist and Wiksell, 1968), chapter 17.

11. Ministerio de Relaciones Exteriores, *Profile of Cuba* (Havana: MINREX, 1966), p. 205.

12. Carmelo Mesa-Lago, *Cuba in the 1970s* (Albuquerque: University of New Mexico Press, 1974), p. 46.

13. Humberto Pérez, "1983 Economic Performance," *Granma Weekly Review*, January 1, 1984.

14. Ibid.

15. Carmelo Mesa-Lago, "Economic Policies and Growth," in Carmelo Mesa-Lago, ed., *Revolutionary Change in Cuba* (Pittsburgh: University of Pittsburgh Press, 1973), p. 292.

16. *Granma Weekly Review*, January 1, 1984; World Bank, *World Development Report 1983*, (Washington, D.C.: 1983), table 23.

17. Ministerio de Salud, *Informe anual de 1979*, (Havana: Ministerio de Salud, 1980).
18. Ricardo Leyva, "Health and Revolution in Cuba," in Rolando E. Bonachea and Nelson P. Valdés, eds., *Cuba in Revolution* (New York: Doubleday, 1972), p. 495.
19. Seers, "The Cuban Experience," p. 262.
20. Robert Bernardo, *The Theory of Moral Incentives in Cuba* (Tuscaloosa, Ala.: University of Alabama Press, 1971), p. ix.
21. Ministerio de Relaciones Exteriores, *Profile of Cuba*, (Havana: MINREX, 1966), p. 120.
22. Ibid.
23. Ibid., p. 121.
24. J.P. Morray, *The Second Revolution in Cuba* (New York: Monthly Review Press, 1962), p. 24.
25. Archibald Ritter, *The Economic Development of Revolutionary Cuba* (New York: Praeger, 1974), p. 107.
26. José-Luis Rodríguez, "Política económica de la revolución cubana (1959–60)," *Economía y desarrollo*, no. 54 (1979), p. 148.
27. O'Connor, *Origins of Socialism in Cuba*, p. 245.
28. Ritter, *Economic Development of Revolutionary Cuba*, p. 107.
29. Claes Brundenius, "Measuring Income Distribution in Pre- and Post-revolutionary Cuba," *Cuban Studies*, vol. 9, no. 2 (1979).
30. Mesa-Lago, "Economic Policies and Growth," p. 211.
31. Dr. Carlos Rafael Rodríguez, vice-president of the Council of State and the Council of Ministers, Havana, November 4, 1980.
32. Brundenius, *Revolutionary Cuba*, p. 109.
33. Ibid., Tables 5.6 and A 2.31.
34. Comité Estatal de Estadísticas, *Anuario estadístico de Cuba 1980* (Havana: Comité Estatal de Estadísticas, 1980).
35. The idea behind the historical wage was that wage or salary earners should not lose with the introduction of the new wage scales in 1962, but the historical wage was attributed to the individual as such and not to any particular occupational group.
36. Fidel Castro, *Informe central al I Congreso del Partido Comunista de Cuba* (Havana: Partido Comunista de Cuba, 1975), p. 149.
37. Shail Jain, *Size Distribution of Income: A Compilation of Data* (Washington, D.C.: World Bank, 1975).
38. Brundenius, *Revolutionary Cuba*, Table 6.3.
39. Streeten, "Growth, Redistribution and Basic Human Needs."
40. Carmelo Mesa-Lago, "Cuba's Centrally Planned Economy: An Equity Trade-Off for Growth," Conference on Models of Political and Economic Change in Latin America, Vanderbilt University, Nashville, Tennessee, November 3–5, 1983.

41. Seers, "The Cuban Experience," p. 262.
42. Norman Hicks, "Growth vs. Basic Needs: Is there a trade-off?," *World Development*, vol. 7 (1979), p. 992.
43. Brundenius, *Revolutionary Cuba*, chapter 3.
44. Ibid.
45. Olga Torres, "El desarrollo de la economía cubana a partir de 1959," *Comercio Exterior*, vol. 31, no. 3 (March 1981), Table 1.
46. Ibid., Table 3.

11

Cuban Economic Planning: Organization and Performance

Andrew Zimbalist

Imagine parenting two sons: a four-year-old and a six-year-old. The four-year-old has taken to hiding and losing puzzle pieces. Further suppose that your younger son has a friend who comes to visit and paints over several of the remaining pieces, creating a different image. Completing such a puzzle is a bit like analyzing Cuba's system of economic planning.

Despite the challenge and complexity of this task, I am impelled to take a stab at it due to the paucity of serious and reliable scholarship on this very important subject. The only detailed studies of economic administration under Castro refer to the early sixties.[1] More recent treatments deal with general development strategy and economic performance.[2] Carmelo Mesa-Lago has included bits of cursory analysis on Cuban planning during the 1970s in some of his more recent work, but I find his comments on the whole to be rather unimaginative, unconvincing, and misleading. For instance, in his 1981 book, *The Economy of Socialist Cuba: A Two Decade Appraisal*, Mesa-Lago, the most prominent U.S. analyst of the Cuban economy, repeatedly refers to Cuba's new, post-1976 planning system as "Soviet-styled."[3] At best, this is an accurate description of the *form* of Cuban planning. The *content* or practice of Cuban planning is quite different from the *content* of Soviet planning.

I shall argue that understanding the content of planning is essential to an appreciation of the system's laws of motion and its performance.

In particular, embodied in the formal structure of planning is a set of power relations and decision-making processes which condition the behavior of the system. Planned economies function on the basis of administrative decision making. Market forces are broadly constrained and circumscribed by the plan. They are not permitted to play the role of providing ubiquitous (price) signals on a decentralized basis to all economic actors.

In economies where market forces dominate, successful economic performance is congruent with self-interested decision making by individuals. Planned economies have attempted to simulate market forces and provide material incentives to motivate desired behavior by managers and workers. Since almost all prices in planned economies are centrally administered, however, the use of material incentives inevitably engenders behavior inconsistent with welfare maximization as defined by the plan. When in 1965, for instance, the Soviets attempted to change their primary enterprise success indicator from physical quantity of output to profitability, the absence of scarcity prices resulted in the distortion of the product mix and the frequent reward of inefficient, laggard enterprises.

The effort in centrally planned economies to use simulated market signals and material incentives is further frustrated by the existence of widespread shortages.[4] For example, it is difficult to motivate greater work effort with higher pay, if the desired goods are not available to be purchased.

In contrast to a decentralized market system, planned economies rely on extensive communication and interagency (also interpersonal) decision making. Any hopes of balancing the economy are contingent on a maximum flow of timely and accurate information (not provided automatically through prices as in a market system). Since material incentives function inadequately in such a system, in order to elicit the desired effort and information other incentives must be present.[5] Coercion and appeals to nationalism or the commonweal may work under special circumstances and in limited ways. Ultimately, however, motivational success will be proportional to the extent of goal internalization by the planners, managers, and workers. That is, economic agents will engage in desired behavior to the degree that they feel identified with the processes, goals, and outcomes of their work center and the entire economy. Furthermore, in the long run such an identification can be sustained only when there is a sense of participation in goal formulation and no violation of prevailing norms of distributional equity in outcomes.[6]

In short, the power relations and decision-making processes embodied in the planning system or the *content* of planning will impact significantly upon economic performance. Although puzzle pieces are sometimes missing and sometimes fuzzy, I will outline below the case that planning in Cuba has evolved in a more decentralized and participatory fashion than in the Soviet Union. These features, in turn, have had a salutary effect on performance. What follows attempts to complement the discussions of economic development and social achievements of the revolution appearing in Sections II and IV of this volume.

PLANNING IN THE SIXTIES

Early efforts at economic planning were frustrated by political instability and lack of leadership coherence. After the attempt to transplant very centralized planning techniques from Czechoslovakia proved unworkable, Cuban economic administration came to be based on poorly coordinated and inefficiently implemented mini-plans which concentrated on prioritized sectors.

In 1963 an extensive debate began over the best use of incentives and methods of planning.[7] Two basic positions were propounded. Ché Guevara argued for central planning, budgetary accounting, and moral incentives. Moral incentives, Guevara maintained, were necessary to create a new socialist consciousness, although he recognized that material incentives could not be abandoned all at once. He urged, therefore, that material incentives be collective (i.e., they should pertain to a group of workers rather than an individual worker) and be limited in scope. According to Guevara, Cuba's low level of material development meant that an extensive use of material incentives, and the corresponding income differentiation, would re-create the widespread poverty of the Batista era.

The other side of the debate was represented most forcefully by Carlos Rafael Rodríguez, a prominent member of the Party's Central Committee. He argued for central planning, economic accounting, and material incentives. Under budgetary accounting, enterprises are financed out of the central budget and are not expected to balance their own costs and revenues or to yield a surplus. Rodríguez believed budgetary accounting encouraged inefficiency. Under economic accounting or self-financing, each enterprise would be expected to balance its budget or yield a net income. Material incentives, he claimed, were imperative to motivate Cuban workers who were not ideologically ready (just five years into the revolution) for the communist principle of distribution: "from each according to their ability, to each according to their need." (This is contrasted with the socialist principle: "from each according to their ability, to each according to their work.") Moral incentives would only be efficacious after the forces of production were more developed.

At the time of the debate, economic management consisted of a rather ad hoc version of central planning, a mixture of budgetary and economic accounting and extensive use of individual material incentives. (Between 1963 and 1966 national wage scales were introduced along with job norms or work quotas. Workers' wages went up .5 percent for every 1 percent production increase above their norm.) Guevara's position was the basis for major economic policy changes beginning in 1966. Indeed, new policies with regard to planning and incentives went considerably beyond the proposals of Ché Guevara.

In 1966, the powers of JUCEPLAN (the Cuban Central Planning Board) were further reduced, and formal one year planning was abandoned. Castro's idea of mini-plans which, in essence, prioritized a few sectors (such as sugar) gained increasing prominence. Non-prioritized sectors, however, fared poorly and bottlenecks spread throughout the economy. The combination of bottlenecks and the high investment ratios of the late sixties (investment as a share of Gross Material Product reached an estimated 27 percent in 1967 and 31 percent in 1968)[8] created serious shortages of consumer goods. Thus, even if the leadership had wanted to, it would have been impossible to meaningfully implement a policy of material incentives. That is, workers could hardly be expected to work harder to earn more when there were insufficient, price-controlled goods on which to spend their income.

The incentive policies of the late sixties, even considering the requirements of Cuba's accumulation strategy, were idealistic in the extreme. The tie between wages and productivity were severed and replaced by a panoply of moral incentives. The economy underwent demonetization as free services were extended to many items. The prices of other basic services and goods were heavily subsidized. The interest rate on credit to enterprises was abolished in 1967 as were income taxes on private farmers. Small private plots on state farms were ended as was overtime pay.

Two additional factors contributed to production problems at the time. First, in 1968 it was decided to nationalize all retail and small businesses, thrusting tens of thousands of workers into the state sector. The organization of the state planning apparatus was already insufficient to plan for and manage large and medium-size industry. Adding this new sector, very dispersed and numerous by nature, made the tasks of coordination overbearing. Moreover, the problems of training and disciplining these new workers were monumental.

Second, the government had placed an irrational emphasis on attaining the ten-million-ton sugar harvest in 1970. This resulted in an enormous diversion of resources, including the use of 170,000 industrial workers in the harvest. In the end, the 1970 harvest reached 8.5 million tons, a record, but short of the goal upon which Castro had staked the honor of the revolution.

Production data series for the 1960s are spotty, and growth estimates from different sources vary widely.[9] National income per capita appears to have increased slightly from 1962 to 1965 and then fallen from 1966 to 1969. After the initial recuperation to 1962, then, there was a seven-year period of stagnation.

If overall production per capita stagnated, then consumer good production per capita fell off appreciably. This, together with the provision of many free services and fixed state prices, led to an excess supply of money in circulation. It was estimated that by 1970 purchasing power exceeded goods supply by 87 percent at existing prices. Before the government could begin to reintroduce material incentives this surplus of money had to be dried up. Beginning in 1970, several measures were taken to accomplish this, including large price increases for non-basic or above-ration goods and a sharp reduction in the investment ratio. More basic, institutional changes were to come.

PLANNING IN THE EARLY 1970s

In Castro's speech of May 20, 1970 on the failure to reach the 10-million-ton sugar harvest, he repeatedly emphasized the problem of bureaucratic leadership and poor economic management. In his speech of July 26, 1970, Castro again alluded to the sugar harvest failure and reiterated that "the leaders of this Revolution have cost the people too much in our process of learning."[10] Castro was quick to add, however, that the problem did not lie with specific individuals; rather, it was a question of the failure of the nation to work as a collectivity:

> We believe this is a problem of the whole people! And we sincerely believe that the only way we can solve the problem we have today is by all working together—all of us—from the men in the highest positions of responsibility in the Party and state right on down to

those in the most humble industrial plant and not just those in leadership positions there....

Why should a manager have to be absolutely in charge? Why shouldn't we begin to introduce representatives of the factory's workers into its management? Why not have confidence? Why not put our trust in that tremendous proletarian spirit?...

...We don't believe that the problem of managing a plant should fall exclusively to the manager. It would really be worthwhile to begin introducing a number of new ideas. There should be a manager, naturally—for there must always be someone accountable—but we must begin to establish a collective body in the management of each plant. A collective body! It should be headed by one man, but it should also be made up of representatives of the advanced workers' movement, the Young Communist League, the Party and the women's front.[11]

Five days later Labor Minister Risquet made a statement on national television criticizing the lack of democracy in Cuba's factories. He made three recommendations: "(a) the unions should be given an opportunity to perform their role; their first duty should be to see that labor legislation is applied and workers' rights protected; (b) the elections of the directorate of the union should not be restricted; there should not be the slightest fear that conditions would be placed on the election of the representatives; there should be no doubt that the election will be free and open; and (c) an investigation should be undertaken on the potential participation of the workers in factory management."[12]

The first actual step along these lines was to revitalize the trade union movement. On November 9, 1970 secret ballot elections were held to choose new union officials. There were 26,427 new locals created and 117,625 officials elected (87 percent for the first time) for two-year terms. Local union officials represent their work centers on higher union bodies confederated along both geographical and product lines.

Cuban trade unions have also been encouraged more and more during the 1970s to serve as autonomous bodies, not subordinate to the Party, the state or to management. (See chapter 15 by Marifeli Pérez-Stable, "Class, Organization, and *Conciencia*: The Cuban Working Class after 1970" and chapter 13 by Rhoda Pearl Rabkin, "Cuban Political Structure: Vanguard Party and the Masses" for further treatment of this and other subjects discussed here.) Figures for 1975 indicate that only around 5 percent of local union leadership belonged to the Party.

Indeed, more recently, unions have been urged to expand their "counterpart" activities, controlling excesses and abuses by local Party leaders, government functionaries, or managers. The more open selection procedures for local leadership and the degree of relative independence of Cuban trade unions stands in contrast to the trade union experience in the Soviet Union.[13]

In early 1973 preparations were made for the 13th National Trade Union Congress (the 12th was in 1966). The "theses" of the Congress were made available at each work center where they were discussed. Delegates were elected to attend the actual Congress in November. Among the major resolutions of the Congress were: (1) the decision to re-invoke the "socialist principle" of remuneration—"from each according to her/his ability, to each according to her/his work"; (2) the decisions to strengthen and extend worker participation in collective management through the union.

The first resolution entailed linking worker income to productivity. Each job was to be assigned an output quota or norm. If the worker fulfilled the norm exactly, he or she would receive the basic wage set for the job established in the national wage scale. For every percent over or under fulfillment the wage would go up or down by the same percent. On the surface, this method resembles the straight-line piece rate system known in many U.S. manufacturing industries. However, the Cubans claim there is one crucial different between the two systems in that the Cuban norms are established in consultation with, and subject to, the approval of the affected workers.

For a variety of reasons these work norms (and their link to income) have been introduced rather slowly. By the last quarter of 1979 only 46.6 percent of the Cuban work force (in the productive sphere) was functioning under this system. One apparent problem is that the norms are generally set unrealistically low. During the last quarter of 1979, 95.5 percent of workers operating with norms either met or exceeded their quotas.[14] It is likely that many of the small percentage who fell below the norm did so due to "external" problems (e.g., production bottlenecks, supply shortages, machinery breakdown, etc.).

Strong emphasis was also placed on collectively based material incentives after 1970. Beginning in 1971, work centers were allocated a number of consumer durables and other items for distribution to the center's workers. In some cases, the size of the allocation was tied to factory performance. Since each year's allocation permitted only a small group of workers to benefit, it was necessary to devise a distribution scheme perceived to be equitable. Through collective discussion in a workers' assembly, beneficiaries would be selected according to merit (attendance and work record) and need (size of family, living conditions, etc.).

The same distribution system was used for housing constructed by "microbrigades." Microbrigades are groups of workers (usually 15 to 40 per work center) who leave their usual workplace to join a state-supplied construction project for a certain period of time. The remaining members of the workplace agree to work harder to maintain production levels. When the housing project is completed, a number of units is assigned to each work center. The microbrigades were begun in mid-1971 and by the mid-seventies were building over 10,000 housing units annually. Their role is less prominent today, being replaced largely by privately contracted housing construction.

The resolution to promote greater popular participation has been implemented on a number of fronts. We shall provide a few examples below. First, as suggested in the speeches of Castro and Risquet, one-man management has been replaced by a Management Council, consisting of the enterprise director, top management assistants, elected representatives from the local Party organization, trade union, and Communist Youth Organization. Generally, this Council meets at least once a week. Second, each production section has a monthly assembly of all workers in the section where matters of production, material supplies, health and safety, worker education programs, labor discipline, etc. are discussed. Attendance at these after-work-hour meetings is optional and appears to be very high (in the 70–95 percent range).[15] Third, each factory workshop elects delegates to attend a quarterly meeting of delegates with the Management Council. In addition, elected trade union committees, labor councils, and other organs are involved in a variety of decisions regarding production, culture, and community at the factory. Popular input into macroeconomic policy and priority setting occurs only indirectly through special commissions of the elected National Assembly of Peoples' Power, the Cuban Federation of Workers, the Institute of Internal Demand, and informal vehicles.

There is some piecemeal evidence of growing worker involvement in enterprise decision making. A 1975 study by Marifeli Pérez-Stable found 85 percent of surveyed workers believed workers must be consulted in enterprise affairs, and 58 percent of this group felt that worker input was already influential and significant.[16] A 1976 survey by José Herrera and Hernán Rosenkranz of 355 workers revealed that 80 percent of their respondents felt they "always or nearly always" made a personal intervention at production assemblies.[17] Moreover, when asked to mention the most important policy areas discussed and decided upon with the direct participation of workers, 95 percent listed production plans. The second highest frequency was education at 57 percent. The entire list is long, but the prioritization is striking. Unlike in Yugoslavia or participatory enterprises elsewhere, Cuban workers appear to take a greater interest in production related matters than in worker benefits.[18]

According to Castro's reports to the First Party Congress (1975) and Second Party Congress (1980), the number of workers participating in the discussion of the annual economic plan in their enterprises rose from 1.26 million in 1975 to 1.45 million in 1980 (or by 15 percent). A 1980 Cuban government study reported that the 1979 economic plan was discussed with the workers in 75 percent of all enterprises, and the 1980 plan was discussed in 91 percent of all enterprises. Workers' suggestions were used to amend the plan's control figures in 42 percent of the enterprises for the 1979 plan and in 59 percent for the 1980 plan.[19] A 1984 study of Cuban unions by Linda Fuller finds that workers have more power today than in the past to dismiss bad managers.[20] All of these results suggest a considerably higher level of actual worker participation in Cuban enterprises than in Soviet enterprises despite the existence of formal legislation in the U.S.S.R. that grants workers significant decision-making rights.[21]

Although similar evidence on worker participation does not exist for the early seventies, impressionistic reports, government documents, and public exhortations make it clear that the process of greater participation began at this time. The early seventies also witnessed sharp increases in labor productivity. In 1972, for instance, economy-wide output per worker jumped by a reported 21 percent.

While some analysts have attributed the early 1970s growth in productivity to the use of material incentives, the relationship between the two is tenuous. The government did not even begin to link wages to worker output until 1974, and the process proceeded very slowly. Moreover, in the first years of the decade there was still considerably excess liquidity held by Cuban households. It is difficult, then, to see a significant connection between the 1972 jump and subsequent increases in labor productivity and material incentives. Nor does it seem probable that the compulsory work law of spring 1971 had much of a net impact on productivity. Whereas the law probably helped to reduce absenteeism, it also brought tens of thousands of new workers into the labor force.[22]

The effect of the latter would be to increase total production, but to lower output per worker as it decreases the capital-labor ratio and brings often reluctant, untrained workers into the production process. It seems plausible to conclude, then, that the shift in enterprise social relations described above helped to promote the development of internal incentives (worker motivation) as well as the elicitation of good ideas for increasing productivity and thereby contributed, along with other factors, to the spurt in productivity growth during the first half of the seventies.

PLANNING SINCE 1975

In 1975, a decentralized system of government, known as Popular Power, was introduced. Popular Power is premised, on the local level, on open, contested elections, although candidates compete on the basis of personal credentials, not policy positions and ideology. The locally elected officials are required to hold meetings at least four times a year at which constituents can discuss matters of concern to them, including the possible recall of incumbents with whom they are dissatisfied. Available information suggests that local meetings are consumed primarily with discussions of bureaucratic deficiencies, including consumer scarcities and complaints about urban services. (For a more detailed analysis of this system, see Rhoda Rabkin's analysis in chapter 13, "Cuban Political Structures: Vanguard Party and the Masses.")

Channels have also been instituted to expand worker and mass participation at the provincial and national levels, but the mechanisms are more indirect and more limited in scope, and they seem, to date, to serve more to strengthen mass identification with the regime and mass responsibility for national decisions than to enable significant input in national decision making. Nonetheless, members of Popular Power at the national level—who are elected by the popularly elected local functionaries—serve on commissions that study economic problems and discuss with JUCEPLAN and the Council of Ministers priorities for the One-Year Plan and Five-Year Plan.

The second half of the seventies also witnessed Cuba's first Five-Year Plan as well as the gradual introduction of an economic reform known as the "New System of Economic Management and Planning" (SDPE). Each represents the evolving maturity and institutionalization of Cuba's economic organizations. The SDPE in many respects is modeled after the 1965 Soviet reforms. It attempts to (1) put enterprises on a self-financing basis, (2) introduce a profitability criterion with its attendant incentives, and (3) generally promote decentralization, organizational coherence, and efficiency.

One interesting organizational change connected with the SDPE has been decentralized control over local enterprises by the elected organs of Popular Power (i.e., municipal or regional governments). Prior to 1976 all enterprises were subordinated to a central state ministry. Currently, some 34 percent of locally oriented enterprises in services, commerce, and industry are responsible to the local organ of Popular Power. The directors of these local enterprises are named and removed by the organ of Popular Power, and this body is the link between JUCEPLAN (the Central Planning Board) and the enterprise. The local government is responsible to JUCEPLAN but is given considerable latitude in its choice and prioritization of projects as well as services and goods production.

Furthermore, the allocation of material supplies for many inputs is being decentralized. The development of direct trading ties between enterprises as well as the initiation of enterprise trade fairs holds significant promise as a vehicle to reduce bureaucratic delays and to encourage the production of properly specified outputs. Any reader familiar with the cumbersome and inefficient system of centralized supplies allocation through GOSNAB in the Soviet Union or with the positive results of Hungary's decentralization of its material supplies system after 1968 will readily appreciate this point. The Cubans have additional plans to introduce more flexibility and further decentralization into other areas of their planning system.[23]

As with the 1965 Soviet reform, the SDPE in Cuba has met with the obstacles of bureaucratic resistance and an "irrational" price structure. The introduction of the SDPE coincides with Cuba's First Five-Year Plan, indicating the youthfulness of Cuba's planning system. Indeed, many of the problems in implementing the SDPE have to do with the need to first develop an adequate statistical network, a legal system for enforcing contracts, an arbitration system, a management training program, proper financial institutions, etc.—none of which existed in satisfactory form prior to 1976.

The Cubans themselves have been very satisfied with the progress of the SDPE. In an introductory summary to a 1980 JUCEPLAN study on the SDPE, Humberto Pérez, JUCEPLAN's head, writes: "There are still several difficulties, but in view of the goals set at the First Party Congress (1975) the final balance of this study is completely positive."[24] More recently, in an early 1983 interview, Pérez states:

> The system has already produced advantageous results. First, it has helped to raise the economic consciousness of all our cadres in administration and management, the consciousness that they must save every possible resource, every *peso*, every *centavo*. The growth in 1981 and 1982 is largely a result of our success in achieving this economic consciousness and the workings of our economic management mechanisms.[25]

It is a curiosity, then, that Carmelo Mesa-Lago read the 1980 JUCEPLAN study and concluded the SDPE's record was disappointingly negative. In his words: "Its [the study's] description of the problems confronted by the SDPE is appalling."[26] Since in the next sentence Mesa-Lago asserts that the SDPE suffers from "excessively centralized control but ineffective coordination," we must conclude, syntax notwithstanding, that Mesa-Lago intends the epithet "appalling" to refer to the SDPE's performance rather than JUCEPLAN's "description" of it.

Mesa-Lago's interpretation can be attributed to a failure to grasp the institutional context (e.g., the inchoate planning apparatus) into which the SDPE was set. He attempts to support his view by selectively presenting the weakest aspects of the SDPE discussed in the report and omitting mention of its manifold accomplishments. Furthermore, there is reason to question the accuracy of Mesa-Lago's reporting on the problem areas. For instance, Mesa-Lago reports that "30 percent of the enterprises lacked [quality] controls altogether, and inspections revealed that 90 percent of the products did not meet the quality norms."[27] Yet the JUCEPLAN study states "el 90% incumplieron lo establecido en las normas *u otros documentos técnicos*" (emphasis mine).[28] That is, 90 percent did not meet *either* the quality norms or other technical instructions or procedures. In fact, this sentence follows an enumeration of seven instructions which were to be followed, including the use of precise weighing scales, the use of scientific measurement procedures, the development of special testing laboratories, etc. In other words, the sentence from the cited JUCEPLAN study refers to a failure in the production of 90 percent of the 507 sampled products to meet any one of the seven instructions—quality norms being just one item on the list.

By overlooking the last part of the relevant sentence, Mesa-Lago turns a very understandable tardiness in developing a complete set of technical and scientific procedures into a stinging indictment of Cuban enterprises.

It is clear to this author anyway that Humberto Pérez has provided a considerably more accurate interpretation of the JUCEPLAN study than has Carmelo Mesa-Lago. A balanced reading does indeed suggest that the SDPE has made significant strides in rationalizing Cuba's planning system. Subsequent evidence tends to confirm this conclusion.[29]

In addition to the organizational change in Cuba's system of planning, the government has also modified its consumer policies during the 1970s. Particularly since 1975 there has been a rapid expansion of the number and variety of consumer goods available to the public. The share of consumer goods which are rationed has also fallen sharply. In addition, the government created the Institute of Internal Demand to survey regularly consumer preferences and to make inventories of available supplies. It has a *formal* Soviet counterpart, but the Cuban Institute is more active and powerful in its impact on planning decisions.[30] The Institute also relies for its effectiveness on a network of thousands of volunteers to provide bi-weekly information on the operation of retail stores, shortages, consumer suggestions, etc. In addition, the Institute publishes its own monthly magazine which reports on new consumer styles, runs campaigns against harmful consumption such as cigarettes and sugar (yes, sugar), and carries eight to ten pages of classified ads. These ads are for a panoply of privately provided services (e.g., repair of appliances, TVs, cars, massages, carpentry, plumbing, cosmetics, gardening, music lessons, magicians and clowns for children's parties) and production (e.g., privately constructed housing—in 1981, 38 percent of new housing units were built by private contractors). These activities have been sanctioned since the late seventies and represent a level of legal decentralization not present in the U.S.S.R. The Institute also runs its own retail clothing stores in downtown Havana to sample the latest fashions.

Beginning in the mid-1970s the government also shifted its rural strategy. It encouraged private farming (involving about 25 percent of all farmland, one-half of which is organized into production cooperatives), by raising prices paid by state procurement agencies and by permitting farmers to market privately all production exceeding the official quotas. Initially farmers could only market their surplus in the countryside, but in 1980 free farmers' markets were permitted in urban areas as well. Moreover, the government reduced the pressure on farmers to work on state farms and to cooperate with official agricultural plans. As a result, the number of private farmers who affiliated with state plans dropped by half between 1973 and 1977.[31] At the same time, the government also reduced its hold over the state sector, first by permitting state farms to sell production in excess of their quotas in the free markets and then by permitting state farm workers to once again have private plots. The new agricultural policies permitted minimal planned agricultural supply, while encouraging additional production consistent with the government's demand-based strategy of the 1970s.

PERFORMANCE AND CONCLUSION

Due to space limitations, we can only raise a few performance-related considerations in this section. According to an August 1982 study by the Cuban Central Bank, Gross Social Product in Cuba grew at a real annual rate of 7.5 percent from 1970 to 1975 and 4.0 percent from 1976 to 1980[32]; real growth in 1981, 1982, and 1983 was reported at 12 percent, 2.7 percent, and 5.2 percent respectively.[33] Mercantile Production (roughly Gross Social Product without commerce) during the first six months of 1984 was 9.9 percent above its level for the same period of 1983.[34] These figures represent a very creditable growth rate, particularly given the severe international recession and low commodity prices over most of the period.

Of course, growth rates by themselves mean little, especially when there are so many methodological questions involved. In this case, the Cuban method of adjusting for price increases is not clear, and the Cubans have been occasionally inconsistent in their own published figures.[35] Fortunately, the Cubans appear to be gathering and reporting data more assiduously than in the past and recent, careful Western studies are refining our understanding of what is available.[36]

Even with improved data, however, several interpretive questions remain. What impact on Cuban growth has the economic blockade had relative to the large amount of Soviet aid and price subsidies?[37] What has been the level of sacrifice of Cuban consumers in order to attain this growth and how has this level changed over the years? How successful have the Cubans been in diversifying their industrial base and export sector? What are the prospects for sustaining recent growth rates in light of the ongoing weakness in world sugar prices?

In this chapter I have attempted to provide a tentative answer to a related question: what effect has Cuba's system of planning and incentives had on its economic performance? After a decade of drifting in the 1960s, the Cubans have been successfully confronting the allocation, coordination, and motivation issues that affect all planned economies. The partial development of internal incentives along with a relatively flexible, pragmatic, and decentralized approach to planning seem to be progressing in spite of the powerful external constraints, both political and economic, affecting Cuba.

NOTES

1. René Dumont, *Cuba: Socialism and Development* (New York: Grove Press, 1970). Edward Boorstein, *The Economic Transformation of Cuba* (New York: Monthly Review Press, 1968). See also Luc Zephirin and Carmelo Mesa-Lago, "Central Planning," in Carmelo Mesa-Lago, ed., *Revolutionary Change in Cuba* (Pittsburgh: University of Pittsburgh Press, 1971), pp. 145–84.

2. See Archibald Ritter, *The Economic Development of Revolutionary Cuba* (New York: Praeger, 1974); Carmelo Mesa-Lago, *Cuba in the 1970s* (Albuquerque: University of New Mexico Press, 1978); Arthur MacEwan, *Revolution and Economic Development in Cuba* (London: Macmillan, 1981).

3. Carmelo Mesa-Lago, *The Economy of Socialist Cuba* (Albuquerque: University of New Mexico Press, 1981), pp. 29, 151, 235.

4. The best economic treatment of this phenomenon in planned economies as well as a useful discussion of reform attempts is Janos Kornai, *Economics of Shortage* (Amsterdam: North-Holland, 1980).

5. For an elaboration of this argument see Sinan Koont and Andrew Zimbalist, "Incentives and Elicitation Schemes: A Critique and an Extension," in Andrew Zimbalist, ed., *Comparative Economic Systems: An Assessment of Knowledge, Theory and Method* (Boston: Kluwer-Nijhoff, 1984), pp. 159–74.

6. The most sophisticated discussion of the importance of worker participation in planned economies is provided in various works by Wlodzimierz Brus, such as *The Economics and Politics of Socialism* (London: Routledge and Kegan Paul, 1973), pp. 31–44.

7. Two good sources on this debate are Robert Bernardo, *The Theory of Moral Incentives in Cuba* (Tuscaloosa, Ala.: University of Alabama Press, 1971); and Bertram Silverman, ed., *Man and Socialism in Cuba: The Great Debate* (New York: Atheneum, 1973). The latter source contains translations of several original articles from the debate.

8. Ritter, *Economic Development*, p. 170. Others have presented data suggesting somewhat lower investment ratios during this period.

9. The estimates of growth for this period vary significantly depending on the source. Mesa-Lago provides a useful discussion of Cuban growth statistics and their problems in *The Economy of Socialist Cuba*, Appendix 1.

Very thorough methodological discussions of Cuban statistics appear in: Claes Brundenius, *Economic Growth, Basic Needs and Income Distribution in Revolutionary Cuba* (Lund, Sweden: Research Policy Institute, University of Lund, 1981) and Wharton Econometric Forecasting Associates, *Construction of Cuban Economic Activity and Trade Indexes* (Washington, D.C.: Wharton, November 1983). See also Banco Nacional de Cuba, *Informe Económico* (Havana: Banco Nacional, August 1982).

10. Fidel Castro, "Report on the Cuban Economy," in *Cuba in Revolution*, eds. R. Bonachea and N. Valdés (Garden City: Anchor, 1972), p. 338.

11. Ibid., pp. 345-49.

12. Cited in R. Hernández and C. Mesa-Lago, "Labor Organization and Wages," in Carmelo Mesa-Lago, ed., *Revolutionary Change in Cuba*.

13. On the counterpart role of unions in Cuba, see Linda Fuller, "Changing Politics of Workers' Control in Post-Revolutionary Cuba: The Work Center and the National Arena" (Ph.D. diss., University of California, Berkeley, 1984), chapter 5.

14. JUCEPLAN, *Segunda Plenaria Nacional de Chequeo de la Implantación del SDPE* (Havana: Ediciones JUCEPLAN, 1980), p. 297. A typographical error in the pertinent table renders the precise percentage somewhat uncertain.

15. This estimate is based on interviews with workers and union leaders conducted by the author during visits to Cuba in July-August 1974 and March 1982.

16. Marifeli Pérez-Stable, "Institutionalization and Workers' Response," *Cuban Studies* 6 (1976), pp. 31-54.

17. A. Herrera and H. Rosenkranz, "Political Consciousness in Cuba," in John Griffiths and Peter Griffiths, eds., *Cuba: The Second Decade* (London: Britain-Cuba Scientific Liaison Committee, 1979), p. 48.

18. I refer here to current experiences with worker participation. Factory councils in Russia in 1917, in Italy in 1918, Catalonia in 1936, or Chile 1970-73 were certainly not guided primarily by an economistic orientation. See Juan Espinosa and Andrew Zimbalist, *Economic Democracy: Workers' Participation in Chilean Industry, 1970-1973* (New York: Academic Press, 1978).

19. JUCEPLAN, *Segunda Plenaria Nacional*, p. 27.

20. Fuller, "Changing Politics of Workers' Control," chapter 5.

21. For additional information on worker participation in Cuba see M. Harnecker, *Cuba: Dictatorship or Democracy?* (Westport, Conn.: Lawrence Hill & Co., 1979), chapter 1; and A. Zimbalist, "Worker Participation in Cuba," *Challenge: The Magazine of Economic Affairs* (November/December 1975). On actual worker participation in the Soviet Union see M. Yanowitch, *Social and Economic Inequality in the Soviet Union* (White Plains, N.Y.: M.E. Sharpe, 1977), chapter 5; M. Yanowitch, ed., *Soviet Work Attitudes: The Issue of Participation in Management* (White Plains, N.Y.: M.E. Sharpe, 1979); and Blair Ruble, *Soviet Trade Unions* (Cambridge: Cambridge University Press, 1981), chapters 4 and 5.

22. Mesa-Lago, *Cuba in the 1970s*, p. 95. Mesa-Lago estimates the law brought over 100,000 new entrants into the labor force.
23. JUCEPLAN, *Segunda Plenaria Nacional*, pp. 22-24 and 87-91.
24. Ibid., p. 4 (author's translation).
25. Humberto Pérez, "On Cuba's Current Economic Problems," *Cuba Update* 4 (August 1983), p. 10.
26. Carmelo Mesa-Lago, "The Economy: Caution, Frugality and Resilient Ideology," in Jorge Domínguez, ed., *Cuba: Internal and International Affairs* (Beverly Hills: Sage, 1982), p. 132.
27. Ibid.
28. JUCEPLAN, *Segunda Plenaria Nacional*, p. 356.
29. I refer here to conversations I had in Cuba in March 1982 and May 1984 with leading economists at JUCEPLAN and elsewhere in the planning hierarchy to public statements by Humberto Pérez such as in the early 1983 interview cited earlier.
30. This is not only my opinion but also the opinion of Eugenio Balari, the head of the Cuban Institute of Internal Demand, as expressed to the author in March 1982. Balari made several trips to the U.S.S.R. to study the parallel institutes there and has maintained close contacts with the Soviet counterpart agencies. Balari's status as head of the Institute has recently been raised to that of a minister.
31. Jorge Domínguez, *Cuba: Order and Revolution* (Cambridge: Harvard University Press, 1978), p. 459.
32. Banco Nacional de Cuba, *Informe Económico*, p. 29. It is noteworthy that the 1970-75 annual growth rate given here is approximately six percentage points below the earlier official estimates cited in Mesa-Lago, *The Economy of Socialist Cuba*, p. 34. Since the 7.5 percent is cited as a *real* growth rate, this suggests that the government either is admitting an inflation rate of around six percent for these years, or it is presenting a revised growth estimate, or some of both. The Cubans have changed their national income accounting methodology several times without providing full explanations of the change.
33. Ibid., p. 38; and Comité Estatal de Estadísticas, *La Economía Cubana, 1982*, p. 17 and 1983, p. 3. The *Anuario Estadístico, 1981* also published by the Cuban State Statistical Committee reports a real 1981 growth rate of Gross Social Product of 14.8 percent, p. 67.
34. Banco Nacional de Cuba, *Informe Económico Primestral*, Junio 1984, p. 2.
35. Mesa-Lago, *The Economy of Socialist Cuba*, pp. 47-49. The absence of an official price index has prompted Mesa-Lago to impute an estimated inflation rate on the basis of excess liquidity. Mesa-Lago's estimate suffers, among other ways, from a conceptual confusion of the absolute price level, which does not denote inflation, with the rate of change of the price level, which does. A more careful discussion of Cuban prices can be found in Wharton Econometric

Forecasting Associates, *Construction of Cuban Economic Activity*, cit., vol. I, pp. 82–100.

36. I refer primarily to: Brundenius, *op. cit.*, Brundenius, *Revolutionary Cuba: The Challenge of Economic Growth with Equity* (Boulder, Colorado: Westview Press, 1984); and Brundenius and Zimbalist, "Recent Studies in Cuban Economic Growth: A Review," *Comparative Economic Studies* (formerly ACES Bulletin) 27 (Spring 1985).

37. For a consideration of this question see A. Zimbalist, "Soviet Aid, US Blockade and the Cuban Economy," *ACES Bulletin* 24 (Winter 1982): 137–46; and Banco Nacional, *Informe Económico*.

Section V
Political Process and Change

12 Continuity and Evolution of Revolutionary Symbolism in *Verde Olivo*

C. Fred Judson

Revolutions continue to be made by organizations with a military component, whether by the M-26-7 (July 26 Movement) in Cuba of the 1950s, Vietnam in the 1940s–1970s, or Nicaragua in the 1970s. Whatever the proportion of the civilian or popular component, revolutionary power is achieved through force of arms. The repressive nature of the state and the armed forces at its disposal dictate that revolutionary military organization is necessary. Some militarization of the struggle to consolidate the revolution and defend its gains against counterrevolution and intervention appears no less common. Thus the class, character, morale, and political education of revolutionary armed forces, whether irregular, militia, conscript, or professional, are critical. In Cuba the leaders of the Rebel Army, from its formation through the struggle in the Sierra Maestra to its institutionalization as the Fuerzas Armadas Revolucionarias (FAR) in 1959, have always regarded the political education of the armed forces as a priority.[1] To consider revolutionary symbolism in Cuba as expressed in *Verde Olivo*, the FAR journal for 25 years, is to study the political essence of that symbolism. The test of the ideological effect of political education and the impact of revolutionary symbolism is the will to sacrifice, and in a world of imperialism and counterrevolution that sacrifice is the ultimate guarantee of a revolution. Hence, although revolutionary symbolism is generalized in Cuban society, *Verde Olivo* offers a distillation of that symbolism.

Revolutionary symbolism, which is both the use of symbols and the body of symbols, is not static; yet neither is it so dynamic as to exhibit no patterns of development. Initially it had the function of recuperating and rehabilitating Cuban national history. It confronted the distortion of history in the legacies of colonialism, in the truncated republic after the 1898 intervention by the United States and in the Batista dictatorship. A manifold enterprise, symbolism sought to make history a living social memory for the nation and to wield it as an ideological weapon in the confrontation with the dictatorship. This task of recuperation continues.

Next, new symbols were sought in the created history of the armed struggle. If history provided mobilizing symbols, ongoing struggle actualized the continuity between past and present that the revolutionaries claimed. After January 1, 1959, continuing struggle in several spheres—military, political, social, economic, cultural—created new symbols to behold, assimilate, revere, and emulate.

Finally, symbolism institutionalized itself in revolutionary society, in politics and popular culture, in the educational materials, and in the revolutionary political discourse that came to achieve ideological hegemony.[2] Nevertheless, institutionalization of revolutionary symbolism has not meant stagnation. Symbols appropriated from history are joined by those created in the revolutionary war and afterwards, while Cuba's national and international life creates new symbols.[3] The dialectic between appropriated, created, and the existentially new is a dialectic of meaning and significance, of mutually enhancing continuity. It is also a dialectic of confrontation with imperialism: "Imperialism is bent on destroying symbols, because it knows the value of symbols, of examples and of ideas... but when their enemies think they have destroyed them, what they have actually done is made them multiply."[4]

CONTINUITY

Continuity of the revolution with Cuban history is the heart of revolutionary symbolism in *Verde Olivo*. There is a central concern to cultivate a radical nationalist historical consciousness, beginning with a revised assessment of the "discovery and conquest." In the early years of *Verde Olivo* there were frequent articles about the aboriginal societies and their socioeconomic development. The purpose was to create a sense of identification with the experiences and struggles of the past, a feeling that the modern revolutionary was part of a long tradition of resistance to exploitation and heir to a rich pre-Columbian culture. Articles from the political education manual of the FAR, *Manual de Capacitación Cívica* (reproduced in *Verde Olivo*), sought to "develop a love for the people as the creators of labor and the source of all social wealth...to indicate the struggle against exploitation and misery."[5] Thus, instead of discovery, Columbus's arrival was disruption and plunder.[6] Colonialism established forms of property and relations of production that determined Cuba's specific underdevelopment.[7] The *Manual* restored dignity to pre-Columbian Cuba and converted it into a symbol of Cuba's inherent human and natural wealth. It did not seek to deny the economic development of the wealth that colonialism objectively meant; rather, it sought to develop a historical understanding of the roots of Cuba's socioeconomic structures prior to the revolution.

On socioeconomic terrain, still, struggles during the colonial period against slavery and racism have been designated by *Verde Olivo* as precursors of the modern revolutionary period. Thus racial prejudice, which the July 26 Movement consciously identified as an obstacle to progress, originated in slavery as a mode of production, and slave revolts have been commemorated.[8] The Cuban defense of Angola was named "Operation Carlota" after the revolt led by the slave Carlota in 1843 until she was martyred.[9]

The reappropriation of colonial history with a nationalist and materialist perspective has been a constant in *Verde Olivo* since 1959, but it is in examining the 1868-98 period that the symbolism acquires additional strength. The armed struggles of those decades—the tactics, strategy, leadership, chronicles, battles—are seen in *Verde Olivo*, as indeed they are throughout the Cuban educational systems, as direct precursors of the 1953-59 struggle. The term *mambí*, which was applied to the guerrilla fighters of the nineteenth century, was later applied to the guerrillas of the 1950s and to the cane-cutters in the campaign for ten million tons in 1970: "We keep machetes as a glorious reminder of the *mambí* cavalry and of the *mambises* of the 20th century, the cane-cutters."[10]

The methods of struggle in the nineteenth century were emulated by the Rebel Army in the 1950s, and the symbolism of both guerrilla campaigns has since been invoked in health and education projects, sports events, and FAR maneuvers. The "incendiary task" of burning sugar cane, initiated by Antonio Maceo, was repeated by the Rebel Army. Breaking out of Oriente and marching westward, which Maceo and General Máximo Gómez undertook in the nineteenth century, was repeated in 1958 by Ché Guevara and Camilo Cienfuegos. Such exploits are chronicled in literally hundreds of *Verde Olivo* articles over the years—diary excerpts from Guevara and Cienfuegos, accounts by members of the invading columns, interviews with M-26-7 militants and others living along the routes. Books about the westward invasion, written by lieutenants of Guevara and Cienfuegos, have appeared.[11] Symbolic continuity is found in such details as Cienfuegos carrying a copy of Miró Argenter's *Chronicles of War* (Argenter was Maceo's chief of staff in 1895) and speaking to his column about Maceo's strategy and tactics.[12] In *Verde Olivo* articles about the battles and politics of 1868–98 are often juxtaposed to those depicting the struggles of 1956–58.

It is even more the case with Jose Martí, considered *the* national hero,[13] that a figure from the nineteenth century has assumed such symbolic significance as to become a Sorelian "revolutionary myth."[14] Martí's thought and life, devoted as it was to achieving not only Cuban independence but social justice, was just that "expression of a determination to act" that Sorel found in revolutionary myths.[15] Martí's life and struggle were mythical in the way that Sorel held that myths "enclose within them all the strongest inclinations of a people, of a party or of a class, inclinations which recur to the mind with the insistence of instincts in all the circumstances of life and which give an aspect of complete reality to the hopes of immediate action by which, more easily than by any other method, men can reform their desires, passion and mental activity."[16] His life was a call to "fulfill the Cuban duty,"[17] to achieve independence and progress. *Verde Olivo* is but one vehicle in which the symbolism of Martí is conveyed to Cubans, though a particularly strong one. The "Apostle's" birthday and anniversary of death under Spanish bullets are remembered annually in *Verde Olivo*, as in virtually every Cuban journal. On those occasions his life and writings are featured.

In Fidel Castro's defense after the July 26, 1953 assault on the Moncada barracks, he claimed that "Martí was the intellectual author" of the assault.[18] When Camilo Cienfuegos's unit entered Palma Soriano, where Martí was killed in 1895, he and his officers signed a pledge to Martí, "faces to the sun, to fulfill the grandiose task which he began and which death kept him from realizing."[19] Fidel Castro and Abel Santamaría, organizers of the Moncada assault, emphasizing the symbolic importance of their attack on the 100th anniversary of Martí's birth, called his corevolutionaries the "Generation of the centenary."[20] The group's political education "was imparted by reading the works of Jose Martí."[21] Since 1959, *Verde Olivo* has participated in the symbolism of Martí, continuing the appropriation Castro and Santamaría carried out in the name of revolution and all Cubans. Phrases from Martí's writings have appeared in almost every issue: "To die for the fatherland is to live"; "To be educated is the only way to be free"; "The best way to speak is to act."

Consciousness of historical continuity is the product of more than symbolism, but symbolism is perhaps the most potent creator of that consciousness. There can of course be no such creation without the raw material of events and personalities, and Cuban history has been rich in raw material. The events and figures of the nineteenth century had been manipulated by the Machados and Batistas of the twentieth century, but their symbolic and mobilizing power was realized only by the nontraditional opposition forces of the M-26-7.[22] With the M-26-7, radical reappropriation of the nineteenth century was matched by events and personalities of equivalent stature, the most powerful symbolic combination possible.

THE CREATION OF SYMBOLS IN STRUGGLE

If the appropriation of Cuban history was for the purpose of its symbolic politicization and conversion into an objective force in revolutionary struggle, the struggle itself created new symbols. That the new set of symbols has acquired the most currency within Cuban symbolism is to be expected, as any revolution celebrates itself. The events and personalities of the struggle against Batista from Moncada to January 1, 1959 have been elevated to symbolic stature.

As with all symbolism, Cuban revolutionary symbolism of the struggle begins with the most inclusive symbols. The very phrase "Generation of the Centenary" identified the revolutionary generation as those who redeemed Cuba and realized Martí's dreams and projects. Thus the Moncada assault is probably the single most significant event in the created symbolism. As such, it has received the most coverage, not only in *Verde Olivo*, but in all vehicles of symbolism. The fact that July 26 is the most symbolic day each year in Cuba is the measure of the significance of Moncada. Every year in *Verde Olivo* the participants are recalled and personal testimonies published. Statements made at the Moncada trial appear on the covers of *Verde Olivo* or are featured in articles.[23] Books and articles on the prison experience and exile in Mexico also commemorate the "Generation."[24]

The voyage of the yacht *Granma* and the struggle of the survivors follow the Moncada assault as symbols. The yacht itself is the main attraction at the Museum of the Revolution in Havana, while *Verde Olivo* leads in publishing accounts of the invasion.[25] Another measure of the invasion's significance is the naming of 1976 as the "year of the twentieth anniversary of the *Granma*." The invasion itself is symbolic of commitment and sacrifice for ideals; Castro had said that "in 1956 we shall be free or we shall be martyrs,"[26] and the invasion was "to fulfill the Cuban duty"[27] in the face of overwhelming odds.

There are two disparate revolutionary symbols linked to the landing of the *Granma*. The first is the personality of Frank País, a young activist who organized an insurrection in Santiago to coincide with the landing. Though it failed, his contribution to the survival and progress of Castro's Rebel Army in the early period of guerrilla struggle, along with his leadership qualities, made him one of the most fondly remembered martyrs of the struggle. After his death at the hands of Batista's police, a second guerrilla front was named for him, as have been many schools, health centers, and other institutions.

The second symbol is the "legend of the twelve," as only twelve survived the landing through the attacks and dispersion that awaited the expeditionaries. Though never openly compared to the twelve Christian disciples, the twelve survivors and their exploits have symbolized determination and sacrifice. Phrases uttered by them and anecdotes about their behavior and actions appear repeatedly in *Verde Olivo*, as well as in other publications, on billboards, or in popular culture. For example, the legend of Camilo Cienfuegos began at the ambush of Alegría de Pío shortly after the landing, when he shouted "No one surrenders here, damn it!"[28]

There are three more general symbols derived from the two years of guerrilla struggle, although these are not as specific as individuals or events: (1) the idea of the *manigua redentora* ("redemptive bushland"), (2) the Sierra Maestra Mountains as teacher and forge of the revolutionaries, and (3) rebel-*guajiro* unity. First, the landscape itself, which sheltered the Rebel Army, symbolized the resistance of the land. It had been so with Maceo's guerrilla struggle, and the phrase dates from that period; thus the celebration of the *manigua redentora* is a conscious connection to the War of Independence.[29]

Second, the Sierra Maestra symbolizes *foquismo* and guerrilla struggle and what the very location of the *foco* there meant for the political education of the Rebel Army—its hardships, relations with the local population, the embryo of land reform carried out after January 1, 1959. Today to scale the highest peak, El Turquino, which was the center of the *foco*, is symbolically to share the Rebel Army experience. The phrase, "in a location in Oriente," which opened many Rebel Army communiques during the struggle, conjures up the images of *barbudos* ("bearded rebels") in the mountains.[30] Those of the original twelve who survived recall the time in the Sierra Maestra with fondness and a near-mysticism: "La Sierra Maestra. That's interesting. Our *maestra*—our teacher."[31] As Castro articulated it, the guerrillas felt a debt to the Sierra Maestra and its inhabitants, a debt that was to be fulfilled in social and economic programs for the region, one of the poorest and most backward in Cuba:

> It was logical that the Sierra Maestra, where the revolutionary spirit of our leaders was forged and where the will and decisions to change the political, economic and social panorama of Cuba was tempered, would vibrate from its roots in support of the Revolution.[32]

It is constantly maintained in political education materials in Cuba that rebel-*guajiro* unity, or revolutionary-peasant unity, is one of the fundamental bases of the revolution. Nothing symbolizes this unity more than Rebel Army-*guajiro* relations during the armed struggle of 1956–58. From the landing of the *Granma* to the final battles of Las Villas province in December 1958, the participation of the peasantry was critical. Rebel Army commitment to the peasantry, rooted in *History Will Absolve Me*, was realized, to begin with, in the treatment of the Sierra Maestra *guajiros* by the guerrillas. Assuming symbolic significance during and since the armed struggle, Rebel Army behavior is part of the political education of Cuba as a whole. Courteous behavior, requests rather than demands for assistance, and prompt, generous payment for supplies received have become legendary:[33] "Castro's people respected the *guajiro*'s property and paid generously for everything consumed."[34] The code of conduct observed by the Rebel Army, reminiscent of the Chinese Communists' "Three Main Rules of Discipline and the Eight Points of Attention,"[35] formed the basis of rebel-*guajiro* unity.

Much has been made of the Rebel Army's political education through their experience in the Sierra Maestra and with the *guajiro* population, to the point that it is enshrined in writings and slogans. For example, Guevara's phrase "the guerrilla put on the straw hat" is symbolic of guerrilla and thus FAR identification with the *guajiros*.[36] The identification was mutual, according to Guevara: "The peasantry recognized those lean men whose beards were beginning to flourish, as companions in misfortune, fresh victims of the repressive forces."[37] As the guerrillas became somewhat more secure, they engaged in more contact with the *guajiros*:

> In order for the peasants to become rebels, the rebels became peasants and took part in field chores. It was not enough to know the need and poverty of rural people. It was necessary to suffer from these hardships and at the same time to combat them. A neat swing of the machete, cutting the stalks like a pro, will do more than a long speech.[38]

When the Rebel Army progressed to becoming the de facto authority, having military successes, imposing justice on informers, thieves, and rapists, and establishing revolutionary civic programs, more *guajiros* joined them: "The *guajiro* who joins the Rebel Army does it not simply for self-defense...but as a means to conserve the gains which are already his own and which no one will ever be able to take away from him."[39]

At the same time, the Rebel Army worked consciously to increase unity with the *guajiros*. This dialectic of conscious guerrilla striving to achieve peasant support and the political education of direct experience with peasant life and struggles there began what would become an ideological and practical mainstay of the revolution—rebel-*guajiro* unity. Guevara spoke of the dialectic in an interview in 1958:

> Much of what we are doing we had not even dreamed of. You could say that we became revolutionaries in the revolution. We came to overthrow a tyrant but we discovered that this enormous peasant zone, wherein our struggle is being prolonged, is the area of Cuba which most needs liberation. We are not fighting for them in the future. We are fighting now and we consider that every meter of the Sierra that is ours...is more theirs than ours.[40]

The rebel-*guajiro* unity thus achieved carried with it an obligation, part of the *deber cubano* ("Cuban duty"), and meeting the obligation has meant institutionalizing the programs undertaken in embryonic form in the Sierra Maestra. In 1958 Castro could say, when asked about programs to be implemented once the revolutionary government was in power, that "much of what we would do we are already doing in the Sierra."[41] The programs of the Segundo Frente Oriental "Frank País," under Raúl Castro—literacy, health, education, union organization, civic administration, peasant militia, agrarian reform—were more complete than those in the original guerrilla *foco* and were more developed precursors of the revolutionary reforms introduced after January 1, 1959.[42] They also expanded the concept of unity to include workers and students, so that the basis of the slogan "*el pueblo unido jamás será vencido*" ("the people united will never be defeated") was set in practice.

Symbols of this expanded unity that appear in *Verde Olivo* and other publications are the Santiago insurrection of November 1956, the March 13, 1957 student Directorio Revolucionario attack on the Presidential Palace, the general strike in Santiago on July 30, 1957 in response to the murder of Frank País, the popular uprising in Cienfuegos on September 5, 1957, and the attempted general strike of April 9, 1958. The events and those martyred are remembered in *Verde Olivo* on every anniversary.[43]

At the most general level of symbolism the Rebel Army/FAR represents the Cuban people and its revolutionary spirit. Derived from the struggle against Batista and built continuously since then by the experience of the revolution, the image of the revolutionary military is that of the Cuban people in arms. Particularly in the early years, *Verde Olivo* contrasted the Rebel Army/FAR with the Batista "mercenaries," with the armies of neocolonial dictatorships, and with the imperialist forces of the United States. The speeches and writings of those who were living symbols, that is, Guevara, Cienfuegos, and Castro, and the remarks of others such as Raúl Castro, Juan Almeida, William Gálvez, Joel Iglesias, stressed the popular character of the FAR.[44] When Castro arrived in Havana in January 1959 and made the famous speech at Campo Columbia, with the white dove settling on his shoulder,[45] he spoke of Rebel Army unity with the people: "Every time I hear of columns, fronts or units, I think to myself: our best column, our best troops, the only ones capable of winning the war are the people. No army can defeat them."[46] Cienfuegos enshrined it in a statement that has become a symbol: "When the *guajiro* with a machete in his belt and the rebel with a rifle on his shoulder embraced, the earth that they stand on, earth soaked with blood, must know that the blood was not shed in vain."[47]

In revolutionary symbolism the general is linked to the specific and individual; each may ultimately represent the same universal values. Thus the Rebel Army/FAR represent the Cuban people and national redemption through struggle, sacrifice, and victory, while individuals, either martyred or surviving, do so also. The Rebel Army/FAR is an army of the people, while figures like Castro, Guevara, and Cienfuegos symbolize and synthesize guerrilla-peasant-worker unity. They also symbolize Sorel's subjective force become objective. Their very lives and actions have assumed mythic dimensions, and symbolism exhorts people to realize and emulate their example. Children are educated about the guerrillas and are encouraged to "be like Ché."[48] The whole nation delivers flowers to the sea on the anniversary of Cienfuegos's disappearance in October 1959, while *Verde Olivo* prints articles by and about him.[49] "The best homage" to figures such as Guevara and Cienfuegos, declared *Verde Olivo*, "is a daily effort,"[50] just as Guevara had said that "the best way to honor Martí is to follow his maxim—'the best way to speak is to act.'"[51]

Symbolism is the vehicle of significance, a means by which a people or a movement communicates to itself its most important experience and messages. The events that comprise a radical break with the past, the revolutionary impact of those events, and the promissory character of the events seem naturally to be the most significant. Thus the created symbolism which the 1953-59 struggle engendered has been the most compelling element of Cuban revolutionary symbolism. This element interprets both the past and the events since 1959 through the meaningfulness of the 1953-59 events and thus is the core of symbolism's coherence.

INSTITUTIONALIZATION, CONSOLIDATION, AND ACCUMULATION OF SYMBOLS

Symbols from Cuban history and those created in the 1953-59 struggle have been institutionalized in a number of ways. They appear in public educational materials as subjects, themes, and examples. In popular culture and the arts, they are frequent subjects and motifs. In political education materials, symbols from the past and those from the 1953–59 period are the most commonly employed. Names of individuals, dates, and places of significant events have been institutionalized in the naming of schools, hospitals, clinics, factories, sugar mills, farms, and public buildings, while military units and maneuvers, Committees for the Defense of the Revolution, neighborhoods, new communities, conferences, sports events, and production units often take their names from the body of symbols. Time measurement itself institutionalizes revolutionary symbols as years are named, confirming an event's symbolic stature or creating a new symbol. "Year of education," "Year of planning," "Year of agriculture"—such designations marked the first years.[52] "Year of solidarity," "Year of heroic Vietnam," and "Year of the heroic guerrilla" characterized the middle and later 1960s. The continuing struggle to create a strong and socialist economy in the late 1960s and early 1970s was reflected in "Year of the decisive effort" and "Year of the 10 million," referring to the campaign for ten million tons of sugar. Consolidation and continuity appear in some of the year names of the 1970s and 1980s: "Year of the twentieth anniversary of Moncada," "Year of the First Party Congress," "Year of the twentieth anniversary of the *Granma* invasion," "Year of the twentieth anniversary of the victory," "Year of the twentieth anniversary of Girón," "Year Twenty-four of the Revolution."

The revolutionary process and Cuba's national and international trajectory since 1959 have created numerous additions to revolutionary symbolism. They are added as elements in a continuum, confirming the past and claiming the past's symbols as precursors. After Guevara's death—following his struggle as an internationalist in Bolivia—for example, one of *Verde Olivo*'s many commemorations appeared in the frontispiece of the April 14, 1968 issue: drawings of Maceo and Guevara with the caption "they now would be like us; we then would have been like them."[53]

The material and subjective gains of the revolution have themselves become symbols of *el deber cubano* realized, as well as symbols of the superiority of socialism, both nationalist and universal symbols. The literacy program, the expansion of health and education services, the provision of employment, public works projects, industrialization, and economic diversification are all frequent topics in *Verde Olivo*, where the military/guerrilla struggle motif is employed to describe the advances.

Often the previously most backward areas of Cuba are the focus when details of progress are presented.[54] Gains of the revolution are seen as symbolic of the contrast between socialism and capitalism[55] with aspects of U.S. society and dependent capitalist societies symbolic of capitalism's inherent inequality and failure to provide Martí's goal, that is, "*una vida de decoro*" ("a life of dignity").

Gains in subjective areas have also achieved symbolic status. The notion of socialist consciousness and the "new man" has been seen as realized in the lives and dedication of national and internationalist martyrs, Cuban volunteers abroad, Cuban sports performers, voluntary labor, and in the victories in the struggle against racism and sexism in Cuban society. References to Guevara's speeches and writings on the topic of the "new man" make him a symbol of progress in these areas. Awards to "exemplary workers" reflect the emphasis on "new man" and "socialist consciousness."

The struggles of the early 1960s against counterrevolution and imperialist intervention consolidated the revolution and created new symbols of determination and resistance. The "*Lucha contra bandidos*" ("struggle against bandits") in the Escambray and other regions made martyrs of some Cubans, who were then commemorated in Verde Olivo.[56] The defeat of the invasion at the Bay of Pigs—Playa Girón— became one of the outstanding symbols, as it was "the first defeat of imperialism in Latin America."[57] The cartoons of René de la Nuez, which since 1959 have contrasted Cuban *barbudos* and *guajiros* with *gusanos* (literally "worms," a despective term applied to Cuban exiles), mercenaries, U.S. Marines and Uncle Sam, employed existing symbols and created new ones at the time of Girón. Speeches made by Castro at the time have become classics, and excerpts appear on the Girón anniversary and throughout the year: "We answered with iron and fire the barbarous aggression"[58]; "What they cannot pardon is that we made a socialist revolution under their very noses."[59] The Girón martyrs have been remembered as much as those of Moncada, the Granma invasion, or the Sierra Maestra. Girón has become symbolic of resistance to imperialism to the extent that Castro called the defeated South African and Central Intelligence Agency operation in Angola "an African Girón."[60]

Cuban internationalism is a major contributor to the body of revolutionary symbolism. From Cubans who fought Franco in the Spanish Civil War[61] to the image of the Andes as Latin America's Sierra

Maestra, the symbolism of internationalist solidarity has been very strong. The sentiment expressed has several elements. First, as a Latin American nation, Cuba owed a debt to the Bolivarian tradition of continental liberation and unity. Ché Guevara, an Argentine, had joined the Cuban struggle and then carried internationalism to Bolivia. Second, Cuba had a debt of internationalist solidarity to repay as regards the assistance received from the Soviet Union, primarily, but from other socialist countries as well. Third, Cuba, as a revolutionary country, had an obligation to act in solidarity with other revolutions and struggles for national liberation. A number of statements articulated this internationalist duty, an extension of *el deber cubano* to *el deber revolucionario*. Two examples include: "The revolutionary movement in whatever part of the world can count on the unconditional and dedicated aid of Cuba"[62]; and "To be internationalists is to meet our own debt of gratitude to humanity."[63]

The outstanding symbol of revolutionary internationalism is Ché Guevara's attempt to wage guerrilla war on Bolivia. Castro designated 1968 the "year of the heroic guerrilla" in tribute to Guevara and Cubans who fell in Bolivia with him: "There is nothing extraordinary nor is there anything more honorable for this country than for its sons to know how to fall fighting to the last drop of blood for the liberation of peoples, which is the liberation of humanity."[64]

In the 1960s and 1970s, Cuban solidarity with guerrilla struggles in Latin America, Southeast Asia, and Africa found frequent expression in the pages of *Verde Olivo*. Martyrs of those struggles were honored, in many ways, from the naming of an FAR unit's participation in the 1965 sugar harvest after the Venezuelan martyr Argimiro Gabaldón[65] to a *Verde Olivo* cover in memory of Ho Chi Minh on the tenth anniversary of his death.[66] When the United States intervened in the Dominican Republic in 1965, *Verde Olivo* brought together disparate struggles in a trenchant statement of anti-imperialist solidarity: "Sandino, the Dominicans, the Vietnamese and the Koreans have proved it: Marines are but flesh and blood... and they die... while perpetrating their crimes in whatever part of the world."[67]

From expression of solidarity with Latin American revolutionaries in the 1960s to the Cuban internationalist presence in Vietnam and Angola in the 1970s, identification with Chile in 1970–73, an internationalist presence in Nicaragua, and the defense of the airfield in Grenada in October 1983, internationalism has been symbolized by Cuban martyrs and material sacrifices. The path of development and the material advances of the revolution have been interpreted as gains for all of Latin America, the Third World, socialism in general, and at the highest level, for all of humanity. As Castro stated, "Our fate will be the fate of the world."[68]

Symbolism is affirmation, and the 25 years of revolution in Cuba have institutionalized the symbols of radically recuperated national history, consolidated and enhanced the stature of symbols emerging from struggle against the dictatorship, and accumulated new symbols to be joined with the latter and former. All of them reinforce each other and communicate coherence and continuity. Cuban revolutionary symbolism's message is that Marxism-Leninism, socialism, anti-imperialism and internationalism are natural to Cuba and are a product of historical forces and processes. Symbolism declares a natural progression of *el deber cubano* from the resistance to Spanish conquest mounted by the chieftain Hatuey to those Cubans who died in Grenada "fulfilling with honor their patriotic and internationalist duties."[69] It is an inclusive symbolism, affirming that Martí's Cuban duty has been realized by the revolution, that Bolívar's Latin American duty is represented by Guevara and Cuba's anti-imperialism, that Marx's liberating socialism is being constructed in Cuba, and that Lenin's proletarian internationalism is an integral part of the Cuban Revolution. Symbolism expresses the continuity of these elements and makes them weapons in the continuing struggles against counterrevolution, imperialism, and capitalism.

NOTES

1. See "El pensamiento revolucionario de Camilo," *Verde Olivo*, October 29, 1960, p. 69.
2. See Richard Fagen, *The Transformation of Political Culture in Cuba* (Stanford: Stanford University Press, 1969), passim.
3. Fidel Castro, "A Pyrrhic Military Victory and a Profound Moral Defeat" (Havana: Editorial Política, 1983), pp. 18-19: "Every day, every hour, every minute...we will remember our comrades who died in Grenada...they are not corpses; they are symbols...their example will be multiplied, their ideas will be multiplied and they themselves will be multiplied in us."
4. Ibid., p. 16.

5. Comisión Nacional Cubana de la UNESCO, *Cuba y la conferencia de educación y desarrollo económico y social* (Havana: Editorial Nacional, 1962), p. 25.

6. See "El descubrimiento," *Verde Olivo*, June 25, 1961; and "La conquista," *Verde Olivo*, July 2, 1961, p. 15

7. See "Lección I: historia de la propiedad de la tierra en Cuba," *Verde Olivo*, p. 81; "El siglo XVI: pacificación y repartimientos," *Verde Olivo*, July 9, 1961, pp. 15–16; "El siglo XVII y la primera mitad del siglo XVIII," *Verde Olivo*, July 23, 1961, pp. 71–72.

8. See "Lección V: el perjuicio racial y la discriminación del negro," *Verde Olivo*, October 22, 1960, pp. 61–62; "Las luchas de los vegueros," *Verde Olivo*, July 30, 1961, p. 58.

9. Gabriel García Márquez, "Operation Carlota," *The Guardian*, January 26, 1977, pp. 14–15.

10. *Verde Olivo*, July 20, 1969, p. 3.

11. See William Gálvez, *Camilo, señor de la vanguardia* (Havana: Editorial de Ciencias Sociales, 1979); and Joel Iglesias, *De la Sierra Maestra al Escambray* (Havana: Editorial Letras Cubanas, 1979).

12. William Gálvez, " Camilo: como lo recordamos," *Verde Olivo*, October 28, 1962, pp. 4–7. See also Guillermo Cabrera Álvarez, *Hablar de Camilo* (Havana: Instituto del Libro, 1970); Gabriel Pérez Tarrau, *Cronología de un héroe* (Havana: Gente Nueva, 1976).

13. See John M. Kirk, *José Martí: Mentor of the Cuban Nation* (Gainesville: University of Florida Press, 1983).

14. See Georges Sorel, *Reflections on Violence*, trans. T.E. Hulme (London: Allen and Unwin, 1925), passim; Georges Sorel, *The Illusions of Progress*, ed. and trans. John and Charlotte Stanley (Berkeley: University of California Press, 1969), passim; see also C.F. Judson, "The Development of Revolutionary Myths in the Political Education of the Cuban Rebel Army 1953–1963," diss. University of Alberta, 1982.

15. Sorel, *Reflections on Violence*, p. 132.

16. Ibid., p. 133.

17. Fidel Castro, *History Will Absolve Me* (Havana: Editorial de Ciencias Sociales, 1975), p. 77: "We are Cubans and to be Cubans implies a duty. Not to fulfill that duty is a crime, it is treason."

18. Marta Rojas, *La Generación del Centenario en el Moncada* (Havana: Ediciones R., 1964), pp. 66–67.

19. Document reproduced in Cabrera Álvarez, *Hablar de Camilo*, p. 106.

20. See Rojas, *La Generación del Centenario en el Moncada*, passim.

21. Rolando Bonachea and Nelson Valdés, "Introduction," *Revolutionary Struggle. Volume I of the Selected Works of Fidel Castro*, Bonachea and Valdés,

eds., p. 42. *See also* Hugh Thomas, *Cuba* (London: Eyre and Spottiswoode, 1971), p. 828: Santamaría was "a fanatic of Martí"; and Haydée Santamaría, *Haydée habla del Moncada* (Havana: Editorial de Ciencias Sociales, 1978), p. 59.

22. The concept of nontraditional opposition is developed by Samuel Farber, *Revolution and Reaction in Cuba* (Middletown, Conn.: Wesleyan University Press, 1976).

23. See *Verde Olivo*, July 29, 1973.

24. See Mario Mencia, *La Prisión Fecunda* (Havana: Editora Política, 1980); Jesús Montané, "Del 26 de julio de 1953 al 15 de mayo 1955—días de combate," *Verde Olivo*, July 28, 1963, pp. 19–23; and Calixto García, "Nuestro deber era permanecer firmes a la orientación trazada por nuestro comandante en jefe," *Verde Olivo*, December 1, 1963, p. 5.

25. E.G. Roberto Roque Núñez, "Relato," *Verde Olivo*, December 1, 1963, pp. 14–15.

26. "Speech in New York" (November 1, 1955), in *Revolutionary Struggle*, pp. 281–84.

27. Faustino Pérez, cited in Armando Giménez, *Sierra Maestra* (Buenos Aires: Editorial Lautaro, 1959).

28. H. de Arturo, "Desde el '56," *Verde Olivo*, December 5, 1971, pp. 68–70.

29. See Julio Antonio Mella, "Glosando el pensamiento de Martí," *Verde Olivo*, January 27, 1963, pp. 30–31. Martí had said to Baliño, later a founder of the Communist Party: "The Revolution? It is not what we will initiate in the *maniguas* but what we shall develop in the Republic."

30. See "En un lugar de Oriente," *Verde Olivo*, January 17, 1965, p. 27.

31. Guillermo García, in Lee Lockwood, *Castro's Cuba, Cuba's Fidel* (New York: Macmillan, 1967), p. 24.

32. In *Cuba Internacional*, May–June 1970, p. 76.

33. See Robert Taber, *M-26, Biography of a Revolution* (New York: Lyle Stewart, 1961), pp. 60–62.

34. Ché Guevara, in *Cuba Internacional*, May–June 1970, p. 14.

35. In *Selected Works of Mao Tse-tung*, vol. IV (Beijing: Foreign Languages Press, 1965), pp. 155–56.

36. See José Mayo, *La guerrilla se vistió de yarey* (Havana: Editora Política, 1979).

37. Ché Guevara, *Reminiscences of the Cuban Revolutionary War*, trans. Victoria Ortiz (New York: Monthly Review Press, 1968), p. 193.

38. Jean-Paul Sartre, *Sartre on Cuba* (New York: Ballantine Books, 1961), pp. 50–51.

39. Jorge Masetti, *Los que luchan y los que lloran* (Buenos Aires: Editorial Jorge Álvarez, 1969), p. 72.

40. Ibid., p. 135.
41. Ibid., p. 150.
42. See José N. Causse, "Relato: El Segundo Frente Oriental 'Frank País'," *Verde Olivo*, March 24, 1963, pp. 5-6; Raúl Castro, "Diario de campaña," in Edmundo Desnoes, *La Sierra y el Llano* (Havana: Casa de las Américas, 1961), p. 213; Ramón Bonachea and Marta San Martín, *The Cuban Insurrection, 1952-1959* (New Brunswick: Transaction Books, 1974).
43. See Castro Valdés-Rodríguez, "El camino de la libertad," *Verde Olivo*, March 17, 1963, pp. 29-31. *See also* the cover photo of José Antonio Echeverría, who led the Palace attack, *Verde Olivo*, March 15, 1970; and "30 de Noviembre de 1956," *Verde Olivo*, November 25, 1982, pp. 4-7.
44. See Raúl Castro, "La patria tiene en las FAR al brazo armado de la clase obrera en el poder," *Verde Olivo*, January 2, 1979, p. 6.
45. See the description in Jules Dubois, *Fidel Castro, Rebel-liberator or Dictator?* (New York: Bobbs-Merrill, 1959), p. 363; and in Bonachea and San Martín, *The Cuban Insurrection*, p. 330.
46. Cited in *Revolución* (Havana), January 10, 1959.
47. Cienfuegos's letter of November 19, 1958 to Castro, cited in Pérez Tarrau, *Cronología de un héroe*, pp. 59-61.
48. See Marvin Leiner, *Children Are the Revolution* (New York: Penguin, 1974), p. 24.
49. See *Verde Olivo*, October 29, 1960, or October 12, 1975.
50. Cover of *Verde Olivo*, October 12, 1975.
51. Cited in *Verde Olivo*, October 7, 1982.
52. In a January 2, 1965 speech, Castro asked the audience to choose between "Year of agriculture," "Year of production," and "Year of struggle against bureaucratism," *Verde Olivo*, January 10, 1965, p. 3.
53. *Verde Olivo*, April 14, 1968.
54. See José Casanas and Jesús Suárez, "Oriente 20 años después," *Verde Olivo*, July 29, 1973, p. 75.
55. E.G. "¿Por qué el Moncada?" *Verde Olivo*, July 13, 1969, p. 25.
56. See *Verde Olivo*, April 11, 1965 (the frontispiece in memory of Misael González González, killed March 22, 1963).
57. Eduardo Yasells, "Primera derrota del imperialismo en América Latina," *Verde Olivo*, April 30, 1961, pp. 6-14.
58. *Verde Olivo*, April 23, 1961, p. 3.
59. Ibid., p. 7.
60. *Verde Olivo*, May 2, 1976, p. 17.
61. See *Verde Olivo*, September 5, 1965, pp. 43-44.
62. Castro, in *Verde Olivo*, January 9, 1966, p. 3.
63. Castro, in *Verde Olivo*, December 3, 1981, p. 92.
64. *Verde Olivo*, January 7, 1968, p. 3.

65. *Verde Olivo*, April 4, 1965, p. 29.
66. *Verde Olivo*, March 4, 1969.
67. *Verde Olivo*, May 30, 1965, p. 61.
68. Castro, cited in *Verde Olivo*, October 10, 1965, p. 3.
69. Castro, "A Pyrrhic Military Victory," p. 18.

13 Cuban Political Structure: Vanguard Party and the Masses

Rhoda Pearl Rabkin

No account of Cuban politics should neglect the central role played, in both theory and practice, by the "vanguard" party. In the 25 years since Castro's revolution triumphed, political change has attempted to improve the effectiveness of the vanguard party, but never to challenge or replace it.

There is obviously something problematic in the concept of a revolutionary vanguard. Party members form, even if only temporarily, a political elite—even as they work to guide society toward its eventual culmination in a completely classless social order. Cuban political life is thus marked by a tension between, on the one hand, the desire for a high degree of mass popular participation, and, on the other hand, the continuing moral/political stratification of society. This tension or paradox must be kept in mind when we seek to understand Cuba's political structures and the processes of mass participation.

CASTROITE SOCIALISM: THE PERSONALISTIC STAGE

The commitment of Castro and his followers to the moral transformation of Cuban society propelled them toward enthusiastic embrace of Leninist political concepts and institutions. Throughout the 1960s, the revolutionary government openly dispensed with competitive electoral politics. It may be inferred that political insecurity led the revolutionaries to prohibit organized opposition. In the late 1960s, Castro told an interviewer, "Do you know how many real revolutionaries there were in Cuba (in 1959) at the moment of the revolution? Well, there wasn't even one percent."[1] Castro explained to another interviewer that denial of the right of political expression to "unreconstructed" social forces and interests was not based on the fear of political challenge, but was "a matter of principle."[2] Yet there appear to have been practical considerations as well, since in an earlier interview, Castro expressed his view that political restrictions would become unnecessary in the future when socialist mores were fully internalized.[3]

Early in the revolution, then, it had become the official goal of the Cuban revolutionary elite to transform Cuban society as a whole into a vanguard, to remake everyone in the vanguard's own image. In Ché Guevara's words, "Our aspiration is that the party become a mass one, but only when the masses reach the level of development of the vanguard, that is, when they are educated for communism."[4] Even in theory, the vanguard, not the proletariat as a whole, exercised the ruling function. Guevara explained with characteristic frankness:

> The vanguard group is ideologically more advanced than the mass; the latter is acquainted with the new values, but insufficiently. While in the former a qualitative change takes place which permits them to make sacrifices as a function of their vanguard character, the latter see only by halves, and must be subjected to incentives and pressures of some intensity; it is the dictatorship of the proletariat being exercised not only upon the defeated class but also individually upon the victorious class.[5]

The power of the vanguard party was thus understood from the beginning to include the power to coerce, and was not *merely* moral and educational through the impact of example.

In view of official expositions of the vanguard's role, one would expect the party to play an important role in formulating policy. But the Cuban vanguard party during the 1960s barely existed as an institution. Although Castro paid lip service to the paramount role of the vanguard party, he was in fact reluctant to subordinate his own considerable personal power to collective decision making. At the end of 1961, after three years of governing without a party, Castro proposed to merge his own 26th of July Movement, the Revolutionary Directorate (a small radical student group), and the traditional Cuban Communist party (PSP) into one organization. An old-line Communist, Aníbal Escalante, was placed in charge of organizational work. A few months later, however, Castro launched a series of vehement denunciations against the activities of the newly formed party. Escalante was blamed for appointing only his own PSP cronies to leadership posts, to the exclusion of Castro's own loyal followers in the 26th of July Movement, many of whom had participated more actively than the PSP is the revolution. Escalante was dismissed and the party ranks purged.

In 1965, the vanguard organization was renamed the *Partido Comunista de Cuba* (PCC), but this did not foretell a regularized institutional life for another 10 years. Until 1975, no party congress had met, and consequently the party had not adopted a program. The eight-person Politburo consisted of trusted *fidelista* loyalists, and the 100-person Central Committee had been handpicked by Castro. The Secretariat presented a semblance of balance between the 26th of July Movement, the Revolutionary Directorate, and the PSP, but neither the Politburo, the Secretariat, nor the Central Committee held frequent or regular meetings. Lacking its own institutional life, the party was ill-equipped to formulate goals and influence government.

To argue that the party was not a policy-setting body is not to say that it did not perform important functions. Even critics of the party's limited influence on policy formulation during this period acknowledged the crucial role of the party cadres in providing the local day-to-day leadership necessary to sustain the revolution's projects. One critic wrote:

> Particularly in small towns, villages, and *bateys* of the island there are numerous effective party secretaries who perform tireless piecemeal work. They mobilize people for volunteer work in agriculture, act as peacemakers in shop disputes, bring some sanity into the planification chaos, fight against disorganization and sloppiness, and act as girl fridays for all and everything during the solution of a thousand everyday problems in the Cuban province. They do this without clearly defined roles, usually on their own initiative.[6]

The Cuban party carried out its functions of mobilization and organization despite the low ratio of its membership to the population and its limited penetration of the economic enterprises. This low coverage was partly the consequence of the tiny size of the Cuban party and partly a result of the promotion of reliable workers into supervisory, administrative positions. Through the 1960s, the PCC was by far the smallest party organization in proportion to population of any Marxist-Leninist regime. In 1969, it comprised a mere 0.8 percent of population, at a time when the Soviet Union averaged 5 percent, and many others (North Korea, East Germany, Czechoslovakia, and Romania) reached 10 percent and more.[7]

Although by comparative standards, the Cuban party was minuscule, after the Escalante affair, Castro developed a new method for involving the public in party affairs. Mass meetings at workplaces were convened to propose new candidates for party membership. The assemblies were not free to nominate just anyone; the standards of eligibility (one had to be an "exemplary" worker and a member of several mass organizations including the militia) were sufficiently stringent that only those of proven loyalty to the revolution qualified. Moreover, nomination by workplace assemblies was neither necessary nor sufficient for party membership. Party commissions proposed to the assemblies candidates who had not been nominated by the assemblies and also excluded those who, although nominated, were deemed "unworthy." Nevertheless, the process did allow for at least some popular participation in party selection of members.

The institutional weakness of the vanguard party was partially compensated for by the charismatic leadership style of Fidel Castro. But reliance on charismatic leadership necessarily entails certain risks for a revolutionary movement or government. In the Cuban case, overcentralization of authority in Castro's hands had a negative impact on economic decision making in the late 1960s. It was at this time that Castro, against the counsel of his technically trained economic advisers, set the goal of harvesting ten million tons of sugar in 1970. Castro believed that a "big push" in the sugar sector was needed to free Cuba from foreign debt and to provide the resource base for ultimate diversification away from sugar. Castro's policy was a failure, however. Not only did sugar output fail to reach the targeted ten million tons, but the all-out effort in sugar diverted resources from other activities, thereby causing production declines in numerous other sectors of the economy.

Responsibility for the economic debacle of 1970 can indeed be traced to the lack of restraint on Fidel Castro's power. Nevertheless, the emotional loyalty of the Cuban masses to their leader made Castro's removal unthinkable. Even the reduction of his power did not alter his preeminence. The events of 1970 were, however, a catalyst for efforts begun much earlier to formalize government structures and to regularize decision-making procedures.

A "NEW" BASIS FOR PARTY-STATE RELATIONS

The important political reforms that began after 1970 were officially described in Cuba as the "institutionalization" of the revolution. New life was breathed into existing organizational structures. The party held its first congress in 1975 and adopted a program and statutes. The Central Committee began to hold more regular meetings. A committee of the party drafted a socialist constitution that, with only minor changes, was adopted by plebiscite in 1976. The document provided for the creation of elected representative institutions. The mass organizations (for citizens, workers, women, and peasants) began to hold more regular meetings and, within the constraints of the system, to lobby on certain policy issues. No change was made, however, in the basic concept of the vanguard party as the most authoritative source of political guidance.

It was now emphasized that party members could not give legally binding orders to state officials; all such orders were to go through the official hierarchy. Raúl Castro explained that the party itself possessed no means of coercion, but was confined to exerting its influence through persuasion.[8] Nevertheless, the legal status of the Communist party of Cuba within the political system remained ambiguous. From Article 5 of the Cuban Constitution, for example, one might deduce that the party did have legal authority over state and society. According to the text,

> The Communist Party of Cuba, the organized Marxist-Leninist vanguard of the working class, is the highest leading force of the society and of the state, which organizes and guides the common effort toward the goals of the construction of socialism and the progress toward a communist society.

In order to make Article 5 consistent with Raúl Castro's explanation of the legal status of the party, one must interpret the constitutional language as a descriptive statement about the de facto role of a voluntary private organization, and not as a constitutional grant of ultimate legal authority.

Ambiguity and confusion have been recurring features in discussion of the relationship between party and state. In early 1981, the official organ of the PCC, *Granma,* gave this startling description:

> The Party is the ruling organ of the entire society, but in order to carry out its function as such it must have the support of an instrument that is essential to it: the state and its institutions. Thus, the Party advises and leads and the organs of People's Power—the highest state authority—administer the state.[9]

Yet in many other presentations (including the 1976 Cuban Constitution), the Organs of Popular Power (especially the National Assembly) are not merely administrative bodies, but decision-making structures that embody the popular will.

Thus, although institutionalization was meant to clarify lines of authority, the statements of Cuban leaders on the relation between party and state remained confused and self-contradictory. Party officials seemed unable to decide which institution—the legislature, which "expresses the sovereign will of the working people," or the PCC, which expresses the class interest of the proletariat—actually "rules." On the whole, however, party leaders betrayed a continued preference for the PCC as a ruling organ. On the very eve of inaugurating Cuba's new representative institutions, Raúl Castro reaffirmed the view that the legitimacy of the vanguard party is more fundamental than that of any other institution. True democracy resides in government for the workers, and, only secondarily, in government of and by them:

> When a state like ours represents the interests of the workers, regardless of its structure, it is a much more democratic state than any other kind which has ever existed in history, because the state of the workers, the state which has undertaken the construction of socialism is, in any form, a majority state of the majority while all other previous states have been states of exploiting minorities.[10]

Procedures and institutions are important, not for their own sake, but insofar as they contribute to political and economic performance, the value of which can be ascertained independently from any process of choosing officials.

INTERNAL PARTY STRUCTURE AND COMPOSITION

By the beginning of the 1980s, the PCC had become a disciplined and well-institutionalized organization. At the top of its hierarchy sat Fidel Castro, his brother Raúl, and a small group of Politburo and Secretariat members.[11] These individuals were responsible for the overall ideological and political direction of society. They consulted in important instances with lower-level party figures but made the final decisions themselves. Officially, the top-ranking party figures were elected from below, but, in practice, internal party elections have been a formality. Although other communist systems have experienced such high levels of political dissatisfaction that shakeups occur in the highest party bodies, the top echelon of the Cuban leadership remained remarkably stable after the early 1960s.

Below the top echelon was the Central Committee, composed after the 1980 Second Party Congress of 148 full members and 77 alternates. In Cuba (as in most other communist countries) Central Committee members have tended to be persons who hold positions of authority in other societal institutions. In other words, the Central Committee has been a collection of leaders from significant social groupings. Some students of communist political systems believe that representation of groups in the Central Committee "can be taken as a measure of the relative influence of various institutions in the political system."[12] Applied to Cuba, this methodological assumption indicates a steady decline for the military since 1970 and relative gains for the party and state apparatus. There has also been an increase in representation of mass organization leaders. Other groups, although noninstitutional ones, which have increased their share of the Central Committee membership are persons who have performed international service and workers linked directly to production.[13]

Below the Central Committee and its staff are the provincial party organizations and the "núcleos" or party cells—the PCC rank and file. The lower party ranks have been necessary instruments of the top party leadership's mobilization and legitimation goals. The activities of the party militants in aid to production, attention to worker living conditions, engagement in mass political education, and general morale boosting and trouble shooting have been extremely important for the maintenance of the system.

Although political and administrative leaders have always been over-represented in the PCC (in comparison to their share of the work force), there was gradual improvement during the 1970s in the percentage of "ordinary" workers who belonged to the party. According to the party's own reckoning, the worker share of PCC civilian membership increased from 55 percent in late 1973 to 62.3 percent in 1980.[14] Nevertheless, as one scholar notes, whereas "the civilian elites account for only 15.2 percent of the State civilian labor force, they account for 37.7 percent of the civilian party membership,..." and while "over one-quarter of the state civilian labor force elites belong to the party, somewhat less than one-seventh of the state civilian labor force mass belongs to the party."[15] In other words, the Cuban political and administrative elite was still over-represented, but to a lesser extent than in the past.

PARTY RELATIONS WITH OTHER INSTITUTIONS

Organs of Popular Power (OPP)

In 1976, a system of local, provincial, and national elected representative institutions was inaugurated with great fanfare. Although institutionally distinct from the PCC, the Organs of Popular Power were not designed to function independently of the party. Instead, restrictive electoral procedures have ensured that delegates are individuals who enjoy the confidence of the PCC. Of the almost 500 delegates to the National Assembly, generally 97 percent have been members of the party or its youth branch, the Young Communists. Party representation has been somewhat less at the provincial level and declined to about 75 percent at the municipal level.

According to the Cuban Constitution, the National Assembly is invested with supreme legislative authority. The assembly elects from its own ranks a Council of State that acts on behalf of the assembly when it is not in session. The president of the Council of State (up to now always Fidel Castro) serves as president of the Council of Ministers (the cabinet) whose membership he chooses, subject to approval by the assembly. In theory, the assembly is empowered, not only to enact legislation, but to supervise every aspect of government performance, from the cabinet down to the local Organs of Popular Power.

In practice, the Assembly has heard reports from various ministers and has criticized some executive performance. The Assembly as a whole has been by-passed, however, on important personnel and policy decisions in favor of the Council of State.[16] In addition, the Politburo customarily reviews draft legislation before it is submitted to the Assembly and decides certain policy matters on its own authority.[17] The Council of State also overlaps with the Politburo—of the council's 31 members in 1980, 19 were either full or alternate members of the Politburo. As of the early 1980s, the National Assembly had yet to develop an identity or political complexion distinct from the top echelon of the PCC leadership.

At the local level, the authority of elected officials has been constrained by the economic and political decision making of elites identified with central state institutions. According to Humberto Pérez, Cuba's Minister of Planning, "The Organs of People's Power were created on the basis that they could manage the country's resources more efficiently than the state's central agencies."[18] In the mid-1970s, a variety of local production, retail and service enterprises passed to the jurisdiction of the local assemblies. The local delegates were told to seek out complaints concerning these enterprises and, within the limits of available resources, find solutions. There is evidence, however, that many delegates felt overwhelmed and helpless in the face of problems brought to them.

Hampering the effectiveness of local government has been the fact that many problems originate in national planning decisions over which the local officials lack control. For example, in one of the main areas of OPP responsibility—restaurant and retail services—the comments of local officials suggest that problems in the local enterprises resulted from poor economic decisions at higher levels.[19] Since Cuba has a centrally planned economy, although local government officially "runs" local enterprises, it may not alter prices, wages, and many other "norms" decided by the central administration. The role of the local assemblies has been officially described as one of implementing methodological guidelines from the center. This is called the principle of "double subordination."

A degree of tension can be observed in the relationship between national officials and those with primarily local responsibilities. Although generally rebuffed, local deputies have attempted to inject local concerns into debates on national policy. In the July 1982 session of the National Assembly, for example, a deputy complained that shoemaking shops transferred from national to local jurisdiction no longer received priority in distribution of raw materials and machinery spare parts. The Minister of Light Industry did not deny the charge, but merely observed that leather assigned to the OPP was frequently diverted from planned use in orthopedic shoes to other purposes.[20] Another deputy in the same session complained that national planning agencies had failed to coordinate the forestry sector with an enterprise in his district manufacturing wooden tool handles. Several high-ranking government leaders took the floor to remind the deputy that the National Assembly was not the proper forum for resolving the problems of a local enterprise. The implications of the problem for larger issues of national economic coordination were firmly ignored. "Our plans will always be deficient plans, and we have to be conscious of that," Politburo member Carlos Rafael Rodríguez remarked philosophically. Humberto Pérez said that local government and the ministries, not his national planning agency JUCEPLAN, were responsible for ensuring coordination of raw material supplies in this case.[21]

There are other indications that local officials have not enjoyed high prestige and influence within the Cuban political hierarchy. For example, the post of PCC provincial first secretary has ranked higher in the Communist Party than the highest posts in local government. In 1980, all the provincial first secretaries were either members or alternates of the Central Committee, but few of the presidents of the provincial OPP served on the Central Committee.[22]

Cuban local officials have failed thus far to utilize their grass-roots connections to expand the role of local government and win for it new powers. At the beginning of the 1980s, many local delegates appeared to believe that instances of waste, disorganization, and mismanagement were the result of failures of planning and coordination at the top. To the extent that their perception was correct, the vague formal grant of "jurisdiction" to local government for local affairs had little substance. As in other communist countries, Cuban local government had been assigned a great many responsibilities, but little effective power.

Administrative and Economic Units

Little progress has been achieved in separating party and government roles at the top of the political hierarchy. The top executive body, the 36-member Council of Ministers has been dominated by its executive committee, consisting of 14 ministers, all of whom were either Politburo, alternate Politburo, or Central Committee members. Most members of this group also served on the National Assembly Council of State. "Ordinary" government ministers could be, and indeed were, held accountable for their performance, as firings and demotions in 1979–80 proved. But the highest leadership echelon, by virtue of its hold over top positions in the party, the National Assembly, and the cabinet, enjoyed the enviable position of playing watchdog over themselves.

In mid-1979, Humberto Pérez delivered a speech that suggested that Cuban thought on the party's role had changed little since the earliest years of the revolution. Pérez described the party as the "motor" of the whole society and the "supervisor" of "every type of work."[23] In the same year, the PCC Politburo passed a resolution criticizing the attitudes and style of work of the party cells. According to the resolution, many party members mistakenly believed that their responsibility was confined to setting a good *personal* example (work discipline, honesty, etc.). The Politburo accused the base organizations of neglecting their duty to uncover and denounce negligence, mistakes, the "buddy-system," and other deficiencies in their work places. The resolution cited the party statutes, according to which the base organizations

> are not empowered to act as administrative organs nor to direct the administrative management; but at the same time it is established clearly that they have the right to supervise the activity of the leadership and administration, whether or not the directors or administrators are members or candidates of the Party.[24]

Apparently, many party members found these "clear" instructions confusing, and preferred cooperation with local managers to conceal problems from superiors over the demands and hazards of attempting improvements.

In 1983, the party carried out a massive program of party meetings from the base up to the national level to discuss economic problems and solutions. The program elicited sharp and wide-ranging criticisms of economic management by party members. Indeed, there is some reason to believe that the volume and scope of the criticisms were not always welcomed by the highest ranking party leaders.[25] Nevertheless, the program was pronounced a success for having increased the economic awareness of the typical party cadre. This campaign of economic education had been undertaken with the goal of augmenting the competence and self-confidence of the base party organizations in carrying out their work of supervision. Only time will tell whether the program will actually have a substantial impact on party effectiveness.

Mass Organizations

The Cuban mass organizations are frequently described as the nation's primary channel for articulating popular demand. There are four major mass organizations: the Committees for the Defense of the Revolution (CDR), the Confederation of Cuban Workers (CTC), the National Association of Small Farmers (ANAP), and the Federation of Cuban Women (FMC).

Each of the Cuban mass organizations enjoys state sponsorship and a monopoly on the organization of the interest it represents. All state workers belong to the CTC, all small farmers to ANAP. Approximately 80 percent of all adult citizens belong to the CDR, and more than 80 percent of women belong to the FMC. The membership for these last two organizations would be even greater were it not for their practice of excluding those citizens of "lower quality" or questionable revolutionary commitment.

Although charged with responsibility for representing interests, the Cuban mass organizations are nonetheless subject to the "leading and orienting role of the Party." The party formulates "general directives concerning fundamental questions of economic, social, political, and cultural development of the country, such as concerning the problems that pertain to the different social sectors."[26] The party also has responsibility for ensuring "the most adequate selection and placement of cadres" on the part of the mass organizations.[27] Lacking autonomy, the mass organizations can with some justice be viewed as agencies of the Cuban government responsible for promoting "nonantagonistic" forms of interest representation.

The leaders of the mass organizations have always tended to enjoy fairly high rank in the party. Their role became even more elevated at the Second Party Congress. Of the 11 new positions made available in the new rank or Politburo alternate, 4 went to the presidents of the major mass organizations. In addition, 17 leaders from the CTC and 8 from the FMC became full members of the Central Committee, a notable increase over previous levels of representation. Overall, the mass organizations increased their share of full Central Committee members from approximately 6 percent at the First Party Congress to about 19 percent at the Second Party Congress in 1980.[28]

In view of the mass organization leaders' dual position in the PCC and their own special interest organizations, it is interesting to question how these leaders handle competing claims and potential conflicts of loyalty. For the most part, these leaders have functioned subordinating particularistic interests to elite definitions of the public good. But this is not to deny that mass organizations also play an important role in channeling opinion from the mass base up the Cuban political hierarchy. Indeed, each of the Cuban interest organizations has at some time publicly advocated policies divergent from the policy preferences of other government leaders. Occasionally, their special lobbying efforts appeared to pay off; it would go beyond what we know, however, to assert that the mass organizations' efforts consistently yielded results.

It is even difficult to say which of the Cuban mass organizations has been the most aggressive and/or effective in pursuing its member interests, much less to specify what organizational or other resources have provided the greatest political advantage. Early in the revolution, the all-purpose Committees for the Defense of the Revolution were the most celebrated of the mass organizations. Once the organs of local government were established, however, the CDR was left with a much narrower role. The responsibility for "vigilance" and good-citizen projects (i.e., neighborhood beautification, inoculation campaigns, glass recycling, etc.) continued undiminished, but the interest-representation function naturally declined.

One scholar believes that the small farmers' group, ANAP, has distinguished itself from other mass organizations through its independent and successful defense of peasant interests.[29] If family income is the standard, there would seem to be great truth in this observation, for the small farmers have been a financially advantaged sector of Cuban society since the mid-1960s.[30] ANAP has achieved this gain despite the small size of its constituency and despite the ideological incompatibility between private farming and Marxism.

ANAP's success derived largely from the coincidence between its members' financial self-interest and policies that promote broader national objectives. At the same time, ANAP's lobbying of the government has been part of a complex give-and-take bargaining process, in which victory is always tenuous. For example, ANAP championed the free farmers' markets (at which beginning in 1980 food was sold at market prices) in alliance with central planning officials who were interested in augmented food supplies. In April 1982, Castro, disturbed by exorbitant prices in these markets, proposed a stiff tax on sales to eliminate profiteering. At the Sixth ANAP Congress in May, however, Castro said that he had been persuaded by the ANAP delegates that price ceilings (at a high level) would achieve the same object without penalizing the consumer or arousing resentment against the farmers. Yet the Sixth Congress did adopt a resolution favoring a tax on gross private sales.

Although still short of complete success, the Cuban government has made notable progress toward abolition of private property in farmland. Almost a quarter million strong in the mid-1960s, the peasant class had shrunk to about 110,000 families by 1981. Hemmed in by legal restrictions on the sale, mortgage, and inheritance of land, many small farmers sold their land to the state. Unable to organize independently of ANAP to challenge these restrictions, the remaining private farmers continue, despite their relatively privileged economic position, to join "more advanced" economic formations, with no reason to expect that the government will relent.

In most respects the Confederation of Cuban Workers is at the opposite end of the spectrum from ANAP. As representative of the entire working class of Cuba, the CTC defends the interests of a huge mass membership, the well-being of which is the ideological raison d'être of the revolution. With 17 leaders on the Central Committee and the right of its secretary general to attend sessions of the Council of Ministers, it is the best institutionally represented at high leadership levels of all of Cuban's mass organizations. The same pattern of strong representation holds also at lower and intermediate levels, since in the early 1980s, CTC leaders at the provincial level were promoted to serve on provincial party committees and their executive bureaus.

The puzzling aspect of the CTC's role in Cuban society is the extent to which, instead of aggressively championing workers' interests, the trade union organization has been criticized—by its own secretary general and others in the government and party—for excessive passivity. Roberto Veiga's report to the Fourteenth Congress denounced the timid role played by the unions and called for eradication of the spirit of the "good neighbor," of "one big family," and of "peace without principles."[32] Veiga's report claimed that labor law violations were frequent, and it requested new legislation to clarify the rights of the unions.[33] According to the Eighth Plenum of the PCC Central Committee in 1979, "there are times when the trade union movement does not contribute energetically enough to carrying out labor legislation and to seeing that the workers' rights are fully respected."[34] In 1980, Politburo member Carlos Rafael Rodríguez offered a critical assessment:

> We don't think, however, that the unions play the role that they should. Our unions are much better at transmitting the party's orientations to the working class than they are at gathering from the working class the desires, the criticisms, the suggestions to which the leadership has to be alert.[35]

In the July 1981 session of the National Assembly, the Commission on Constitutional and Judicial Affairs recommended special emphasis "on the struggle for the adequate observance of labor legislation on the part of state enterprises and agencies."[36]

A plausible explanation of this strange pattern is that the criticism of CTC performance has been hypocritical and inconsistent. In practice, union leaders have had to respond not only to criticisms of their passivity but also to denunciations of "lax" worker discipline and exhortations that the CTC should function as the "nonantagonistic counterpart of the management," and that it should be primarily concerned with raising productivity.[37] To some extent, then, CTC leaders may have served as a convenient scapegoat for deeper ills.

Cuban leaders frequently refer to the CTC as "the most important of the mass organizations." The high (relative to other mass organizations) participation of union representatives at all levels of the party, state, and government testifies to the importance and prestige accorded the CTC. But the CTC's spotty record in defense of workers' interests suggests that the special attention given the organization and its high degree of integration into the structure of governance has been a mixed blessing for its working class membership. (For a more detailed study of the role of the CTC, see chapter 15 by Marifeli Pérez-Stable, "Class, Organization, and *Conciencia*: The Cuban Working Class After 1970.")

If the chief obstacle to peasant aspirations is the PCC commitment to abolish private property, and if the chief barrier to worker benefits lies in the financial limitations of the country and concern for productivity, then, for the Federation of Cuban Women, the chief impediment is the ingrained traditional outlook of many Cubans in regard to appropriate sex roles.

The FMC's commitment to sexual equality has been officially endorsed by the PCC, and in many respects the government has been more favorably disposed toward FMC aspirations than has the population as a whole. For example, in the 1981 municipal elections, 11.3 percent of those nominated for local office were female, but the voters elected only 7.2 percent females for these posts.[38] Elections at the provincial and national level are more subject to PCC manipulation, and the number of women at these higher levels is larger. In 1981, of the 143 women candidates nominated as National Assembly delegates, 113, or 79 percent, were elected. But of 660 male nominees, only 386, or 58 percent, were elected.[39]

The FMC has criticized administrative decisions when it has viewed these as insufficiently sensitive to women's concerns. For example, at the Third FMC Congress (in March 1980), the main report criticized discontinuation of an experimental program that had opened stores and service units during evening hours for the convenience of working women. According to the report, the FMC was not consulted on the decision. In a closing address to the Congress, Castro took note of the FMC's complaints on the issue and expressed support for their position.[40] The FMC has also had something of a running feud with government ministries and the CTC over jobs classified as "too dangerous" for women to perform. This issue seems to be perpetually "under study."[41]

If sexual equality in education, work force participation, and political status is the standard, Cuban women have significantly improved their position in Cuban society since the revolution. One may question the independent contribution of the FMC to this change, emphasizing instead, for example, the impact of underlying modernization trends, but there is no question that the FMC has adopted a public posture that is critical, not only of "tradition," but of ongoing institutional practices and decisions.

In theory all Cuban mass organizations are the organized expression of distinct constituencies whose interests they represent and defend in the policy-making process. In practice, however, representation takes place through a "consultation" process that leaves political initiative and control largely in the hands of trusted political lieutenants who cooperate closely with the highest party leadership. *What* is an acceptable interest to be organized and *who* will lead it are questions with which the party considers itself properly concerned. Consequently, the mass organizations encourage citizens to watch and report on their neighbors, urge workers to produce faster and better, encourage peasants to join cooperatives, and exhort women to join the paid labor force, despite their continued special responsibility in the home. It is unlikely that spontaneous voluntary interest associations would pursue the same agenda. As a result of low autonomy, the mass organizations to a substantial degree represent the interests of the government to its members.

CONCLUSION

Formally, the Cuban regime consists of three or four major institutional elements—the Communist Party, the state (Organs of Popular Power), and the government (the administration or executive branch). In addition, the semiofficial mass organizations serve as regime-sanctioned channels of political communication and demand articulation. But since party leaders greatly influence the selection and promotion of individuals for positions in the OPP, administration, and mass organizations, the PCC must be considered the preeminent or governing institution.

The problem of Cuban politics is how to combine opportunities for mass participation with a protracted process of elite-sponsored moral and social transformation. The ideology of the PCC requires both transformation and participation, but in practice (and theory as well), mass participation in Cuba has been subordinated to the requirements of socialist transformation.

In theory, democracy has been "proletarian," that is, structured so as to exclude bourgeois influences that are by definition antithetical to collective interests. From the beginning, the authority of the proletarian vanguard party has been understood (despite considerable vacillation in public expositions of this point) as including the power, not only to inspire and persuade, but also to rule and coerce.

In practice, Cuban society presents to outside observers a highly participatory surface, with impressive numbers attending meetings, voting for leaders, debating legislation, managing local activities, and so forth. Many political scientists question, however, whether the enormous quantity of political activity in Marxist-Leninist regimes such as Cuba translates into qualitative opportunities for popular influence on government decisions.

By their own account, Cuban political institutions have been extremely successful in pursuing both the goal of social transformation and the goal of mass participation. Officially, the supervision and guidance provided by the vanguard party are not considered a hindrance to the effective articulation of citizen demands. This is not the most credible of claims; it hardly seems likely that such an elaborate apparatus of restraints would exist where there is little or nothing to be restrained.

In the official Cuban view, political restraints are of limited duration, destined to disappear with full communism, although during the transitionary period they are necessary and beneficial. It is of course not self-evident that the moral and political stratification of society, implied in the vanguard role, is the best means—or even a possible means—of fostering a fraternal egalitarian social order. Many observers, however, will consider a quarter century (and even several quarter centuries) too short a period to reveal fully all the potential of the Cuban system. Therefore, all that can be said with some confidence is that a considerable distance remains between the social and political realities of Cuban life and the goal of the Cuban elite that all participate in that life on equal terms.

NOTES

1. K.S. Karol, "Where Castro Went Wrong," *New Statesman*, August 1979, p. 46.
2. Frank Mankiewicz and Kirby Jones, *With Fidel: A Portrait of Castro and Cuba* (New York: Ballantine Books, 1975), pp. 85-86.
3. Lee Lockwood, *Castro's Cuba, Cuba's Fidel* (New York: Random House, 1969), p. 112.
4. Ernesto Ché Guevara, "Man and Socialism in Cuba," in John Gerassi, ed., *Venceremos! The Speeches and Writings of Ernesto Ché Guevara* (New York: Simon and Schuster, 1968), p. 397.
5. Ibid., pp. 392-93.
6. Hans Magnus Enzensberger, "Portrait of a Party: Prehistory, Structure and Ideology of the PCC," in Ronald Radosh, ed., *The New Cuba: Paradoxes and Potentials* (New York: William Morrow, 1976), p. 135.
7. Richard C. Gripp, *The Political System of Communism* (New York: Dodd, Mead, 1973), p. 46.
8. *Órganos de Poder Popular* (La Habana: Edit. Orbe, 1974), pp. 130-31. See also *Granma Weekly Review*, supplement, January 18, 1981, p. 4.
9. *Granma Weekly Review*, January 18, 1981, p. 4.
10. Ibid., September 8, 1974, p. 3.
11. The Politburo consists of 16 members. In 1980, the rank of alternate Politburo member (filled by 11 individuals) was created. Because of overlapping membership, the Politburo, alternates, and the Secretariat consist of only 29 people.
12. William M. LeoGrande, "Continuity and Change in the Urban Political Elite," *Urban Studies* 8 (July 1978), p. 3.
13. Jorge I. Domínguez, "Revolutionary Politics: The New Demands for Orderliness," in Jorge I. Domínguez, ed., *Cuba: Internal and International Affairs* (Beverly Hills: Sage Publications, 1982) pp. 24, 31-33.
14. Jorge I. Domínguez, *Cuba: Order and Revolution* (Cambridge: Harvard University Press, 1978), p. 320; and *Granma Weekly Review*, December 28, 1980, p. 12.
15. Domínguez, "Revolutionary Politics," pp. 60-62.
16. In late 1979 and early 1980, major dismissals and demotions of ministers were timed so as to precede and follow the Assembly session in December 1979, thereby reducing that body's role to one of ratifying the decisions of the Council of State. Many of the vacated posts were filled by members of the executive committee of the Council of Ministers, a body that overlapped with the Politburo. The PCC elite responded to political difficulty by concentrating authority in its own hands, not by enlarging the role of the national legislature.
17. *Granma Weekly Review*, January 11, 1981, p. 2; and William M. LeoGrande, "The Communist Party of Cuba Since the First Congress" (Paper

presented to the Institute of Cuban Studies, Washington, D.C., August 13-17, 1979), p. 22.

18. *Granma Weekly Review*, July 13, 1980, p. 2.
19. See, for instance, articles in *Bohemia*, July 27, 1979, p. 20; and August 5, 1980, p. 61.
20. *Granma*, July 5, 1982, p. 2.
21. Ibid., July 3, 1982, p. 3.
22. Domínguez, "Revolutionary Politics," p. 39.
23. Humberto Pérez, "Discurso," *Economía y Desarrollo*, no. 53 (August 1979), p. 137.
24. *Bohemia*, July 20, 1979, p. 44.
25. See the rather sarcastic comments of Julio Camacho Aguilera in *Granma*, December 21, 1983, p. 1; *see also* the positive assessment of Politburo member José Ramón Machado Ventura in *Granma*, January 18, 1984, pp. 2-3.
26. *Plataforma Programática del Partido Comunista de Cuba* (La Habana: Departamento de Orientación Revolucionaria del Comité Central del Partido Comunista de Cuba, 1976), pp. 137-38.
27. Ibid., p. 138.
28. Domínguez, "Revolutionary Politics," p. 24.
29. Ibid., pp. 50-52.
30. Carmelo Mesa-Lago, *The Economy of Socialist Cuba* (Albuquerque: University of New Mexico Press, 1981), p. 156.
31. *Granma*, February 22, 1984, p. 4.
32. Ibid., November 29, 1978, p. 3.
33. Ibid., December 2, 1978, p. 3.
34. Ibid., May 23, 1979, p. 7.
35. "Entrevista: Carlos Rafael Rodríguez," *Areíto* 7 (1981), p. 10.
36. *Granma Weekly Review*, July 5, 1981, p. 2.
37. *Granma*, November 30, 1978, p. 5; and *Granma Weekly Review*, December 15, 1979, p. 3.
38. *Granma Weekly Review*, August 30, 1981, p. 3; and *Granma*, October 25, 1981, p. 3.
39. *Granma Weekly Review*, December 6, 1981, p. 3.
40. *Granma*, March 6, 1980, p. 2.
41. Max Azicri, "Women's Development through Revolutionary Mobilization: A Study of the Federation of Cuban Women," in Irving Louis Horowitz, ed., *Cuban Communism*, 4th ed. (London: Transaction Books, 1981), p. 297; and *Granma*, February 23, 1984, p. 3.

14 The Organs of People's Power and the Communist Party: The Nature of Cuban Democracy

Archibald R.M. Ritter

INTRODUCTION

On February 24, 1976, Cuba adopted by referendum a new socialist constitution which established new representative institutions—the *organós del poder popular*, or the Organs of People's Power (OPP). In national elections on October 10 of the same year representatives for municipal assemblies were selected. On December 2, 1976, the National Assembly held its inaugural session. The establishment of the Organs of People's Power (OPP) ended a sixteen year period in which there had been no formal electoral institutions for the governance of the Cuban state.

The objective of this essay is to review the structure and functioning of the new representative institutions, and to examine the relationship between the Organs of People's Power and the *Partido Comunista de Cuba* (PCC). The central issue which is explored here is the nature of democracy in the operation of the OPP. In what senses and to what extent are the new assemblies "democratic"? Do the OPP constitute effective decision-making and initiative-taking bodies? What is the role of the Party in the new assemblies?

Assessing the nature of democracy in Cuba's representative institutions is a difficult task. There is a major debate as to what constitutes genuine democracy and democratic participation. Many analysts from the Western world would quickly reject the notion that political democracy could exist in a system characterized by a monopolistic political party; monopolistic control of all organs of communication by that party; intense purveying of a single ideology and party line, through the educational system and the media; and thorough penetration and substantial manipulation of the civil organs of society by the party. On the other hand, other observers would reject the idea that authentic democracy could exist in Western systems characterized by highly unequal ownership and control of financial resources by citizens, generating unequal capabilities for manipulation of the system; the presence of large and vociferous private business establishments, with disproportionately large powers to shape legislative processes and policy formulation; and private ownership and financing of the communications media.

I will not try to resolve the debate between Western pluralistic and Communist conceptions of the meaning of democracy. Instead, the criterion I will employ for "democratic participation" will be the degree of control and influence that ordinary citizens are able to exercise over (1) the selection of those in leadership positions, and (2) the decisions, policies and procedures adopted in relevant groups or collectivities.[1]

On the basis of this criterion, a one-party state could constitute a genuine political democracy if it were possible for citizens to exercise influence or control over policy formulation and leadership selection. Such control or influence perhaps could be exercised at least to some extent through electoral procedures, if there were open selection of candidates and voting for delegates for representative assemblies, if the assemblies wielded autonomous decision-making power, and if there were other consultative processes concerning new legislation and the formulation of public policy. On the other hand, a single party state often is one in which elections are stage-managed and controlled by the monopoly party, in which electoral assemblies are empty shells which rubber stamp decisions reached by the party, and in which meaningful public discussion and influence over policy formulation is narrowly circumscribed by the party with its monopoly control over the media, over the civil organs of society, and over the right to aggregate and articulate the interests and choices of a group of citizens.

On the basis of this criterion also, a Western liberal multiparty system could be either democratic or undemocratic politically. The mere existence of multiple parties with open political competition, does not guarantee meaningful influence or control over policy formulation and leadership selection by the majority of an electorate. A multiparty system can, under some circumstances, serve as a means by which powerful interest groups or classes effectively dominate the state, shaping public policy and influencing leadership selection through their control of economic resources. On the other hand, Western pluralistic multiparty systems can also be genuinely democratic to a significant degree according to the above definition of democracy. Thus the definition of participatory democracy employed here is largely neutral as between Western political systems and Soviet-type systems.

THE POLITICAL SYSTEM OF THE 1960s

The essence of the political system throughout the 1960s was the direct personal relationship between Castro and the Cuban people. This relationship expressed itself through a variety of media, the most important of which may have been the mass rallies. But while the public could respond in the rallies with cheers and shouted slogans, the mass rallies were essentially one-way, top-down events. This was totally the case with televised and radio presentations of speeches and with the write-ups in *Granma*. A second mechanism of popular communication for Castro was through the frequent tours and visits he made throughout Cuba, speaking directly to a broad range of people and listening to their views. Finally, Castro had had intimate contact with rural people, especially those of the Sierra Maestra, during the guerrilla campaign of 1956 to 1958.

The political system throughout the 1960s, and especially in the latter half of that decade, cannot be considered to be democratic in the sense that mechanisms were used or even existed for the popular selection of the leadership, or in the sense that people were able to influence policy-making through formal mechanisms. It is important to emphasize that despite this, policies were formulated that were highly beneficial to the large majority of the population. With surprising success, these policies redistributed income, reduced urban-rural disparities, reduced unemployment, and achieved universal access to education and public health.[2] Presumably, the system generated beneficial results because of the identification of the revolutionary leadership with the interests of the bulk of the population, the commitment to improve the well-being of the people, and the character of the socialist ideology of the Castro regime.

In the latter half of the 1960s, and especially from 1968 to mid-1970, the nonparticipatory nature of the political system aggravated other difficulties encountered by the revolution. It is very difficult to disentangle the impacts of the political system from economic factors such as excessive centralization, heavy reliance upon nonmaterial incentives, and the fixation on the 10-million-ton sugar-harvest target. The lack of representational machinery in the state, the party and the mass organizations, together with a lack of other means for influencing policy formulation likely contributed to growing public apathy in the face of the strenuous exhortation to work harder and to accept intensified austerity. If people had no meaningful input into the formulation of national objectives or plant-level targets, could it be expected that they would behave as the planners desired, on the basis of exhortation and moral incentives rather than according to their perceptions of their own costs and benefits? The symptoms of the difficulties arising from a lack of meaningful participation (and other factors) were high levels of absenteeism, low on-the-job productivity, and "indiscipline."[3]

By mid-1970, the shortcomings of the existing system were apparent to the revolutionary leadership. A decision was made to establish formal electoral mechanisms. Democratization and institutionalization became the hallmarks of the system that was to be constructed. Movement toward a new system began with public discussion of the problems of the late 1960s, and continued with public consideration of new pieces of legislation (such as the Anti-Loafing Law), with elections in the labour unions, with work on the drafting of a new constitution, and finally with the establishment of the Organs of People's Power in 1976.

THE NEW POLITICAL INSTITUTIONS

The Organs of Popular Power consist of a five-tiered set of assemblies beginning at the neighbourhood level, and moving through the *circunscripción* (district) electoral level, the municipal level, and the provincial level to the national level.[4]

At the level of the neighbourhood, citizens select, by a show of hands at a general public meeting, a secretary and president, whose task is to run the nomination proceedings for the rest of the meeting. Potential candidates for the later elections at the *circunscripción* level are then nominated from the floor. Of the several potential candidates (the minimum being two), one is elected at the meeting, again by a show of hands. The individual chosen then becomes the neighbourhood nominee for the *circunscripción* election. In these elections, one representative is selected by secret ballot in enclosed voting booths and by a simple majority (with a runoff, if necessary), to represent the *circunscripción* in the Municipal Assembly.

The municipal assemblies, and not the citizens directly, select the delegates to the 14 provincial assemblies (one delegate for every 10,000 inhabitants and for a portion of people greater than 5,000) and the deputies for the National Assembly (one for every 20,000 inhabitants and for a portion exceeding 10,000). *Circunscripciones electorales* may select candidates from outside the relevant area. Similarly, the municipal assemblies may choose delegates to the provincial assemblies and deputies for the National Assembly who are neither delegates to the municipal assemblies, nor residents of the relevant municipalities.[5]

On October 11, 1976, some 10,725 delegates were elected in the national elections for the 169 municipal assemblies. These assemblies then elected 1,084 delegates to the provincial assemblies and 481 deputies for the National Assembly.[6] In the National Assembly, a Council of State was selected, with Fidel Castro as president and Raúl Castro as first vice president; five other vice presidents, a secretary, and 23 other members were named.

The modes of operation and the responsibilities of the municipal and provincial assemblies and the National Assembly and of the Council of State are outlined in the constitution. According to the constitution, the National Assembly is the supreme organ in the political system. It selects the Council of State, and is also the ultimate constituent and legislative body. It is the supreme economic authority, being empowered to discuss and approve the national economic and social plans, the state budget, and the nature of the economic-management system. It is the foremost authority on such matters as the general outline of foreign and domestic policy. It selects the members of the Supreme Court and the attorney general. It "exercises the highest supervision over the organs of state and government."[7]

The executive body of the National Assembly is the Council of State, which represents the former when it is not in session, and which is charged with overseeing the implementation of its decisions. However, another body, the Council of Ministers, is the highest-ranking administrative and executive organ. Members of this body are appointed by the president of the Council of State and approved by the National Assembly. The Council of Ministers includes the president, vice president, and secretary of the Council of State, together with all ministers, the head of the *Junta Central de Planificación* (JUCEPLAN), and some others.

At the provincial and municipal levels, the assemblies are charged with overseeing and controlling the administrative leadership and local enterprises in their relevant jurisdictions, with aiding in plan formulation and implementation in their relevant areas, with upholding the constitution, and defending the rights of citizens and socialist property, and with other legal and appointive tasks.[8] The municipal and provincial assemblies do not, however, possess independent revenue-raising capabilities.

Two important mechanisms exist to ensure that delegates to municipal and provincial assemblies and deputies for the National Assembly continue to be in close contact with their constituents and responsive to their needs, suggestions, and criticisms. First, delegates must be "accountable" to their electors. In practice, this means that they must meet every four months with their electors and listen to complaints, grievances, and proposals they then may transmit upward. They also report back to their constituents on their own activities and those of their respective assemblies. Municipal-assembly delegates are required to set aside a specific time every few weeks for consultation with constituents, although often this consultation may occur also on a more informal and frequent basis. Second, delegates and deputies are subject to recall by their electors. If a delegate or deputy is thought to have been negligent in his or her duty, those who elected that delegate or deputy can remove that person from office and select another representative.

THE COMMUNIST PARTY AND THE ORGANS OF PEOPLE'S POWER

Cuba's Constitution guarantees a number of fundamental political rights and freedoms to the citizenry, and the OPP provide an institutional framework for the selection of political leadership and for shaping public policy. However, the *Partido Comunista de Cuba* (PCC) plays a dominant role at all levels of the OPP, and especially in the National Assembly. In view of the Party monopoly over interest aggregation and articulation, over the media, and over the mass organizations, can genuine participatory democracy, as defined here, be meaningfully exercised? The evidence so far suggests that the answer to this question is a qualified "yes" at the municipal level, and a qualified "no" at the national level.

The Constitutional Relationship

The tension and, ultimately, the contradiction between the Organs of People's Power and the Communist Party is enshrined in the Constitution. Article 4 asserts the supremacy of the people, as exercised through the OPP:

> In the Republic of Cuba all the power belongs to the working people, who exercise it either directly or through the assemblies of People's Power and other organs of the state which derive their authority from these assemblies.[9]

On the other hand, the Party is meant to provide guidance or control over the OPP. As stated in Article 5 of the Constitution:

> The Communist Party of Cuba, the organized Marxist-Leninist vanguard of the working class, is the highest leading force of the society, which organizes and guides the common effort toward the goals of the construction of socialism and the progress toward a communist society.[10]

The text of the First Party Congress Resolution on the Organs of Popular Power contains the following statement:

> The Party must guide, promote and control the work of state organs, control the policy for the promotion and training of cadres and perfect the mechanisms of the state; but the Party should never replace the state in the exercise of its power and functions.[11]

It would thus appear that it is the responsibility of the Party not only to ensure the correct functioning of the OPP, but also to ensure that leadership selection and policy formulation are consistent with, and further the progress of the development of, the Communist society. However, Party members are supposed to participate in the OPP purely on a personal basis, and not as representatives of the Party.

While the Party is charged by the Constitution with this important guidance function, it is also exhorted to respect the supremacy of the

OPP institutions: "We must bear in mind that the Organs of People's Power are the highest state authority on the territories under their jurisdiction."[12]

Articles 52 and 53 of the Constitution guarantee basic political freedoms to the citizenry:

> Citizens have freedom of speech and of the press in keeping with the objectives of the Socialist State.

> The rights to assembly, demonstration and association are exercised by workers, both manual and intellectual; women; students; and other sectors of the working people, and they have the necessary means for this.[13]

However, the electronic and print media are controlled by the Party. The national newspaper, *Granma*, is the "Official Organ of the Central Committee of the Communist Party of Cuba," and is part of one of the Departments of the Central Committee, namely the Department of Revolutionary Orientation. The electronic media are part of the same Department. The second major newspaper, *Juventud Rebelde* is a part of the National Committee of the *Unión de Jóvenes Comunistas* (UJC). The establishment of publications which could propound analyses, world views or policies not in harmony with those of the Party is prohibited. Freedom of speech and of the articulation of alternate views is therefore seriously curtailed.

Freedom of "assembly, demonstration and association" for political purposes is also limited. It is not possible for groups to organize for political purposes outside the established mass organizations. The mass organizations are effectively controlled by the Communist Party, in keeping with the responsibility of the Party as enunciated in Article 5 of the Constitution, as cited previously. The paramount guidance function of the Party in the civil organs of society is also confirmed in the Statutes of the Communist Party of Cuba. Chapter VIII, Article 73 of the Statutes reads as follows:

> The Party guides and directs the work of the mass and social organizations, based on the principle of full and conscious acceptance of its leadership role and of the influence its members and aspirants have in the mass organizations, while recognizing the organic independence and autonomy of those organizations.

> The method of Party leadership and guidance is to promote the broad, democratic discussions in these organizations; to reason with and convince people of the correctness of the Party line and its agreements; and to respect the autonomy of those organizations and the interests of the sectors of the population they represent.[14]

What happens when the "correctness of the Party line" is not in harmony with the "autonomy of the organizations" and the interests of the people therein? Although detailed research on this does not seem to have been published yet, it would appear that the Party line takes precedence, judging from the absence of any disarticulation or clashing of sectional interests.

The Party in the Municipal Assemblies

The Party has a strong presence in the Municipal Assemblies. In 1979, about 76 percent of all elected delegates were members or aspirants of the Party or of the UJC. Over 95 percent of the members of the Executive Committees also had a Party affiliation at this level (see Table 14.1).

It is difficult to know for sure why the Party presence is so strong at the municipal level, but some conjecture is possible. To some degree, it may be due to superior individual characteristics of Party and UJC members. Collusion, either implicit or explicit, among party members is probable, however, in view of the organizational monopoly of the Party and its junior affiliate, together with the old-boy networks it nurtures, and the certification of good character and ideological correctness it provides.

There are a number of mechanisms that facilitate the work of the Party in shaping electoral outcomes. First, no uncontrolled campaigning is permitted before the municipal-level public votes occur, or before the indirect selection of provincial delegates and national deputies. Instead, election commissions write up and distribute biographies of all candidates at the local level. While the makeup of these commissions is not known for sure, it is not likely that the roles of the Party, the UJC, and the mass organizations therein would be very different from their roles in the commissions that scrutinize and approve or disapprove of nominees for the positions of provincial delegate or national deputy. Under these circumstances, it is highly unlikely that a candidate with a questionable background, of a noncompliant disposition, or openly hostile, would

TABLE 14.1 Political Affiliation in the Organs of People's Power, 1979 (Percent of Totals)

Political Affiliations	Municipality		Province		National Assembly	
	Assemblies	Executive Committees	Assemblies	Executive Committees	Assembly	Council of State
Communist Party:						
Members or Aspirants	64.7	90.4	90.6	99.2	91.7	100.0
Young Communist League						
Members	11.1	5.2	3.3	0.4	5.0	0
Nonaffiliated	24.2	4.4	6.1	0.4	3.3	0
Total	100.0	100.0	100.0	100.0	100.0	100.0

Source: Comisión Electoral Nacional, 1979, cited in B. Jorgensen, "The Interrelation Between Base and Superstructure in Cuba," *Ibero-Americana: Nordic Journal of Latin American Studies*, vol. 13, 1 (1983), p. 39.

let his or her name stand as a nominee, thereby risking public embarrassment.

A second important factor in the apparent Party/UJC predominance at the municipal level arises from the organization of the elections. Each of the four-to-eight neighbourhoods within a *circunscripción* selects a nominee for the election. Because of the organizational monopoly of the Party, any support for noncompliant nominees is likely to be of a neighbourhood favourite-son nature. With no possibility of overt campaigning, and great obstacles to covert political action, support for noncompliant nominees is likely to be fragmented and neighbourhood-specific. On the other hand, the Party/UJC machine, of course, continues to function during elections, and can ensure without difficulty that its members throughout the *circunscripción* support the certified candidate(s).

Third, the mechanism of the recall or revocation could be utilized to enforce delegate compliance. By February 1979, 108 out of 10,725 municipal-level delegates had been recalled. For at least a few others, recall proceedings had been initiated but the relevant body of electors had refrained from voting the delegates out of office.[15] The recall is intended to ensure that delegates are responsive and responsible to their electors. It is possible that this mechanism could be used to induce conformity and, in the extreme, to weed out troublemakers and upstarts.

There is little concrete evidence concerning the authenticity of participatory democracy at the municipal level. Perhaps the only political study by 1984 is based on a survey conducted in Nuevitas in 1979 by B. Jørgensen.[16] On the basis of his survey, Jørgensen concluded that the

> OPP has been an important instrument in improving local service systems.... The OPP seem to have functioned effectively in leading people's energies towards making solutions to their own problems. At this level, the OPP decentralize decision-making and place the discussion of problems close to the problems themselves.[17]

Conjecture also supports the conclusion that the OPP have enhanced local-level policy formulation and decision-making. Matters of municipal concern such as transport, sanitation, and water provision are seldom ideologically contentious, and efficiency as well as equity in their provision requires substantial local input into problem-solving. It is therefore probable that Jørgensen's conclusions are generalizable to many or most municipalities.[18]

With respect to leadership selection at the local level, I would conclude that the local-level OPP assemblies do permit local initiative and participation. As argued previously, however, the Party plays a prominent role in the process of delegate selection.

The Party in the Provincial and National Assemblies

Membership in both Provincial and National Assemblies consists almost entirely of Party members or aspirants and UJC members (see Table 14.1). In 1979, 6 percent of Provincial delegates and 3.3 percent of National delegates were unaffiliated. 99.2 percent and 100 percent of Provincial Executive Committee and National Council of State members respectively were Party members. It is also of interest to note that about 45 percent of the members of the National Assembly were selected by the Municipal Assemblies from outside those assemblies themselves.[19]

While it is difficult to know exactly why such Party/UJC dominance exists, one can infer how it is generated. To begin with, a substantial proportion of municipal-assembly delegates are Party or UJC members. Indirect selection of National Assembly deputies permits the municipal delegates to select Party members, both from within and from outside the municipal assemblies. It is likely that in view of the role of the Party in providing a certification of good behaviour and of ideological rectitude for its members, Party members, rather than nonmembers, are likely to be chosen by other Party members.

The result of this overwhelming presence of Party members in the National Assembly is that a clear separation between the Party apparatus and the organs of the state has not been achieved, as some observers had hoped and expected. What appears to have happened instead is that the OPP, especially the National Assembly, provide a public and legitimate forum for discussions and decision making by the Party. The National Assembly is likely to have only as much participatory democracy as the Communist Party itself.

The permanent executive organ of the National Assembly is the Council of State, the members of which are elected by the Assembly. Of the 31 members of the Council of States in 1983, 29 were also members of the Central Committee of the Party, including the positions of president, first vice-president, secretary and the five vice-presidents. This overlap in the membership of the Council of State and the Central Committee is outlined in detail in Table 14.2.

TABLE 14.2. Cuban Party, Government and State Leadership in 1983

Name	Party Apparatus			Council of State National Assembly	Council of Ministers
	Politbureau	Secretariat	General Committee		
Castro Ruz, Fidel	First Secretary	First Secretary	Member	President	President
Castro Ruz, Raúl	Second Secretary	Second Secretary	Member	First Vice President	First Vice President and Minister, FAR
Almeida Bosque, Juan	Member		Member	Vice President	
Camacho Aguilera, Julio	Member		Member		Advisor to VPs
Cienfuegos Gorriaran, Osmani	Member		Member	Member	Vice Pres., Finance, Labor and Minister Secretary
Dorticós Torrado, Osvaldo	Member			Member	Vice Pres. and Minister of Justice
García Frías, Guillermo	Member		Member	Vice President	Vice Pres. & Minister of Commun. & Transport
Hart Dávalos, Armando	Member	Member		Member	Min. of Culture
Machado Ventura, José	Member		Member	Member	
Milián Castro, Arnaldo	Member		Member	Member	Vice Pres. Agriculture & Food
Miret Prieto, Pedro	Member		Member	Member	Vice Pres., Basic Industries
Risquet Valdés, Jorge	Member	Member	Member		
Roca Calderón, Blas	Member		Member	Vice President	
Rodríguez Rodríguez, Carlos Rafael	Member		Member	Vice President	Vice Pres., Foreign Rel'ns and Trade
Valdés Menéndez, Ramiro	Member		Member	Vice President	Vice Pres. & Min. Interior
Valle Jiménez, Sergio del	Member		Member	Member	Min. of Public Health

Acosta Cordero, Armando	Alternate		Member	
Batista Santana, Sixto	Alternate		Member	
Cano Blanco, Miguel José	Alternate		Member	
Casa Requeiro, Senén	Alternate		Member	
Colomé Ibarra, Abelardo	Alternate		Member	
Espín Gaillois, Vilma	Alternate		Member	
Montané Oropesa, Jesús	Alternate	Member		
Peréz Herrero, Antonio	Alternate	Member		Vice Pres. & Min. Central Planning
Peréz González, Humberto	Alternate		Member	
Ramírez Cruz, José	Alternate		Member	
Veiga Menéndez, Roberto	Alternate		Member	(President, CTC)
Crombet, Jaime		Member		
Rizo Alvarez, Julián		Member		
Soto Prieto, Lionel		Member		
Aguirre del Cristo, Severo			Member	
Bravo Pardo, Flavio		Member		
Castilla Mas, Belarmino			Member	
Castro Yedra, Reinaldo		Member		
Deprés Arozarena, Marta			Member	
Domenech Benítez, Joel			Member	Vice Pres. no Portfolio
Domínguez Muñoz, Luis			Member	
Fernández Álvarez, José Ramón			Member	Vice Pres. & Min. Education

283

TABLE 14.2. (continued)

Name	Party Apparatus			Council of State National Assembly	Council of Ministers
	Politbureau	Secretariat	General Committee		
Lezcano Pérez, Jorge			Member	Member	
Maza Oliva, Braulio			Member	Member	
Torralba González, Diocles			Member	Member	Vice Pres. & Min. Sugar Industry
Esquivel Yedra, Antonio			Member		Vice Pres. Light Industries
López Moreno, José A.			Member		Vice Pres. & Min. Construction
Portal León, Marcos J.			Alternate		Min. of Basic Industry
Guelmes González, Pedro			Member		Min. of Communications
Vila Sosa, Manuel					Min. of Domestic Trade
Fernández, Jorge A.					Min. of Fishing Ind.
Roca Iglesias, Alejandro					Min. of Food Ind.
Malmierca Peoli, Isidoro			Member		Min. of Foreign Relations
Cabrisas Ruiz, Ricardo					Min. of Foreign Trade
Vecino Alegret, Fernando			Member		Min. of Higher Education
Milleros Rodríguez, Manuel					Min. of Light Industry
Lage Coello, Marcos					Min. of Steelworking
Rodríguez Cruz, René			Member		(President, ICAP)
Ramírez Cruz, José			Member		(President, ANAP)
			(plus 25 other members or alternates)		(plus 10 other Ministers)

Source: Government of the United States, Directorate of Intelligence, Directory of Officials of the Government of Cuba, CR 83-11555, Washington, U.S.A., June 1983.

Perhaps it should not be surprising that Party heavyweights occupy virtually all the Council of State positions, in view of the Party predominance in the National Assembly. What seems to happen is that Party members in the Assembly select their Party superiors for the leadership positions in the Council of State. Table 14.2 also illustrates some of the detail of the overlap that exists between the Council of Ministers, the Central Committee, and the Council of State. All Politbureau members except two were also members of the Council of State.

In view of the fact that virtually all Council of State members are members of the Central Committee of the Party, with key Council positions being occupied by Politbureau members, it is difficult to envisage how the National Assembly could take initiatives or adopt policies that had not been decided upon previously within the higher echelons of the Party.

The predominance of the Party in the National Assembly likely means that serious debate on difficult issues occurs before the legislation reaches the Assembly for approval. One would anticipate that the National Assembly should have little problem in dealing with the large number of pieces of legislation that are likely to come before it, in its two two-day sessions each year.

THE FUNCTIONING OF THE NATIONAL ASSEMBLY

The National Assembly meets twice annually, in June and/or July and in December. Its sessions lasted for three or three and one-half days each from 1976 to 1978. Since 1979, each session has lasted two days. Each session has a heavy workload, with substantial pieces of legislation, state budgets, and socioeconomic plans to approve; with various reports to consider; with important appointments to approve; with decree-laws, passed by the Council of State between sessions of the Assembly, to approve. The sessions of the Assembly have been amazingly productive. The December 21-22, 1983 session, for example, discussed and approved a Law on National Symbols and a bill concerning road transport; ratified several decree-laws and resolutions adopted by the Council of State; approved some Ministerial appointments; heard reports by the Minister of Communications and by the City of Havana Provincial Assembly; discussed and approved report-backs by the Council of Ministers and a summary of the international activities of the National

Assembly; and approved the Budget and the Integral Plan for Economic and Social Development for 1984.

The heavy agenda and high "productivity" (defined in terms of approvals and ratifications) of each session would not be likely to permit much time for serious appraisals and discussions of legislation such that major modifications could be introduced. This creates a strong impression that due to workload and time constraints, the Assembly usually performs what is essentially a rubber stamp function, approving or ratifying what is placed before it.

A second factor that may limit the potency of the National Assembly (and perhaps also the provincial assemblies) is the part-time nature of the deputy's position. According to the constitution, deputies continue to hold their regular jobs, and are given leave from these when their work as deputies demands.[20] (Deputies are given leave without pay from their regular tasks, but receive as deputies a daily allowance equivalent to their regular salary plus expenses.) There also appear to be insufficient time, support staff, and financial resources to permit individual members to scrutinize problem areas, pieces of legislation, and reports independently and carefully, or to take major initiatives in the Assembly independently.

There is one encouraging feature of the National Assembly, which permits more continuous work by Assembly delegates. This is the existence of approximately 20 working commissions dealing with such issue areas as Child Care and Women's Rights; Culture and Art; Defense and Internal Order; Constitutional and Legal Affairs; Work, Social Security, Social Prevention, and Aid; Young People and Children; Construction and Construction Materials; and Complaints and Suggestions.[21] Judging from the accounts of the Assembly proceedings in the Cuban press, these commissions play an active role.[22] The commissions are charged with examining drafts of legislation and proposing modifications for discussion and approval at the assemblies. They also are charged with following and reporting upon the particular issue areas with which they are identified by their names. This was done, for example, with considerable effectiveness by the Transportation and Communications Commission, whose report on the national passenger-transportation service was presented and debated in the July 1979 meeting of the Assembly. Its report appears to have been comprehensive, thorough, and critical of the transportation system and, by implication, the Ministry of Transportation. After some debate, the report was approved and submitted for action by the Executive Committee of the

Council of Members.[23] This type of scrutiny of a particular aspect of Cuba's socioeconomic system may be invaluable as a means to put the pressure on parts of the economic bureaucracy, in order to improve economic performance from the standpoint of citizens in their position as consumers. The commissions may come to play an important role in permitting the views and interests of the public on specific issue areas to find expression in the National Assembly.

Before 1979, a deputies' question period was used as a means of raising issues of importance to the deputies and their constituents. This mechanism was discontinued in 1979 for unknown reasons. In the first four regular sessions of the Assembly, however, time was set aside for deputies to bring up a variety of topics for discussion. In the third regular session, for example, the matters raised by the deputies included problems of "broken water mains which are repeatedly discussed at grass-roots assemblies but not solved"; problems relating to gas service, urban transportation, the quality of bread, and the domestic distribution of goods; and "buck-passing" from one official to another, among other things.[24] This opportunity may have had some effect on the shape of the Assembly's agenda in future sessions, and on future budget and plan priorities. It is possible that the questions and proposals pertaining to housing, urban transport, the distribution system, and official buck-passing in the first four regular sessions likely had a reinforcing impact upon how the problems and priorities are perceived by the Junta Central de Planificación, which constructs the annual socioeconomic plans. It is unfortunate that the delegates' discussion period has been terminated.

CONCLUSION

This essay has examined the structure and functioning of the Organs of People's Power and has explored the relationship between the Communist Party and the electoral institutions in Cuba. On the basis of the meager evidence available so far on the actual functioning of the OPP and the Party, an attempt was made to determine tentatively the extent to which Cuba's electoral system is genuinely "democratic," where that term is defined as the ability of citizens to influence and ultimately to control the selection of their leaders and the formulation of public policy.

The new electoral system is a significant improvement over the system of the 1960s in terms of permitting active participation and more direct influence by the public on leadership selection and policy formulation. In the 1960s era of "revolutionary paternalism" there were no adequate formal mechanisms for public participation in the governance of Cuban society. (But public policies were introduced which were highly beneficial in meeting the basic needs of the population.)

The most serious problem concerning the authenticity of participatory democracy in Cuba arises from the dominant role played by the Party in the OPP. The Party is empowered by the Constitution to play a pervasive guidance function in Cuban society generally, and the OPP and mass organizations specifically. Judging from the high proportion of OPP delegates and deputies who are Party and UJC members, the Party would appear to be fulfilling its constitutional guidance responsibilities effectively. However, in my view, it would be an exaggeration to view the OPP at all levels as only a front or facade, to be used for legitimizing the actions of the Party, and improving the efficiency with which Party decisions can be implemented.

Despite the monopoly position of the Party, I conclude tentatively that at the local level, where citizens directly elect neighbourhood leaders, and at the municipal level, where citizens elect candidates and directly elect their representatives, democracy defined in terms of control over leadership selection exists to some degree. Accountability and recall reinforce the influence of the electors, although recall conceivably could be employed to keep elected delegates in line with Party policy. Direct elections, the importance of neighbourhood and *circunscripción* electoral meetings, and the practice of accountability sessions appear to operate so as to ensure some responsiveness on the part of elected delegates to their electors' wishes.

In the National Assembly, the role of the Party is paramount. About 92 percent of the deputies, and 100 percent of the Council of State members are Party members. The key executive positions within the Council of State are all filled by members of the Politbureau of the Central Committee of the Party. The predominance of the Party within the National Assembly would lead one to conclude that the democratic centralism, as practiced within the Party, is simply transferred to the Assembly. Separation of powers between the Party and the national-level Organs of People's Power has not been achieved.

Deputies to the National Assembly are not directly elected by citizens but are chosen by the municipal assemblies. It would seem that municipal delegates select party members and superiors for the National Assembly, and that deputies for the latter select their Party leaders for Council of State positions.

So far, the National Assembly has had a heavy agenda and now has only four days each year to complete its tasks. Undoubtedly, the workload and time constraint have limited discussion on new legislation, reports, budgets, development plans, and matters raised by deputies. This lends support to the conclusion that the National Assembly is not an organ within which independent initiatives can be taken. However, the formation of some 20 working commissions and their active work so far, in and between assemblies, generate some optimism that the Assembly might acquire an activist dynamic of its own.

At present, then, I conclude that at the level of the National Assembly, a large proportion of the processes of leadership selection and policy formulation is carried out by the Party within the shell or framework of the Assembly.

Effective public participation at the level of the National Assembly could be improved in a number of ways, so as to make it more independent, self-activating and responsive. First, the duration of the Assembly's sessions could be increased drastically, from four days to perhaps six months annually. This would permit more thorough analysis and more complete discussion of major pieces of legislation and other items of business than is now possible. It would provide time for deputies to develop more expertise on specific issue-areas and the work of the Assembly generally. Second, some support facilities for the deputies in their legislative work could be provided. Third, the question period for deputies could be reestablished, as this may facilitate the timely raising of issues of concern to the electorate. Fourth, direct elections with multiple candidates for the National Assembly could be established, in order to intensify the responsiveness of the deputies directly to the citizenry. Direct elections with a choice among candidates would not necessarily be incompatible with the continuation of single party rule, but it could provide an element of meaningful choice with the single party system. However, the domination of the National Assembly by the Party is likely to remain as long as the Party monopoly over the aggregation and articulation of citizens' interests, over the mass organizations, over the media, and over the formulation and dissemination of world views and ideology continues.

NOTES

1. This definition is borrowed largely from W.R. Schonfeld, "The Meaning of Democratic Participation," *World Politics*, vol. 28, no. 1 (October 1975).
2. See A. Ritter, *The Economic Development of Revolutionary Cuba: Strategy and Performance* (New York: Praeger, 1974), for substantiation of this statement. Also see appropriate chapters of this book (in particular the essays by Ross Danielson, Claes Brundenius, Marvin Leiner, and Joseph Collins and Medea Benjamin) which deal with these successful redistribution plans.
3. A. Ritter, *The Economic Development of Revolutionary Cuba*, pp. 282-94.
4. "Constitution of the Republic of Cuba," *Granma Weekly Review*, March 7, 1976.
5. See First Congress of the Party, "Resolution on the Organs of People's Power," *Granma Weekly Review*, January 11, 1976; and *Granma*, February 16, 1979, p. 4.
6. "Cuba: Su Institucionalización Histórica," *Cuba Internacional, Suplemento Especial*, 1976; and *Granma*, February 16, 1979, p. 4.
7. "Constitution," chapter VIII.
8. Ibid., chapter IX.
9. Ibid., p. 2.
10. Ibid.
11. First Congress, "Resolution," p. 9.
12. Ibid.
13. Ibid., p. 6.
14. 2nd Congress of the Communist Party of Cuba, *Documents and Speeches* (Havana: Political Publishers, 1981), "Statutes of the Communist Party of Cuba," Article 73.
15. *Granma*, February 16, 1979, p. 4.
16. B. Jørgensen, "The Interrelationship Between Base and Superstructure in Cuba," *Ibero-Americana: Nordic Journal of Latin American Studies*, vol. 13, 1(1983):333.
17. Ibid., p. 37.
18. M. Azicri comes to a similar conclusion. See M. Azicri, "The Institutionalization of the Cuban State," *Journal of Interamerican Studies and World Affairs*, vol. 22, no. 3 (1980), p. 333.
19. *Granma Weekly Review*, December 12, 1976.
20. "Constitution," Article 80, p. 8.
21. *Granma Weekly Review*, July 24, 1977, p. 9.
22. Ibid.
23. *Granma Weekly Review*, July 15, 1979, p. 3.
24. *Granma Weekly Review*, July 9, 1978, p. 3.

15 Class, Organization, and *Conciencia:* The Cuban Working Class After 1970

Marifeli Pérez-Stable

> The labor movement's role is decisive. Don't anyone ever think that the Revolution can even be conceived without the role of trade unions. Whatever management may do, workers are fundamental, decisive.
>
> Fidel Castro at the 1978 CTC Congress

> We have to understand that occasionally we cannot say what would be most pleasing to some workers, but what promotes the Revolution's interests which correspond to workers' interests: we all know that.
>
> Roberto Veiga, interview in Bohemia, 1984

The Cuban working class has grown to nearly three million persons in the mid-1980s. Founded in 1939 in the aftermath of the frustrated 1933–35 revolutionary upheavals, the Cuban Workers' Confederation (CTC) counts over 99 percent of the labor force as members in its 18 trade unions. Before 1959, Cuba's workers were highly syndicalistic (50 percent) and militantly trade unionist. While organized working class actions may not have been decisive for the demise of the old order in the 1950s, workers' mobilizations were, to be sure, imperative for the consolidation and defense of the Cuban Revolution and the socialist organization of the economy.[1] Nevertheless, the issue of working class organization in the revolution was problematic.

During the 1960s the Cuban leadership sought to steer away from the paths trodden in the socialist countries, in search of more dynamic and responsive institutions that would stave off bureaucratism and its concomitant "petit-bourgeois" *conciencia*. Contingent upon the success of the 10-million-ton sugar harvest in 1970, the Cuban model resorted to highly centralized planning, mass mobilizations, and moral incentives. Economic development and a communist *conciencia* were to have been its outcome. The 1970 debacle—a seriously dislocated economy and a tired population—sobered the Cuban leadership into the institutionalization of the revolution and the establishment of a more decentralized economic management and planning system. A call for the revitalization and democratization of the CTC was a top item in the post-1970 revolutionary agenda.

The 1960s had exacted a heavy toll from the trade union movement. Grass-roots organizations had either disappeared or responded only to vanguard workers, then a mere 10 percent of the labor force. The struggle against bureaucracy had eliminated the provincial and local structures of the sectoral trade unions and reduced the number of professional cadres. Thus the CTC could muster neither the expertise nor the personnel to even attempt to defend workers' interests. The trade union movement had simply become an adjunct of enterprise administrations and the Cuban Communist Party (PCC).[2] Its institutionalization entailed a reconsideration of the functions of trade unions in the transition to socialism, the role of workers in the economy, and relations with management. Although the 1970s undoubtedly rescued trade union authority from its ebb in the 1960s, economic development and national defense continued to be its primary objectives. Issues of workers' control were couched to respond to the exigencies of the economic management and planning system.

THE FUNCTIONS OF TRADE UNIONS

The first step toward restoring trade unions to the mainstream of Cuban society was the reconstruction of the labor movement. Local trade unions were created in nearly 40,000 enterprises, more than 280,000 grass-roots leaders were elected and national trade unions were established. CTC congresses in which up to 68 percent of the delegates were rank-and-file workers were held in 1973, 1978, and 1984.[3] The 1970s gradually institutionalized the trade union movement.

The question of the role of trade unions in the transition to socialism was addressed in terms of their nature as *mass* organizations which recognize the *vanguard* leadership of the Communist Party. While the balance sheet of the 1960s clearly underscored the need to define trade unions as organizations concerned with all workers, not just the most conscientious and politicized, the post-1970 institutionalization pivoted on strengthening the PCC as overseer of the state apparatus and mass organizations. In 1973, Raúl Castro underlined the reason for the party's pre-eminence:

> It is necessary to keep in mind that the working class considered as a whole... cannot exercise its own dictatorship since,... originating from bourgeois society, it is marked by flaws and vices from the past. The working class is heterogeneous in its consciousness and social behavior.... [O]nly through a political party that brings together its conscious minority can the working class conduct its dictatorship and construct a socialist society.[4]

Consequently, the realm and scope of trade union activity in Cuba reflected the need for the party's guidance and supervision. Raúl Castro reiterated the point in 1974:

> One of the principal functions of trade unions under socialism is to serve as a vehicle for orientation, directives and goals which the revolutionary power must convey to the working masses.... The Party is the vanguard. Trade unions are the most powerful link between the party and the working masses. That is one of their principal missions under socialism.[5]

The 1980 Party congress emphasized the importance of trade unions as veritable mass organizations:

> The CTC's structure and work methods are geared towards improving the work of grass-roots organizations and strengthening links between top leadership bodies and rank and file organizations. There is a growing awareness of the importance and need for maintaining and reinforcing these efforts in the future.[6]

Working class membership in the party was a crucial element in strengthening the "transmission belt" relationship between the PCC and the trade unions. Throughout the 1970s, the party made notable gains in working class militancy within its ranks—from 36 percent in 1975 to almost 50 percent in 1980. (For a study of the composition of party membership and of labor force distribution, see Tables 15.1 and 15.2.) The party targeted its main growth in key sectors, such as the sugar industry, construction, transportation, and education and, to a lesser extent, agriculture and public health. Workers in production and services nearly tripled their absolute numbers in the PCC's rank and file between 1975-80. However, critical questions were not publicly addressed by the party leadership. The exact proportion within the party of workers directly linked to production remained at approximately 47.3 percent comprising industrial, agricultural, construction, and service workers. While socialism undoubtedly increased the demand for service workers (education and health, for example), under conditions of scarcity and austerity it was particularly important to be attuned to those who actually produced society's wealth. Moreover, although working class membership was a necessary prerequisite for the PCC's claim to be the revolutionary vanguard, it certainly was not sufficient to guarantee its effectiveness and responsiveness as a vanguard. The transition to socialism in the twentieth century has quite evidently underscored that raising the proletariat to the position of the ruling class and winning the battle of democracy is a long process. An understanding of the Cuban experience within such a perspective is beyond the confines of

TABLE 15.1. Comparative Analysis of Party Membership Composition (Figures Given in Percentages)

	June 1975	Dec. 1978	July 1980
Workers in industry, agriculture, construction and services	35.9	44.9	47.3
Professional & technical workers	9.2	13.5	15.0
Administrative cadre	33.4	26.2	n.a.
Political cadre	8.7	4.8	n.a.
Workers in administrative functions	4.1	4.8	n.a.
Peasants	1.8	1.3	n.a.
Others	6.9	4.8	n.a.

Sources: *Tesis y Resoluciones: Primer Congreso del Partido Comunistsa de Cuba* (Departamento de Orientación Revolucionaria: (La Habana) 1976) p. 23; Isidro Gómez, "El Partido Comunista de Cuba," Paper presented at the 1979 seminar of the Institute for Cuban Studies, p. 28; Fidel Castro, *Main Report: Second Congress of the Communist Party of Cuba* (New York: Center for Cuban Studies, 1981), p. 27.

this chapter. Nevertheless, a partial analysis that identifies issues pertinent to the revitalization of the trade unions after 1970 is presented.

The ninth thesis of the 1973 CTC Congress laid out the basis for subsequent practical elaborations of the character of trade unions:

> In the recent past, some comrades expressed doubts about the character and role of trade unions as mass organizations of all workers and committed grave errors in the system of relations of trade union organizations with state organizations. These doubts and errors have been criticized by Comrade Fidel...especially in 1970, when he launched the slogan of strengthening trade unions and other mass organizations and personally participated in many trade union assemblies and urged them to act as counterparts to the administration.[7]

The thesis further detailed trade unions' relations with the state apparatus, management, and the party in view of their being representative and respondent to working class interests. Relationships between trade unions and other institutions "are fundamentally cooperative relationships for a superior common objective. But it is a type of cooperation in which each component has its own sphere of action and its own distinct method of action to arrive at the common goal."[8] As counterparts to management, trade union leaders were bound to defend workers' legitimate interests against possible infractions, especially given that "a petit-bourgeois spirit still permeates public administrations. ...[S]ometimes public officials are not at all like workers.... It is undeniable that an antiworker spirit, a bit of disdain for workers, exists among some managers."[9]

Nevertheless, trade unions were not empowered to control the economy or its management. The determination of plan priorities,

TABLE 15.2. Labor Force Distribution in Cuba, 1980 (Figures Given in Percentages)

Total labor force 1979: 2,733,100

Production workers	54
Administrative & service workers	20
Professional & technical workers	18
Administrative & political cadres	8

Source: Joaquín Benavides Rodríguez, "La ley de la distribución con arreglo al trabajo y la reforma de salarios en Cuba," *Cuba Socialista* II (marzo de 1982), pp. 70–73.

including the wage fund and management personnel policies, were beyond the bounds of union authority. These substantive matters were first the jurisdiction of top party and government echelons and then were entrusted to enterprise management councils for their implementation. Trade unions, however, were represented at all levels of this policy-making process, which implied the "cooperative relationships for a superior common objective."[10] The underlying thrust of these relationships was unequivocally articulated at the 1978 CTC Congress:

> With the elimination of exploitation, the people's standard of living depends on the economy's development. Consequently, the labor movement should guide its fundamental activity to strengthening its participation in fostering and consolidating the economy.... We Cuban workers are keenly aware that we own our country's wealth ...and that we are in power since the oppressive yoke of imperialism and its bourgeois and landlord allies was broken forever....[W]e therefore willingly sacrifice those immediate and particular interests ...for the benefit of the collective good.[11]

The unions' primary objective was clearly to join in the struggle to increase production. Fidel asserted this responsibility at the 1978 event: "we have to concentrate our efforts and our thoughts on developing the economy and think more about it than about consumption.... Our country's development is this generation of workers' most sacred commitment."[12] Within this struggle, the strengthening of trade unions was imperative for the efficient implementation of economic plans. Defense of workers' rights was understood from the vantage point of greater autonomy accorded to enterprises under the post-1975 economic management and planning system. Concomitantly, greater decentralization allowed for an enhanced role for trade unions in work centers: the new system created a "space" for trade unions and required their systematic input for its optimal operation.

WORKERS AND THE ECONOMY

Cuba's experience with highly centralized economic planning, mass mobilizations, and moral incentives induced the revolutionary leadership to adopt a more orthodox economic management and planning system. Large scale absenteeism (an average of 20 percent of the labor force in 1970), severe shortages, and an economy gravely dislocated by the abortive 10-million-ton sugar harvest demanded that productivity and efficiency become the order of the day. Campaigns were launched to encourage a stricter enforcement of labor discipline, an antiloafing law was enacted, and measures were taken to promote efficient investment allocations. "Socialist inflation" was slowly curbed through a policy of price increases for nonessential goods. The 1973 CTC Congress provided a forum for the first full-fledged discussion of the economic reorganization that the 1975 PCC Congress formalized.

The CTC Congress in 1973, like the subsequent events in 1978 and 1984, focused largely on matters relative to workers' contributions to economic development. However, the 1973 event marked a special occasion. As noted above, trade unions were restored as viable institutions in Cuban society. More importantly, the policies that led to the 1970 failure were assailed, if only by default. While the policies were by no means minutely analyzed, the theses and resolutions presented to the CTC Congress constituted their de facto condemnation. "From each according to his ability, to each according to his work" was certainly a distinct departure from the motto "constructing communism with *conciencia*" that had inspired the radical experiment of the late 1960s. Linking work performance to payment was hailed as "an inexorable law in the construction of socialism." In his speech to the congress, Fidel said: "we should have the courage to correct the idealistic mistakes we made...in certain cases, we tried to make more headway than we were prepared for."[13] Thus, the CTC Congress introduced payment for overtime, double-shifts, and hazardous conditions. "Socialist inflation" was further undercut by eliminating Law 270 (full-time salary retirement for workers in vanguard work centers) and abrogating "historical salaries" (salaries prior to the 1963 wage scales). Socialist emulation was reorganized both collectively and individually: improvements in production and productivity were sought by individual workers and enterprises "competing" with one another. Voluntary work—a symbol, to be sure, of the radical 1960s—was revamped to respond to productive criteria. The gains registered by the Cuban economy by the mid-seventies were indeed partially attributable to the program adopted at the 1973 CTC congress.[14]

However, less than a year into the first Five Year Plan of 1976–80, the economy ran into difficulties. Sugar prices, which in 1974–75 had reached an all-time high, plunged in 1976 and have generally remained low until the present. Worldwide inflation and the deterioration of trade relations with capitalist countries forced a readjustment of development prospects.[15] The economic slowdown threatened to refuel inflationary tendencies: the "inexorable" law of socialist construction—from each according to his work—was leading Cuba to internal financial imbalances. Wage raises soon equaled or surpassed productivity increases, while the supply of consumer goods declined. Wage measures adopted at the 1973 CTC Congress could not be fully applied. Roberto Veiga, CTC general secretary, observed in 1978:

> Reality forced us to stop implementing some of these measures. The point wasn't that they were no longer just, but rather that their implementation was economically irrational. We wouldn't have achieved anything if in their application we caused an internal financial imbalance. Increasing money in circulation without providing an adequate supply of goods and services would have constituted a step backwards to the situation we faced between 1967 and 1970.[16]

Consequently, the 1978 CTC Congress recommended the enforcement of wage-related measures at a pace and extent that promoted growth and increased labor productivity. Particular concern was expressed with the persistence of "historical salaries," which undercut the effectiveness of material incentives, and with the organization of socialist emulation and the coordination of the inventors' and innovators' movement which were not yielding the expected savings and productivity increases.[17]

Nonetheless, a general wage reform was decreed in 1980 to fine-tune the use of material incentives. Although enforcement was slow initially, by November 1981, the reform had been applied to 94 percent of the labor force. The new scales widened the ratio between the highest and lowest salaries from 4.33:1 in 1963 to 5.29:1. Salaries increased an average of 15 percent, while productivity registered a 35 percent improvement after 1977. The wage reform stipulated that 15–25 percent of salaries be "mobile," that is, bonuses either for individuals who exceed work norms or for enterprises' collective performance.[18] A corresponding retail price reform enacted in December 1981 raised the cost of over 1,500 products; on 64 sample items listed in *Granma*, the average price increase was 60 percent.[19]

The 1984 CTC Congress gathered under relatively auspicious economic circumstances. The economy had grown 5 percent in 1983, and the revolutionary leadership was confident that modest growth rates could be maintained, the adverse economic and political international situation notwithstanding. Consumption had improved notably as well.[20] Nonetheless, the congress focused on furthering the role of workers and trade unions in abetting the cautiously optimistic economic forecast of the mid-1980s. The struggle to make each enterprise "profitable" through higher productivity rates and overall savings of raw materials was its overriding concern. A particularly thorny issue before the congress was the law granting laid-off workers 70 percent of their salaries, a provision that quite obviously cut into productivity increases. *Disponibles* ("unemployment") first became a problem in the mid-1970s due to the rationalization imperative of the economic management and planning system. Although the congress fell short of recommending the law's repeal, it did predict substantial modifications to reduce both its costs and its irregularities. A similar concern was expressed with proposals to permit women's early retirement and to allow full payment to retirees hired on a contract basis. Both proposals were rejected as detrimental to the objective of prolonging a worker's productive life.[21]

WORKERS AND MANAGEMENT

At the 1978 CTC Congress, Fidel Castro pointed out the unions' twin objectives in the revolution: the construction of socialism and the defense of workers' rights. He noted: "Today a manager does not belong to another class, he is not the workers' enemy; he came forth from the workers' ranks and is friend, relative, neighbor of those who work with him.... We have to demand him to be demanding... his job is to be demanding and to control."[22]

However, the virtual disappearance of trade unions in the 1960s imposed upon the institutionalization of the labor movement the careful and formal delineation of local union-management relations. The need for specificity and clarity in those relations was further enhanced by the establishment of the economic management and planning system, the demands of which created the potential for significant tensions. The 1978 CTC Congress pointedly signaled the likelihood of contradictions:

> The reorganization of enterprises on the basis of an economic management system which underscores the urgency to improve efficiency and to attain profitability can result in contradictions between workers and management on issues of work conditions and other problems. Undoubtedly, we need to develop our economy in order

to improve our working and living conditions. But, differences and even contradictions can arise. In those cases, trade unions are obliged to seek an honest clarification... on the basis that workers' rights be respected, without lessening our inescapable obligation to fulfill our duties. The defense of workers' rights, correctly interpreted, strengthens proletarian power.[23]

Collective work agreements regulated worker-management relations after the 1973 CTC Congress. Their main objective was to guarantee conditions (raw materials, labor, etc.) to meet production plans. The agreements bound management to enforce safety regulations, maintain workers' lounges and recreational areas, establish a timetable for workers' vacations and time off to study, and the like. Workers were commensurately committed to punctuality, discipline, and care of their work instruments. While collective work agreements were generally extended throughout the economy, their establishment and implementation often ran into difficulties. Vague commitments, weak procedures for assigning responsibility for unkept records, and poor disclosure of their content among workers were typical obstacles encountered. More seriously, managers occasionally refused to ratify the agreements.[24] Labor unions were particularly sensitive to safety violations. Job-related accidents increased alarmingly between 1977 and 1980 and later declined somewhat. The CTC partially attributed the rise to management's use in production needs of funds allotted to safety equipment. Unions called for the inclusion in the budget of a safety category with nontransferable funds.[25] Most accidents (about 88 percent), however, were not caused by the lack of proper safety equipment, but rather by ignorance about rules and regulations, worker indiscipline in using the equipment, and a lackadaisical attitude from trade unions and management in enforcing safety regulations.[26]

Monthly production (or service) assemblies conducted by enterprise councils, which included the trade union general secretary, checked upon plan fulfillment, analyzed the quality of production, and sought to improve plant upkeep, upgrade labor discipline, and further workers' political and technical education. These assemblies were meant to spur "workers' enthusiastic and active participation... in the struggle to improve economic efficiency" and help them "to acquire consciousness of themselves as owners."[27] While trade unions rightfully could encourage workers to exercise criticism of enterprises' problems, labor leaders had to educate workers that their input could "not pry into things which are not their concern... be concrete and precise, contribute to solve problems."[28] Being a counterpart to management in these assemblies did not mean prompting antiadministration tendencies. Not surprisingly, production assemblies were beset by difficulties. The 1978 CTC Congress exhorted that these assemblies should not be "meetings in which a mechanical rattling off of figures is presented and where the analysis of fundamental problems is omitted."[29] Two years later a similar observation underscored the weaknesses in the monthly assemblies: "There are work places in which workers express their concerns and disagreements in these assemblies... and they are not heard by management.... [A] climate of malaise and indifference is generated to the considerable detriment of our economic endeavors."[30]

The yearly discussion of enterprise plans undoubtedly represented a cardinal instance of workers' involvement and education in the economic management and planning system.[31] Between 1974 and 1978, 85 percent of the work force discussed the yearly plans. Many ministries, however, either belatedly or only partially released the necessary data; often management failed to seriously consider workers' input. Roberto Veiga warned in 1978 that such practices resulted in the "mere formality of discussing plans with workers and their unions."[32] Humberto Pérez, minister-president of the planning board JUCEPLAN, subsequently divulged salient information relative to plan discussions. In 1978, 35 percent of all enterprises never held assemblies to discuss the 1979 plan, and only 42 percent revised it to include workers' suggestions. The 1980 plan showed some improvement: 9 percent failed to discuss the plan, and 59 percent included workers' input.[33] The 1984 CTC Congress emphasized a parallel theme on the absence of feedback to workers' suggestions: "Such a situation understandably irritates workers because they consider that their opinions and suggestions have been underestimated. It conspires against the objective of attaining the increasingly active and conscious participation of workers in planning and the economy."[34]

Until 1980 worker-management disputes were arbitrated by work councils empowered to hear two types of grievances: infringement of workers' rights and labor indiscipline. Between 1974 and 1978 the councils handled an average of 80,000 cases a year, 25 percent of which dealt with workers' grievances.[35] In 1977, the National Popular Power Assembly placed work councils under CTC jurisdiction. A year later, the CTC Congress pledged to strengthen their effectiveness as instruments of arbitration and labor justice.[36] Labor indiscipline and low productivity had been persistent problems in Cuba. After 1976 productivity failed to grow at the planned rate. There were many reasons for this failure: the incongruence in wage policies and the *disponibles* mentioned previously, historically low productivity of Cuban labor, work stoppages caused by shortages of raw materials, and work indiscipline. The discipline issue became a focus of public discussion. A 1979 National Popular Assembly meeting heard Fidel note that a better labor discipline had been achieved by capitalism in Cuba. "Maybe we have been too utopian and our own labor legislation... and our system of labor justice are deficient.... But we have to establish discipline one way or another."[37]

In 1980, the Council of Ministers stripped work councils of their power to resolve cases of labor discipline. Bureaucratic red tape had often bogged down the councils, rendering them extremely slow in settling disputes. In order to expedite matters, the 1980 decree bestowed upon management full authority in establishing work discipline and arresting falling productivity. The decree (number 32) required managers to submit workers' sanctions in writing prior to their enforcement and recognized a worker's right to appeal to the corresponding municipal court. The Council of Ministers simultaneously enacted another decree (number 36) regulating management infractions that were sanctioned by their corresponding ministries, however.

Four years after their enactment, these two decrees were deemed highly effective. By 1983 productivity increases were surpassing projected rates.[38] As could have been expected, decree law 32 was initially enforced with vigor and in excess; management resorted to dismissal as a first sanction against a lax worker, for example. The lenient application of decree law 36 was likewise foreseeable. Measures were taken to achieve a balance in the enforcement of these two decrees. First, labor inspections and workers' appeals obtained compensation (out of enterprise funds) for workers who had been unfairly sanctioned by management. Some workers' assemblies demanded that compensation be made from managers' salaries, but the suggestion was flatly discarded as counterproductive to the just application of decree law 32.[39] Second, disciplinary rules and regulations were elaborated for the various sectors and state enterprises. More than two million workers participated in the discussion of these rules and regulations, which by their mere existence curbed the margin of management arbitrariness in enforcing labor discipline.[40] Third, decree law 36 was more regularly enforced, especially against managers who exceeded their authority under decree law 32.[41]

Notwithstanding the effectiveness of decree law 32, its enactment was politically disturbing. While the demoralizing impact of habitually undisciplined and unsanctioned individuals could not be underestimated, was the *political* solution to the problem the extension of full authority to management? Labor discipline was temporarily expedited, but the long-term political and social consequences were unforeseeable. Indeed, the combination of international and national circumstances at that time encouraged solutions conducive to immediate, tangible results without full consideration to issues of workers' control. However, it was heartening that the CTC voiced serious objections over the decree's initially overzealous applications and that some corrections were instituted.

CONCLUSION

The remaining decade and a half before the twenty-first century pose an historic challenge to the Cuban Revolution. Trade unions have been restored to the mainstream of Cuban society through institutionalization and the implementation of the economic management and planning system. From the vantage point of the 1960s, the working class has certainly gained in organization and improved its standard of living. The struggle for *conciencia* continues. Workers' economic *conciencia* has surely been enhanced with the institution of material incentives. Strengthening workers' *conciencia* as owners and the vanguard class of Cuban society is an ongoing process both advanced and limited by post-1970 reforms. Cuba has yet to fully realize Fidel Castro's exhortation of 1970: "We don't believe that the problem of administering an enterprise should be only management's.... Someone should bear ultimate responsibility... but we should begin to establish a collective body, a collective body!"[42] Establishing and strengthening institutions conducive to more meaningful participation—not just mere involvement—in the management of enterprises and the development of economic plans is imperative for the continuing struggle for a revolutionary *conciencia* in the Cuban working class.

NOTES

1. Maurice Zeitlin, *Revolutionary Politics and the Cuban Working Class* (New York: Harper & Row, 1970).

2. Marifeli Pérez-Stable, "Whither the Cuban Working Class?" *Latin American Perspectives*, 2 (supplement, 1975).

3. In 1970, Fidel Castro and other leaders called for open and free elections of local trade union leaders. Between 1970 and 1973, elections resulted in a 40 percent turnover of the old leadership. Some "unqualified" persons were elected and subsequently removed by the CTC or party hierarchies or recalled by workers. The party exerts close supervision over all electoral processes in Cuba. Jorge I. Domínguez, *Cuba: Order and Revolution* (Cambridge: Harvard University Press, 1978), pp. 291-95; Nelson P. Valdés, "The Cuban Revolution: Economic Organization and Bureaucracy," *Latin American Perspectives* 6 (Winter 1979), pp. 22-24. Fifty percent of the 1973 Congress delegates were rank and file, *Granma* (November 11, 1973), p. 5. Sixty-eight percent of the 1978 Congress delegates were grass-roots representatives, *XIV Congreso de la CTC: Memorias* (La Habana: Editorial Orbe, 1980), pp. 87, 94. Fifty-four percent of local union leaders were newly elected. Data for the 1984 Congress were not yet fully available. In his main report to that congress, Roberto Veiga noted that labor leaders with more than 10 years experience had increased from 28 percent in 1978 to 47 percent in 1983. The average age was 40 in 1983, 37 in 1978. Given the dismemberment of the labor movement in the 1960s, continuity and experience were important accomplishments. Now the CTC and the trade unions faced a different problem, that is, turnover to ensure responsiveness and fresh blood from a work force in which one-third of all workers were young. Roberto Veiga, "Informe Central," *Trabajadores* (n.d.), p. 13.

4. Fidel Castro and Raúl Castro, *Selección de discursos acerca del Partido* (La Habana: Ciencias Sociales, 1975), p. 59.

5. *Granma Weekly Review* (September 26, 1974). This official position coincided with Lenin's position in the 1921 Bolshevik party debate on trade unions between Workers' Opposition and Trotsky.

6. Fidel Castro, *Main Report: Second Congress of the Communist Party* (New York: Center for Cuban Studies, 1981), p. 20.

7. *Memorias: Congreso de la CTC* (La Habana: Departamento de Divulgación de la CTC Nacional, 1974), p. 58.

8. Ibid.

9. Fidel Castro, "Discurso pronunciado el 23 de agosto de 1970—X aniversario de la FMC," *Pensamiento Crítico*, (October 1970), pp. 45, 91.

10. After the 1980 Second Party Congress, Roberto Veiga and the other mass organizations' general secretaries became alternate members of the Politbureau. Nineteen of the 148 full members of the Central Committee were trade union leaders. Veiga also attended Council of Ministers meetings at which wage and price policies were discussed. Corresponding representation of trade union leaders was also instituted at the provincial and municipal levels. Local unions' general secretaries also became members of enterprise councils.

11. XIV Congreso de la CTC, pp. 42, 44.
12. Ibid., pp. 30-31.
13. Memorias: Congreso de la CTC, p. 12.
14. Ibid., pp. 38-46.
15. Granma Weekly Review, October 10, 1976, pp. 2-6.
16. XIV Congreso de la CTC: Memorias, p. 97.
17. Ibid., pp. 42-56.
18. Joaquín Benavides Rodríguez, "La ley de la distribución con arreglo al trabajo y la reforma de salarios en Cuba," *Cuba Socialista* 2 (March 1982), pp. 62-93. Interview conducted with Felino Quesada, JUCEPLAN economist, July 1982. Eugenio Rodríguez Balari, president of the National Institute for Internal Demand, told me in July 1982 that average wages have doubled since 1970. With 1970 as the base year, wages had risen 36.2 percent by 1975, 67.8 percent by 1979, 75.5 percent by 1980, and 107.6 percent after the 1981 wage reform. By 1984, less than 1,000 enterprises were creating individual and collective bonus funds. The CTC Congress emphasized that an actual overfulfillment of plans had to correspond to the disbursement of bonuses. The 1981 reform inequality spread was potentially much greater than 5.29:1 once bonuses were fully operant.
19. *Granma*, December 14, 1981, pp. 1-3.
20. See "Informe de Humberto Pérez," *Granma*, December 24, 1983, p. 2; "A Unique Kind of Consumer Boom," *Latin American Regional Report*, September 30, 1983, p. 8. Rationing accounted for only 30 percent of individual consumption.
21. Veiga, "Informe Central," pp. 8-9.
22. XIV Congreso de la CTC, p. 16.
23. Ibid., p. 66.
24. Ibid., p. 67. The Council of State established a decree law regulating collective work agreements. Problems in their contracting and in their implementation persisted nevertheless. *Proyecto Tesis XV Congreso*, p. 10.
25. *Bohemia*, November 13, 1981, p. 55.
26. Veiga, "Informe Central," p. 7.
27. XIV Congreso de la CTC, p. 53. Representative assemblies were also permanently constituted as a means to enhance workers' involvement.
28. Memorias: Congreso de la CTC, p. 69.
29. XIV Congreso de la CTC, p. 53.
30. Roberto Veiga, "Clausura del octavo curso para directores de empresas, celebrado en la Escuela Nacional de Dirección de la Economía," *Cuestiones de la Economía Planificada*, 3 (March/April 1980), p. 29.
31. Prior to 1974, plans were not regularly drawn up, hence there was no discussion. Workers discussed their enterprises' output goals, not the national economic plan in its entirety.
32. XIV Congreso de la CTC, p. 102.

33. See *Plenaria Nacional de Chequeo sobre el sistema de dirección y planificación de la economía* (JUCEPLAN: La Habana, 1979), pp. 36-37; and Humberto Pérez González, "Clausura de la Segunda Plenaria Nacional sobre la implantación del sistema de Dirección y Planificación de la Economía," p. 26.

34. *Proyecto Tesis XV Congreso*, p. 6.

35. CTC, *Dirección de Justicia Laboral* (CTC: La Habana, 1981). Cases nearly doubled after the early 1970s. Two reasons were apparent: (1) grievance procedures were strengthened after the late 1960s, and (2) material incentives spurred both workers and managers to abide more closely by the new regulations. For more information on work councils in the 1960s, see Carmelo Mesa-Lago, *The Labor Sector and Socialist Distribution in Cuba* (New York: Praeger, 1968).

36. *XIV Congreso de la CTC*, p. 67.

37. *Juventud Rebelde*, July 5, 1979, p. 1. See Raúl Castro's speech, *Granma*, August 7, 1979, p. 2, on the same subject.

38. "Informe de Humberto Pérez," p. 2.

39. "Entrevista con Roberto Veiga: la rentabilidad en el centro de las tareas," *Bohemia*, February 17, 1984, p. 45.

40. *Proyecto Tesis XV Congreso*, p. 6.

41. "Informe Central," p. 8.

42. Fidel Castro, "Discurso pronunciado el 26 de julio de 1970—XVII aniversario del asalto al Cuartel Moncada," *Pensamiento Crítico*, October 1970, p. 40. While raising the proletariat to the position of the ruling class and winning the battle for democracy certainly goes beyond issues of workers' control, the transition to socialism *must* address these issues to overcome the division between production and consumption inherited from capitalism.

16 Socialist Legality and Practice: The Cuban Experience

Max Azicri

Notwithstanding codes and laws still in force from prerevolutionary days, today's Cuban legal and judicial system is mostly the product of the revolutionary laws enacted during the 1960s and the comprehensive institutionalization of the state that followed in the 1970s. By now, the newly created political and socioeconomic institutions have been integrated into a coherent legal and judicial structure under a socialist constitution—the 1976 charter. The institutionalization drive was the belated outcome of the nation-building and state-building process undertaken since the revolutionary government came to power in 1959. The third decade of the revolution, the 1980s, corresponds to the postinstitutionalization period. Thus the regime is now living under its own formalized political, legal and judicial, and socioeconomic order.

This chapter examines the legal and judicial system as the normative and institutional outcome of a comprehensive societal change process that involved the polity as a whole. In addition to discussing the applicability of these two related conceptual constructs to the Cuban legal and judicial engineering experience, some of the major changes in this area and salient legislation and codification are examined. Also discussed is the "sovietization of Cuba" thesis (with particular attention paid to the legal change process in which Marxist juridical principles were applied and added to Cuba's legal culture and traditions), and an evaluation is provided on whether or not this is a valid criticism of the institutionalization of the state and legal judicial system.

The first years, approximately from 1959 to 1963, represent a founding stage of profound social change that was underscored by a series of revolutionary laws aiming at political and economic goals, such as the redistribution of wealth, agrarian reform, nationalization of private enterprises, and others. Notwithstanding their social significance, these laws were basically of a populist nature; they were not by themselves sufficient to build and deliver a socialist polity. Nevertheless, they were able to provide the legal and socioeconomic ingredients needed in ulterior stages of socialist development.

A DUAL CONCEPTUAL FRAMEWORK

The legal and judicial record of the revolution follows an irregular path. Despite its significant historical peculiarities, this path still follows from the legal and judicial experience of other nations. Cuba's original civil (Roman) law jurisdiction was the creation of the three-century-long Spanish colonial government that lasted until the Spanish-Cuban-American War in 1898. Spain's domination, in turn, was followed by a conflictive U.S. military government for over three years, from 1899 to 1902. This first American intervention ended with the proclamation of the republic a year after the first Cuban Constitution was approved in 1901. A second military intervention by the United States, from 1906 to 1909, had an equal, if not more disruptive, impact on the island's political development. There were additional landings of American Marines in 1912 and 1917. Under Washington's rule there were serious attempts to cast Cuban society in a North American image. Therefore, some common law judicial practices were established, such as trial by jury, which lacked support and failed. Other judicial initiatives dating from this period were more successful, such as the *Tribunales Correccionales* ("Correctional Tribunals"), a system of lower level nonappellate courts used until the revolutionary government replaced them with the People's Tribunals in the 1960s.[1]

The Law and Development Framework

As a theoretical category, law and development are part of, or definable as, a (limited) form of "progressive social change," which then becomes more inclusive. In spite of its apparent simplicity, this characterization implies a hierarchical differentiation between law and development and progressive social change by subsuming the former under the latter. Whereas legally induced social change has a broader scope and meaning, legal development is more specific; thus it is mainly seen here as a kind of legislation seeking legal and judicial reform.

The inner, direct relationship that allegedly exists between law and development in a legal and social change context acquired certain specific behavioral patterns in revolutionary Cuba. The initial social change-oriented law and development role played by the revolutionary laws during the first 10-year period, shifted to an increasingly social reinforcement-oriented law and development role during the second decade, the 1970s. The regime used the 1970s as a supportive and stabilizing legislative period reinforcing the social changes accomplished earlier by building permanent legal and judicial institutions, such as the 1973 and 1977 judicial reforms, the 1975 Family Code, the 1976 Constitution, the 1979 Penal Code, and others. The 1960s was a period of legally induced social change, whereas the 1970s represented better legal development. Altogether, this period provides a panoramic view of legal development evolving through different phases of social and legal engineering.

Cuba has been a contributing actor in the growth and expansion of its newly chosen legal family—socialist law—while simultaneously engaging in a comprehensive law and development and social change program. Highly industrialized nations provide a less than definite record regarding the impact that law and development have had on their social systems.

The empirical examination of the Cuban legal and judicial experience found in this chapter may shed some light on some of the broader and more abstract theoretical questions related to law and development, both legally and socially. Societal change under the revolutionary government represents a complex and comprehensive social engineering process in which initially the law was used as a "tool of directed social change." This was followed by a phase in which the law was used as a tool reinforcing societal change already accomplished, as well as defining the conditions and scope of future change—that is, the institutionalization of the state, including its legal and judicial system. Whether the regime will be able to successfully balance the opposing forces, pitting stability against change within the system during the present postinstitutionalization phase and in the future, will be decided in the actual course of the revolution. Socialist legality, as well as the official Marxist-Leninist ideology upon which it is based, is not recognized as a value system standing against or limiting progress; rather, it is understood in Cuba, and in other socialist countries, as an invaluable asset for steering socialist polities into the future. Nonetheless, critics of Marxist-Leninist systems disregard such an interpretation on the grounds that it is another sign of official orthodoxy, ideologically and otherwise.

The Socialist Law Framework

Upon examining the Marxist legal record in new African nation-states, John Hazard made rather critical comments, perhaps more so than on other occasions.[2] After recognizing that there are significant historical differences among Marxist-Leninist countries' legal and social changes, he nevertheless made a sweeping generalization regarding these countries' political legitimacy, as well as their legal systems: "The history of states led by Marxists, of whatever degree of acceptance of the faith and on whatever continent, is written in the struggle between a determined leadership and a recalcitrant people."[3]

By the time Cuban revolutionaries decided in the 1960s to build a socialist system using Marxism-Leninism as its official ideology, there already were several Communist party-states in existence with a long-established political and legal and juridical record. Early Soviet perceptions, or misconceptions, about law, questioning its social function and the scope of its applicability in a socialist state, had been substantively modified by the time Cuban socialism came into existence. Soviet claims that socialist law constitutes a new legal family had been properly established by then, as evidenced by its own legal system and the growth of socialist jurisprudence in general.

Nonetheless, a serious legal and cultural problem developed in Cuba when the populace publicly demonstrated a general disregard for the law of the revolution. This was mainly in response to the all-encompassing societal changes brought about by the revolutionary process itself, which unexpectedly provoked a social by-product of poor compliance with the emerging legal system. The population was acting on the belief that past and present social and political institutions, the legal system in particular, were of only relative import. What really mattered was to be a true revolutionary in both thought and action—especially whenever there was a discrepancy between the values. Therefore, the people disregarded the notion that respect for the law—being law-abiding citizens—was important or made any real difference. A Cuban jurist characterized this practice as a serious danger to the revolution. In his view, revolutionary (socialist) legality had become so relative, and respect for the law so lax, that it had been subordinated to "revolutionary usefulness" (i.e., expediency), which many regarded as a primary and overriding consideration.[4]

Initially, the Soviet approach to law, even revolutionary law, was that it was at best a temporary phenomenon for a socialist state. In the historic writings of E.B. Pashukanis, law was seen as being "ninety-per cent political," and as a "capitalist institution destined to wither away ...once socialism is established."[5] This erroneous approach to law changed drastically in the 1930s, when finally "Pashukanis's nihilistic theories of law were denounced." Later, under A.Y. Vyshinsky's legal theories, law was regarded as performing an "active, creative role," including the "tasks of legal protection of personal, property, family, testamentary, and other rights and interests." Since then, however, Soviet law has played a central role in the country's planned economy, hence becoming recognized as a "positive feature of Soviet socialism ...and as part of a general stabilization of social relations."[6]

Since the mid-1930s, Soviet jurists have made the claim that "socialist law" is a "new type of law," that is, workers' law or the law of the Soviet ruling class—the proletariat. Nevertheless, recognition of socialist law by the West as a new type of law, or as a new legal family, did not come fast or easily. Even today, after it has been generally established and recognized as such, there still are Western scholars who look at socialist legality as a "branch of the civil law system"—the legal tradition from which most socialist countries came—even if recognizing "its own distinct characteristics."[7]

Also, there is the question of whether to accept or reject the socialist legal system's legitimacy and, moreover, whether this decision is made on the basis of a juridical or political judgment. Although only a small number of jurists today would agree upon rejecting the system's legitimacy for juridical reasons, a larger number of political analysts still share political objections as the basis for such a rejection.

Applying Soviet Legal Modalities to Cuban Law

Harold Berman summarizes the main features of the Soviet legal system as: (1) the institution of the procuracy, established by Lenin in 1922 (besides being responsible for criminal prosecutions, it is in charge of overseeing that socialist legality is properly enforced); (2) the adjudication of contractual disputes between the different state enterprises and organizations by administrative courts (the so-called *Arbitrazh* tribunals, which arrive at their judicial decisions on the basis of contract law, administrative regulations, and state economic plans); and (3) the educational function performed by socialist law, particularly criminal law (both substantive and procedural law are expected to legally and politically guide the citizenry so they will comply with socialist legality and support "the aims of society as formulated by the Communist party").[8] All these three major characteristics of the Soviet system, and others, have been applied to Cuban law and society, thereby making the Soviet system part of its legal and judicial system. In this case, as had happened with other socialist countries, the Soviet legal system was used as a model from which operational principles and institutional structures were drawn—notwithstanding local differences, some of a historical nature, which, after some adjustments were incorporated into the new legal system.

Developing a Body of Socialist Jurisprudence. Hazard's and Aleksandr Makhnenko's Soviet public law studies, although following different and, to some extent, opposing academic and philosophical perspectives, arrived at rather similar conclusions.[9] Upon applying Hazard's and Makhnenko's conceptualization to the Cuban case, including its preinstitutionalization and postinstitutionalization periods, it becomes clear that there are substantive similarities and differences between both countries, including past and present legal practices.

After visiting in 1979 with some law professors in Havana, Berman and Van Whiting compared the office of the Cuban prosecutor (the *fiscalía* which dates back to Spanish colonial days) to the office of the Soviet prosecutor (the *prokuratura*, which dates back to prerevolutionary days). According to their present ombudsman, an all-embracing function, both the Cuban *fiscalía* and the Soviet *prokuratura* have changed so they can respond satisfactorily to pressing legal and sociopolitical needs; thus their traditional structure has been transformed while their jurisdictional scope has been expanded.

The second feature of the Soviet legal system, the adjudication of contractual disputes among state enterprises, was adopted in a series of statutes in 1976, 1977, and 1978.[10] The educational objective of the socialist legal system present in Cuban law, particularly the behavioral modification and rehabilitation function of the criminal law and penal system, has been enforced and has been amply recognized and examined in the literature.[11]

The Emergence of Cuban Socialist Jurisprudence. Cuban jurists were highly influenced by legal and political thinking and practices from the Soviet Union and other socialist countries. Their successful transition to socialist jurisprudence allowed them later to provide the principle guidelines featured by socialist constitutionalism, upon which the Cuban state was later organized. These juridical and political guidelines determine: who will exercise state (political) power; what kind of organic principles should be applied (in the organization of the state); what types of political methods should be used (revolutionary politics acquired a socialist character); and the legal and political limitations to be followed by the different state organs (within an organically unified state structure, governmental-administrative and political functions were differentiated).[12] These guidelines were incorporated into the 1976 Constitution as constitutional principles (socialist constitutionalism) governing the organization of a socialist institutionalized state.

A Havana University law professor characterized public law principles present in Cuba's socialist jurisprudence and legal system in the following way:

> The law in a socialist society, as well as the state, constitutes a necessity.... Socialist law is a new form of law because of three main reasons: the nature of the social relations covered by it; the new function assigned to it; and its known political character. This does not mean that bourgeois law could not be used again in whatever contribution it may take that is technically or formally useful. *More than anything else, it is the conception and the function of the law that became different* (emphasis added).[13]

As indicated by Fernando Diego Cañizares and fellow Cuban jurists—most notably as expressed in the *Revista Cubana de Derecho* ("Cuban Law Review"), the Union of Cuban Jurists' scholarly journal, in which for over a decade a Cuban school of socialist jurisprudence has been collectively developed—they are seeking to reconcile the apparent contradictory juridical influences. That is, they are applying the Marxist-Leninist doctrine of socialist jurisprudence while still preserving some juridical continuity with bourgeois law in general, and Cuban prerevolutionary law in particular, in today's legal system. This eclectic approach represents Cuba's main contribution to the broader field of socialist law. It lies at the heart of its legal system. By being able to preserve a sense of national identity, in keeping with the country's judicial past, in spite of, or in addition to, the colossal changes undertaken by the revolution, it was possible for Cuba to implement its own political modality in the transformation of the state—from its prerevolutionary stage to its present socialist stage.

In retrospect, the 1960s stand today as a period of legal and judicial creativeness under extremely difficult conditions; that is, in the midst of sweeping social change and general confusion. Those years were also characterized by a commonly shared yearning among the country's lawyers, judges, and jurists for an adequate judicial-philosophical conceptualization of the emerging revolutionary society. While President Fidel Castro, then prime minister, decided what political and socioeconomic direction the country would take under his regime, the late Osvaldo Dorticós, then president, and Alfredo Yabur, Minister of Justice, were responsible for inducing serious thinking in different quarters, regarding not only the operational and practical questions but also the ideological and philosophical questions of revolutionary law.

It was Yabur's initiative that led to the formation of the *Tribunales Populares* ("Popular Courts") movement around 1963 (it is no longer in existence). In the 1973 and 1977 reorganization or institutionalization of the judicial system, under their strong influence some of the main features of these courts would remain—most notably, the utilization of lay judges next to professional ones throughout the different levels of the judicial structure. But, above all, the Popular Courts were an instrument of the revolutionists leading the populace into playing an adjudicatory role in the judicial system. By doing so, the populace was gaining an educational experience of the new legal system and judicial practices, while increasing its integration and identification with the revolution.

From the outset, Cuban jurists provided some of the intellectual groundwork needed for conceptualizing the theoretical-juridical framework supporting the revolution's legal and judicial system. This happened, in many instances, as a result of pure individual initiative and ingenuity. In a country like Cuba, with a tradition of well-trained lawyers and knowledgeable jurists but with no background in Marxist law to speak of, such a drastic change in collective legal thinking was expected to be more difficult (assuming lawyers to be less resilient) than proved to be the case. A plausible explanation for this phenomenon is that whereas many disaffected lawyers and judges went into exile, those who remained in Cuba were either more sympathetic to or prone to go along with the ideological and juridical changes demanded by the political course pursued by the revolutionary leadership. Therefore, they were willing to convert their legal and judicial and political thinking. This entire episode has not yet been properly chronicled.

Examination of positive law (a sanctioned statute that has not been superseded by successive legislation) as a juridical empirical indicator of the kind of law and law-making practices characterizing a political system and, to a large extent, as a measurement of the political nature of the regime itself shows the 1975 Family Code, the 1976 Constitution, and the 1979 Penal Code, among other laws and codes, to be relevant examples of Cuba's individualized version of socialist jurisprudence and of the political and socioeconomic features of its socialist state.[14]

THE SOVIETIZATION OF CUBA THESIS

The socialist (Soviet) and Marxist-Leninist philosophical influence exerted upon and accepted by Cuba as the ideological and operational rationale for its own transformation under the revolution has been criticized by many analysts, among them the supporters of the sovietization of Cuba thesis. This thesis includes some social science studies that are either antagonistic or at least decisively critical of the historical changes that have taken place since 1959, particularly during the institutionalization of the revolution in the 1970s and thereafter (i.e., the changes and transformation of the Cuban polity examined in this chapter).

In 1970 when the 10-million-ton sugar harvest goal was not achieved—it was short by 1.465 million tons—the regime finally moved toward the institutionalization of the state, including the Communist Party and the revolution as a whole. As far back as 1966, however, Castro was apologetically explaining the reasons for not moving sooner into such institutionalization of the state: "We have not rushed into setting them up [the new legal and political institutions] because we would like them to conform to [social] reality, and not the other way around." Also, he said that, "There are many things...which demand definitions, concepts, and ideas, which should come from our revolutionary ideology and our Marxist view of society."[15] Basically, the process involved substituting new political structures providing rational, stable, and continuous channels of decision making for the centralized and charismatic dominance of the revolution by Castro's leadership.

What characterizes this thesis—analytically and ideologically—is its interpretation of the meaning and significance of the institutionalization of the revolution. Essentially, that interpretation asserts that the revolutionary leadership adopted as its own a Soviet bureaucratic decision-making model that defines power relations within the political system according to its pyramidal and hierarchical structure. Hence the institutionalizing process has allowed the power-holding elite—Castro and his close associates—to position itself at the top and control the Communist Party, even much more so than before. Rather than decentralizing the regime's decision-making practices and bringing a more meaningful political participation by the populace, this political change allegedly brought Cuba closer to the Soviet bureaucratic model. The newly created socioeconomic, political, and—particularly significant for this study—legal and judicial institutions amount to not much more than a Cuban version of the main features of the Soviet model, copied and applied with some adjustments. Finally, the institutionalization—or sovietization, according to this thesis—of the revolution increased the Soviet Union's grip on Cuba, thereby formalizing Havana's increasing dependency on Moscow.

The sovietization thesis is mainly the work of political rather than legal analysts.[16] A reason for this distinction seems to be that there are more of the former dedicated to studying the Cuban Revolution than there are of the latter. While Cuba's allegedly controversial treatment of political prisoners and dissidents and other violations of human rights have been extensively publicized, by contrast the strictly juridical and legal aspects of the revolution (e.g., its legal and judicial changes and development process) have not been publicized. This is particularly true when one considers the limited number of comparative law, jurisprudence, legal development, and even socialist law studies examining legal changes in contemporary Cuba. This has created an imbalance regarding both the number of studies produced in the different disciplines and the extent to which different subjects have been covered by them. To some extent, this asymmetrical distribution of scholarly concern and research efforts is the revolutionary government's responsibility. As indicated earlier, throughout the 1960s, revolutionary laws were primarily used in pursuance of ambitious societal programs and not for the more specific purpose of building a new legal system based on a legal family different from the one to which the country's pre-revolutionary legal system belonged.

Even as compelling as this explanation seems to be, it does not address itself to the main thrust of the sovietization thesis as it is discussed here, that is, the meaning and significance of institutionalizing the state and the judicial and legal system. As I have previously expressed, this thesis seems to signify primarily the existence of "a Soviet-look-alike nation and state-building process...during the institutionalization movement." Also, "More than a serious oversimplification of a complex phenomenon, this interpretation constitutes a gross distortion of the real nature and meaning of the socioeconomic and political (and legal and judicial) development, and institutionalization, achieved under the revolution."[17]

There is substantive political, ideological, and juridical influence in Cuba as well as other kinds of influence of Soviet and other socialist countries. The real question for social scientists is to understand properly the nature, the extent, and the implications of such influence within the revolutionary process. By the time the institutionalization drive started in the 1970s, the island had already established itself as a recognized member of the socialist camp. Ideological principles supportive of present juridical practices and institutions characteristic of socialist legality became central to the country's emerging legal and political culture. They had been alien philosophical values to the prerevolutionary society, but they had been assimilated by the population as part of the newly created revolutionary culture. This happened initially during the massive cultural changes of the 1960s, but continued with some modifications in the 1970s and since.

The Popular Courts movement was instrumental in popularizing the revolution's approach to justice and legality, bringing the people into the judicial and decision-making process by involving them. The central role played by popularly elected lay judges was equally helpful. Under the new system, lay and professional judges, working together with lawyers, law students, and, on occasion, with the public attending the court's proceedings, adjudicated minor grievances at the local level. Revolutionary legal and political culture played a decisive role in legitimizing the new legal and judicial institutions established during the ambitious process of legal development and legally induced social engineering. The revolution's legal development policy was initially aimed at achieving legally induced social change; ultimately, it established an institutionalized socialist legal and judicial system.

It is significant and troublesome in some quarters that the Soviet Union's political, socioeconomic, and legal systems serve as models for other countries whose official ideology is equally Marxist-Leninist—the so-called Communist Party states. A common political ideology shared by the regimes involved seemingly provides the bedrock policy deciding this important transference of organizational modalities, which is not as such a unique historical phenomenon. Whether this happens because of a political decision freely made by the receiving country (Cuba and socialist countries other than the U.S.S.R.) or under some form of pressure exerted by the country serving as the model state (the U.S.S.R.)

is something that should be decided on a case-by-case basis, according to objectively evaluated facts and avoiding prejudicial generalization.

Exercising ideological, political, or juridical influence (providing an organizational state or constitutional model that could/should be emulated) upon other regimes (who will respond willingly or unwillingly, positively or negatively, to such influence) is not a new or strange experience, nor is the traditional influence exerted by any of the major legal families upon different political and legal systems. This is the history of the civil (Roman) law and (Anglo) common law legal families and the way in which they were assimilated (emulated) by countries all over the world.

John H. Merryman examined how the American Constitution exerted such a significant and lasting influence upon so many countries— including Cuba and its first constitution in 1901—and how the U.S. Constitution is still used in contemporary constitutional studies:

> The amount of "leading" law reform activity in the West in the past two centuries is enormous. An early example is the Constitution of the United States, a law reform that had extraordinary influence, establishing a style of constitution-making later emulated in many parts of the world. The constitutions of the Latin American nations that achieved independence in the 19th century, and that frequently used the U.S. Constitution as a model, are further early examples.[18]

The Soviet Union is providing a constitutional, legal, and juridical (as well as socioeconomic and political) model for today's world that follows the experience of the United States constitutional (and political and economic) model in the nineteenth century and since. So far, Cuba is the only country in the Western hemisphere to receive the political and juridical influence of both countries; it modeled its first constitution after the United States', and its last one after the Soviet Union's.

THE 1973 AND 1977 REORGANIZATION OF THE JUDICIAL SYSTEM

Government leaders had recognized that the reorganization of the judiciary was long overdue when a new law institutionalizing the judicial system came into effect on June 23, 1973. Law 1250 brought a new sense of order and harmony into what otherwise amounted to a confusing and sometimes contradictory mosaic of juridical instruments representative of prerevolutionary and revolutionary stages of the Cuban polity. Nevertheless, from the perspective of the overall institutionalization of the state, the 1973 Law was premature; it failed to anticipate the forthcoming stage of revolutionary state building and the new institutions that emerged from it (especially since this law preceded the 1976 Constitution, which unified the state's institutions under its legal and political structure).

The movement toward the institutionalization of the judicial system was based on eight principles: (1) socialist legality; (2) people's participation (initiated earlier through the Popular Courts movement); (3) the administration of justice on behalf of the people and in defense of their interests; (4) the integration of the judicial system into the revolutionary government; (5) the independence of judges in dispensing justice; (6) the administration by the courts of their own sentences; (7) social prevention agencies working in coordination with the courts; and (8) the dispensation of justice free of charge for all citizens (legal counseling, provided by *bufetes colectivos* ["collective law firms"] attorneys, was based on fees officially set by government).

Law 1250 secured the administration of democratic centralism, as an operational practice between the government (Council of Ministers) and the judiciary, by determining that policies and orientations issued by the former to the latter, as well as any decision related to their implementation, were channeled downward to the entire judicial system through the Council of Government of the People's Supreme Court. (According to the 1977 organization of the judicial system, the nation's courts system, as well as the People's Supreme Court, did not fall under the supervision of the government, but instead it came under the new highest state organ and its executive body, the National Assembly of People's Power and the Council of State, respectively.)

Under Law 1250, all existent legal jurisdictions became unified. Thus, four different jurisdictions such as the ordinary, revolutionary, people's, and military, which had been handled by courts administered separately, were all integrated into a unified judiciary. The only exception to this policy was the system of labor justice, which was not incorporated into the unified judicial system until 1977, under Law Number 4.

Article 2 of Law 1250 established a hierarchy of four judicial layers that included from the top to the bottom: (1) the People's Supreme Court, (2) the People's Provincial Courts, (3) the People's Regional Courts, and (4) the People's Courts at the Base. Also the People's

Supreme Court had a military chamber with first instance and appellate jurisdiction, which reviewed sentences from the armed forces and the Minister of Interior Courts (articles 37 and 38). This system was changed in 1977 to a simplified version of only three layers, including (1) the People's Supreme Court, (2) the People's Provincial Courts, and (3) the People's Municipal Courts (by then, under the new politico-administrative division of the country, there were 14 instead of 6 provinces, the municipalities were reduced to 169, and the regional division had been eliminated). There was also a Military Chamber of the People's Supreme Court, which had first instance and appellate jurisdiction to sentences given by Military Territorial Courts (article 29 of Law Number 4).

There seems to be an agreement on matters of principle between the 1973 and 1977 reorganization of the judicial system, including the avowal that socialist legality should be preserved and reinforced and that professional and lay judges should be side-by-side forming part of the collegial courts. In 1977, however, a higher level of institutionalization of the judicial system was achieved than in 1973. Law 4 (1977) encompasses both the reorganization of the judiciary and the advanced stage of institutionalizing the state accomplished throughout the 1970s (including the 1976 Constitution), which brings, in that way, an element of increased coherence into the process.

The 1977 institutionalization of the judicial system recognizes the value of autonomy in the courts by separating the administrating (governmental) functions of the judiciary from the actual administration of justice (judicial decision making); hence, the former is entrusted to the Ministry of Justice (government), and the latter remains as the sole domain of the courts. Furthermore, these legal changes took place at a moment when the government (administration) and the state (political) structures were separated from one another by the 1976 Constitution, differentiating their respective jurisdictions (and when the incumbents of state political organs are elected directly by the people at the municipal level of the Organs of People's Power). Later, the municipal delegates would elect the deputies for the Provincial and National assemblies of the Organs of People's Power; the parliamentary structure system includes three different levels: municipal, provincial, and national. Altogether, throughout the 1970s the regime accomplished an advanced stage of institutionalization for the state and the judicial and legal system.

THE 1976 CONSTITUTION

The popular approval of the socialist constitution through a national referendum held on February 24, 1976 was a carefully calculated political step by the regime. In addition to the previous nationwide discussion of the constitutional draft, which took place in a myriad of meetings held by mass organizations and collective legal offices and in work centers and informal gatherings, and beyond the fact that it satisfied legal formalities, the referendum was held to bring popular participation into the institutionalization process. This participatory process allowed for a channel of grass-roots recommendations requesting changes in the final draft. However, it is difficult to ascertain with fairness how many of these recommendations were actually heeded by the drafters of the constitution.

With the new constitution the regime sought to increase the institutional cohesiveness of the state, formalizing its socialist nature as well as the character of the society and economic system. Constitutional principles governing the organization of the state under the new charter included: the recognition of the Cuban Communist Party (PCC) as the only political party in the political system; the implementation of democratic centralism as the organizational principle behind the system of hierarchical relations among the different state organs; the exercise of the dictatorship of the proletariat (workers' and peasants' political power) through such political bodies as the Organs of People's Power (national, provincial, and municipal levels), and other lesser, but still important, sociopolitical organizations, such as the different mass organizations. Also, they provided for: (1) the establishment of an economic system based on the public ownership of the means of production (with the exception of privately owned farms, the economy has almost been totally socialized); (2) a socialist reward system (which accepts the existence of income differentials: "from each according to his ability, to each according to his work"); and (3) the recognition that proletarian internationalism functions as a central political value guiding the country's international relations with fellow socialist countries and with progressive states and national liberation movements (particularly those among the latter that are actively engaged in national liberation wars).

Some of the political organizational arrangements under the 1976 Constitution departed from those of other socialist countries, particularly in the case of a single person heading both the state and the government. This person would function as president of both the Council of State (political organ) and the Council of Ministers (governmental/administrative organ) for a five-year period, the same period for which the deputies of the National Assembly of the Organs of People's Power have been elected. On both occasions in which presidential elections have been held by the National Assembly, Castro has been elected, as he was expected to be. In addition to expressing present revolutionary political realities, this kind of unified power arrangement is more in line with Latin American political practice of favoring a strong executive.

Paradoxically, in spite of the well-known dominance by Castro's personalized leadership style of the revolution's decision-making modalities, the 16 years of provisional revolutionary government that ended with the new institutionalized phase under the constitution—1959–76—meant an end too for the type of formal division that existed separating the head of the state and the government. Under the initial revolutionary government structure, they functioned separately with a president and a prime minister, respectively. The 1976 charter separated the political-state from the administrative-governmental organs structurally and institutionally, but unified them under a single presidential head; it also established communication links at different levels of their respective structures according to the principles of democratic centralism.

Furthermore, under the new constitution the Cuban Communist Party (PCC) was carefully excluded from the administrative-governmental functions it had performed before 1976. Its central and guiding political function for the state and the society as a whole was recognized, however, characterizing it as the foremost political force in the nation. In keeping with the political practices of a Marxist-Leninist state, the Communist Party assumed a leading and central position as the ideologically and politically guiding institution in a socialist state.

As the real political engine in a socialist society, the Communist Party assumes multiple responsibilities which, in addition to the high level of national expectation awaiting effective and inspiring leadership, become almost overwhelming. This leaves little room for a failing party, sometimes not even for minor mistakes. This is so if the nation is expected to fare well politically, socially, and economically. Under this type of political arrangement, it is impossible for the country to be steered satisfactorily under poor party leadership and performance. In recognition of this multifaceted and sensitive political reality, the First Congress of the PCC, held in December 1975, moved initially to institutionalize itself (the party), proceeding then to the approval of the draft constitution, which was used as the legal foundation for the institutionalization of both the party and the state. The people's participation in the decision-making process was secured by holding a national referendum the following year, in which the new charter was decisively approved. This paved the way for the national election of delegates for the Municipal Organs of People's Power held later in October, the first one ever held under the revolutionary government.

The Second Party Congress in December 1980—they are held every five years—covered a broad agenda: a comprehensive rendition of accounts of the party's performance since 1976; a critical evaluation of the national and international state of the country politically, socially, and economically; and agreeing on political and socioeconomic guidelines for the next five-year period, until the Third Party Congress is held. But above all, it fulfilled the need for energizing the party, so it can perform effectively the central political role that is expected from it under the 1976 charter.

Cuba's socialist constitution blends effectively in its 12 chapters and 141 articles Marxist-Leninist ideology with political pragmatism and some previous national constitutional experience with the influence of other socialist countries, particularly the Soviet Union. It claims to represent a linear progression of Cuban history, which finally leads to its present socialist state organization. This is done by recognizing its present domestic and international reality and its historical and cultural heritage, and above all by incorporating in its different articles the changes that have occurred during the revolution. Also, it enhanced the institutional cohesiveness of the state by integrating it further into the newly established political structures, as well as with the newly institutionalized socialist legal and judicial system. Even without these significant achievements, the 1976 Constitution has its place guaranteed in the history books: it is the first socialist constitution in the Western hemisphere.

TWO MAJOR CODES FROM THE 1970s

The number and importance of the laws and codes legislated during the 1970s were impressive. Two major pieces of legislation, the 1975 Family Code and the 1979 Penal Code, represent legal landmarks of Cuban socialist jurisprudence. A third major piece of legislation, the new Civil Code, has been under study and public discussion since the mid-1970s. The present draft of this code has been discussed in public meetings attended by lawyers, judges, law students, party members, and the public in general. Presently, it is close to a final draft stage.[19] When the new Civil Code is approved by the legislative bodies, it will be the first of its type in the republic. The Civil Code inherited from Spain (July 31, 1889), with substantial modifications before and after 1959, is still in force.

The Family Code

The legal framework for family relations within the revolutionary process was finally formalized with Law 1289, the 1975 Family Code. This code superseded not only the 1889 Civil Code regarding family matters, but such legislation as the 1934 Divorce Law, and Law 9 of 1950, which advanced women's rights in both marital and family life. The code became effective on February 14, 1975, International Women's Day of the International Women's Year. The Federation of Cuban Women (FMC) was highly instrumental in bringing the Family Code into existence.

The Family Code has been characterized as being revolutionary as well as conservative, as being innovative as well as traditional, and as being under the influence of socialist (particularly Soviet) legal experience as well as being a continuation of the latest modification in prerevolutionary Cuban civil law. I have characterized the Family Code as follows: "A revolutionary law toward which the FMC and its leadership had been working for a long time, (it) was designed by the regime to counter traditional attitudes rooted in cultural values, held by both females and males, which inhibit the acceptance of equality in practice as well as in theory."[20]

According to a Havana University law professor, Daniel A. Peral Collado, the family should be examined following a historico-judicial approach, including an analysis of the differences between the bourgeois and the socialist family. For him, the bourgeois family would express the "decisive influence (that) in family life (is) exercised by private property" (thus love and sexual relations would usually take second place). Meanwhile, for Peral Collado the socialist family would express the proper "features of a socialist society, in which private property and man's exploitation by man have been abolished" (thus allowing love and sexual relations to manifest themselves as human feelings and desires with no ulterior economic motives).

The Family Code brought some legislative innovations to Cuban socialist law while still providing for some continuities in its prerevolutionary legal tradition. How close it could bring family life, women's equality, and human relations in general to Peral Collado's perceptive vision of the socialist family is something that might lie beyond the legislative scope of the Family Code itself. In this sense, it is a law recognizing social changes already accomplished in Cuban society, as much as a guide for future change, both normative and behavioral.

The 1979 Penal Code

The National Assembly of People's Power, during its second session of December 28–30, 1978, approved Law 21, the 1979 Penal Code. It took effect on November 1, 1979. The previous criminal code, the Social Defense Code of 1936 (*Codigo de Defensa Social*), and all the amendments and revisions implemented before and during 20 years of revolutionary government, with some exceptions, is no longer in effect.

For years, jurists, judges, and revolutionary leaders recognized that a new criminal statute was long overdue and that the preservation of public order demanded a well-integrated system of criminal law, akin to the problems faced by their new social reality. Moreover, most of the criticism raised against the revolution's legal record, after public law and constitutional issues were exhausted, was precisely in the criminal justice area. The rule of law under the revolutionary government seemed so arbitrary and appalling to some individual-rights and due-process minded (within a Western judicial, and political, context) legal scholars and attorneys that the International Commission of Jurists passed a final judgment that "the rule of law has disappeared from the Cuban scene."[21] Similarly, from an adversary position, serious charges have been made for what is considered "the existence of a double standard of legality":

> [I]n Cuba something took place that...is characteristic of communist regimes, particularly at their consolidation stage...the apparent order of written law, and the real legal order stemming from decisions made by government officials.[22]

What is missing from such politically motivated criticism is a proper understanding of the dynamics of a social change process as comprehensive as the one experienced by Cuba; laws intended to define acceptable and unacceptable behavioral norms were also expected to be applied with the resilience needed in a society undergoing an intensive state of flux. Therefore, particularly in the early years, the meaning, scope, and applicability of the laws were adapted on occasions to changing political and social circumstances. This was particularly true in the early period of massive legally induced social change. As indicated earlier, the emphasis was placed on the social and developmental aspects of the change process, not on legal development and the rule of law as such. Not surprisingly, charges were also made that the revolution failed to live within the legal boundaries of its own self-made constitutional framework—the Fundamental Law of the Republic of 1959. The tension between strict legality and revolutionary dynamics increased when the process of social change became progressively radicalized, moving beyond the transformation originally intended and/or expressed.

Nevertheless, representing the socialist character of the Cuban polity today, the 1979 Penal Code defines some of its legal and social goals in the criminal justice area as: the increased protection of society and the people; the reeducational rather than the repressive nature of sanctions; fostering the individualization of sanctions, so they become more equitable; recognizing as crimes such actions as genocide, apartheid, and mercenary actions; sanctions for crimes against the rights of the workers; and protecting socialist property.

The implicit challenge for the 1979 Penal Code, including its two Books (General Part, and Special Part) and 404 Articles, is to rehabilitate the wrongdoer effectively; that is, the new criminal law individualizes sanctions and programs seeking to improve the capacity for social adjustment of the offender during and after the completion of his sentence. Consequently, the regime is bent on deemphasizing punishment as a viable alternative in combatting crime—this policy is particularly worthy insofar as the death penalty is still on the books, even if it is applied on a rather limited basis.[23]

CONCLUSIONS

The legal development experience under the revolutionary government is, indeed, an impressive one. After far-reaching social, political, and economic changes were in place, a new legal and judicial order finally emerged. Initially, laws were primarily used as tools inducing social change. Later, however, they were used to safeguard and consolidate earlier societal change, while also defining the course of future change (within the modalities of a Marxist-Leninist system). Thus the revolutionary state became institutionalized, as did the legal and judicial system. Moreover, according to the ideological and political identity of the revolution, a Marxist-Leninist legal and judicial system was also established. The overall process of social and legal engineering led to the creation of the first socialist jurisdiction in the Western hemisphere. The vitality demonstrated by the Cuban revolutionary process, particularly by its legal development record, represents also a major contribution to socialist legality, fostering its status as an established legal family in contemporary jurisprudence.

NOTES

1. Calixto C. Masó, *Historia de Cuba* (Miami, Fla.: Ediciones Universal, 1976), pp. 421-23.
2. John N. Hazard, "Law and Social Change in Marxist Africa," in Stuart S. Nagel, ed., *Law and Social Change* (Beverly Hills, Cal.: Sage, 1970), p. 97; and his *Communists and Their Law—A Search for the Common Core of the Legal Systems of the Marxian Socialist States* (Chicago: The University of Chicago Press, 1969).
3. Hazard, "Law and Social Change," p. 97.
4. Fernando Diego Cañizares, *Teoría del Estado* (La Habana: Editorial Pueblo y Educación, 1979), p. 398.
5. Harold J. Berman, "Socialist Legal Systems—Soviet Law," *International Encyclopedia of the Social Sciences*, vol. 9 (New York: Macmillan, 1968), p. 217.
6. Ibid., p. 219.
7. Mario P. Goderich and Jan Stepan, "Foreign and Comparative Law," in Morris L. Cohen, ed., *How to Find the Law* (St. Paul, Minn.: West Publishing, 1976), p. 391.
8. Berman, op. cit., p. 220.
9. Max Azicri, "An Introduction to Cuban Socialist Law," *Review of Socialist Law* 6 (1980), pp. 153-63.
10. See *Sistema de Arbitraje Estatal y Normas Básicas para los Contratos Económicos* (La Habana: Editorial Orbe, 1978); Raúl Martel, *La Empresa Socialista* (La Habana: Editorial de Ciencias Sociales, 1979); and Harold J. Berman and Van R. Whiting, "Impressions of Cuban Law," *American Journal of Comparative Law* 28 (1980), pp. 475-86.
11. See Michael E. Tigar, "The Educative Function of Criminal Law: Cuban Reforms in Comparative Perspective" (Paper presented at the National Conference on Cuba, New York, 1979); Max Azicri, "Crime and Law Under

Socialism: The 1979 Cuban Penal Code," *Review of Socialist Law* 6 (1980), pp. 5-29.

12. See Fernando Álvarez Tabío, *Política y Legalidad* (La Habana: Editorial de Ciencias Sociales, 1977), p. 305; and his *Comentarios a la Constitución Socialista* (La Habana: Editorial de Ciencias Sociales, 1981).

13. Fernando Diego Cañizares, op. cit., p. 100.

14. In conversations with the director of the juridical counseling office of the Cuban Ministry of Higher education, Dr. Denio Camacho, first during his visit to the United States in April 1982, and later during my visit to Cuba that summer, I asked him what, in his opinion, were the main contributions made so far by Cuba to socialist legality. His response included the following points: Cuban jurists had a higher technical level than Soviet jurists did (the reference seems to be to the time when each country's revolution took place and/or came to power; it could have been made to their juridical systems as well); Cuba achieved social change while still preserving its original level of juridical (technical) rigor; and, "without implying a lack of appreciation for the U.S.S.R.'s juridical development," *Cuban jurisprudence (since the revolution) has never departed from the country's legal traditions*. He added that the 1975 Family Code implemented revolutionary social changes while still maintaining the tradition of the family (as a social institution). Dr. Camacho said: *"Socialism must be adjusted to the country's culture and traditions."* Finally, he mentioned how Cuba has preserved in its civil law (the new Civil Code is still under discussion) some important components of private property, including items destined for personal use and consumption, and even for production, as it is a small tract of land owned privately by farmers (three *caballerías*; 1 *caballería* equals 13.4 hectares). Among the socialist countries the private property issue is not uniquely Cuban. (Emphasis added)

15. Cañizares, *Teoría del Estado*, p. 303.

16. For social science analysis that directly or indirectly supports the sovietization thesis, see: Jorge Domínguez, *Cuba—Order and Revolution* (Cambridge, Mass.: Harvard University Press, 1978); Edward González, "Castro and Cuba's New Orthodoxy," *Problems of Communism*, 1976, pp. 1-19; Edward González, "The Party Congress and *Poder Popular*: Orthodoxy, Democratization, and the Leader's Dominance," *Cuban Studies/Estudios Cubanos*, 1976, pp. 1-14; Carmelo Mesa-Lago, *Cuba in the 1970s—Pragmatism and Institutionalization*, rev. ed. (Albuquerque: University of New Mexico Press, 1978); and Carmelo Mesa-Lago, *The Economy of Socialist Cuba—A Two Decade Appraisal* (Albuquerque: University of New Mexico Press, 1981). For studies dealing with legal, constitutional, and criminal justice matters that equally support directly or indirectly the sovietization thesis, see: Luis Salas, "Juvenile Delinquency in Postrevolutionary Cuba: Characteristics and Cuban Explanations," *Cuban Studies/Estudios Cubanos* 9 (1979), pp. 43-61; Luis Salas, *Social Control and Deviance in Cuba* (New York: Praeger, 1979); L.B. Klein, "The Socialist

Constitution of Cuba," in Irving L. Horowitz, ed., *Cuban Communism*, 5th ed., (New Brunswick, N.J.: Transaction, 1984), pp. 452-74; and William T. D'Zurilla, "Cuba's 1976 Socialist Constitution and the *Fidelista* Interpretation of Cuban Constitutional History," *Tulane Law Review* 55 (1981), pp. 1223-84. For a critical evaluation of this thesis and its supporters, see Frank T. Fitzgerald, "A Critique of the 'Sovietization of Cuba' Thesis," *Science and Society* 42 (1978), pp. 1-32.

17. Max Azicri, "On the Widsom of Scholarly Criticism: 'Thou Shalt Not Beleaguer Fellow Cubanologists...'," *Cuban Studies/Estudios Cubanos* 12 (1982), pp. 101-03.

18. John H. Merryman, "Comparative Law and Social Change: On the Origins, Style, Decline and Revival of the Law and Development Movement," *The American Journal of Comparative Law* 25 (1977), p. 463.

19. "Anteproyecto de Código Civil" mimeographed, (Ciudad Habana: Dirección Provincial de Bufetes Colectivos, February 1982), pp. 1-158.

20. Max Azicri, "Women's Development Through Revolutionary Mobilization: A Study of the Federation of Cuban Women," in Irving L. Horowitz, ed., *Cuban Communism*, 5th ed. (New Brunswick, N.J., Transaction, 1984), pp. 268-300; and Max Azicri, "The Cuban Family Code: Some Observations on Its Innovations and Continuities," *Review of Socialist Law* 6 (1980), pp. 183-91.

21. International Commission of Jurists, *Cuba and the Rule of Law* (Geneva, Switzerland: International Commission of Jurists, 1962), pp. 1-267. See also "Report on the Situation of Political Prisoners and Their Relatives in Cuba," Inter-American Commission on Human Rights, Pan American Union, Washington, D.C., OEA/Ser. L/V/II. 7, Document 4 (English) (1963), pp. 1-64; and *Questions and Answers About... Political Prisoners in Cuba* (Washington, D.C.: n.d.).

22. Alberto A. García-Menéndez, "Estructura Jurídica del Castrismo," in Carlos Alberto Montaner, ed., *Diez Años de Revolución Cubana* (San Juan, Puerto Rico: Editorial San Juan, 1970), p. 59.

23. Azicri, "Crime and Law Under Socialism," pp. 9-25; and Max Azicri "Change and Institutionalization in the Revolutionary Process: The Cuban Legal System in the 1970s," *Review of Socialist Law* 6 (1980), pp. 164-82. The comparison made between the 1960s and 1970s legal development policy of the Cuban regime examined throughout this chapter has been based on this study.

Section VI
Foreign Policy Developments

17 U.S.–Cuba Relations: Twenty-Five Years of Hostility

Wayne S. Smith

INTRODUCTION

Relations between the United States and Castro's Cuba have long been characterized by emotionalism and hostility. The intensity of feelings on both sides can hardly be exaggerated. In part, this has to do with their geographic proximity and disparity in size. For the United States, a superpower, the presence of a small Marxist-Leninist state only 90 miles off its shores is taken as an unpleasant reminder of the limitations of power and influence. As many Americans see it, this "upstart" has defied us and gotten away with it for almost a quarter of a century. That perception goes a long way toward explaining American emotionalism with respect to Cuba. On Cuba's side, it is just the opposite. Cubans' emotionalism stems from the sense of being constantly threatened by the hostile giant that blacks out the entire northern horizon.

The animosity between the two is also a product of history. There were decades of Cuban resentment against U.S. domination—as manifested by the Platt Amendment, the military occupations, and the overpowering U.S. economic presence. From the American viewpoint, there is a continuing myth that the United States selflessly gave Cuba its independence from Spain and that if the Cubans harbor resentments against Americans, it must be because they are ingrates.[1] Also, Cuba's revolutionary ethos inevitably clashes with the American quest for stability and world order. The two see themselves and the world around them from very different points of view. Added to this is the fact that Cuba is the ally of Washington's principal global antagonist, the Soviet Union.

Given these attitudes, Washington and Havana could not but view one another as adversaries. However, even the bitterest of adversaries frequently find it to be in their mutual interests to seek accommodation rather than accept the costs and risks of continued confrontation. Such accommodation between Cuba and the United States is feasible, and there have been several indications over recent years of a disposition on Cuba's part to seek one. Except for brief moments during the Ford and Carter administrations, however, the U.S. approach to Cuba has changed little over the past 20 years. If anything, it became less analytical and more hostile during the Reagan administration than it was during the Johnson administration.

GENESIS OF HOSTILITY

A break of relations between the United States and Castro's Cuba was perhaps inevitable, but it was preordained as much by the early drives and objectives of the Cuban Revolution as by U.S. reaction to them. It was not simply, as some have insisted, that the United States drove Castro into Moscow's arms, nor was it, as declared by others, that Castro had been Moscow's agent all along. Rather, it was a mix of Castro's goals and U.S. reaction to them that initially led him to align with the U.S.S.R.

Despite what he says today, Castro was not a Marxist-Leninist when he came to power in 1959.[2] Rather, he saw himself as a nationalist Third World leader. He was inspired by the ideas of Simón Bolívar, José Martí, and, to some extent, by those of Nasser and Nehru, not by the doctrines of Marx and Lenin. His early governmental program was moderate and not undemocratic. Certainly, it contained nothing from the Soviet model. His proclamations also were those of a progressive—a progressive nationalist. According to Castro, his was a "humanist" revolution. He did not agree with communism. For him, democracy, which was his goal, was by no means compatible with communism. "The problems which confronted Cuba were the same which confronted all Latin American countries. The case of Cuba was the same as that of the Congo...of Egypt...of Algeria...of Panama."[3]

Cuban Foreign Minister Raúl Roa's first speech before the United Nations General Assembly in September of 1959 holds the same inspiration. For the first time, he said, Cuba was really free and would have an independent foreign policy. Cuba no longer accepted the inevitability of choosing between capitalism and communism; now there were other paths and other solutions. Cuba's path would be that of the other Latin American states and of the peoples of Africa and Asia.[4]

Castro's ambitions ranged beyond Cuba. The centerpiece of these ambitions was the "liberation of Latin America," a goal encapsulated by the slogan "the Andes will become the Sierra Maestra of South America." Castro's ambitions, however, were not limited to the liberation of the Americas. Even that was only a means to still a greater end. Castro yearned to play a major role on the world stage and instinctively understood that it was in the milieu of the Third World that his charismatic style could best be brought to bear. Ghana might have been a small unimportant country, for example, but Nkrumah had been able to project himself onto center stage through the force of his own personality. Egypt was not powerful economically or militarily, yet Nasser was one of the foremost leaders of the Third World. It was a matter of having ideas, charisma, and force of will. That suited Castro ideally.

Castro saw clearly that the pursuit of his objectives in Latin America was likely to lead him, in time, to a direct confrontation with U.S. power. Castro knew the United States would not watch passively as he curtailed its economic interests and political influence in the hemisphere. Initially, Castro counted on a show of Latin American unity to restrain the United States. Cuban survival was seen to depend on the triumph in the near term of other revolutionary movements in Latin America. Such revolutions, however, did not occur. Thus, by late 1959, Castro had to reassess the situation. Obviously it was going to take much longer than he had expected to bring the great new Latin American revolutionary bloc into existence.

Meanwhile, the United States had become increasingly concerned over Castro's radical rhetoric and his efforts to foster other revolutions. Despite its suspicions of him, once Castro was in power, the U.S. State Department made a number of friendly overtures. Recognition had been quickly extended and Philip Bonsal, a highly respected career diplomat, was sent to Havana in February 1959 with instructions to establish a good working relationship with the new government. He tried.[6] And although Castro was not received by President Eisenhower, during his "unofficial" visit to the United States in April 1959, U.S.

officials at that time did express a willingness to consider economic assistance for Cuba. They invited Castro's economic advisers to indicate how the United States might be helpful. There was never any response from the Cuban side.[7]

As these early overtures were not successful, latent U.S. suspicions of and hostility toward Castro were soon revived. Perhaps in the last analysis, the policy of constructive forebearance never really had a chance, for it required more flexibility and patience than could reasonably have been expected of the Eisenhower-Nixon administration. In any event, by the summer of 1959, the United States, rightly or wrongly, had become convinced it could not work with Castro. It began to plan actions of its own against him, and it encouraged the Organization of American States (OAS) to take up the "Cuban problem." The Fifth Meeting of OAS Foreign Ministers, held in Santiago de Chile in August 1959, did exactly that by raising what it saw as the cause of tensions in the Caribbean.

Castro knew who the "cause" was and drew his own conclusions. He assumed the United States was beginning to gear up through the OAS to confront him. Future Cuban efforts to export revolution would almost certainly provoke a devastating response, cloaked by the mantle of the OAS. If he continued to pursue his objectives in Latin America, he would find himself face to face with the most powerful nation in the world, and he would stand alone. His choice was either to give up his broader foreign policy objectives or to seek a shield against U.S. power—at least until he could develop the other Latin American revolutionary governments of which he dreamed. In order for such a shield to be credible, the nation providing it had to be a powerful one. To which of the world's powers could Castro turn with any hope that his request would be honored? Obviously, only to the Soviet Union. Only the Soviet Union had both the power and an intense interest in undercutting U.S. influence in the area. Castro's choice was obvious, and in late 1959 he took it. Anastas Mikoyan's visit to Cuba in February 1960 marked the first public manifestation of the new relationship. It was one that would develop quickly.

Cuba's growing ties to the Soviet Union, of course, simply confirmed Washington's worst fears. If it had not already resolved to move decisively against Castro, it now became so resolved. Relations between the two countries deteriorated rapidly, and on January 4, 1961, in reaction to Castro's demand that the U.S. embassy in Havana be reduced to 11 employees, Washington broke diplomatic relations.

Even after he turned to Moscow for assistance, Castro may not have intended to go beyond a political-military alliance. There was nothing in his statements from the fall of 1959 until April 1961 to suggest he intended to align himself ideologically as well as politically with the Soviets. Indeed, in 1960 Ché Guevara declared the Cuban Revolution to be left-wing nationalist, rather than Marxist-Leninist.[8]

Castro soon saw, however, that the Soviets were not likely to provide the defense umbrella he wanted unless Cuba were a Marxist-Leninist state. Only then would there be a doctrinal imperative for them to come to his defense. Thus the day before the Bay of Pigs invasion, in a transparent effort to force the Soviets to guarantee Cuba's security, Castro declared his revolution to be socialist. That was the beginning; all else flowed from that step. But it did not get him the defense commitment he wanted. The Soviets have never vowed to defend Cuba, and Castro continues to pursue such a commitment even 25 years later. Once having declared himself to be a socialist, he became one and over the years transformed Cuba into a full-fledged Marxist-Leninist state.

Needless to say, the Latin American governments also reacted angrily to Castro's efforts to export revolution, that is, to overthrow them. After the meeting of foreign ministers held at Punta del Este, Uruguay, in January 1962, at which Cuba's membership in the OAS was suspended, it became something of a pariah state. Castro retaliated the following month with his famous "Second Declaration of Havana" calling for revolution throughout the hemisphere—a statement regarded as a virtual declaration of war against all the Latin American governments except the Mexican (the single Latin American country that refused to break relations with Havana).

For their part the Soviets had misread the U.S. failure at the Bay of Pigs. They believed it reflected lack of will and tried to take advantage of this perceived weakness by moving to position intercontinental ballistic missiles in Cuba. They did not realize until it was too late that the United States would defend itself vigorously and effectively when its security was really threatened.

So much has already been written about the missile crisis of 1962 that it would be redundant to discuss it here again.[9] What is interesting to note, however, is Castro's reaction to it. Upon learning that Nikita Khrushchev had struck a deal behind his back, Castro was furious. That much might have been expected. But it might also have been expected that his antagonism toward and his resolve not to deal with the United States would also have deepened. Instead, his pique with the Soviets was profound enough to start him thinking of rapprochement with the United States. This was not too surprising, for as he must already have become convinced that he could not count on the Soviets to defend him, he must have begun to ask himself what good the relationship really was to him. Did it protect him or simply increase the danger from the United States?

Thus he put out some tentative feelers to the United States,[10] and just prior to John Kennedy's assassination in 1963 he received a French newsman, Jean Daniel, who was acting as Kennedy's emissary. Castro was receptive to what Daniel had to say, but even before Daniel could return with Castro's reply, Kennedy was dead.[11] Even then Castro did not drop the idea of repairing bridges. In 1964, in an interview with Dick Eder of the *New York Times*, Castro proposed to withhold material support from Latin American revolutionaries, if the United States would cease its own hostile actions against Cuba.[12] In a speech on July 26, 1964 Castro repeated the proposal publicly.[13]

Was he serious? Perhaps at least in part, but it seems most unlikely that he would have willingly given up his foreign policy objectives at that point. He may simply have been playing for time; or perhaps, having assessed what he was up against, he decided to scale down his objectives to see if that would open the way for a deal with the United States. He may have calculated that at the very least, the active possibility of such a deal would increase his bargaining power with Moscow.

The United States was, and should have been, suspicious of Castro's motives, but one would have thought the offer worth exploring, even if only through confidential talks. However, no such actions were taken. The United States was already immersed in a clandestine war against Castro (one that led to such extremes as contracting Mafia hit men to assassinate Cuban leaders) and was trying to isolate him in the hemisphere. The United States feared that any vacillation on its part would affect the momentum of that campaign. Thus the United States unceremoniously rebuffed Castro's overtures, noting that it would be willing to talk to him only after he had halted all export of revolution and severed his ties of dependency on the Soviet Union.

The latter condition closed off any discussion, for Castro could not sever his ties to Moscow even *before* reaching some accommodation with Washington—even if he had wished to do so. He would have left himself defenseless and at the mercy of the United States, not a position in which any reasonable leader could be expected to place himself.

With his overture to the United States rebuffed, Castro returned with a vengeance to the export of revolution as a policy and to armed struggle as a tactic. Not that this pleased the Soviets. They probably would have preferred to see some reduction in U.S.-Cuban tensions, and certainly they did not approve of what appeared to them as Castro's reckless and counterproductive support for revolutionaries anywhere and everywhere. From their point of view, this smacked of "infantile adventurism." And they were right. Castro's approach did not pay off. Guerrilla movements failed in country after country. Nowhere in Latin America did armed struggle succeed in duplicating the Cuban model. On the other hand, by the late 1960s the more patient "popular front" tactics advocated by the Soviets were beginning to bear fruit. In 1968, a progressive military government came to power in Peru. Castro had insisted that "the forces of progress" could reach power only through the barrel of a rifle. Now he had to admit there might be other paths as well.[14] The Peruvian variant, moreover, was followed shortly by the victory of Allende's popular front in Chile, which came to power through elections, not through armed struggle.

With his own tactics a failure (symbolic of this failure was the death of Ché Guevara while leading a futile guerrilla operation in Boliva), with other methods apparently succeeding, and with increased pressure from the Soviets, Castro moved to de-emphasize export of revolution and armed struggle. Instead, he began to concentrate on breaking out of his isolation in the hemisphere through the establishment of diplomatic and trade relations with "progressive" governments. The shift did not take place overnight to be sure, but the trend was nonetheless clear. By 1970 Cuban assistance to guerrilla groups and other subversive efforts had been cut back to very low levels.[15]

It was against this background of declining Cuban aggressiveness that the other governments of the hemisphere, which had once felt themselves to be the targets of this activity, began to resume diplomatic relations with Havana and to insist that the multilateral sanctions imposed by the OAS be lifted.

BEGINNINGS OF A U.S.-CUBAN THAW

It was against this background that the U.S. attitude toward Cuba began to soften. In 1973 the two sides signed an antihijacking agreement under which each agreed either to prosecute aerial hijackers or to return them to the other country for prosecution. The successful negotiations leading to this agreement were followed by secret talks in 1974 and

1975 which explored the grounds for some deeper improvement in relations.

There were also overt signs of a thaw. On January 9, 1975 Castro commented to visiting newsmen that the United States seemed to be interested in contacts with Cuba. "We view this," he said, "with pleasure."[16] Henry Kissinger responded in kind two months later during a major policy speech in Houston. The United States was willing to move in a new direction if Cuba would meet halfway, he said, adding that, "we see no virtue in perpetual antagonism between Cuba and the U.S."[17]

On July 29 the United States voted with the majority in the OAS to end multilateral diplomatic and economic sanctions that had been in place against Cuba for 17 years. Henceforth, each member government would be free to carry on relations with Cuba if it so chose. The United States did not follow up by establishing relations or lifting its own embargo against Cuba. In keeping with the spirit of the OAS vote, however, in August it did lift a number of so-called third-country sanctions (e.g., foreign subsidiaries of U.S. companies would be permitted to trade with Cuba under certain conditions). As late as September 23, 1975, Assistant Secretary William D. Rogers reaffirmed U.S. willingness to improve relations with Cuba. Resolution of the various issues in disagreement would not be easy, he said, but the United States was prepared to begin a dialogue to address those disagreements.[18]

ANGOLA

Unfortunately, the dialogue envisaged by Assistant Secretary Rogers did not get off the ground, for as the United States and Cuba had been moving toward better relations in this hemisphere, a new irritant was developing in Africa. On November 5, 1975 for the first time Kissinger stated that Cuba as well as the Soviet Union was supplying assistance to the Popular Movement for the Liberation of Angola (MPLA) in its war for control of Angola (against Holden Roberto's FNLA and Jonas Savimbi's UNITA).[19] By November 11 Kissinger was saying this Cuban assistance "gave us pause," and by November 24 he had come around to the position that U.S. efforts at rapprochement with Cuba would end should "Cuban armed intervention in the affairs of other nations struggling to decide their own fate" continue.[20]

President Ford put an end to the thaw in a surprise press conference on December 20. "The action of the Cuban government in sending combat forces to Angola destroys any opportunity for improvement in relations with the United States," he stated heatedly.[21] On February 28, 1976 he called Castro "an international outlaw" and described the deployment of Cuban troops to Angola as "a flagrant act of aggression."[22]

Neither President Ford nor Secretary Kissinger, of course, had anything to say about the intervention of South African troops in Angola, much less about the role the United States had played in touching off the conflict in the first place. Indeed, the Ford administration did such an effective job of obfuscating events in Angola that even today most Americans believe that Cuban intervention was unprovoked and that Castro ordered his troops into Angola while the United States was seeking to promote a peaceful solution there. Nothing could be further from the truth. From the eyewitness account of the chief of the CIA's Angola Task Force and from various other sources, it is known that the United States, far from seeking a peaceful solution, was instrumental in starting the fighting.

Three principal groups had carried on the liberation struggle against the Portuguese, and, as the latter prepared to withdraw, they were in competition with one another—often armed competition—for the reins of government. These were Agostinho Neto's MPLA, Jonas Savimbi's UNITA, and Holden Roberto's FNLA. Under pressure from the Organization of African Unity, the three leaders met in January 1975 in Alvor, Portugal and agreed to settle the issue peacefully—following Portuguese withdrawal, the three would coexist until elections could be held. This gave rise to hopes that Angola's transition from colony to nation could be accomplished without a civil war.

The United States, however, was not content to let well enough alone, to wait and see if the Alvor agreement worked. The MPLA was regarded as too closely associated with the Soviets and Cubans. Apparently, the U.S. government did not want to take any chances that the MPLA might come to power. Hence, at the strong urging of the CIA, only days after the Alvor agreement was signed, the National Security Council's 40 Committee authorized substantial assistance to Holden Roberto. (The CIA had been supporting Roberto even before, without authorization.) The results were rapid and dramatic. The MPLA had made no aggressive moves against the FNLA. On the contrary, both the MPLA and UNITA gave evidence of intending to adhere to the Alvor agreement.[23] However, in March, Holden Roberto's forces, encouraged by the CIA and accompanied by 1,200 regular Zairean troops and later joined by CIA advisers and European mercenaries paid by the CIA, crossed into Angola and attacked the MPLA. Outnumbered and outgunned, MPLA forces retreated south.

The Cubans, of course, were not blind to what was going on. They knew that CIA advisers were cooperating with the FNLA and that the United States was supporting its offensive. In June Havana responded by sending 200 advisers of its own to help the beleaguered MPLA. This prompted the 40 Committee on July 17 to authorize still more covert support to both Holden Roberto and Savimbi, the recruitment of mercenaries, and the expanded use of CIA advisers. On August 9, South African forces intervened for the first time, crossing into Angola and occupying the Cunene hydroelectric project.

In the wake of the South African incursion, the MPLA asked the Cubans for increased assistance, which was not long in coming. In late August, more Cuban military personnel arrived. Whether they were regular troops or simply advisers is a hotly debated question. Regardless, the numbers were small, and they arrived on the scene *after* regular South African troops had crossed into Angola.

Until then, the war had remained limited. However, on October 23 the South Africans crossed the border in force and launched a drive on Luanda, sweeping the demoralized MPLA before them. The South Africans appeared to be unstoppable and were expected to reach Luanda easily. The United States was fully aware of this South African intervention. Indeed, according to ex-CIA officer John Stockwell, there was close liaison between the United States and the South Africans.[24]

Two weeks later, in response to desperate appeals from the MPLA, Havana began airlifting troops to Angola. In mid-November, these newly arrived forces were instrumental in turning back the FNLA and its foreign allies at the battle of Quifangondo. Eventually, approximately 30,000 Cuban troops arrived in Angola and turned the tide in favor of the MPLA. The MPLA was left in sole possession of power in Angola. U.S. bungling had accomplished exactly the opposite of what we should have wished to achieve.

The Ford administration's outraged protests that Cuba had committed an international crime by sending its troops to Angola were extremely hypocritical. The Ford administration itself had been instrumental in starting the civil war. It had applauded and been in secret liaison with the South Africans as they intervened on a massive scale. The MPLA would have been utterly destroyed by the South Africans if the Cubans had not come to their aid. When they did, the Ford administration petulantly cried foul. But it had only been beaten at its own game.

Since 1975 Americans opposed to a more pragmatic approach to Cuba have pointed to Cuban intervention in Angola as proof that trying to talk to Castro accomplishes nothing. According to this argument, "We tried to open the door to better relations, and Castro responded by intervening in Angola."

This argument is without merit. There is strong evidence that Castro was indeed interested in improving relations with the United States in 1975 and his moves in Angola did not signify to the contrary. If we expected him to give us a free hand in return for a more normal relationship with us, we were being exceedingly unrealistic. Castro was no more willing than the United States to opt out of the game of international politics.

The lesson we should have learned from the Angola debacle was the opposite of what apparently registered with the Ford administration. The Alvor agreement may have been imperfect, but it offered the best hope of avoiding a civil war in Angola and of excluding direct external intervention. The United States might have been expected to launch a diplomatic campaign aimed at engaging other African states and the Organization of African Unity in support of the Alvor agreement and aimed at laying ground rules to make certain it was respected by foreign powers. This would have included conversations with the Soviets and Cubans as well as the South Africans. Instead of talks, we launched an ill-conceived and essentially frivolous clandestine military operation, which led to disaster. What Angola suggests, therefore, is not that dialogue with the Cubans accomplishes nothing but that dialogue might indeed have been preferable to the approach we actually took in Angola (and which the Reagan administration has taken again in Central America).

THE THAW BRIEFLY RESUMES

The Ford administration had broken off all contacts with the Cubans. The Carter administration, however, was more flexible. It wished to establish a new and more harmonious relationship with the

Third World in general. More normal relations with Cuba were seen as an important part of this effort, a sign of the seriousness of U.S. intentions.

The withdrawal of Cuban troops from Angola was a stated objective of the new administration, but it was no longer a precondition to talks with Havana. On February 3, 1977 Secretary of State Cyrus Vance emphasized U.S. readiness to begin discussions on a wide range of issues.[25] The Cubans responded positively, and in late March U.S. and Cuban diplomats opened discussions in New York on the subjects of maritime boundaries and fishing rights in one another's waters. These were concluded the following month in Havana with the signing of agreements on both subjects. During its April stay in Havana, the U.S. delegation also discussed with the Cuban foreign minister the desirability of opening diplomatic missions below the embassy level in one another's capitals. This was not only a sensible step but a very necessary one, for the two sides had taken mutually exclusive positions that could only be resolved through dialogue. Cuba said normal diplomatic relations could not exist between the two until the United States lifted its economic embargo. The United States, on the other hand, said it could not raise the embargo until Cuba had compensated American owners of goods and properties that had been nationalized by the Castro government in the early 1960s. Yet neither issue could be resolved until the two governments had direct communications with one another. Interests sections (the Cuban to be in the Czechoslovakian Embassy in Washington and the American to be in the Swiss Embassy in Havana) were the solution to the problem. With their opening in September 1977, diplomats of the two countries were stationed in one another's capitals for the first time in over 16 years.

Even as relations were improving in Washington and Havana, however, new complications were developing in Africa. Somalia had been an ally of Cuba and the Soviet Union, but its leader, Siad Barre, was irritated by their efforts to establish a relationship with the Ethiopian revolutionary military junta—the Dergue—which had overthrown Emperor Haile Selassie in 1974. The United States was prepared to enter the dispute. On June 11, 1977 President Carter indicated the United States would "aggressively challenge" the Soviet Union for influence in Somalia and a number of other countries.[26] Siad Barre requested U.S. assistance to supply him with arms, and, perhaps to his surprise, he received a positive response. In a speech in St. Louis on July 1, Secretary Vance suggested that the United States would indeed give favorable consideration to Somalia's requests for arms.[27] Other U.S. spokesmen stated that the United States had made the decision, in principle, to become an arms supplier in the area.[28]

U.S. spokesmen emphasized that the arms would be for defensive purposes, but to Siad Barre the U.S. response meant that he now had the backing he needed for his irredentist war. It was not simply a coincidence that he invaded Ethiopia on July 17, 1977.

The United States had not really intended to encourage the Somali attack on Ethiopia. However, given the chronology of events, and against the background of United States and British statements during the month of the invasion, the Soviets and Cubans assumed that Washington (and London) had encouraged it—perhaps were directly behind it. The United States did not in fact provide arms for Siad Barre's invasion; in November the Carter administration announced that no arms would be forthcoming so long as Somali troops were in Ethiopia. The Soviets, however, may well have believed this was simply an empty moral posture on the part of the United States, given that Somalia seemed well on the way to winning the war. Not at all disposed to give Washington a cheap victory in the Horn, Havana and Moscow dramatically increased their support to Ethiopia as Somali forces penetrated deeper into its territory. When the Somali invasion began in July, there had only been a handful of Cuban medical personnel in Ethiopia. By January 1978, however, there were several thousand Cuban troops on the ground, supplied with tanks, artillery, and other heavy weapons provided by the Soviet Union. They were instrumental in defeating Siad Barre's forces and driving them back behind their own borders.

With Cuba's intervention in Ethiopia, any willingness on Washington's part to continue the normalization process with Havana ended. The interests sections remained open, but the United States took no more substantive steps toward improvement of relations, not even reciprocating those taken by the Cubans.

The United States could only react adversely to the Soviet-Cuban intervention in Ethiopia. The presence of still another Cuban expeditionary force in Africa had to be a matter of concern to Washington. As in the case of Angola, however, U.S. policies had helped to bring about the crisis that provoked Cuban intervention. Not that U.S. policymakers were inclined to acknowledge any responsibility for the turn of events; rather, they again cried foul, describing events in Ethiopia as proof of a Soviet-Cuban blueprint for world conquest, and at one point were considering the dispatch of a U.S. naval carrier group[29] (surely one of the most ineffectual steps we might have taken; the war, after all, had already been lost). Yet, there was no question at all but that Somalia was the aggressor. The Cubans had come to the defense of a government and of boundaries recognized by the United States as well as the rest of the international community.

Other developments created new obstacles to improved relations between the United States and Cuba. One of the most dramatic was the "discovery" of the Soviet brigade in Cuba during the summer of 1979.

At the time of the 1962 missile crisis, there had been at least 20,000 Soviet troops in Cuba. Their withdrawal was not covered by the Kennedy-Khrushchev understanding, but as the missiles were withdrawn, so too, gradually, were most of the troops, as their mission had been to protect the missile sites. Over the years, U.S. intelligence gave little attention to the few remaining Soviet ground personnel in Cuba; rather, it concentrated on determining what kinds of weapons were on the island—most specifically, on trying to detect the possible reintroduction of nuclear armaments. When the question of Soviet personnel was occasionally raised (e.g., in congressional correspondence to the Pentagon), the standard reply was that there were several thousand Soviet military personnel on the island, "mostly in an advisory capacity."

In the early summer of 1979, however, there were reports that at least some of those Soviet personnel constituted an organized unit. These same reports also emphasized that there had been no significant new arrivals of Soviet troops in Cuba. In other words, whatever was there had been there all along.

There might have been no brouhaha if the Department of State had been more forthright about these reports and if it had taken the position from the beginning that regardless of the role of Soviet ground personnel, they posed no threat to the United States. As it was, however, the Department first assured a number of concerned senators that there was no such unit in Cuba, then reversed course and acknowledged that there was, and, finally, left it up to one of the senators to go public with news of the unit's presence.

Having allowed others to set the tone of public reaction, the administration then tried to regain the initiative by striking a tough posture and asserting that "the status quo was unacceptable." Some administration officials portrayed the brigade (even though it had been there all along) as evidence of Soviet-Cuban aggressiveness so threatening that it would be extremely dangerous if the United States did not react. Moscow and Havana were testing the United States, the argument ran;

accordingly, the administration had to demand the brigade's withdrawal. But the Soviets and Cubans, for their part, had no intention of removing it simply because Washington wished them to do so.

The Carter administration had spun a public relations problem for itself with which it then had to live. The status quo later became acceptable after all, but not before the administration had done tremendous harm to its own credibility and to important American priorities. The SALT II treaty was shelved, and détente was dealt a mortal blow. The Soviets and Cubans were not, in fact, testing the United States at all. The administration simply chose to portray the situation in those terms and was then caught in its own trap.

The exodus of Cubans through the port of Mariel in the spring and summer of 1980 was cited as conclusive evidence that dialogue with Cuba accomplishes nothing. According to the American argument, "We tried to talk with them, but while we did so, they opened Mariel and dumped 125,000 refugees on us, including criminals and mental patients." However, Mariel was evidence of exactly the opposite—of a *breakdown* in communications. In the months prior to the Mariel incident, the Cubans had complained that while the United States welcomed anyone who arrived in Florida by small boat, it offered very few immigrant visas. In other words, it encouraged illegal departures even as it restricted legal channels of entry. The Cubans indicated a desire to discuss with the United States the establishment of a normal flow of immigration. The United States never really replied.

Of even greater urgency was the issue of boat hijackings. Beginning with a hijacking in October 1979, the Cuban government insisted that the United States define its position toward such acts. Cuba was cooperating with the United States in discouraging aerial hijackings, they pointed out. Planes and passengers were immediately returned, and hijackers were prosecuted. They did not expect the United States to return boat hijackers, but surely it could prosecute them under existing U.S. laws, thus discouraging the practice.

Between October 1979 and April 1980, when the Mariel exodus began, there were five additional hijackings. On each occasion, the Cuban government presented a protest note and asked for a clarification of the U.S. position. The United States never provided any such clarification. In fact, it never responded to a single one of the Cuban protest notes.

In February 1980, the U.S. Interests Section in Havana was warned by Cuban Vice President Carlos Rafael Rodríguez that the U.S. position on maritime hijackings had come to be seen within the Cuban government as a litmus test of U.S. intentions. U.S. failure to respond was taken by many Cuban officials as confirmation that the United States was trying to use illegal departures as an instrument of destabilization. If the United States did not soon define itself, Rafael Rodríguez went on, the Cuban government might take defensive measures, such as opening a new Camarioca (the Mariel of 1965). If the United States wished to encourage the arrival of people in small boats, he said, Cuba could give it more than it could handle.[30]

The U.S. government did not pay any heed. It was only in July, some three months after the exodus had begun, that it finally issued a statement that in effect simply condemned maritime hijacking as an act of terrorism and said anyone who arrived in the United States as the result of such an act would be prosecuted consistent with U.S. law. But by then it was too late.

The problem prior to Mariel, then, was not that the United States was talking with the Cubans; on the contrary, it was precisely that it *did not talk to them.* Had it addressed the maritime hijacking issue and discussed other Cuban complaints in a sensible, straightforward manner, the whole situation might have had a different outcome. Mariel might well have been avoided.

This does not mean that omissions by the United States justified Cuban actions at Mariel. On the contrary, Mariel represented an outburst of anger and frustration on the Cuban side, and anger is always dangerous in international politics. Mariel was handled in a way that was deeply offensive to the American people. Sending refugees to the United States was one thing; including criminals and the mentally ill was something else again.

The Cubans appear to have realized that they went too far and to seem to have wished that they could retract their objectionable actions. They closed Mariel in September 1980 and subsequently offered to discuss with the United States modalities for the return of the criminals and the establishment of a normal flow of immigrants which they would commit themselves to respect. Two rounds of talks were held with the outgoing Carter administration. Agreement had not been reached, but in February 1981 the Cubans indicated the United States had not heard its final offer and urged a third round of talks with the new Reagan administration. The latter, however, did not even respond; rather, it adopted a policy of inflexible hostility toward Cuba and made it clear that it wished to discuss nothing with Havana—not the return of the criminals, not other bilateral problems, not even the situation in Central America. Indeed, under the Reagan administration, U.S.-Cuban relations reached perhaps their lowest point since the open conflict at the Bay of Pigs and the near cataclysm of the missile crisis. American policymakers seem to have learned nothing. Tactics of intimidation that had failed when they were tried 20 years before were now tried again.

CONCLUSION

The Carter administration's opening to Cuba failed ultimately because it was based on unrealistic expectations. Rather than seeing the moderation of Cuban foreign policy as a goal that could only be achieved, at best, over time and through a process of gradual and cautious engagement, the Carter administration seemed to expect that Castro would quickly and drastically scale back his foreign policy objectives in return for and almost as a prerequisite for a more normal relationship with the United States. When Castro did not pull his troops out of Africa and, instead, sent a new expeditionary force to Ethiopia, the Carter administration retreated to the rigid attitudes of its predecessors.

Any sensible engagement between the two countries would have to begin with the recognition that there are real and serious problems between them, that the two are likely to remain in something of an adversarial relationship for a long time to come, and that even when their diplomatic and trade relations have been "normalized," the atmosphere between them is not likely to be cordial. Still, many of the problems between them, especially those of a bilateral nature, can be resolved. The two sides should, in their mutual interests, begin negotiations to address them. And even in those cases in which no immediate solution is possible, the areas of disagreement, through negotiations, might at least be reduced. New problems have arisen in Central America, for example, where a government sympathetic to Cuba has emerged in Nicaragua and where leftist guerrillas are battling the government of El Salvador. Cuba did not create the crisis in Central America, but it does support the Nicaraguan government and at least in the past has given some degree of support to the Salvadoran guerrillas. Cuba, however, has on several occasions indicated its willingness to discuss the matter with the United States and to contribute to political solutions in the area. It would seem to have been in the interests of the United States to begin such a dialogue and to engage Cuba in the search for peace in Central America. Instead, the Reagan administration has rebuffed all such Cuban overtures, apparently on grounds that diplomacy is not an appropriate instrument for dealing with Cuba. Hostility for the sake of hostility, like the unchanging season of the rain forest, still appears to be an immutable condition in U.S.-Cuban relations.

NOTES

1. For a very different view, see Louis A. Pérez, Jr., *Cuba Between Empires, 1878–1902* (Pittsburgh: University of Pittsburgh Press, 1983).
2. Deputy CIA Director C.P. Cabell, in testimony to the Senate Internal Security Subcommittee in November 1959, stated that based on all the evidence available to the CIA, Castro was not a Communist.
3. See *Revolución* (Havana), April 18, 1959, April 20, 1959, and September 27, 1960 for the texts of several of Castro's early speeches.
4. *Revolución*, September 25, 1959.
5. *Revolución*, January 22, 1959.
6. See Bonsal's own account of his mission. Philip W. Bonsal, *Cuba, Castro and the U.S.* (Pittsburgh: University of Pittsburgh Press, 1972).
7. In addition, Justo Carillo, Castro's first finance minister, has revealed that as early as February 1959, Treasury Secretary Robert Anderson indicated that the United States was willing to be helpful to Cuba economically (*Miami Herald*, February 24, 1984, p. 8A).
8. *Bohemia* (Havana), January 31, 1960.
9. See Henry M. Pachter, *Collision Course: The Cuban Missile Crisis and Coexistence* (New York: Praeger, 1963); Abram Chayes, *The Cuban Missile Crisis* (London: Oxford University Press, 1974); and Herbert Dinerstein, *The Making of a Missile Crisis, October 1962* (Baltimore: Johns Hopkins Press, 1976).
10. See William Atwood, *The Reds and the Blacks* (New York: Harper and Row, 1967), pp. 142–44.
11. Frank Mankiewicz and Kirby Jones, *With Fidel* (Chicago: Playboy Press, 1975), pp. 160–66.
12. Maurice Halperin, *The Taming of Fidel Castro* (Berkeley: University of California Press, 1981), pp. 93–101.
13. Ibid., pp. 101–11.
14. See text of Castro's speech in *Revolución*, July 19, 1969.
15. See my testimony before the Subcommittee on Inter-American Affairs of the House of Representatives Committee on International Relations, April 5, 1978. In the committee report entitled "Impact of Cuban-Soviet Ties in the Western Hemisphere," p. 57.

16. "Toward Improved United States-Cuban Relations," the report of a special study mission to Cuba, printed for the use of the Committee on International Relations, May 23, 1977, p. 72.
17. Ibid., p. 71.
18. Ibid., p. 65.
19. Ibid., p. 64.
20. Ibid., p. 65.
21. Ibid., p. 63.
22. Ibid., p. 62.
23. John Stockwell, *In Search of Enemies: A CIA Story* (New York: W.W. Norton & Co., 1978), p. 67.
24. Ibid., pp. 187–88.
25. "Toward Improved U.S.-Cuban Relations," p. 45.
26. *New York Times*, June 12, 1977, p. 1.
27. *New York Times*, July 27, 1977, p. 3.
28. *New York Times*, July 28, 1977, p. 1.
29. Zbigniew Brzezinski, *Power and Principle* (New York: Farrar-Straus-Giroux, 1983), pp. 181–85.
30. *Miami Herald*, October 5, 1982, p. 11A.

18 Cuba, the Soviet Union, and Third World Struggle

Marjorie Woodford Bray and Donald W. Bray

One overriding concern has dogged Cuban international life since the revolution—survival. In its attempted overthrow of a noncapitalist society on its doorsteps, the United States has expended a great deal of money and energy, even resorting to contracts with Mafia hitmen and a poisoned milkshake in murder attempts against Cuba's chief of state. Clearly, much of the literature of conventional interstate relations does not apply to relations between the United States and Cuba. Incredibly, despite its adversarial relationship with the strongest power, Cuba has become a world actor. It has done more then just survive.

No Latin American nation, probably not even Brazil, has been a more influential international force than Cuba. Paradoxically, before 1959 Cuba was one of the least influential. The chemistry of this change is complex. One determining factor is the nature and experience of the revolutionary leadership. Prior generations of Latin American revolutionaries, many radical in their youth, accommodated U.S. interests once they came to power (leaders such as Betancourt, Haya de la Torre, and Figueres). After overrunning the largest military in the Caribbean, the Cuban guerrillas would not be intimidated. Their audacity was projected into the world theater. A second factor is that once defiance of U.S. power had caused the Congress to end the sugar quota in 1960, Cuba had no real alternative but to establish a profound relationship with the U.S.S.R.

Cuba's unique international role would have been practically impossible without its association with the Soviet Union. One is tempted to make comparisons with Israel and its enlarged influence related to U.S. support; however, the ends differ. Since 1967 Israel had been preoccupied with self-interest and self-preservation, whereas Cuba has continued to promote liberation around the globe.

Of course, liberation is a loaded concept. Nicaraguan diplomat Edgar Parrales provides a good analysis of Third World liberation. He posits the logic of the majority against the logic of the minority. As long as a minority's interests are in power in a region such as Central America and as long as these interests also protect those of the United States, all is well. When the needs of a broad base of the population come to be represented in government (as in Nicaragua) the United States responds like a wounded bear.

Cuba's natural economic and cultural relations are tied to the Western hemisphere, as they well know. They must study the subtropical agriculture of Louisiana and Hawaii. They need spare parts by air the same day from Florida. García Márquez of Colombia and Vargas Llosa of Peru are their literary compañeros. Angela Davis is a compelling symbol for Cubans. Yet, the U.S.S.R. has been their lifeline.

CUBAN ACTIVISM

Cuban attempts to overthrow right-wing governments in the Western hemisphere soon after the revolution were not successful. The only effort the Cubans had their heart in was against Trujillo in the Dominican Republic. Ironically, the CIA (under Kennedy) disposed of Trujillo because he stood in the way of a hemisphere-wide effort to isolate Cuba. Yet Cuba was not to be isolated. Under the U.S. gun, boycotted and threatened Cuba needed other friends. Rendering technical assistance to many states helped offset U.S. pressure. This is not to deny that the motivation was primarily political principle, but overseas aid did win support in world forums. Cuba could not offer money, but it could offer skilled workers in considerable numbers. For example, there are more medical doctors in Africa from Cuba then from the United States. Cubans are popular military trainers to other Third World nations. They have earned their spurs in combat, particularly in Angola. And Cuba is not a superpower or a former colonial master country. Cuba's commitment to the liberation struggle and protection of progressive governments began soon after the triumph of the revolution. As early as 1963 Cuba sent troops and equipment to Algeria when the latter was involved in a border skirmish with Morocco.

Cuba has achieved an impressive record for an underdeveloped country. It is clearly a leader in the areas of education, public health, culture, and athletics. Its superskilled populace has lent technical assistance to 37 countries (see chapter 19 by Susan Eckstein). Its leadership has designated Cuba as "medical power" because of its numerous health programs abroad. Perhaps most astonishing, since the revolution its artists have produced the lion's share of notable films, novels, poems, short stories, and songs for all of Latin America.

THE POLITICAL ECONOMY OF CUBA'S WORLD ROLE

The fact that Cuba has become an authentic leader in the arena of international politics has not been an automatic consequence of the success of the Cuban experiment. It has also been the result of changes in world conditions and the astute appreciation of these changes by the Cuban leadership who seized opportunities provided by these changes and guided events into outcomes made possible by historic forces. It is an advantage of Marxism that it affords those who are guided by its analysis a world view that permits policy adjustments to the fluidity of the world political and economic situation without the concern that underlying principles have been abandoned.

The most important aspects of the world situation 25 years after the revolution are the economic crisis and the growing global concern of nuclear destruction—concerns that are interrelated. Past periods of severe economic dislocation have given rise to the tensions that have led to world war. The existance of nuclear weapons makes the potential outcome of conflict generated by economic factors too dangerous to be pursued. Alternative paths must be found if the world is to survive. However, without a solution to the acute economic problems of Third World countries, the possibility that the underlying structural crisis could lead to a war with world repercussions is a constant concern.

Fidel Castro recognized this problem in his speech to the United Nations reporting on the Sixth Conference of the Movement of Non-aligned Countries held in Havana in October 1979:

> World financial bankruptcy would be very hard, most of all for the underdeveloped countries and the workers in the developed capitalist countries. It would also affect even the most stable socialist economies. But it is doubtful that the capitalist system would be able

to survive such a catastrophe. And it would be difficult for the resulting dreadful economic situation not to inevitably engender a world conflagration.[1]

This is the analysis that underlay Castro's words to the World Peace Council as it met in Havana in 1981:

> ...[T]he struggle to avert the outbreak of a new world war is the most urgent, necessary and decisive task of our time. Peace itself is not the solution to all problems. Peace is only the basic condition in order to turn over the colossal wealth of energy and resources needed so that all of humanity, not just a part of it, can live honorably, decently and decorously. Peace is an indispensable prerequisite for the great battle against underdevelopment....[2]

Such awareness has provided the Cuban leadership with the ability to recognize the issues upon which many countries can unite and to provide direction that will be accepted by nations with diverse social systems, but which have all undergone an historical experience characterized by underdevelopment. It is also in this context that today the Cubans no longer advocate the recapitulation of their own revolutionary ideas as guides for the revolutionary practice of other nations. These are the conditions that have given rise to the "new revolutionary theory."

It is true that the foreign policy of the revolutionary state involves a fundamental contradiction. For its own economic and political survival it is essential that any nation develop a basis for interaction with other states that involves observation of the fundamental norms that have evolved under international law. Nevertheless, to sustain internal and external legitimacy as a revolutionary force, Marxist states also must maintain a stance of continued commitment to change in the social and economic systems of capitalist countries. After the revolution, it appeared to the Cuban leadership that such change was possible in other Latin American countries in that period. Consequently, Cuban policy espoused such movements in the region even though its main ally, the Soviet Union, did not endorse such efforts. By the end of the 1960s the Soviet Union clearly opposed such support because of its own estimation of world forces, its self interest as a great power, and the requirements of peaceful coexistence dictated by the possibility of nuclear war.

The failure of the Latin American revolutions to materialize, which culminated in the tragic death of Ché Guevara in Bolivia in 1967, was partially due to the very success of the Cuban venture. This success impelled the United States into active opposition on a hemispheric scale to the movement which, if successful, would have provided Cuba with a more supportive environment in the region. This intervention began with military support against revolutionary groups in Venezuela, Peru, Guatemala, Nicaragua, and Bolivia; and it included support of the overthrow of the constitutional government of Brazil in 1964, occupation of the Dominican Republic in 1965, and the destruction of the elected government of the Unidad Popular in Chile in 1973. It continued with CIA efforts to overthrow the Sandinista regime in the mid-1980s and the invasion of Grenada in 1983.

In Latin America the critical situation that had given rise to the movements for change continued to intensify. The economic conditions in the region had created a situation in which all social sectors recognized the need to alter the status quo. As early as the late 1940s the United Nations Economic Commission for Latin America (ECLA), under the direction of Argentine economist Raúl Prebisch, began to provide an analysis of the role of the underdeveloped countries in the world economy. The analysis provided by ECLA was such a powerful framework upon which to mount international economic negotiations that it became the foundation for proposals elaborated in the United Nations Conference on Trade and Development (UNCTAD). Established in 1964 and also headed by Raúl Prebisch, it became the principal forum in which all Third World nations sought to achieve equity in the world economy.

The cooperation among the Latin American countries in developing the program implied by the ECLA analysis was carried on in various regional and international organizations. Cuba's new government was naturally interested in these initiatives. Fidel Castro attended a meeting of the Committee of the Twenty One, sponsored by the Organization of American States, in Buenos Aires in May 1959. There he called for a ten-year aid program of $30 billion, to be built along Marshall Plan-type lines and that in fact was similar to the format that would be adopted by the Alliance for Progress in 1961. The Cubans, with Guevara as head of their delegation, also actively participated in the 1961 meetings at Punta del Este, Uruguay, which set up the Alliance for Progress. The Cubans called for an emphasis on industrialization, which was not explicitly dealt with at the conference, contending that economic and social development were synonymous with industrialization and that the establishment of nationally owned industries for capital goods production should be given top priority. Guevara's address to the conference criticized the emphasis on improving social conditions as an almost "colonial" attitude that assumed what poor Indians, Negroes, and other Latin Americans needed most was sanitation.[3]

However, the United States was determined to exclude Cuba from any benefits of the foreign aid provided under the Alliance and to isolate the island nation from the rest of the hemisphere. The success of the United States in enrolling the countries of the area in the economic blockade of Cuba (to the extent that Cuba was expelled from the OAS in 1962), and the severance by 1964 of diplomatic and commercial relations by all nations except Mexico, meant that Cubans were in general unable to participate in the further development of the regional analysis and strategy. Although Cuba continued to be a member of ECLA, other regional economic ventures of the 1960s such as the Latin American Free Trade Agreement (LAFTA), excluded Cuba. It was also barred from the Special Latin American Coordinating Committee (CECLA), the vehicle for Latin American cooperation with the rest of the Third World, organized as the Group of 77. Cuba did not become a member of the Group of 77 until 1971. This made it impossible for the Cubans to exercise a leadership role in the development of UNCTAD, since these organizations were instrumental in making UNCTAD the arena in which Third World economic demands were agreed upon and presented to the industrialized countries.[4]

CUBA AND THE NONALIGNED MOVEMENT

Meanwhile, however, the Cubans were forging their own leadership role in another international organization, the Movement of Nonaligned Countries. This movement evolved out of the meeting of Asian and African nations in Bandung, Indonesia in 1955. The First Conference of Nonaligned Countries was held in Belgrade, Yugoslavia in September 1961, and Cuba was the only Latin American state present. The movement continued to grow with 31 developing nations participating in the third meeting in Cairo in 1962, including four from Latin America— Cuba, Bolivia, Brazil, and Mexico. However, the organization never achieved the almost universal Third World membership of UNCTAD and the Group of 77.

Although in its early years the Nonaligned Movement put more emphasis on the goal of independence, making it a forum in which nations without alliances with either the West or the socialist bloc sought to sustain freedom of action and to promote world peace, economic concerns were also present. The Cairo meetings were designated the Conference on the Problems of Economic Development, and it was there that a call was issued for a conference to be held under the auspices of the United Nations that would consider international trade, primary commodities trade, and relations between developed and developing countries, the response to which was the establishment of UNCTAD.[5]

The Cuban rise to leadership in the Nonaligned Movement was not meteoric. The Cuban relationship with the Soviet Union made for inevitable tensions with other members. Its activities in Africa alienated some states so greatly that even after Cuba had been designated the site of the Sixth Summit Conference, to be held in 1979, unsuccessful efforts were initiated to expel Cuba from the organization in 1978.[6] Nevertheless, the meeting in Havana did take place, and the subsequent role of Fidel Castro as president of the organization presented increased opportunities for Cuba to influence world opinion. In the report that Castro presented to the Seventh Summit Conference in New Delhi in 1981 he compared the Cuban Revolution and its practice of leadership in the Third World with the economic struggle as developed in previous decades, but with a Cuban flavor.[7]

How did Cuba come to this position of leadership? Certainly for some, willingness to back ideological support with military assistance was a factor. Also important has been the economic assistance that the Cubans provided to various Third World countries. Although limited in number, the fact that an underdeveloped nation is willing to provide aid to others less advanced demonstrates Cuba's genuine commitment to Third World development. Nevertheless, more than these activities would be required to propel Cuba into the forefront of Third World activity, especially when actions that won it support from some nations threw it into disrepute with others with more conservative governments. The major change in the constellation of Third World forces lies in the failure of the programs and strategies devised under the UNCTAD banner to alleviate the unequal economic relationship between the developed and the underdeveloped world.

In Latin America the failure of the Alliance for Progress, the Latin American Free Trade Area, and the similar Central American Common Market (CACM) to promote balanced economic growth also contributed to the disappointment with the strategies that had evolved through the process begun by ECLA and continued in UNCTAD. While participating in the UNCTAD movement, the Cubans consistently questioned the uncritical reliance on private investment to provide resources that would promote development in Third World nations.

The world inflation of the early 1970s, the increase in petroleum prices as a result of the action of OPEC, and the growing debt crisis of many Third World nations made the goals of UNCTAD even more urgent. In 1974 the issues were elevated to the UNCTAD General Assembly at the Sixth Special Session, the first to deal with economic matters. At this session a document calling for a "new international economic order," basically the agenda developed in UNCTAD, was adopted.[8]

The success of OPEC as a producer cartel inspired great fear in the industrialized nations, and in the primary commodity-producing countries, it inspired great hope of the possibilities of using similar mechanisms to achieve leverage with their customers. The Cubans read other lessons into the actions of OPEC. On September 28, 1974 Castro indicated his clear understanding of the situation in an address to a meeting of representatives of the Committees for the Defense of the Revolution. First he noted that the world inflation was not due to the oil crisis. Instead, it was due to the policies of the United States, which imposed a monetary system on the rest of the world that gave the dollar a privileged position. He also cited the arms race and the Vietnam War as roots of the inflated monetary crisis.[9] He said that increased prices charged by the developed countries for the manufactured goods they exported were greater than the added energy costs, and the situation was especially difficult for nonindustrialized countries without oil. The danger was that the strategy of the "imperialists" to force down petroleum prices "might find acceptance in many poor countries. This could result in tremendous division among the countries of the Third World," constituting a "defeat" for the oil producers, and in the long run for all producers of raw materials and leading to a "worsening in the unequal terms of exchange."[10] Castro continued: "If all of the underdeveloped countries are to make the battle of petroleum theirs it is imperative that the oil producing countries make the battle of the underdeveloped world theirs."[11] This they should achieve by investing their increased incomes in the nations of the Third World.

In March 1975 at the meeting of the Coordinating Bureau of the Nonaligned Countries, Castro called attention to the fact that less than five percent of the $60 million accumulated by oil-producing countries had been invested in the underdeveloped nations, and that the amount received by most of these countries for their exports had been declining. He stated that the OPEC countries must have a strategy of economic cooperation with the underdeveloped world.[12] However, in December 1976 the failure of OPEC, "especially the largest producers with the smallest populations," to follow Castro's advice elicited sharp criticism from the Cuban leader in an address to the meeting that organized the Assembly of People's Power in Cuba.

The analysis that Castro presented in his report to the Nonaligned Movement in 1981 took the facts presented in conventional Third World discussions and gave them a new and more critical interpretation. He said the current situation showed a "new trait" of "monopolist extraction." In addition to unequal trade and private investment, the problems were now to be resolved by "financial means, that is... external debt."[13] He observed that "capital prefers to remain as financial capital drawing high interest rates, rather than as investment in production." Then he made his fundamental critique.

> Third World external debt, considered by many... to be uncontrollable and unpayable... is probably one of the clearest expressions of the irrationality and unviability of an obsolete international economic order.[14]

He was highly critical of the new practice of "industrial redeployment," which used "the headquarters-subsidiary system to take advantage of... the cheap abundant work force in the Third World for the production of industrial goods for export." He said, "The transnational corporations have found a kind of external reserve army which... fulfills its role as a mechanism of plunder encouraging the accumulation of capital."[15] All of these problems represent outcomes reached by achieving the very objectives sought by the Third World at UNCTAD—more credit, more investment, and preferential tariffs for industrial products.

One of Castro's major recommendations for remedying this situation was Third World economic cooperation. He criticized opinions expressed in some market economy countries that such cooperation was costly or ineffective. He noted that "recommendations that appear to be of a technological nature" portrayed cooperation to be "an unrealizable dream or a mere propagandistic slogan."[16] He held that the potential for cooperation to provide "concrete benefits" had a sound basis in the diverse material and human resources and capacities of the Third World, which indicated "important possibilities for efficient economic complementation."[17] Castro said that such a cooperation must not "become a mechanism for transnationals... to control most of the benefits of a broadened market...." He also noted that "unequal distribution of benefits" among countries with different development levels had led to the failure of previous regional or subregional economic integration efforts (presumably such as LAFTA and CACM), so that cooperation had to include "preventing a few countries with a certain level of industrialization and exporting capability from reaping most of the benefits."[18] In addition, he admonished that cooperation "could not be used as a pretext for not carrying out the domestic structural transformation which... constitutes the main prerequisite for a genuine development process."[19]

The focus on economic issues was not a repudiation of the Cuban concern with the need for revolutionary change, nor did the growing participation of Cuba in international organizations imply an abandoning of support for revolutionary movements. Castro publicly recognized the contradictions of the Nonaligned Movement:

> Of course, we, the group of underdeveloped countries, do not constitute a homogeneous whole. Some oppose imperialism... others are... very close to imperialism and in many cases even act as its allies.[20]

Also prominent in the Cuban analysis was the fact that activities of imperialism were not attacked only as phenomena of the nation-state system. The importance of the role of transnational corporations was a constant theme. Nevertheless, the strategy being pursued by Cuba did mean that postures constrained by the tension between being a state and being a revolutionary force seemed to reflect considerations of state interest to a somewhat greater degree than in other periods of Cuban history. The continuing friendship of Cuba with the Forbes Burnham government of Guyana[21] and the lack of an official position on the Ferdinand Marcos government of the Philippines may be symptoms of this situation.

The Cuban public stance in regard to the Soviet Union has continued to be laudatory. Soviet activities in Afghanistan are not subject to condemnation because they are supporting "the revolutionary victory of the Afghan people, who overthrew the despotic, semifeudal regime in their country."[22] Cuba was unable to achieve support in the Nonaligned Movement for the concept that the socialist bloc was the "natural ally" of developing nations.[23] However, the Cubans steadfastly maintained that the Soviet role was qualitatively different from that of the West, rejecting the notion of two imperialisms:

> The socialist countries do not have transnational enterprises, nor do they own mines, oil deposits or factories beyond their borders. Not one single socialist country exploits a worker or peasant in another country.[24]

The growing Cuban international leadership was supported by the changing situation in the Caribbean. The establishment of the Latin American Economic System (SELA) in 1975, under the leadership of Mexico and Venezuela, restored Cuba to a role in hemispheric activities in a setting that explicitly excluded the United States. The development of the independent nations of the English-speaking Caribbean had also increased the supportiveness of the international environment for Cuba.[25] Severe reversals occurred when Cuba lost its close alliances with Jamaica under Michael Manley and Grenada under Maurice Bishop.[26] However, the presence of the Sandinista government in Nicaragua and the strength of revolutionary movements in El Salvador and Guatemala still contributed to a regional balance of forces that was more favorable to Cuba than in the early years of the revolution.

THE U.S. RESPONSE TO CUBAN WORLD ACTIVISM

All U.S. administrations since Dwight Eisenhower have regarded Cuban foreign involvement as troublemaking. In effect, a new corollary to the Monroe Doctrine has emerged: A Latin American nation must confine its political and military initiatives to the Western hemisphere, and in the hemisphere only the United States (or friendly right-wing regimes) may undertake to destabilize other regimes.

Cuba was the first Latin American state to play an independent international military role.[27] The charge that in this role Cuba is simply a "proxy" or "surrogate" for the Soviet Union is rejected by scholars most knowledgeable on the subject.[28] Cuban overseas military activities have at times been supported by the U.S.S.R. when there has been a convergence of interests, but in general the Cubans have developed their own military agenda, sometimes in conflict with Soviet interests.

With its enormous phosphates investment in Morocco, for example, the U.S.S.R. must be disquieted by continued military support of the Polisario liberation movement fighting Morocco in Spanish Sahara. The presence of military advisors from Cuba and other socialist countries in besieged Nicaragua is presented as evidence by the U.S. government that the longstanding struggles in Central America are a Soviet-Cuban creation. Former Jamaican Prime Minister Michael Manley comments tellingly:

> The theory which sees Soviet and now Cuban expansionism as the root of popular revolutionary activity misconceives the nature of popular revolutions, underrates the quality of patriotism that inspires recently liberated peoples and misunderstands a new kind of internationalism among third world countries in which cooperation is seen as the answer to big-power domination and local tyranny alike.... A policy that flows from an analysis based upon myths is likely to be crazy. Action that flows from such an analysis is bound to be dangerous.[29]

THE NEW REVOLUTIONARY THEORY

Revolutionary theory has been transformed since 1959. The New Theory includes:

1. Policies that will hold the skilled middle class in the country after victory even if they are settlers (e.g., Zimbabwe);

2. Commercial and diplomatic relations with all states to avoid dependence on one country (under the New Theory, revolutionary states, such as Mozambique and Nicaragua, do not give military base rights to superpowers);

3. Retention of the small-sized and medium-sized private sector in agriculture, industry, and commerce;

4. Religious freedom;

5. Open public discussion; and

6. Socialist democracy.

Under the New Revolution Theory, Grenada and Nicaragua experienced the most humane revolutions in history, virtually without retributive killing and with the preservation of a high level of free speech. Political pluralism is accepted, but the interests of the broad base of the population must take precedence. That is not negotiable.

The new approaches, revised from the "war of national liberation" thinking of the 1960s, are now advocated by the Cuban government. Indeed, Cuba has helped elaborate on them. Nicaragua has seriously pursued these goals. The program of the FMLN-FDR (The Farabundo Martí Front for National Liberation-Democratic Revolutionary Front) in El Salvador is similar to that of the Sandinistas in Nicaragua and retains a defined private sector. The Reagan strategy has been to use economic and military pressure to force a decrease in the existing openness in Nicaraguan society and to force the destruction of the private sector by denying it access to credit from abroad. The Reagan administration described the Central American struggle as if it were an earlier revolution, while attempting to stifle its democratic and pluralistic features.

Drawing upon the Cuban example, recently triumphant revolutionary regimes (e.g., Nicaragua, Guinea-Bissau, Mozambique, Angola, Grenada, Ethiopia, etc.) have instituted literacy and health campaigns, but sooner after victory than happened in Cuba. These campaigns have received financial and technical assistance from many nations, both capitalist and socialist, but only a pittance from the United States. The U.S. government simply cannot relate to wars of national liberation, even though they are a most important phenomenon of this epoch.

THE CUBAN-SOVIET ENCOUNTER

The giving of an extraordinary amount of assistance to Cuba is not without precedent for the U.S.S.R. Within the Soviet Union, people in the Slavic-speaking republics have had their living standards reduced by subsidization of the "Islamic" republics. Externally, Soviet aid has transformed the People's Republic of Mongolia from a land of tents and ponies into one of schools, hospitals, and industries. (The U.S.S.R. has ensnared itself in Afghanistan in such a way that it probably will some day have to pay to "Mongolianize" that country.) Still the case of Soviet aid to Cuba is somewhat unique. It exceeds the total amounts granted to India, Egypt, or Vietnam, countries with large populations. It does not seem likely that (apart from Afghanistan) other countries will be given such incredible largesse. Nicaragua, for example, receives only modest assistance from the U.S.S.R.

In addition to credits and other assistance, the Soviet Union buys Cuban sugar above the world price and sells Cuba its oil below the market price. What is the political cost of all this? What would the politics of the Cuban Revolution be without the Soviet encounter? This can only be answered by intuition or witchcraft. Is Cuba doing "unnatural" things? A few. The three issues that have done the most to harm Cuba's standing in the Third World have all involved invasion—Czechoslovakia, Afghanistan, and Kampuchea. Soviet armed forces led the first two invasions and the last was led by Vietnam. On Czechoslovakia the Cuban response boiled down to: It had to be done but we would never let them (the U.S.S.R.) do it to us. On Afghanistan: Publicly we will not condone the U.S.S.R., but privately we are "worried." On Kampuchea: We have always felt the utmost solidarity with Vietnam, besides, the Pol Pot regime was genocidal. Still, the country *was* invaded. These Cuban responses demonstrate ambiguity in all three instances. Their positions were a little "unnatural."

The Cuban analysis that the socialist bloc is naturally the ally of the Third World has also been controversial. Since most of the commercial relations of Third World states are with the West, the "natural ally" concept has met with resistance. This resistance has softened with the world recession, the Third World debt traps, and the smashing of efforts to forge price-stabilizing organizations for Third World exports. For now, attempts to create the New International Economic Order have ended in almost unconditional victory for the industrialized states.

Since in the Nonaligned Movement Cuba has stressed the inequities of North-South economic relationships, events have validated the Cuban position, and this together with Cuba's heroic role in Angola, helping to stop the South Africans 70 miles from Luanda, have overridden the "natural ally" problem to project Cuba into the leadership of the Nonaligned Movement. In Angola, Cuba changed the course of events in southern Africa. Cuba's contribution in Angola would not have been possible without Soviet logistical and material support. Turning around the history of the region away from white South Africa's dominance has to be measured against a bit of Cuban ambiguity in the matter of the three invasions. In recent years Cuba has downplayed its "natural ally" stance at international gatherings.

CUBA AND REAGAN

Normalization of Cuban-U.S. relations was ruptured during the Ford administration. With the South African racists stabbing into Angola, the Cubans were presented with an agonizing choice: Come to the defense of the Angolan independence or proceed with the negotiations that would eventually lead to access to the U.S. market, technology, and tourists. After 12 hours of continuous discussion, the Cuban leadership decided to support the M.P.L.A. (Popular Movement for the Liberation of Angola) in Angola. It was one of those rare instances in international relations where principle triumphs over economic advantage. In any case, the dye was cast. The United States would maintain hostility as long as thousands of Cuban troops remained in Africa. United Nations Ambassador Andrew Young was open-minded about the Cuban military presence in Africa, but he was fired for talking to the PLO. Carter left office with a military build-up in the Caribbean, "exposure" of a phony new Soviet brigade in Cuba, and by sending helicopters to the Salvadoran military.

When Ronald Reagan took office, his self-proclaimed "vicar" of U.S. foreign policy, General Alexander Haig, proposed a hawkish desire to "go to the source," allegedly Cuba, in Reagan's crusade of socialism-prevention in Central America. A new effort, reminiscient of the 1960s, was launched to isolate Cuba in the hemisphere. For the more easily intimidated countries, being anti-Cuban became the price of continued U.S. military and economic assistance. The rulers of Ecuador, Colombia, Costa Rica, Panama, Jamaica, and Venezuela caved in under U.S. pressure, suspending or "revising" relations with Cuba.[30] Each country has shopping lists in Washington to protect.

Reagan's policy of isolating Cuba was carried to the extreme; even U.S. diplomats in the UN would not respond to a "good afternoon" in the men's room by a Cuban diplomat. Communication virtually ceased. General Haig advocated the preposterous action that the U.S. Navy take the Cuban prisoners in Atlanta ("Marielitos") back home and defy Cuba to prevent their unloading.

U.S. nastiness toward Cuba, which has included weather modification to induce drought, ruination of a sugar cargo on a ship seeking emergency help in San Juan, introduction of animal diseases, not to mention attempted murder of the president, are part of a tradition continued by Reagan in his efforts to end U.S. tourism to Cuba. The Cubans have invested heavily in tourism. They now are building toward providing facilities to accommodate all Cubans' right to a month's vacation in the finest resorts plus facilities to serve a prerevolution volume of U.S. tourists. (Can you imagine a Mexican *campesino* pondering whether to take his vacation this year in Cancún, Cabo San Lucas, or Acapulco?)

In Central America the Cuban role has been helpful, and grossly misrepresented. Hundreds of Nicaraguan youths who were in need of prosthetic devices and special medical treatment were taken care of in Cuba. Hundreds more Nicaraguans are studying there. Meanwhile, Cuban nurses, teachers, and doctors are providing care in Nicaragua, often in remote places without electricity or running water. The United States charges that Cuban technicians in Nicaragua are actually military personnel in another guise, even though half of them are women. If Cuba had not helped overthrow Somoza, it would have belied its principles. If Cuba does not lend assistance to the Sandinista government, it belies its principles. That is too much to demand. But the Cubans are willing to end their military-advisory role in Nicaragua. This is implicit in their endorsement of the Contadora approach to achieving peace in Central America.

Cuba is willing to withdraw its military advisors in Nicaragua if the United States will do the same in El Salvador and Honduras. Since this would remove the pretext for U.S. gunboat, Green Beret, and Secret War diplomacy, it would make Reagan's military build-up look silly. It would puncture his Colonel Blimp. The real goal, of course, is to maintain capitalism in Central America, with or without a Cuban presence. If Cuba withdraws, new bugaboos will have to be found.

North Americans should give careful thought to Carla Anne Robbins's 10 myths about Cuba:

1. The Cubans are Soviet pawns;

2. The Cubans are everywhere;

3. The Cubans are always subversive;

4. The Cubans always win;

5. The Cubans are international outlaws;

6. The Cubans are inevitably anti-United States;

7. Anyone who is Cuba's enemy is our friend;

8. Anyone who is Cuba's friend is our enemy;

9. The Cubans never change; and

10. Everyone agrees with our view of the Cubans.[31]

The resumption of normal U.S.-Cuban relations will come, but not under Reagan. His mind-set belongs to some other era, some dark period of jingoism and ignorance. The Reagan administration, García Márquez laments, is "not interested in just solutions to our countries' problems" but, "wants only to use us as another chip in the war of nerves between the United States and the Soviet Union."[32]

CONCLUSION

False conceptualization of reality is commonplace. Reagan's thinker Jeane Kirkpatrick's analysis of Central America is a flaming example of falsity. Some years from now American observers and activists will focus on the *real* issues in Central America and the Third World in general: job creation (for the 600 million new job seekers by the year 2000), education, public health, desertification, nutrition, housing, and power for the dispossessed. Reagan, Kirkpatrick, and Kissinger have no real solutions for the real issues. The latter would create a "stable world order," presumably by stabilizing poverty in the Third World. And they have the gall to criticize *Cuba's* world role.

It is notable how many of the key pronouncements of the Cuban leadership on international issues have been formulated in statements made at meetings of internal Cuban institutions (e.g., the Assembly of Popular Power, the Committee for the Defense of the Revolution, and the Cuban Communist Party). The positions were elaborated in great detail and included large amounts of factual supporting material. This reflects the conviction that it is the consciousness of the people that will lead to fundamental change. As Castro stated: "When the masses have access to culture, when they have the opportunity to study, when they have access to knowledge... there are ten thousand geniuses. There is no one genius at all, there is a collective genius."[33]

With this view of the world and faith in the "laws of history" Cuban international policy can be guided by the conviction that "sooner rather than later, the people will choose an increasingly democratic social organization and finally opt for a system with no exploitation or exploited."[34]

NOTES

1. Fidel Castro, speech to the 34th session of the United Nations General Assembly, October 12, 1979, in Michael Taber, ed., *Cuba's Internationalist Foreign Policy 1975-1980: Fidel Castro Speeches* (New York: Pathfinder Press, 1981), p. 201.
2. Fidel Castro, April 12, 1981, in *Granma Weekly Edition*, May 3, 1981, p. 2.
3. Organization of American States (OAS), *Reunión Extraordinaria del Consejo Interamericano Económico y Social al Nivel Ministerial: Actos y Documentos*, Punte del Este, Uruguay, August 5-17, 1961 (Washington D.C.: Pan American Union, 1962), p. 44.
4. For the history of the CECLA and Latin American participation in UNCTAD see Marjorie Woodford Bray, "The International Economic Policy of Latin America: The Genesis and Limits of Third World Cooperation" (Ph.D. diss. Claremont Graduate School, 1981).
5. A.S. Friedeberg, *The United Nations Conference on Trade and Development of 1964: The Theory of the Peripheral Economy at the Centre of International Political Discussions* (Rotterdam: Rotterdam University Press, 1969), p. 11.
6. Carla Anne Robbins, *The Cuban Threat* (New York: McGraw Hill, 1983), p. 235.
7. Fidel Castro, *The World Economic and Social Crisis: Its Impact on the Underdeveloped Countries, Its Somber Prospects, and the Need to Struggle If We Are to Survive* (Havana: Oficina de Publicaciones del Consejo de Estado, 1983).
8. The Cuban economist who headed the Association of Third World Economists, Oscar Pino Santos, has said "I don't believe that the entire plan for a New International Economic order should be approved, but many of its demands are well grounded and therefore should be given our support." (*Granma Weekly Edition*, February 8, 1981, p. 6.).
9. The respected and acute observer of the international monetary scene, economist Robert Triffin, held similar views on the causes of world inflation. See "Reshaping the International Monetary Order" in Anthony J. Dolman and Jan van Ettinger, eds., *Partners in Tomorrow* (New York: E.P. Dutton, 1978), pp. 246-50.
10. Fidel Castro, *This Is the Hour in Which the Countries of the Third World Must Unite Their Forces and Confront the Imperialist Challenge* (Havana: Editoral de Ciencias Sociales, Instituto Cubano del Libro, 1974), p. 25.
11. Ibid., pp. 26-27.
12. Fidel Castro, "At Nonaligned Ministerial Meeting, March 19, 1975," in *Speeches*, p. 15.
13. Castro, *The World Economic and Social Crisis*, p. 15.
14. Ibid., p. 47.
15. Ibid., p. 133. In a speech on April 26, 1981 to the Association of Third World Economists held in Havana, Castro was even more critical of

redeployment, which, he said, tightened neocolonial ties and was a "new international division of labor that turns the backward south into a depot of industries of relatively low technical level and abundant manpower, and of industries whose polluting effects are not tolerated by people of their respective metropolises" (*Granma*, May 10, 1981, p. 5).

16. Castro, *The World Economic and Social Crisis*, p. 157.
17. Ibid., p. 159.
18. Ibid., p. 160.
19. Ibid., p. 159.
20. Castro, "At Nonaligned Ministerial Meeting," p. 157.
21. For a discussion of Cuban-Guyanese relations, see Ronald E. Jones, "Cuba and the English-Speaking Caribbean" in Cole Blasier and Carmelo Mesa-Lago, eds., *Cuba in the World* (Pittsburgh: University of Pittsburgh Press, 1979), pp. 139–41.
22. Castro, "Resolution on International Policy," adopted by the Second Congress of the Communist Party of Cuba, December 17–20, in *Speeches*, p. 361.
23. Robbins, *The Cuban Threat*, pp. 201, 251.
24. *Granma*, May 10, 1981, p. 5.
25. For an analysis of the development of official bilateral contacts with the Caribbean region and other areas, see Jones, "Cuba and the English-Speaking Caribbean." *See also* Jorge Peréz-López and René Pérez-López, *Cuban International Relations: A Bilateral Agreement Perspective* (Latin American Monograph Series 6, The Northwestern Pennsylvania Institute for Latin American Studies, Erie, Pa.: Mercyhurst College, 1979).
26. Cuban lack of awareness of Bishop's problems with his fellow revolutionaries belies U.S. accusations of direct Cuban participation in revolutionary movements of the region.
27. There has, of course, been Latin participation in U.N. peace-keeping forces: the Colombian batallion in the Korean War, Brazilian involvement in the Italian campaign in World War II, and the participation of a few Mexican aviators in the Philippines in World War II.
28. Jorge Domínguez, "Cuban Foreign Policy," *Foreign Affairs* 57 (Summer 1978), pp. 83–108; William J. Durch, "The Cuban Military in Africa and the Middle East: From Algeria to Angola," *Studies in Comparative Communism* 11 (Spring-Summer 1978), pp. 3–33; Edward González, "The United States and Castro: Breaking the Deadlock," *Foreign Affairs*, July 1972, pp. 722–37; William LeoGrande, "Cuba Policy Recycled," *Foreign Policy* 46 (spring 1982), pp. 105–19; Abraham F. Lowenthal, "Why Cuba is in Angola (and What's Next)," in Martin Weinstein, ed., *Revolutionary Cuba in the World Arena* (Philadelphia: Institute for the Study of Human Issues, 1979); José A. Moreno and Nicholas O. Lardas, "Integrating International Revolution and Detente: The Cuba Case," *Latin American Perspectives* 21 (spring 1979), pp.

36–61; Carla Anne Robbins, *The Cuban Threat* (New York: McGraw Hill, 1983); and Nelson P. Valdés, "Revolutionary Solidarity in Angola," in Cole Blasier and Carmelo Mesa-Lago, eds., *Cuba in the World* (Pittsburgh: University of Pittsburgh Press, 1979).

29. Michael Manley, "More Pluralist Than Thou," *The Nation*, August 1981, pp. 106–08.

30. Colombia, under President Betancur, and Costa Rica, under Monge, regained some of their self-respect vis-à-vis Washington.

31. Robbins, *The Cuban Threat*, p. 280.

32. Penny Lernoux, "Haig's Cuban Quarantine," *The Nation*, June 1981, pp. 784–86.

33. Castro, "Closing Speech to First Party Congress," December 22, 1975, in *Speeches*, p. 73.

34. *Granma*, May 10, 1981, p. 5

19 Cuban Internationalism

Susan Eckstein

Why does Cuba, despite low domestic living standards, have extensive overseas commitments? Although most Americans believe Cuba extends aid to foreign countries at the behest of the Soviet Union, in fact the island has its own independent reasons for aiding Third World countries, including to compensate for Soviet bloc limitations. This chapter first describes Cuba's "socialist internationalist" programs, above all its relatively unknown civilian assistance projects. Then, the two most commonly held explanations of Cuba's overseas activities, ideological commitment to global socialist solidarity and Soviet pressure, will be discussed. The two will be shown to be insufficient, for domestic material considerations have also induced the island to engage in overseas activities.

CUBAN OVERSEAS ACTIVITIES

The Castro government has extended military and civilian aid to Third World countries since its first years of rule. Militarily, it has aided national liberation and guerrilla movements, and it has helped train "people's militias" to protect "progressive" governments in power. Castro's military activism tapered off in the latter 1960s, only to resume once again in the 1970s. During Castro's second decade in office Cuba sent military missions to many African countries, the largest to Angola and Ethiopia. It also sent modest contingents to

Southeast Asian countries, and more substantial ones to some Middle Eastern countries. It did not, however, concomitantly strengthen its Latin American missions.

Only in late 1978 did Cuba begin once again to provide material aid to guerrilla movements in Latin America: namely in Central America. Cuba reinstituted its policy of "exporting revolution" in the hemisphere because the prospects of its success, under changed political conditions, appeared good. Then, in 1980, Cuba also provided Maurice Bishop's socialist New Jewel Movement with light arms and a few dozen military advisors to defend the small island against any attempt by his predecessor to return to power.[1] Unlike in the late 1960s, in the late 1970s, Cuba targeted its aid to movements with a strong political base. The policy shift backfired by 1983, however, leaving the island isolated once again in the hemisphere.

The size and nature of Cuba's overseas commitments changed in the seventies. Military programs began to include large numbers of combat troops for the first time, and the size of the missions accordingly increased. Consequently, whereas Cuba had an estimated 750 to 1,000 military advisors and troops in Africa in 1966, twelve years later the number rose to a record high of about 38,000 to 39,000.[2] The size of the military missions subsequently declined, but only slightly. In 1979 Cuba still apparently had about 34,000 to 36,000 military personnel in Africa, all but 830 in Angola and Ethiopia.[3]

The Castro regime has operated civilian missions since the early 1970s as well. It has had programs in 37 countries, on three continents.[4] Western sources have had difficulty assessing the size of the civilian programs because military and non-military personnel are not always easily distinguishable. Most civilian personnel in overseas assignments have had military training, as has the population at large. The fighting capacity of civilian internationalists became apparent after the U.S. invasion of Grenada, when Cubans who were constructing an airport there participated in Grenadian resistance efforts. Yet available evidence suggests that Cuba had an estimated 5,400 civilian personnel in Africa and another 600 in other parts of the world in 1977, twice as many in Africa and nearly six times as many in Asia, the Middle East, and Latin America in 1978-79,[5] and about 20,000 civilian internationalists abroad in the early 1980s.[6]

In the latter half of the 1970s the island's largest African civilian mission was in Angola, and the next largest in Ethiopia, Libya, and Mozambique.[7] The Angolan program rose rapidly from several hundred persons in the first half of 1976 to an estimated 6,000 at the year's end, and to 8,500 two years later.[8] At the same time, Cuba's civilian aid programs to Vietnam and Nicaragua expanded and diversified markedly, following the civil wars in the two countries. In the Caribbean, Guyana, Grenada, St. Lucia, Jamaica, and Surinam received small but important civilian contingents.

Civilian programs involve medical, construction, and educational cadre, along with some economic and other assistance. Construction, however, constitutes the principal component of the civilian program.[9] Construction aid includes topography studies, materials, organizational and planning advice, and building assistance. The overseas construction program began modestly in the early 1970s, when island construction workers built six hospitals in Peru after the South American country had been hit by an earthquake. The program expanded in 1974-75 with the building of a hospital, highway, hotel, several poultry complexes, and 13 milking barns in North Vietnam.[10] By the late 1970s, about 3 percent of Cuba's construction workers were involved in overseas assignments.[11] The number rose from about 4,500 in 1978 to 7,900 year later, with Angola and Ethiopia receiving especially large contingents.

The educational and medical assistance programs involved the second and third of the larges number of personnel, respectively. In 1979, at least 2,300 Cuban teachers were abroad, and in 1980 about 3,500 were—the equivalent of about 2 percent of the island's stock of teachers.[12] In addition, more than 9,000 foreign students, mainly from Africa, studied on Cuba's Isle of Pines in 1980.[13] Nicaragua received the largest contingent of teachers between 1979 and 1983: 2,000 went there, for example, in 1983 alone.[14] As with education, medical assistance increased in the late 1970s. There were 700 medical cadre abroad in 1977, nearly 1,200 in 1979, and about 2,000 in 1980.[15] The 1980 overseas program employed between 7 and 13 percent of the island's entire supply of doctors,[16] as well as dentists, nurses, technicians, and support personnel. Three years later the health missions included an additional 1,000 in 26 countries on three continents. Six hundred of the health cadre were in Nicaragua alone.

Cuba's economic programs, in turn, involve specialists in agriculture, sugar cultivation and refining, mining, fishing, transportation, cattle raising, irrigation, industry, economic and physical planning, and management. The island has sent large numbers of specialists abroad, where they have trained local personnel. Beneficiary countries include Vietnam, Guinea-Bissau, the Republic of Equatorial Guinea, Somalia,

Ethiopia, Mozambique, the People's Republic of the Congo, Angola, and South Yemen.[17]

Why has Cuba, with such a limited domestic resource base, expanded its overseas civilian and military commitments? Has the expansion occurred because of a genuine commitment to socialist internationalism, because of Soviet bloc pressures, or because the Castro regime believes its own material interests are at stake? Each of these possibilities will be analyzed.

IDEOLOGICAL BASES OF CUBA'S OVERSEAS INVOLVEMENT

The Cuban government asserts that it aids other Third World countries because it is committed to internationalist solidarity. While official views may conceal underlying motives, if the island *primarily* supports overseas activities for moral and ideological reasons, Cuba should receive no regular quid pro quo for its assistance, and it should limit its aid to ideologically sympathetic countries. If Cuba gains materially from its involvement, the benefits should be minor and they should have been unanticipated at the time the aid was extended. The island should risk receiving no economic pay-offs.

Most of the aid programs described above can be viewed, in part, as government efforts to fulfill its internationalist commitment. The Castro regime has a long history of assisting revolutionary and national liberation movements, and the governments to which they have given rise, possibly because its own social transformation depended on the assistance of other socialist countries. Yet its identity with progressive, anti-imperialist states has not been contingent on the adoption of a Marxist-Leninist model or membership in the socialist camp.[18] Indeed, even when Cuba took steps to institutionalize the revolution in the mid-1970s, it continued its official commitment to internationalism. The First Party Congress Resolution on International Policy asserts that Cuba subordinates its interests to the general interests of socialism and communism and national liberation of peoples, so as to defeat imperialism and eliminate colonialism.[19]

Cuba's *espoused* commitment to internationalist solidarity is indisputable. But ideological commitment alone cannot explain several aspects of the island's foreign policy. It cannot, for example, explain why Castro, with his longstanding commitment to internationalism, stepped up overseas activities in the middle 1970s. The step-up reflected changing global opportunities, not a greater commitment to ideological principles. This structural interpretation does not deny the importance of ideology; it merely implies that ideology alone does not determine foreign policy. Conditions facilitating Cuba's overseas involvement in the 1970s included an improvement in the island's national security situation, so that defense was a less pressing domestic concern; professionalization of the island's armed forces; and impressive improvements in the island's economic performance and the size of the island's skilled labor force. Consequently, the government could afford, more than ever before, significant overseas commitments.

CUBA AS A SOVIET SURROGATE

Cuba's actual and professed commitment to internationalist solidarity might, of course, reflect U.S.S.R. influence over the island. The Soviets might either compel Cuba to engage in overseas activities as a prerequisite for continued island subsidies and financing, or the dynamics of Soviet bloc relations might induce Cuba to assist certain countries. In the United States, where the government and press tend to depict Cuba as a helpless pawn of Soviet imperialist interests and as a willing Soviet collaborator, the Soviet hegemony thesis is widely believed.

While it is impossible to determine the precise nature of Cuba's ties to the Soviet Union, if Cuba is a Soviet surrogate, or if its foreign policy is determined by Soviet bloc dynamics, Cuba should not extend aid to countries hostile to the U.S.S.R. Also, there should be evidence of Cuban-Soviet overseas coordination, and Cuban overseas involvements should vary with ups and downs in Cuban-Soviet relations. Moreover, if Cuba operates *primarily* as a Soviet puppet, the Castro regime should have no major reasons of its own for engaging in foreign activities. The following evidence suggests that most of Cuba's overseas activities are consistent with the Soviet Union's global interests, but that Cuba has had its own reasons for overseas programs, and the Soviet Union at times has extended its involvements because of Cuba, and not the converse.

The Cuban regime publicly recognizes its close alliance with the Soviet Union. It even claims that the alliance is a permanent element of its international policy. Illustrative of their ties, the two countries have collaborated in Somalia, Ethiopia, Angola, Syria, and Indochina, agreeing to a complementary division of labor. The Soviet Union has provided equipment and financing while Cuba has provided personnel.

Yet Cuba has not operated merely as a puppet of the superpower. There is evidence that Cuba dispatched 36,000 combat troops to help the MPLA in Angola at is own initiative,[20] and that Cuba formulated its own foreign policy toward Central America, with the Soviet Union more a follower than a leader.[21] Yet, in all the large-scale overseas operations, the support of both countries has been crucial. In the absence of the collaboration, Cuba might well have extended aid, but not in the same manner or to the same extent.

Most important, Cuba has its own reasons for cooperating with the Soviet Union. In demonstrating its political-military worth to the Soviet Union, Cuba undoubtedly enhances the likelihood of continued Soviet military and economic support; Cuba's main value to the Soviet Union is political, not economic.[22] U.S. foreign policy has the effect, even if not the intent, of inducing Cuba to ally with Soviet concerns. In view of U.S. hostility, the small vulnerable island needs a protector. President Reagan's threat to impose a naval blockade on Cuba in retaliation for the Soviet's intervention in Afghanistan, for example, gave Castro security reasons to strengthen its ties with the Soviet Union. Overseas activities are one way to do so. Accordingly, global as well as specifically Soviet bloc dynamics contribute to Cuban internationalism.

Despite commitment to and conformity with Soviet imperial interests, nearly all U.S. studies of Cuba's overseas activities—including studies by such agencies as the Center for Naval Analysis, which does classified research—conclude that Cuba has not been an undeviating puppet.[23] Studies note, for one, that Cuba's foreign policy has been consistent for over a decade, despite changes in Cuban-Soviet relations. In 1966–67, when Cuban-Soviet relations were at their postrevolutionary low, Cuba pursued policies in Africa and Latin America which in most respects were indistinguishable from its policies in the 1970s.[24] If the Soviet Union had had its way, Cuba would not have engaged in guerrilla activities at the time, especially in the Western hemisphere. The Soviet Union then advocated "peaceful coexistence"; it tacitly recognized the Western hemisphere as the U.S.'s sphere of influence.

Studies also note that the Castro regime has aided some revolutionary and national liberation movements and "progressive" governments which the Soviet Union rebuffed, even when Cuba and the Soviet Union were on good terms. In particular, in 1974 Cuba extended aid to Angola just as the U.S.S.R. pulled out of the country and gave the then MPLA-leader, Agostinho Neto, a "chilling reception" in Moscow. In view of how close Cuba and the Soviet Union were at the time, Castro's independent policy was striking. The Soviets resumed their aid to Angola only *after* the Cuban military build-up had begun.[25]

In sum, available evidence suggests that the Castro regime has expanded its overseas activities not simply at the behest of the U.S.S.R. Generally, though, Cuban and Soviet foreign interests have converged. In serving Soviet interests Cuba has undoubtedly increased its worth to the socialist bloc superpower, and in doing so increased the probability of continued Soviet economic and military subsidies. And because Third World countries have perceived the Castro regime to be helpful and influential, the overseas activities have enhanced the island's stature in the less developed world. Moreover, the Castro regime has also had material reasons for its overseas adventures, including the need to compensate for Soviet bloc deficiencies.

MATERIAL BASES FOR CUBA'S OVERSEAS INVOLVEMENTS

In 1978 Castro declared that the "exportation of technical services is becoming an important factor in the economic development of the country."[26] Why might this be so? And do the economic benefits exceed the costs? Arguably, the Cuban government has sacrificed certain domestic resources for its overseas projects, but it has made use of the revolution's greatest accomplishment: its human capital. The Castro regime has exported labor both because Soviet aid has restricted the island's capacity to diversify its commodity exports and because it needs foreign exchange to purchase desired Western goods. In short, the economic limitations—and not merely the political-military strength—of the Soviet bloc give Cuba reason to expand its overseas programs.

Economic Benefits

In principle, overseas military and civilian programs could open up new trade and investment opportunities, and they could generate foreign exchange revenues if the host countries paid for services rendered. The island might thereby expand its resource base and acquire goods and technology unavailable from COMECON. Its material interests would accordingly be advanced.

Whatever Cuba's intentions, thus far the island derives no *immediate* trade pay-off from its aid programs. Since the revolution Cuba has traded mainly but not exclusively with COMECON countries. The volume of Western trade has varied over the years, conditioned by world market opportunities and the willingness of Western countries to engage in commerce with Cuba. Since 1975 Third World countries have accounted for only 4-7 percent of total Cuban trade.[27] Non-COMECON countries that receive Cuban military and civilian assistance appear to be responsible for a declining portion of that trade.

While some Cubanologists have argued that the main economic benefit accruing to the island from its overseas programs is increased Soviet aid,[28] there is only limited evidence to substantiate their claims. In the 1970s Soviet technical assistance to Cuba expanded, and the Soviet Union continued to subsidize sugar and nickel exports from, and oil imports to, the island. But the superpower cut back the size of its oil subsidy following post-1973 OPEC price hikes. The U.S.S.R. apparently raised the rate it charged Cuba for petroleum and petroleum products to the level charged Eastern Europe. Moreover, Soviet financial aid did not rise after Cuba stepped-up its involvement in Angola and Ethiopia. The superpower offered Cuba more new and inexpensive financing in 1972 than later in the decade. While the Soviets provided Cuba with perhaps its largest delivery of weapons in the early 1980s, presumably freeing up Cuba's own resources for other purposes, the increase is as likely a response to Reagan security threats as a reward for overseas activity. Even though the Soviets might have cut back island subsidies more, had Cuba not proved itself an ideal ally, there is no evidence that the U.S.S.R. has compensated Cuba materially for its overseas collaboration.[29]

Although the overseas ventures have not, to date, led to significant new trade or bilateral economic ties, they have generated foreign exchange. Cuba receives hard currency for some of its military and many of its civilian programs. In 1977, when the island apparently began charging the more developed countries in hard currency for projects, Cubans overseas generated an estimated $50 million in hard currency, about 9 percent of the value of commodity exports to capitalist countries.[30] And two years later Cuba received $115 million in U.S. dollars for a construction and technical aid contract with Libya, and $25 million (apparently also in U.S. dollars) for another contract with Angola.[31] The two agreements alone generated 18 percent of the value of Cuba's 1979 hard currency trade.[32] However, in 1980 both the earnings generated by overseas programs and their share of hard currency trade earnings apparently declined. According to a Department of Commerce source, that year Cuba's overseas human capital ventures possibly generated $100 million, 6 percent of the value of the island's Western commodity exports.[33] Yet the following year, Cuba allegedly received $250 million for its military and civilian operations in Angola alone.[34] Cuba even seems to have earned some foreign exchange from its internationalist mission in Nicaragua, for according to an official source the island received "favorable financing terms" for a contract to build a sugar mill, primarily with Cuban machinery, in the Central American country in 1983.[35] Moreover, in at least one country, the Congo, a donation of a plant to build pre-fabricated housing sectors led to a contract to construct a highway and several farms and towns.[36]

The Domestic Opportunity Costs of Cuban Foreign Involvements

Although all countries experience domestic opportunity costs when they export goods, capital, and personnel, as an underdeveloped country Cuba unquestionably could use all possible resources to improve its own economy. In what ways are Cuba's overseas activities a drain on the economy?

The island, for one, incurs costs from its military program. While the Soviets provide Cuba with weaponry for domestic use free of charge, the Castro regime must absorb other military expenses. Even though not all military expenditures go to Cuba's foreign aid program, the military budget did increase more than the national budget between the eve of the Angolan war and 1978, when Cuba's overseas military commitments expanded considerably and domestic security was not a problem.[37] The military aid program, in addition, utilizes labor which could otherwise be deployed in civilian activity. Since overseas missions draw upon reservists, they drain the country of civilian personnel. For this reason, some enterprise managers have apparently been reluctant to release employees for internationalist assignments.[38] However, since surplus labor probably contributes more to the island economy through foreign exchange-generating overseas activities, than it does at home, the labor costs of the military aid program in the 1970s and the 1980s, on balance, may be low.

The overseas civilian programs, which involve skilled workers, probably drain the domestic economy more. In terms of island shortages, Cuba can least afford to export construction workers. The number of housing units constructed on the island fluctuated yearly between about 14,000 and 20,000 from 1974 to 1980,[39] although new housing would not necessarily have been constructed were the workers kept at home. The Castro regime undoubtedly sends builders and supplies abroad because it can thereby generate foreign exchange. Its international building program is profitable, producing more hard currency revenue than other civilian programs.[40] To take advantage of the earning opportunities abroad the government has not only allocated scarce domestic supplies to overseas projects, but it also sends its best workers abroad. Because the island must compete for foreign building assignments, it otherwise risks losing contracts.[41] Thus, the island's continued dependence on capitalist markets compels the country to send workers and supplies overseas for hard currency at certain costs to the domestic economy.

Cubanologists have argued that the various overseas civilian and military programs affected the country's overall development capacity.[42] The domestic economic growth rate, which had reached a record high in the early 1970s, indeed declined when the island's overseas commitments expanded. However, the drop in export earnings, with the decline in world market sugar prices from over 60 cents a pound in November 1974 to 8 cents two years later, plus the rapid rise in import costs, particularly after successive OPEC price hikes, undoubtedly contributed more to the economic contraction than the expansion of overseas programs. In fact, the island's annual economic growth rate (as measured by the gross social product) reached one of its highest postrevolutionary levels (9 percent) in 1978, the peak year of overseas military commitment.[43] The foreign programs seem to have had only a minor impact on domestic economic performance measures because Cuba's military mobilizations draw on surplus labor and because civilian projects include teachers and medical personnel, contributors to the service sector; the service sector, according to Marxist economic principles, is nonproductive and therefore excluded from national product estimates.

Finally, Cuba's overseas involvements have set back negotiations with the United States. In the mid-1970s, Castro and U.S. businessmen had begun to discuss trade and investment possibilities, and political relations between the two countries had begun to improve. However, by the end of the decade business and diplomatic discussions subsided. Although Cuba's widescale aid to Ethiopia unquestionably contributed to the cooling off of diplomatic negotiations, the drop in the world market sugar price and its devastating effect on the Cuban economy undoubtedly also did. U.S. business cut back its lobbying efforts to improve economic relations with the island when business opportunities contracted. It is difficult to assess the effect of the step-up in island overseas military ventures independently from the deterioration in trade and investment opportunities.

In sum, Cuba's overseas programs impose certain domestic opportunity costs, but they generate needed foreign exchange earnings. Yet, as detailed below, Cuba has expanded its foreign aid program not entirely under conditions of its own choosing. Global economic constraints compel the island to seek new sources of hard currency earnings.

Global Economic Dynamics and Cuba's Aid Program

If Cuba needs foreign exchange, why has it not expanded its commodity exports? It has not done so because integration into the Soviet economic bloc restricts Cuba's capacity to produce marketable exports at the same time that Soviet bloc deficiencies require Cuba to trade with Western countries. Meanwhile, Cuba's human resource development has been exceptionally impressive.

Castro initially subordinated production for export to production for domestic consumption. However, imports needed to fuel domestic expansion and diversification had an extremely negative effect on the island's balance of payments. Consequently, beginning in 1963 the revolutionary government concerned itself with exports. Efforts to diversify exports notwithstanding, the island ranks second among Latin American countries in monoproduct export dependence. The country has been unable to produce many items that Western or COMECON countries are willing to purchase. Cuba, for example, has not moved into the low cost, labor-intensive industrial export market, as have such other traditional Latin American agricultural exporters as Brazil and Colombia. Since 1959 sugar has accounted for 74 to 90 percent of Cuban exports,[44] and it is Cuba's principal export to capitalist as well as socialist economies.

Were Cuba still centrally integrated in to the Western bloc, it probably would have moved more into the industrial export market. Foreign direct investment, which was high by Latin American standards under Batista, undoubtedly would be more important now than in 1959. Because of its proximity to the U.S., Cuba most likely would have turned to industrial consumer export promotion when the negative effects of industrial import-substitution became apparent. Using Western technology and cheap domestic labor the island would have been able to produce competitive consumer exports, but with similar social and economic costs as in Brazil. In Brazil, the industrial export strategy has been associated with a highly inegalitarian distribution of wealth and a balance of payments deterioration owing to the growth in capital goods imports (and foreign borrowing) exceeding the value of export earnings.

While the Castro regime has sought to eliminate the exploitative aspects of multinational capitalist development, it exports few industrial goods, not for lack of effort.[45] Cuba *has* built up its industrial base, by restricting Western import competition. However, the island cannot shield itself from Soviet production and marketing disadvantages, the loss of access to the U.S. market, and the negative effects of the reorganization of the domestic economy on the quality of local production. As a consequence, the revolution has served to marginalize the country's ability to compete in international export markets. The small amount of industrial goods that Cuba exports is limited to such items as cement, metal scrap, and alcohol.[46] The Cuban experience suggests that the best technology and marketing capabilities remain within the Western bloc.

Given Cuba's failure to diversify commodity exports, and its persistent need for foreign exchange, its overseas civilian program is creative and sensible. The Castro regime has been unusually successful at human resource development, to the extent that it can afford to export trained personnel. Also, it can do so at low cost.

Since 1959 the island's per capita supply of teachers and medical personnel improved markedly more than in other Latin American countries. The development of domestic human capital resources declined somewhat during Castro's first years of rule, owing to the emigration of trained personnel (e.g., one-third to one-half of the country's stock of doctors left). But by the latter 1970s, when the island expanded its overseas military and civilian activities, its skilled resource base was impressive. There was one doctor for every 2,839 inhabitants and one nurse for every 365 inhabitants in 1980.[47] Its population to doctor and nurse ratios ranked fourth and second, respectively, among Latin American countries in the latter 1970s. Therefore, the island can afford to export skilled personnel more than can most Latin American countries, even if the manpower could be used at home to improve the domestic living standard. According to a Cuban official, with the education system now producing more scientists, doctors, and engineers than the country can absorb, "internationalism" is seen as a potentially important source of foreign exchange.[48]

Thus, Cuba has material as well as ideological and pragmatic political reasons for its overseas involvements. Cuba needs and wants to trade with the West. On the one hand, the regime's dependence on the Soviet Union constricts the country's capacity to diversify commodity exports. On the other hand, the government has successfully developed internationally marketable human resources. The island is concerned with internationalist solidarity and with improving economic relations with the West, at the same time that it advances general COMECON bloc interests.

FUTURE PROSPECTS OF CUBA'S FOREIGN-EXCHANGE GENERATING OVERSEAS INVOLVEMENTS

Are Cuba's overseas foreign-exchange generating ventures a viable long-term strategy? Cuba's prospects for expanding its human capital export program are likely to hinge more on global political events than on domestic resource developments and domestic priorities.

Domestic support appears to be no obstacle to the aid program. While some Cubans may be averse to additional overseas military activities, especially if friends and family lose their lives in battle, the island's overseas civilian programs seem to have popular support. When Castro called for volunteers to serve in Nicaragua in 1980, for example, 29,500 teachers offered to go.[49] And since Cuba's current health care cadre are a product of the revolution, they too are undoubtedly committed to the government's overseas humanitarian and patriotic concerns. Moreover, Cuban surveys report that more than 300,000 persons had been willing to go to Angola and Ethiopia.[50] Probably commitment to the revolution, prestige, and search for adventure, and material and political incentives account for the enthusiasm. To encourage participation in civilian programs, the government offers overseas workers a salary 20 percent higher and better pension benefits than equivalent workers receive at home, plus priority access to housing and scarce and valued consumer goods upon return.[51] Overseas service also offers a channel of access to the selective membership of the Communist Party.

The expansion of Cuba's foreign aid program, however, requires a proliferation of friendly, "progressive" governments in the Third World. Developed countries are unlikely to be interested in Cuban technical assistance; they have their own trained personnel. And Third World regimes that do not sympathize with the Cuban revolution are likely to feel threatened by Cuban programs, particularly by the human services which Cuba can best provide. Third World capitalist countries could indeed make use of Cuban health and education personnel, given how little they have done to develop their own supply of teachers and health care workers. But because such countries are more preoccupied with short-run economic gains than with long-term human investments, they are unlikely to want to allocate scarce resources to social welfare. Moreover, governments in countries opposed to Castro's politics would undoubtedly be reluctant to allow Cubans to work in the socially and economically depressed countryside. The idealism and revolutionary zeal of the Cubans might foment revolutionary turmoil there.

With respect to many of the moderately friendly governments that could afford Cuban aid, cultural barriers are likely to stand in the way, especially in the field of education. Cultural barriers are not a problem in Latin America, at least not in the Spanish-speaking region of the continent. The common religious, linguistic, and general Spanish heritage that the Cubans and Nicaraguans share may help explain the speed with which the Sandinistas turned to Cuba for aid after Somoza was ousted. However, cultural differences do stand between Cuban and the oil-rich Arab states which—since post-1973 price hikes—have hosted millions of foreign laborers and their families. Undoubtedly cultural as well as political barriers have kept Cuba from getting many Middle Eastern labor contracts.

Global political constraints also threatened Cuban internationalism in the 1980s, but not merely because Third World countries became more conservative. Jamaica ended its aid program in 1980, with the election of Edward Seaga. Since Jamaica is the largest English-speaking Caribbean island this break was a severe blow to Castro. That left Grenada, Cuba's one remaining close ally among the English-speaking states in the region, and the U.S. invasion of Grenada in 1983 brought the 784-person operation on the small Caribbean island to an abrupt halt. More than 600 of the workers had been involved in construction projects, and only 43 had been military personnel (22 officers, with the remainder translators and service workers).[52] Moreover, in the wake of the Grenada experience both the Cuban and the Nicaraguan governments became more fearful of a U.S. invasion of the Central American country. Consequently, the Cubans—according to U.S. estimates—reduced their civilian and military force in Nicaragua in early 1984 from 6,000 to 5,000 and they arranged to send younger civilians with better military training who would be able to resist "acts of aggression." Both the Reagan administration and the Latin American countries involved in the Contadora Group (Panama, Mexico, Colombia, and Venezuela) stress that Cuban military forces must be removed before a Central American peace settlement can be reached.[53]

U.S. pressure threatens Cuban projects in other parts of the world as well. In particular, the Reagan administration is insisting that Angola oust all Cuban troops before it will support Namibian independence and establish diplomatic relations with the former Portuguese colony. While Angola has thus far refused to acquiesce to the pressure, in early 1984 the Cuban government began to consider withdrawing its troops from Angola amid new promise for peace agreements in southern Africa.[54]

Cuba's renewed international activism, combined with U.S. efforts to isolate, in Reagan's words, the "communist virus," have even damaged Castro's normal state-to-state relations. Cuba's military involvement in Africa may have contributed to the suspension, reduction, or nonrenewal of economic and technical aid to the island in 1976-78 from Sweden, Holland, Norway, West Germany, and Canada. Moreover, Costa Rica and Colombia severed diplomatic ties with Cuba in the 1980s, and its relations with Venezuela, Ecuador, Peru, and Panama have deteriorated. Only Mexico has been willing to strengthen its ties with Cuba in light of U.S. hostility.[55]

Cuba's capacity to advance both its ideological commitment to internationalist solidarity and its material interests in hard currency earnings to compensate for Soviet trade bloc deficiencies accordingly depend both on the growth of the number of Third World governments that want and can afford to contract Cuba for assistance, and on reduced U.S. hostility. By the early 1980s Castro had little basis for optimism. The U.S. may pressure even more countries to sever whatever ties they have with Cuba and avoid establishing new relations with the island.

CONCLUSION

This analysis has shown that ideological, geopolitical, and economic considerations have above all shaped the nature of Cuba's foreign aid program. While foreign aid programs of other countries may address similar concerns, Cuba's particular mix and its ability to maximize all three are rather unique, especially for a country of its size.

Most of Castro's recent overseas programs have been consistent with the regime's long-term commitment to assist foreign national liberation and revolutionary movements. The programs merely increased in scope and scale in the 1970s, as the island's resource base expanded and international conditions became propitious.

The projects also enhanced the island's geopolitical interests, at least until the Reagan administration undermined its global efforts. The aid programs have strengthened Cuba's ties with the Soviet Union and served to win the island new Third World allies and Third Word prestige, after the Kennedy administration forced Cuba into hemispheric isolation. However, at the same time that Cuba has proven itself to be a dependable and useful ally to the Soviets, the island has not operated as a mere superpower puppet.

While Cuban foreign aid programs have advanced Soviet imperial interests, they have been designed, in recent years, to improve the island's relations with the capitalist world as well. In certain countries civilian and, to a lesser extent, military projects have generated foreign exchange that has helped reduce the island's outstanding Western debt and permitted the country to purchase goods not available from the Soviet bloc. The Castro regime has devised a foreign policy which makes use of its greatest accomplishment, an unusual accomplishment for a Third World country: a skilled labor force.

For a country of its size its aid program is impressive and well designed to address moral, material, and geopolitical concerns. However, its future ability to expand its overseas commitments as its own resource base improves is not promising. It faces political and cultural obstacles. In particular, it stands to suffer from U.S. policy that penalizes countries receiving Cuban aid. In short, global market dynamics induce Cuba to expand its aid program at the same time that the hegemonic Western power undermines its efforts.

NOTES

1. William LeoGrande, "Foreign Policy: The Limits of Success," in Jorge Domínguez, ed., *Cuba: Internal and International Affairs* (Beverly Hills: Sage, 1982), p. 181.
2. William LeoGrande, "Cuban-Soviet Relations and Cuban Policy in Africa," *Cuban Studies* 10 (January 1980), pp. 1–37.
3. Sergio Roca, "Economic Aspects of Cuban Involvement in Africa," *Cuban Studies* 10 (January 1980), pp. 50–80.

4. *Granma Weekly Review*, November 30, 1980, p. 3.

5. Jorge Domínguez, "The Armed Forces and Foreign Relations," in Cole Blasier and Carmelo Mesa-Lago, eds., *Cuba in the World* (Pittsburgh: University of Pittsburgh Press, 1979), p. 62; and Roca, "Economic Aspects of Cuban Involvement in Africa," p. 60.

6. *New York Times*, June 23, 1983, p. 2; and Lawrence Theriot, "1980 Estimated Cuban Hard Currency Income," U.S. Department of Commerce, International Trade Administration, Department of East-West Trade, typescript, 1981.

7. Roca, "Economic Aspects of Cuban Involvement in Africa," pp. 56–58.

8. Domínguez, "The Armed Forces and Foreign Relations," p 64; and William Durch, *The Cuban Military in Africa and the Middle East*, Occasional Paper No. 201 (Arlington, Va.: Center for Naval Analysis, 1977), p. 50; and Roca, "Economic Aspects of Cuban Involvement in Africa," p. 56.

9. Ibid., p. 60.

10. Jorge Pérez-López, "Comment: Economic Costs and Benefits of African Involvement," *Cuban Studies* (July 1980), p. 81.

11. Roca, "Economic Aspects of Cuban Involvement in Africa," p. 59.

12. *Granma Weekly Review*, November 16, 1980, p. 4.

13. Ibid., November 30, 1980, p. 3.

14. Ibid., February 13, 1983, p. 3.

15. Roca, "Economic Aspects of Cuban Involvement in Africa," p. 58; and *Granma Weekly Review*, September 21, 1980, p. 2.

16. *Granma Weekly Review*, August 3, 1980, p. 3; and September 21, 1980, p. 2.

17. Domínguez, "The Armed Forces and Foreign Relations," pp. 66, 67; *Granma Weekly Review*, November 30, 1980, p. 4; November 23, 1980, p. 8; December 21, 1980, p. 12; and Roca, "Economic Aspects of Cuban Involvement in Africa," p. 60.

18. LeoGrande, "Foreign Policy: The Limits of Success," p. 169.

19. *Granma Weekly Review*, November 1980, p. 2, Supplement.

20. LeoGrande, "Foreign Policy: The limits of Success," p. 172.

21. Jorge Domínguez, "Cuba's Relations with Caribbean and Central American Countries," *Cuban Studies* 13 (summer 1983), p.100.

22. Lawrence Theriot and Jenelle Matheson, "Soviet Economic Relations with Non-European CMEA: Cuba, Vietnam, and Mongolia," in *Soviet Economy in a Time of Change* (Washington, D.C., Joint Economic Commission of the U.S. Congress, October 1979), p. 567.

23. Gordon Adams, "Cuba and Africa: The International Politics of the Liberation Struggle—A Documentary Essay," *Latin American Perspectives*, winter 1981, pp. 109–12; Cole Blasier, "The Soviet Union in the Cuban-American Conflict," in Cole Blasier and Carmelo Mesa-Lago, eds., *Cuba in the World*

(Pittsburgh: University of Pittsburgh Press, 1979), p. 40; and "Comment: The Consequences of Military Initiatives," *Cuban Studies* 10 (January 1980), p. 40; Durch, *The Cuban Military in Africa and the Middle East*; Domínguez, "The Armed Forces and Foreign Relations,"; Edward González, "Comment: Operational Goals of Cuban Policy in Africa," *Cuban Studies* 10 (January 1980), pp. 43-48; and LeoGrande, "Cuban-Soviet Relations and Cuban Policy in Africa."
    24. Durch, *The Cuban Military in Africa and the Middle East*, pp. 3, 38.
    25. Ibid., pp. 46-47.
    26. Roca, "Economic Aspects of Cuban Involvement in Africa," p. 67.
    27. LeoGrande, "Foreign Policy: The Limits of Success," p. 179.
    28. González, "Comment: Operational Goals of Cuban Policy in Africa," p. 44; LeoGrande, "Cuban-Soviet Relations and Cuban Policy in Africa," p. 9; and Roca, "Economic Aspects of Cuban Involvement in Africa," pp. 60-63.
    29. Domínguez, "The Armed Forces and Foreign Relations."
    30. Theriot and Matheson, "Soviet Economic Relations with Non-European CMEA," pp. 556, 567.
    31. Roca, "Economic Aspects of Cuban Involvement in Africa," p. 66.
    32. Theriot, "1980 Estimated Cuban Hard Currency Income."
    33. Ibid.
    34. *New York Times*, October 3, 1981, p. 20.
    35. *Granma Weekly Review*, April 3, 1983, p. 12.
    36. Ibid., February 27, 1983, p. 9.
    37. Jorge Domínguez, "Political and Military Limitations and Consequences of Cuban Policies in Africa," *Cuban Studies* 10 (July 1980), p. 24.
    38. Jorge Domínguez, "The Cuban Operation in Angola: Costs and Benefits for the Armed Forces," *Cuban Studies*, January 1978; "The Armed Forces and Foreign Relations"; and "Cuban Military and National Security Policies," in Martin Weinstein, ed., *Revolutionary Cuba in the World Arena* (Philadelphia: Institute for the Study of Human Issues, 1979), pp. 84-85.
    39. Claes Brundenius, *Economic Growth, Basic Needs and Income Distribution in Revolutionary Cuba* (Lund, Sweden: Research Policy Institute, 1981), p. 116.
    40. Roca, "Economic Aspects of Cuban Involvement in Africa," p. 60.
    41. Pérez-López, "Comment: Economic Costs and Benefits of African Involvement," p. 83.
    42. Blasier, "Comment: The Consequences of Military Initiatives," p. 38; Domínguez, "Political and Military Limitations and Consequenses of Cuban Policies in Africa," p. 25; Carmelo Mesa-Lago, "The Economy and International Economic Relations," in Cole Blasier and Carmelo Mesa-Lago, eds., *Cuba in the World* (Pittsburgh: University of Pittsburgh Press, 1979), p. 178; and Roca, "Economic Aspects of Cuban Involvement in Africa," pp. 74-75.
    43. Roca, "Economic Aspects of Cuban Involvement in Africa," pp. 57, 74.

44. William LeoGrande, "Cuban Dependency: A Comparison of Pre-Revolutionary and Post-Revolutionary International Economic Relations," *Cuban Studies* 9 (July 1979), p. 10.
45. *Granma Weekly Review*, January 15, 1978, p. 3; July 24, 1977, p. 10; and November 9, 1980, p. 6.
46. Lawrence Theriot and Carol Callahan, *Cuban Trade with Industrialized West 1973-78*, East-West Trade Policy Staff Paper (Washington, D.C.; Department of Commerce, International Trade Administration, 1980), p. 16; Roca, "Economic Aspects of Cuban Involvement in Africa," p. 73.
47. Susan Eckstein, "Structural and Ideological Bases of Cuba's Overseas Programs," *Politics and Society* 11 (1982), table 9.
48. *New York Times*, June 23, 1982, p. 2.
49. *Granma Weekly Review*, March 16, 1980, p. 2.
50. Ibid., p. 2.
51. Roca, "Economic Aspects of Cuban Involvement in Africa," p. 67.
52. *Granma Weekly Review*, November 6, 1983, p. 1.
53. *The Boston Globe*, March 13, 1984, p. 6.
54. Ibid., p. 1.
55. LeoGrande, "Foreign Policy: The Limits of Success," p. 184.

Section VII
Overviews

20 The Cuban Revolution Twenty-Five Years Later: A Survey of Sources, Scholarship, and State of the Literature

Louis A. Pérez, Jr.

The Cuban Revolution celebrated its twenty-fifth anniversary in 1984 amid assessments of its performance and problems and appraisals of its success and setbacks. Both in and out of Cuba, both among friends and foes, the quarter-century mark seemed to offer a significant benchmark at which to pause and take stock of the course completed by the revolution these two and a half decades. The practice of assessing the Cuban Revolution has become something of an annual ritual, and the pronouncements of the twenty-fifth year have differed only in kind from previous appraisals. On 24 previous occasions, the passing of each anniversary provided the opportunity to assess the state of the revolution. And in the course of these 25 years, a literature of rather formidable proportions has accumulated.

But it was not always so. The Cuban Revolution erupted into something of a literary void, and quite suddenly the deficiencies of the scholarship about Cuba were set in sharp relief. These shortcomings were especially conspicuous in the United States. In no other Latin American country had the United States been so thorough a presence; nowhere else had the United States so totally penetrated the economy, so completely dominated the political process, so fully influenced cultural forms. Despite this omnipresence, perhaps because of it, Cuba remained largely unknown to all but a dedicated group of *aficionados* of things Cuban. Fifty years of intimate political and economic relations had generated little more than casual and passing interest in Cuba. There were many exceptions, of course,[1] but the corpus of the scholarship remained rather meager and singularly inauspicious.

That was 25 years ago, and much has happened since then. The successful climax in January 1959 of a popular rebellion led by a charismatic personality served immediately to fix attention on Cuba. And in the years that followed, this attention has remained fixed. The revolutionary processes deepened, and ultimately Cuba evolved into the first Marxist-Leninist state in the Western hemisphere and the first New World nation to align itself totally with the Soviet Union—all this occurring 90 miles from the United States, in a region traditionally secure as an American sphere of influence, in a country historically secure as an American client state.

In the more than two decades that have passed, the corpus of the literature inspired by the Cuban Revolution has reached extraordinary proportions. It is a literature that has passed through several distinctive stages and developed in several different directions. Virtually all of this vast body of literature falls within two categories. One important achievement of the postrevolutionary scholarship was the development of a new historiography on Cuba. Until 1959 historical research on Cuba was confined largely to articles appearing in scholarly journals dealing with important but highly specialized subjects.[2] After the revolution, historical research on Cuba expanded rapidly and became something of a flourishing enterprise. In a very real sense, this was research inspired by a search for the antecedents of the revolution—an inquiry that rested on the unstated assumption that somewhere in the unrevealed Cuban past was to be found the sources of the Cuban conversion to the socialist faith. Exploration of the past became the means through which to locate the origins of revolutionary change in Cuba and to determine, in the words of one anthology title, "what happened in Cuba?"[3]

At the same time, however, the very developments that stimulated new research interest in the Cuban past also served to close off the island to foreign scholars. The isolation of Cuba after 1961–1962 meant that access to Cuban archival and manuscript holdings and library collections was beyond the reach of outside researchers. These developments had far-reaching consequences, for they effectively served to limit the nature of research materials available to scholars. This, in turn, influenced decisively the direction of historical inquiry. The records most accessible to historians were those located in the document collections in United States depositories—largely those located in presidential libraries, the official records of such governmental agencies as the Department of State, the Department of Defense, and the Department of Commerce, and the vast collection of personal papers of diplomats, soldiers, administrators, and businessmen, all of whom at one time or another had something to do with Cuba.

In many important ways, these records, rich and diverse as they are, served to skew the direction of historical research. Inevitably, and of necessity, the vast body of the scholarship came to reflect the very sources available for research. The preponderance of articles, monographs, and dissertations tended to cluster around those aspects of Cuban history for which there existed sufficient research resources in the United States. Emphasis fell on political and diplomatic history within a period spanning the late nineteenth and mid-twentieth century. The principal areas of scholarly work included the Spanish-Cuban-American War and the subsequent military occupation of Cuba (1989-1902),[4] the second intervention (1906-1909),[5] and the revolutionary upheavals of the 1930s.[6] Considerable research was also directed toward the examination of various aspects of U.S.-Cuban relations for all or part of the period from 1895 to 1959/1961.[7]

The second major category of the postrevolutionary literature, and by far the most extensive of the two (and continuing to expand), is the work dealing with the politics, policies, and performance of the revolutionary government during the past 25 years. No other period has so closely and continuously engaged the attention of writers and researchers. These resulting publications have assumed vast proportions and continue to account for the better part of current research on Cuba.

Almost from the outset, the literature examining developments after 1959 acquired several notable characteristics. During the first several years, as the revolution traversed the full course from its humanist origins to its Marxist-Leninist destination, the principal themes of the literature reflected accurately the policy debate and political dispute prevailing in the United States and Cuba. As the revolution radicalized, it polarized, and through the early years produced a literature that was largely polemical in format and policy-oriented in function. Sides were quickly chosen, and almost from the outset the Cuba literature became possessed of one of its most enduring qualities—engagement.[8] Defenders and detractors participated in lengthy, often passionate, disputes over the virtues and vices of revolutionary developments in Cuba. An extensive literature resulted to exonerate one side or excoriate the other.[9]

A part of this polemic, but largely independent of the policy debate, were the writings produced by Cuban exiles. A vast emigré literature emerged in the months and years following the fall of Fulgencio Batista and the radicalization of the revolution, and it was divided into two distinct categories. One body of writing consisted almost entirely of the books and articles produced by the first group of political refugees from Cuba, principally *batistianos*, Cubans who had supported Fulgencio Batista and/or were members of the discredited government. They constituted the first wave of exiles during the early part of 1959. The writings of this group of emigrés represented a polemic within a polemic. The literature was certainly antirevolutionary; but it also tended toward rancor and recrimination, as this first wave of displaced and dispossessed Cubans sought to locate responsibility for the calamity that had overtaken them. Some blamed the army command for military defeat. Some blamed Batista for political incompetence. Some accused the United States of abandoning loyal allies. But all agreed that something had gone terribly wrong, and that someone was responsible. It became a highly charged atmosphere as Cubans in exile engaged in a spirited exchange of epithets. It was an intense debate, often in public and always acrimonious, one that occurred entirely within the community of exiled *batistianos*. This environment provided special incentive for former public officials to document for the record the part they played in the last crucial months and years of the Batista government. Personal accounts came to constitute in quantity and quality an impressive part of the early literature dealing with the revolution. Key political and military leaders during the Batista years chronicled, often in great detail, accounts as a means of vindicating their part in the ill-starred regime. They surfaced in the form of books, tracts, and articles. But it was on the pages of the exile press and periodicals that the debate acquired its most formidable proportions. So vast is the volume of the literature published in this fashion that it is perhaps not an undue exaggeration to suggest that thorough research on the closing years of the Batista government would be impossible without consultating this material. Regrettably, however, there are no guides to this extensive literature, making its use a great task; but the rewards are well worth the labor.[10]

Shortly thereafter, a second wave of political refugees augmented the swelling ranks of Cubans in exile, and the emigré literature took a slightly different turn. The newest exile group included active participants in the early years of the revolution, many who had become disaffected and disenchanted during the period of radicalization and subsequently defected. Many had been active in the anti-Batista struggle, either in the 26 of July Movement or other revolutionary organizations. Some had served briefly in various positions of government. A few were high-ranking colleagues and collaborators of Fidel Castro. This literature lacked the internecine acrimony of *batistiano* writing, but not the acrimony. It directed its ire toward the leadership of the revolution, stressing ideological questions and leveling charges of the revolution betrayed.[11]

Together, these two categories of exile literature have served as important sources for the study of the final years of the Batista government and the early years of the revolution. In a very real sense, these writings fall within a broader genre of literature, that of memoirs and reminiscences. Almost all key actors in the Cuban drama have written a memoir in some form, and these first-person accounts serve as an important source of information for the early years of the Cuban Revolution.[12]

A third variant of the first-person narrative, and perhaps the most extensive body of writings, is the literature published in Cuba. Indeed, nowhere do memoirs provide as rich and diverse a source of information as in the scores of published accounts of the revolutionary war between 1956 and 1958. Virtually all key Rebel Army commanders and urban resistance leaders penned their recollections and memoirs of the revolutionary struggle in the period immediately following the triumph of the revolution.[13]

Akin to formal memoirs and autobiographies are the first-person accounts obtained through transcribed interviews and oral histories. The formal interview technique has lent itself principally for use with Cuban leaders, past and present, in and out of Cuba. It is a format, too, that lends itself well to the style of Fidel Castro. Indeed, several book-length interviews have been published in recent years that provide remarkable personal and political portraits of the *Jefe Máximo*.[14] Oral histories, on the other hand, have served to provide detailed views of important aspects of life in socialist Cuba from all sectors of society.[15]

Related to memoirs, reminiscences, and oral histories are the first-person accounts of visitors and travelers to Cuba in the past 25 years. The travelogue represents a separate genre of literature, and in the hands of skilled researchers it can yield a wealth of enormously useful information. The literature of travel and description was particularly popular during the 1960s and 1970s and provided a steady, if often uneven, flow of impressionistic views of life in socialist Cuba during some of the most difficult moments of the revolution. These first-person accounts tend to be generally sympathetic, for during these years travel to Cuba was restricted largely to outsiders known for their sympathy toward or, at least, lack of hostility toward the revolution. This caveat notwithstanding, however, many travelogues offer a useful perspective of Cuba in the throes of revolutionary change and stand as important sources of information for these years.[16]

Equally important as a primary research source, but requiring no less circumspection, are the numerous statistical compilations published under the auspices of the Cuban government.[17] Virtually every government ministry has published, more or less regularly, statistical series containing vital data relating to population and demography, production and manufacturing, commerce and trade, transportation and communication, industry and agriculture.[18]

During the mid-1960s, the literature underwent several significant changes. The Cuban Revolution increasingly became the subject of serious research and scholarly inquiry. This is not to suggest that the polemical tide of the early years totally abated. It did not. Nor did the prevailing partisanship end. Indeed, much of the scholarship on Cuba has been unabashedly sympathetic to the revolution. Some have been openly hostile. However, for those who desired official access to Cuban research materials and formal permission to undertake field work on the island, political credentials were often almost as important as professional credibility. Certainly, too, several researchers arrived in Cuba initially sympathetic to the revolution, only to leave the island disillusioned by the findings of their investigation.

The changes of the mid-1960s foretold of other developments. The failure of the United States to overthrow the Cuban government in April 1961 at the Bay of Pigs and the American promise not to invade Cuba after the missile crisis seemed to guarantee the permanence of the revolution. These were years, too, in which the consolidation of power in Cuba was complete and with a measure of security guaranteed from without, and with the Revolution uncontested from within, other changes followed. Cuban willingness to permit foreign scholars to travel to the island served to stimulate new research interest. The literature of the last two decades has tended to conform to one of two broad categories: those works examining international relations and those dealing with internal developments.

Perhaps no aspect of Cuban foreign policy has been the subject of as much sustained discussion and recurring debate as relations with the United States. The literature has tended to be uneven, and has itself often served as an indicator of the state of relations between Cuba and the United States. The early literature tended to reflect principally American policy perspectives, while later writing has developed a much more balanced approach to bilateral relations.[19] Two aspects of U.S.-Cuban relations in particular have been the subject of continuing interest: the Bay of Pigs[20] and the subsequent covert war against Cuba in the 1960s and early 1970s.[21] This latter research has produced some first-rate studies—publications that have skillfully used documents obtained through the Freedom of Information Act.

Cuban international relations generally also have been the subject of considerable research. This work has proceeded under an obvious handicap, for information and data is often limited and always incomplete. Therefore, findings are typically tentative and almost always speculative.[22] This is research, too, that has followed the trends set by developments in Cuban foreign policy. During the 1960s Cuban foreign policy centered on Latin America. By the 1970s, the focus of Cuban internationalism had shifted to Africa. In the 1980s attention was again given to Latin America, specifically Central America and the Caribbean.[23]

Studies dealing with the internal aspects of the revolution, by far the most extensive portion of the literature published in the 1960s, fall into several distinctive groupings. One topic of active, if not belated, research interest was the nature of the Cuban guerrilla insurgency. Through the early years of the revolution, as Havana extolled the efficacy of armed struggle as the principal means of social change, attention returned to the Cuban insurgency of 1956 and 1958. For many, this experience offered a model worthy of emulation elsewhere. Fidel Castro's summons to transform the Andes into the Sierra Maestra of Latin America was more than idle rhetoric. But study of the seizure of power in Cuba offered at least as much to those who sought to combat revolution as it did to those who sought to promote revolution. During the 1960s and the early 1970s, for revolutionaries and counter-revolutionaries alike, the Cuban guerrilla experience became a subject of considerable research and the object of much theoretical formulation.[24]

By the end of the 1960s attention shifted again, this time to internal political developments. The Cuban Revolution appeared to have acquired a certain permanence, and the socialist experiment if not entirely flourishing was nevertheless still functioning. During the late 1960s and early 1970s research emphasis was on the study of the consolidation of political power and the transition to socialism. This literature stressed such diverse aspects as political mobilization, leadership—specifically the role of Fidel Castro—and domestic policies.[25]

But if the revolution had succeeded in political terms, such was not the case with economic programs. Problems persisted and deepened. The 1960s had been characterized by the debate over the nature of incentives, erratic production strategies, and the traumatic process of disengaging from North American capitalism within the context of the blockade. The results were less than reassuring. The 1960s ended with Cuba mobilized for the record sugar harvest of 10 million tons. The 1970s began under the pall of what must be considered one of the great calamities of socialist planning in Cuba. The effects went far beyond the failure to meet the 10-million-ton quota. No aspect of Cuban society was left unaffected by the debacle. The economy was left in ruins, poised on the brink of collapse. Cuban international relations changed as the necessity of massive economic assistance increased Cuban dependency on the Soviet Union. Internal policies changed as Cuba became more vulnerable to Soviet pressure.

The literature of these years concentrates on these problems and reflects accurately the vagaries of economic developments in Cuba. This is an enormously rich literature, much of it a critical chronicle of the failures of the Cuban experiment. Several key themes predominate, including changing production modes, the debate on incentives, development strategies (particularly as they involved sugar), and economic performance.[26]

The 1970s were characterized by several new trends and developments in Cuban literature. On one hand, the larger scholarly synthesis began to make its appearance. The revolution was now entering its second decade, and a sufficient body of data had accumulated to permit the integration of the monographic literature and specialized studies into a broader narrative approach to Cuban developments. These works typically adopted an historical format, tracing the origins of the revolution to the colonial past and/or the early twentieth century republic. The narrative was carried through the early 1970s and tended to focus upon political, economic, and social aspects of the revolutionary change in Cuba.[27]

A second important development during the 1979s (and continuing through the 1980s) has been the growth of specialized studies. Even as the popularity of the narrative synthesis increased, the range of the specialist enlarged. One noteworthy development has been registered in the successful fusion of both these approaches in the form of the anthology, bringing together breadth for generalists by providing depth by specialists. Indeed, the anthology has offered one of the most versatile and valuable formats through which to publish new research and report the findings of works in progress.[28]

Overall, however, it has been the literature of specialization that has prevailed in the last 15 years. Scholars have been prolific, producing a vast body of books, articles, and dissertations. These efforts have themselves reflected increasing research opportunities. First, and most important, travel to Cuba no longer presents the insurmountable obstacles of previous years. Scholars in growing numbers have traveled to Cuba for the purpose of research and study. As part of this process, collaboration between scholars in and out of Cuba has increased.[29] Sufficient data has accumulated to permit longitudinal research projects. Much of this research concentrates on assessments of the performance and progress of the revolution in a variety of fields; and most of this has been devoted to the study of social developments, including the state of education,[30] housing,[31] religion,[32] the status of women,[33] labor,[34] condition of blacks,[35] and medicine and health care delivery systems.[36] A second focus of the literature has been on the examination of the development of the principal institutional structures of the revolution[37] and the institutionalization of the revolution.[38] A third area of interest has been Cuban cultural and artistic achievements in the last 25 years, specifically literature, music and dance, cinema, and art.[39]

The net result of these developments has been to produce a body of literature of such vast proportions that it has in turn served to summon an equally vast body of bibliographical compilations and research guides. Indeed, the publication of bibliographical aids has itself become a large enterprise, without which research on the Cuban Revolution would be a daunting proposition indeed.[40]

The achievements of the scholarship on Cuba have been nothing less than spectacular. Over the past 25 years, often under difficult circumstances and frequently with formidable obstacles, the scholarship has advanced, and the advances have been constant and noteworthy. This is not to suggest that research on Cuba is free of problems, for such certainly is not the case. Research remains subject to the vagaries of larger foreign policy developments. Travel to and from Cuba is often uncertain and almost always cumbersome. Over the long run, these obstacles may prove to be of sufficient nuisance to discourage new research on Cuba at the graduate level and ultimately deter new researchers from entering the field of Cuban studies altogether.

For the time being, however, these obstacles notwithstanding, *cubanólogos* have demonstrated themselves to be a persistent lot, and more often than not their persistence has prevailed. The scholarship has tended to adjust well to the difficulties long associated with research on Cuba. More than resilience, however, the literature has accomplished balance. It has been representative of virtually all academic disciplines in the social sciences and the humanities. However, it is not only academics who have made important contributions to the Cuban literature. Novelists, clergy, journalists, playwrights, and policymakers have also contributed to advancing our understanding of the Cuban past and present.

Notwithstanding these achievements, the scholarship on Cuba must still be viewed as fragmentary and incomplete. Vital sources of data and research materials have remained consistently beyond the reach of the investigator. The information that is available must be utilized always with skepticism and circumspection, for it represents only part of the whole, and often not the most important part. Obviously the study of current developments in Cuba must proceed under the pall of a host of caveats. Conclusions must be advanced tentatively if not often speculatively, subject always to revisions as new information becomes available.

In the end, however, the passing of 25 years has resulted in the development of great maturity in the literature. A sound historiography has emerged. A rich and diverse bibliography has been compiled. The first 25 years have witnessed an auspicious beginning, and there is every reason to believe that this foundation will provide the sound basis for even greater accomplishments during the second 25 years of the Cuban Revolution.

NOTES

1. These include Irene A. Wright, *Cuba* (New York: Macmillan, 1910) and *The Early History of Cuba, 1492-1586* (New York: Macmillan, 1916); Russell H. Fitzgibbon, *Cuba and the United States, 1900-1935* (Menasha, Wis.: George Banta Co., 1935); Charles E. Chapman, *A History of the Cuban Republic* (New York: Macmillan, 1927); David A. Lockmiller, *Magoon in Cuba: A*

History of the Second Intervention (Chapel Hill, N.C.: University of North Carolina Press, 1938); Leland H. Jenks, *Our Cuban Colony* (New York: Vanguard Press, 1928).

2. These would include such excellent pieces as Duvon C. Corbitt, "'Mercedes' and 'Realengos': A Survey of the Public Land System in Cuba," *Hispanic American Historical Review* 19 (1939), pp. 262-85 and "Immigration in Cuba," *Hispanic American Historical Review* 12 (1942), pp. 280-308.

3. Robert Freeman Smith, ed., *What Happened in Cuba? A Documentary History* (New York: Twayne Publishers, 1963).

4. David F. Healy, *The United States in Cuba, 1898-1902* (Madison, Wis.: University of Wisconsin Press, 1963); James H. Hitchman, *Leonard Wood and Cuban Independence, 1898-1902* (The Hague: Martinus Nijhoff, 1971); Philip S. Foner, *The Spanish-Cuban-American War and the Birth of American Imperialism*, 2 vols., (New York: Monthly Review Press, 1972); Louis A. Pérez, Jr., *Cuba Between Empires, 1898-1902* (Pittsburgh: University of Pittsburgh Press, 1983); Jack C. Lane, "Instrument of Empire: The American Military Government in Cuba, 1899-1902," *Science and Society*, 36 (1972), pp. 314-30.

5. Allan Reed Millett, *The Politics of Intervention: The Military Occupation of Cuba, 1906-1909* (Columbus, Ohio: Ohio State University Press, 1968).

6. Luis E. Aguilar, *Cuba, 1933: Prologue to Revolution* (Ithaca, N.Y.: Cornell University Press, 1972); Francis V. Jackman, "America's Cuban Policy During the Period of the Machado Regime" (Ph.D. diss., Catholic University, 1965); Peter Frederic Krogh, "Sumner Welles and United States Relations With Cuba: 1933" (Ph.D. diss., Fletcher, 1966).

7. Robert F. Smith, *The United States and Cuba: Business and Diplomacy, 1917-1960* (New Haven, Conn.: College and University Press, 1960); Irwin Gellman, *Good Neighbor Diplomacy in Cuba, 1933-1945* (Albuquerque: University of New Mexico Press, 1973); Lester D. Langley, *The Cuban Policy of the United States* (New York: John Wiley, 1968); Jules Robert Benjamin, *The United States and Cuba: Hegemony and Dependent Development, 1880-1934* (Pittsburgh: University of Pittsburgh Press, 1976).

8. For a brief but provocative discussion of this phenomenon see Carmelo Mesa-Lago, "Revolutionary Empathy vs. Calculated Detachment in the Study of the Cuban Revolution," *Cuban Studies/Estudios Cubanos* 11 (January 1981), pp. 90-92.

9. The defenders included C. Wright Mills, *Listen Yankee* (New York: Ballantine, 1960); Herbert L. Matthews, *The Cuban Story* (New York: George Braziller, 1961); Jean Paul Sartre, *Sartre on Cuba* (New York: Ballantine, 1961); William Appleman Williams, *The United States, Cuba, and Castro* (New York: Monthly Review Press, 1961); Waldo Frank, *Cuba, Prophetic Island* (New York: Marzani and Munsell, 1961); Leo Huberman and Paul M. Sweezy, *Cuba: Anatomy of a Revolution* (New York: Monthly Review Press, 1961). Detractors

included Nathaniel Weyl, *Red Star Over Cuba* (New York: Devin-Adair, 1972); James Daniel, *Cuba, the First Soviet Satellite in the Americas* (New York: Avon, 1961); Irving P. Pflaum, *Tragic Island: How Communism Came to Cuba* (Englewood Cliffs, N.Y.: Prentice Hall, 1961); Edwin C. Stein, *Cuba, Castro and Communism* (New York: McFadden Bartell, 1962).

10. Representative of this literature are Alberto Baeza Flores, *Las cadenas vienen de lejos* (México: Ed. Letras, 1970); L.P. Elizalde, *La tragedia de Cuba* (México, 1959); Fulgencio Batista, *Cuba Betrayed* (New York: Vantage Press, 1962); Florentino Rosell Leyva, *La verdad* (Miami, Fla.: 1960); José Suárez Núñez, *El gran culpable* (Caracas, 1963). Some of the periodical and newspaper literature includes Pedro A. Barrera Pérez, "Por qué el ejército no derrotó a Castro," *Bohemia Libre* (Caracas) 53, July 9, 1961–September 3, 1961; Rafael Guas Inclán, "Todos erramos," *Cuba Libre* (Miami), 2, October 28, 1960, pp. 1, 3; Florentino E. Rosell Leyva, "Confirme el acuerdo Batista-Cantillo," *La Crónica* (Miami), August 16, 1968, p. 19 and "El tren blindado," *La Crónica* (Miami), July-August, 1960; Francisco Tabernilla Dolz, "Carta abierta," *Cuba Libre* (Miami) 2, October 28, 1960, p. 2.

11. This literature is best represented by Teresa Casuso, *Cuba and Castro* (New York: Random House, 1964); Manuel Urrutia Lleo, *Fidel Castro and Company, Inc.* (New York: Praeger, 1964); Rufo López Fresquet, *My 14 Months with Castro* (Cleveland, Ohio: World Publishing Co., 1966); Mario Llerena, *The Unsuspected Revolution* (Ithaca, N.Y.: Cornell University Press, 1978). An important recent contribution to the literature is Carlos Franqui, *Diario de la revolución cubana* (Madrid: R. Torres, 1976) and *Retrato de familia con Fidel* (Caracas: Seix Barral, 1981).

12. The memoirs of the last two American ambassadors to Cuba offer valuable information for the period of the late 1950s and early 1960s. See Earl E.T. Smith, *The Fourth Floor* (New York: Random House, 1962); and Philip W. Bonsal, *Cuba, Castro, and the United States* (Pittsburgh: University of Pittsburgh Press, 1971).

13. Perhaps the most well known is Ernesto Ché Guevara, *Reminiscences of the Cuban Revolutionary War* (New York: Merit Publishers, 1968). See also Neill W. Macaulay, Jr., *A Rebel in Cuba* (Chicago: Quadrangle, 1970); Faure Chomón, *La verdadera historia del asalto al Palacio Presidencial* (Havana: Prensa Estudiantil, 1959); Luis Pavón, ed., *Días de combate* (Havana: Instituto Cubano del Libro, 1970); Camilo Cienfuegos, *Páginas del diario de campaña* (Havana: Ministerio de Educación, 1962); José Quevedo Pérez, *La batalla del Jigüe* (Havana: Instituto Cubano del Libro, 1973); José Pardo Llada, *Memoria de la Sierra Maestra* (Havana: Editorial Tierra Nueva, 1960). Like the exile literature, the vast proportion of these works also appeared in newspapers and periodicals. Numerous first-person accounts of the war appeared in Cuba during the early 1960s and 1970s in *Bohemia, Juventud Rebelde, Granma, Verde Olivo,* and *Revolución*. The authors included various leaders of the revolutionary struggle,

among the most prominent of whom were Raúl Castro, Juan Almeida, Faustino Pérez, Armando Hart, Antonio Enrique Lussón, Efigenio Ameijeiras, William Gálvez, José Caussé, Raúl Menéndez, and Joel Iglesias. Unlike the exile literature, however, there is a guide to this work. See Louis A. Pérez, Jr., *The Cuban Revolutionary War, 1953–1958: A Bibliography* (Metuchen, N.J.: Scarecrow Press, 1976).

14. See in particular Lee Lockwood, *Castro's Cuba, Cuba's Fidel* (New York: Random House, 1969); and Frank Mankiewicz and Kirby Jones, *With Fidel: A Portrait of Castro and Cuba* (New York: Playboy Press, 1975).

15. Among the more important contributions to oral history are Francisco García Moreira, *Tiempo muerto. Memorias de un trabajador azucarero* (Havana: Instituto Cubano del Libro, 1969); Andrés D. García Suárez, *Los fundidores relatan su historia* (Havana: Orientación Revolucionaria del Comité Central del PCC, 1975); Julián Sánchez, *Julián Sánchez cuenta su vida*, ed. Erasmo Dumpierre (Havana: Instituto Cubano del Libro, 1970). Also important sources in the form of oral history are the three volumes prepared by Oscar Lewis, Ruth Lewis, and Susan Rigdon, *Four Men: Living the Revolution. An Oral History of Contemporary Cuba* (Urbana, Ill.: University of Illinois Press, 1977); *Four Women: Living the Revolution. An Oral History of Contemporary Cuba* (Urbana, Ill.: University of Illinois Press, 1977); and *Neighbors: Living the Revolution. An Oral History of Contemporary Cuba* (Urbana, Ill.: University of Illinois Press, 1978). Equally valuable is Douglas Butterworth, *The People of Buena Vista: Relocation of Slum Dwellers in Postrevolutionary Cuba* (Urbana, Ill.: University of Illinois Press, 1980).

16. Among the most informative accounts are Warren Miller, *90 Miles from Home* (Boston: Little, Brown, 1961); Victor Franco, *The Morning After* (New York: Praeger, 1963); Mohammed A. Rauf, *Cuba Journal* (New York: Crowell, 1964); Elizabeth Sutherland, *The Youngest Revolution* (New York: Dial Press, 1969); Matilde Ladrón de Guevara, *Diario de una mujer* (Buenos Aires: Editorial Goyanarte, 1964); José Yglesias, *In the Fist of the Revolution* (New York: Pantheon, 1968); Charles K. McClatchy, *Cuba Revisited 1967* (Sacramento, Cal.; n.p., 1967); Fred Ward, *Inside Cuba Today* (New York: Crown Publishers, 1978); Fernando Morais, *La isla de Cuba: Cuba y los cubanos* (México: Editorial Nueva Imagen, 1978); Frank Mulville, *In Granma's Wake* (London: Seafarer's Books, 1970); Joe Nicholson, *Inside Cuba* (New York: Sheed and Ward, 1974); Ernesto Cardenal, *In Cuba* (New York: New Directions Publishing Co., 1974); Lee Chadwick, *Cuba Today* (Westport, Conn., Lawrence Hill and Co., 1975).

17. See Carmelo Mesa-Lago, "Availability and Reliability of Statistics In Socialist Cuba," *Latin American Research Review* 4 (spring 1969), pp. 53–91 and (fall 1969), pp. 47–81; Carmelo Mesa-Lago, "Cuban Statistics Revisited," *Cuban Studies/Estudios Cubanos* 9 (July 1979), pp. 59–62.

18. Some of the more important statistic sources include Cuba, Junta Central de Planificación, *Anuario demográfico de Cuba, 1961* (Havana, 1965)

and *Censo de población y vivienda, 1970* (Havana, 1970); Cuba, Comité Estatal de Estadística, *Comunicado acerca de los resultados preliminares del censo nacional de población y viviendas de 1981* (Havana, 1981); Cuba, Dirección Central de Estadística, *Compendio estadístico de Cuba* (Havana, 1965-); Cuba, Dirección Central de Estadística, *Estadísticas quinquenales de Cuba, 1965-1980* (Havana, 1982); Cuba, Junta Central de Planificación, Dirección Central de Estadística, *Anuario estadístico de Cuba* (Havana, 1972) and *Boletín Estadístico de Cuba* (Havana, 1965-1971); Cuba, Departamento de Demografía, *Características de la divorcialidad cubana* (Havana, 1976) and *Las estadísticas demográficas cubanas* (Havana, 1975); Cuba, Dirección Central de Estadística, *La situación de la vivienda en Cuba en 1970 y su evolución perspectiva* (Havana, 1976) and *Anuario demográfico en Cuba* (Havana, 1961-). Perhaps the best statistical compilation in English is Susan Schroeder, *Cuba: A Handbook of Historical Statistics* (Boston: G.K. Hall and Company, 1982).

19. See Robert D. Crassweller, *Cuba and the United States: The Tangled Relationship* (New York: Foreign Policy Association, 1971); Lester D. Langley, ed., *The United States, Cuba, and the Cold War* (Lexington, Mass.: Heath, 1970); Lynn Darrell Bender, *Cuba vs. the United States: The Politics of Hostility*, 2nd ed. (San Juan, Puerto Rico: Interamerican University Press, 1981); Mario Lazo, *Dagger in the Heart* (New York: Twin Circle Publishing Co., 1968); Carla Ann Robbins, *The Cuban Threat* (New York: McGraw-Hill, 1983).

20. For accounts of the Bay of Pigs see Karl E. Meyer and Tad Szulc, *The Cuban Invasion* (New York: Praeger, 1962); Haynes B. Johnson, *The Bay of Pigs* (New York: Norton, 1964); Hans M. Enzensberger, *The Havana Inquiry* (New York: Holt, Rinehart, Winston, 1974); Peter Wyden, *The Bay of Pigs: The Untold Story* (New York: Simon and Schuster, 1979). E. Howard Hunt provides a first-person account of the Bay of Pigs as a CIA organizer in *Give Us This Day* (New Rochelle, N.Y.: Arlington House, 1973). A first-rate documentary collection is found in Paramilitary Study Group, *Operation Zapata: The "Ultrasecretive" Report and Testimony of the Board of Inquiry on the Bay of Pigs* (Frederick, Mc.: Alethia Books, 1981). For Cuban accounts see Justina Álvarez, *Héroes eternos de la patria* (Havana: Ediciones Venceremos, 1964); Rafael Pino, *Amanecer en Girón* (Havana: Ediciones Venceremos, 1964); Raúl González, *Gente de Playa Girón* (Havana: Casa de las Americas, 1962); Lisandro Otero, *Playa Girón, derrota del imperialismo*, 4 vols. (Havana: Ediciones Venceremos, 1961-1962).

21. See Warren Hinckle and William W. Turner, *The Fish is Red: The Story of the Secret War Against Castro* (New York: Harper and Row, 1981); Bradley E. Ayers, *The War that Never Was* (Indianapolis: Bobbs Merrill, 1976); and Taylor Branch and George Crile, "The Kennedy Vendetta: How the CIA Waged a Silent War Against Cuba," *Harper's*, 1975, pp. 49-63; Philip Brenner, "The Assassination Report: Congress and the Investigation of Intelligence," *Cuba Review* 6 (June 1976), pp. 3-15; Joe Eldridge, "Undercover

Foreign Policy," *Cuba Review* 6 (June 1976), pp. 16-20. For a U.S. government report see U.S. Congress, Senate, Select Committee to Study Government Operations, *Alleged Assassination Plots Involving Foreign Leaders*, 94th Cong. 1st sess. (Washington, D.C.: Government Printing Office, 1975).

22. See D. Bruce Jackson, *Castro, the Kremlin, and Communism in Latin America* (Baltimore, Md.: Johns Hopkins Press, 1969); Cole Blasier, "The Cuban-U.S.-Soviet Triangle, Changing Angles," *Cuban Studies/Estudios Cubanos* 8 (January 1976), pp. 1-9; Ángel García and Piotr Mironchuk, *Esbozo histórico de las relaciones entre Cuba-Rusia y Cuba-URRS* (Havana: Instituto Cubano del Libro, 1976); Blanca Torres Ramírez, *Las relaciones cubano-soviéticas* (Mexico: Institute for the Study of Human Issues, 1978); Jacques Lévesque, *The U.S.S.R. and the Cuban Revolution* (New York: Praeger, 1978); Edward González, "The Cuban Revolution and the Soviet Union, 1959-1960" (Ph.D. diss., University of California, Los Angeles, 1966).

23. For general works dealing with Cuban foreign policy see Carmelo Mesa-Lago, ed., *Cuba in the World* (Pittsburgh: University of Pittsburgh Press, 1979); Jorge I. Domínguez, ed., *Cuba: Internal and International Affairs* (Beverly Hills, Cal.: Sage, 1982); Martin Weinstein, ed., *Revolutionary Cuba in the World Arena* (Philadelphia: 1979). The topic of Cuban relations with Latin America is dealt with in Barry B. Levine, ed., *The New Cuban Presence in the Caribbean* (Boulder, Colo.: Westview, 1983); Boris Goldenberg, *The Cuban Revolution and Latin America* (New York, Praeger, 1965); J.H. Ferguson, "The Cuban Revolution and Latin America," *International Affairs* (London), July 1961, pp. 285-92. Studies dealing with individual countries include Miles P. Wolpin, *Cuban Foreign Policy and Chilean Politics* (Lexington, Mass.: Heath, 1972); Julio Portillo, *Venezuela-Cuba, 1902-1980* (Caracas: Editorial Arte, 1981); Olga Pellicer de Brody, *México y la revolución cubana* (Mexico: 1972). Works dealing with Africa include William M. LeoGrande, *Cuba's Policy in Africa, 1959-1980* (Berkeley, Cal.: University of California Press, 1980); Carmelo Mesa-Lago and June Belkin, eds., *Cuba in Africa* (Pittsburgh: University of Pittsburgh Press, 1982); Phillip A. Luce, *The New Imperialism: Cuba and the Soviets in Africa* (Washington, D.C.: 1979); Michael A. Samuels, et al., *Implications of Soviet and Cuban Activities in Africa for United States Policy* (Washington, D.C.: Center for Strategic and International Studies, Georgetown University, 1979); Danny Schecter, "The Havana-Luanda Connection," *Cuba Review* 6 (March 1976), pp. 5-13; Gordon Adams and Michael Locker, "Cuba and Africa: The Politics of the Liberation Struggle," *Cuba Review* 8 (October 1978), pp. 3-9; William M. LeoGrande, "Cuban-Soviet Relations and Cuban Policy in Africa," *Cuban Studies/Estudios Cubanos* 10 (January 1980), pp. 1-37; Nelson P. Valdés, "Cuban Involvement in the Horn of Africa: The Ethiopian-Somali War and the Eritrean Conflict," *Cuban Studies/Estudios Cubanos* 10 (January 1980), pp. 49-89; Jorge I. Domínguez, "Political and Military Limitations and Consequences of Cuban Policies in Africa," *Cuban Studies/Estudios Cubanos* 10 (July

1980), pp. 1-35; Sergio Roca, "Economic Aspects of Cuban Involvement in Africa," *Cuban Studies/Estudios Cubanos* 10 (July 1980), pp. 55-79.

24. Early works include the two studies by Robert Taber, *M-26, Biography of a Revolution* (New York: Lyle Stuart, 1961) and *The War of the Flea* (New York: Lyle Stuart, 1965); Harold R. Aaron, "The Seizure of Political Power in Cuba, 1956-1959,"(Ph.D. diss., Georgetown University) and "Why Batista Lost," *Army* 15 (September 1965), pp. 64-71; Merle Kling, "Cuba: A Case Study of a Successful Attempt to Seize Political Power by the Application of Unconventional Warfare," *The Annals of the American Academy of Political and Social Sciences* 341 (May 1962), pp. 43-52. One of the most recent studies of the insurrectionary war is Ramón L. Bonachea and Marta San Martín, *The Cuban Insurrection, 1952-1959* (New Brunswick, N.J.: Transaction Books, 1972). The two works central to the theoretical formulation for armed struggle (*foquismo*) are Ernesto Ché Guevara, *La guerra de guerrillas* (Havana: Departmento de Instrucción del MINFAR, 1960); and Regis Debray, *Revolution in the Revolution?* (New York: Monthly Review Press, 1968). The literature dealing with *foquismo* is voluminous and includes Leo Huberman and Paul M. Sweezy, eds., *Regis Debray and the Latin American Revolution* (New York: Monthly Review Press, 1968); José A. Moreno, "Ché Guevara on Guerrilla Warfare: Doctrine, Practice, and Evaluation," *Comparative Studies in Society and History*, April 1970, pp. 114-33.

25. See Andrés Suárez, *Cuba: Castroism and Communism, 1959-1966* (Cambridge, Mass.: MIT, 1967); Loree A. Wilkerson, *Fidel Castro's Political Programs: From Reformism to Marxism-Leninism* (Gainesville, Fla.: University of Florida Press, 1965); Richard Fagen, *The Transformation of Political Culture in Cuba* (Stanford, Cal.: Stanford University Press, 1969); David D. Burks, *Cuba Under Castro* (New York: Foreign Policy Association, 1965); K.S. Karol, *Guerrillas in Power* (New York: Hill and Wang, 1970); Edward González, *Cuba Under Castro: The Limits of Charisma* (Boston: Houghton Mifflin, 1974); Carlos Rafael Rodríguez, *Cuba en el tránsito al socialismo, 1959-1963* (Havana: Editorial Política, 1979).

26. This literature is voluminous. Some of the better representative works include, Claes Brundenius, *Economic Growth, Basic Needs, and Income Distribution in Revolutionary Cuba* (Lund, Sweden: Research Policy Institute, 1981); Heinrich Brunner, *Cuban Sugar Policy from 1963 to 1970* (Pittsburgh: University of Pittsburgh Press, 1977); Lowry Nelson, *Cuba: the Measure of a Revolution* (Minneapolis: University of Minnesota Press, 1972); Arthur MacEwan, *Revolution and Economic Development in Cuba* (New York: St. Martin's Press, 1981); Archibald R. Ritter, *The Economic Development of Revolutionary Cuba* (New York: Praeger, 1974); Edward Boorstein, *The Economic Transformation of Cuba* (New York: Monthly Review Press, 1968); Carmelo Mesa-Lago, *Cuba in the 1970s* (Albuquerque: University of New Mexico Press, 1978) and *Cuba: A Two Decade Appraisal* (Albuquerque: University of New Mexico

Press, 1981); Bertram Silverman, ed., *Man and Socialism in Cuba: The Great Debate* (New York: Atheneum, 1971); Juan F. Noyola, *La economía cubana en los primeros años de la revolución* (México: Siglo Veintiuno, 1978); Alberto Recarte, *Cuba, economía y poder, 1959-1980* (Madrid: Alianza, 1980).

27. See Hugh Thomas, *Cuba, The Pursuit of Freedom* (New York: Harper and Row, 1971); James O'Connor, *The Origins of Socialism in Cuba* (Ithaca, N.Y.: Cornell University Press, 1970); Ramón Ruiz, *Cuba: The Making of a Revolution* (Amherst, Mass.: University of Massachusetts Press, 1968); Jaime Suchlicki, *Cuba: From Columbus to Castro* (New York: Scribner's, 1974); Herbert L. Matthews, *Revolution in Cuba* (New York: Scribner's, 1975); Jorge I. Domínguez, *Cuba: Order and Revolution* (Cambridge, Mass.: Harvard University Press, 1978); Ovidio García Regueiro, *Cuba: raíces, frutas de una revolución* (Madrid: Imp. Romero-Requejo, 1970).

28. The most balanced and comprehensive anthologies include: Carmelo Mesa-Lago, ed., *Revolutionary Change in Cuba* (Pittsburgh: University of Pittsburgh Press, 1971), which deals with ideology; Cuban relations with the United States, the Soviet Union, and Latin America; labor, economic planning, art, literature, and theater; Ronald Radosh, ed., *The New Cuba: Paradoxes and Potentials* (New York: William Morrow, 1975), which examines the role of intellectuals, the development of the Communist Party, United States-Cuban relations, and economic issues; David P. Barken and Nita R. Manitzas, eds., *Cuba: The Logic of the Revolution* (Andover, Mass.: Warner, 1973) which treats education, economic organization, urban policies, and the revolution in Latin America; Irving L. Horowitz, *Cuban Communism*, 3rd ed. (New Brunswick, N.J.: Transaction Books, 1977), which deals with ideology, agriculture, military organization, race relations, students, and incentives; and John Griffiths and Peter Griffiths, eds., *Cuba: The Second Decade* (London: Writers and Readers Cooperative, 1979), which covers aging, women, agriculture, housing, media, sports, and culture. Other useful anthologies include Jaime Suchlicki, ed., *Cuba, Castro, and Revolution* (Coral Gables, Fla.: University of Miami Press, 1972); Nelson P. Valdés and Rolando Bonachea, eds., *Cuba in Revolution* (Garden City, N.Y.: Anchor, 1972); Lester A. Sobel, ed., *Castro's Cuba in the 1970s* (New York: Facts on File, 1978); James N. Goodsell, *Fidel Castro's Personal Revolution in Cuba, 1959-1973* (New York: Knopf, 1975).

29. One of the most recent collaborative efforts is Stanley L. Engerman, Manual Moreno Fraginals, and Herbert S. Klein, "The Level and Structure of Slave Prices on Cuban Plantations in the Mid-Nineteenth Century: Some Comparative Perspectives," *The American Historical Review* 88 (December 1983), pp. 1201-18. Recent professional meetings, including the Latin American Studies Organization and the American Historical Association, have included Cuban scholars in the program.

30. Martin Carnoy and Jorge Werthein, *Cuba: Economic Change and Educational Reform 1955-1974* (Washington, D.C.: World Bank, 1979); Marvin

Leiner, *Major Developments in Cuban Education* (Andover, Mass.: Warner, 1973); Jonathan Kozol, *Children of the Revolution* (New York: Delacorte, 1978); John Griffiths, *The Education System of Revolutionary Cuba* (London: 1977); Karen Wald, *Children of Ché: Childcare and Education in Cuba* (Palo Alto, Cal.: Ramparts Press, 1978); Carl J. Dahlman, *The Nationwide Learning System of Cuba* (Princeton, N.J.: Princeton University Press, 1973); Donna Katzin, "Education and Revolution are the Same Thing," *Cuba Review* 5 (June 1975), pp. 3-10; John L. Hammond, "Adults and Higher Education: Every Worker a Student, Every Student a Worker," *Cuba Review* 5 (June 1975), pp. 27-32.

31. Maruja Acosta and Jorge E. Hardoy, *Urban Reform in Revolutionary Cuba* (New Haven, Conn.: Yale University Antilles Research Program, 1973); Tony Schuman, "Housing: 'We Don't Have the Right to Wait,'" *Cuba Review* 5 (March 1975), pp. 3-22.

32. Leslie Dewart, *Christianity and Revolution* (New York: Herder and Herder, 1963); Alice Hageman and Philip E. Wheaton, eds., *Religion in Cuba Today: A New Church in a New Society* (New York: Association Press, 1971); Margaret E. Crahan, "Salvation Through Christ or Marx: Religion in Revolutionary Cuba," *Journal of Inter-American Studies* 21 (February 1979), pp 156-84; Mary Lou Suhor, "Free to be Christian and Revolutionary," *Cuba Review* 5 (March 1975), pp. 23-26; Jim Wallace, "Christians in Cuba," *Cuba Resource Center Newsletter* 3 (April 1973), pp. 3-11; Larry Becker, "Jews in Cuba," *Cuba Resource Center Newsletter* 3 (April 1973), pp. 12-13; Donna Katzin, "Cuban Jews: Continuity and Change," *Cuban Resource Center Newsletter* 3 (December 1973), pp. 25-28.

33. Margaret Randall, *Cuban Women Now* (Toronto: Women's Press, 1974); Silvio de la Torre, *Mujer y sociedad* (Havana: Editorial Universitaria, 1965); Inger Holt-Seeland, *Women of Cuba* (New York: Lawrence Hill, 1982); Margaret Randall, *Women in Cuba—Twenty Years Later* (New York: Smyrna Press, 1981); Guillermo Wasmer Miguel, ed., *La mujer en Cuba socialista* (Havana: Instituto Cubano del Libro, 1977); Anna Ramos, "Women and the Cuban Revolution," *Cuban Resources Center Newsletter* 2 (March 1972), pp. 3-11; Carollee Benglesdorf and Alice Hageman, "Emerging from Underdevelopment: Women and Work," *Cuba Review* 4 (September 1974), pp. 3-12.

34. Maurice Zeitlin, *Revolutionary Politics and the Cuban Working Class* (New York: Harper and Row, 1970); Marifeli Pérez-Stable, "Institutionalization and Workers Response," *Cuban Studies/Estudios Cubanos* 6 (July 1976), pp. 31-54; Carmelo Mesa-Lago, *The Labor Force, Employment, Unemployment and Underemployment in Cuba, 1899-1970* (Beverly Hills, Cal.: Sage, 1972) and *The Labor Sector and Socialist Distribution in Cuba* (New York: Praeger, 1968).

35. Terence Cannon, *Free and Equal: The End of Racial Discrimination in Cuba* (New York: Venceremos, 1978); Rafael L. López Valdés, "Discrimination in Cuba," *Cuba Resource Center Newsletter* 2 (January 1973), pp. 6-14; John Clytus, *Black Man in Red Cuba* (Coral Gables, Fla.: University of Miami Press,

1970); Joseph North, "Negro and White in Cuba," *Political Affairs*, July 1963, pp. 34-45.

36. Ross Danielson, *Cuban Medicine* (New Brunswick, N.J.: Transaction Books, 1979); Cuba Study Group, *Cuba's Health System: An Alternative Approach to Health Delivery* (Houston: CSG, 1975); Margaret Gilpin and Helen Rodríguez-Trias, "Looking at Health in a Healthy Way," *Cuba Review* 7 (March 1978), pp. 3-15; Evan Stark, "Overcoming the Diseases of Poverty," *Cuba Review* 7 (March 1978), pp. 23-30; Roy John, et al., "Public Health Care in Cuba," *Cuba Resource Center Newsletter* 2 (May 1972), pp. 4-10.

37. Emilio T. González, "The Development of the Cuban Army," *Military Review* 61 (April 1981), pp. 56-64; Louis A. Pérez, Jr., "Army Politics in Socialist Cuba," *The Journal of Latin American Studies* 12 (November 1976), pp. 251-71; Jorge I. Domínguez, "The Cuban Operations in Angola: Costs and Benefits for the Armed Forces," *Cuban Studies/Estudios Cubanos* 8 (January 1978), pp. 10-21 and "Institutionalization and Civil-Military Relations," *Cuban Studies/Estudios Cubanos* 6 (January 1976), pp. 39-65; Edward González, "The Party Congress and Poder Popular: Orthodoxy, Democratization and the Leader's Dominance," *Cuban Studies/Estudios Cubanos* 6 (July 1976), pp. 1-14.

38. Leonel-Antonio de la Cuesta, "The Cuban Socialist Constitution: Its Originality and Role in Institutionalization," *Cuban Studies/Etudios Cubanos* 6 (July 1976), pp. 15-30; Nelson P. Valdés, "Revolution and Institutionalization in Cuba," *Cuban Studies/Estudios Cubanos* 6 (January 1976), pp. 1-38; Irving Louis Horowitz, "Institutionalization as Integration: The Cuban Revolution at Age Twenty," *Cuban Studies/Estudios Cubanos* 9 (July 1979), pp. 84-90. For a general discussion of this literature see Max Azicri, "The Institutionalization of the Cuban Revolution: A Review of the Literature," *Cuban Studies/Estudios Cubanos* 9 (July 1979), pp. 63-77.

39. Anna Veltfort, "Toward a Genuine Culture," *Cuba Resource Center Newsletter* 3 (October 1973), pp. 3-6; Andrés R. Hernández. "Cinema and Politics: the Cuban Experience," *Cuba Resource Center Newsletter* 3 (October 1973), pp. 19-22. Miguel Cabrera, *Órbita del Ballet Nacional de Cuba: 1948-1978* (Havana: Editorial Orbe, 1978); Magali Muguercia, *Teatro: en busca de una expresión socialista* (Havana: Letras Cubanos, 1981).

40. Among the most useful general bibliographical guides are Edwin Lieuwen and Nelson P. Valdés, *The Cuban Revolution: A Research Guide, 1959-1969* (Albuquerque: University of New Mexico Press, 1971); Jaime Suchlicki, *The Cuban Revolution: A Documentary Bibliography, 1952-1968* (Coral Gables, Fla.: University of Miami Press, 1968); Research Institute for Cuba and the Caribbean, University of Miami, *Revolutionary Cuba: A Bibliography* (Coral Gables, Fla.: University of Miami Press, 1959-). Specialized bibliographies include Roberto Nodal, *The Cuban Presence in Africa: Bibliography* (Milwaukee, Wis.: University of Wisconsin Press, 1980); Jan Czarnecki, *Cuba in Soviet Writings, 1959-1972: An Annotated Bibliography of Soviet Publications on*

Cuba in the Collection of the University of Miami Library (Coral Gables, Fla.: University of Miami Press, 1977); Nelson P. Valdés, "A Bibliography on Cuban Women in the 20th Century," *Cuban Studies Newsletter* 4 (June 1974), pp. 1-3; Gilbert V. Fort, *The Cuban Revolution of Fidel Castro Viewed from Abroad* (Lawrence, Kan.: University of Kansas Press, 1969); Arthur Gillingham and Barry Roseman, *The Cuban Missile Crisis* (Los Angeles: Center for the Study of Armament and Disarmament, 1976); Teresa Anderson, *Cuban Agrarian Economy: Bibliography* (Madison, Wis.: Land Tenure Center, 1974); *Bibliografía de asalto al cuartel Moncada* (Havana: n.p., 1975); Terry J. Peavler, "Prose Fiction Criticism and Theory in Cuban Journals: An Annotated Bibliography," *Cuban Studies/Estudios Cubanos* 7 (January 1977), pp. 58-118; Aleida de los Santos Quilez, *El campesinado cubano: breve bibliografía* (Havana: Editorial Politica, 1980); Louis A. Pérez, Jr., *Historiography in the Revolution: A Bibliography of Cuban Scholarship, 1959-1979* (New York: Garland Publishing, 1982); Tomás F. Robaina, *Bibliografía de bibliografías Cubanas* (Havana: Biblioteca Nacional "Jose Martí," 1973). By far the most complete and updated bibliographical guide is *Cuban Studies/Estudios Cubanos*, published on a semiannual basis by the Center for Latin American Studies at the University of Pittsburgh.

21   Cuba: A Revolution of the People (November 23, 1960)

A. Gunder Frank
Sagua de Tánamo and Holguín
Oriente Province, Cuba

THE OLD CUBA—A LIFE OF HELPLESSNESS AND HOPELESSNESS

Before the revolution, Cuba was a land of tyranny where 20,000 people were murdered; a land of justice only for those rich enough to buy it, of hunger for most eight months of the year (during the *tiempo muerto* of the sugar industry), and squalor all of the time. It was a land of little education (and an American stranglehold on the economy maintained this misery), of government-enforced discrimination against the colored (of a whole people more repressed than are the rural Negros of Mississippi), and maybe worst of all, of a life without future, a life of helplessness for today and hopelessness for tomorrow. Years of revolutionary activity, two years of guerrilla warfare in the mountains, and only less than two years of the revolution and its government has completely transformed Cuba into a land of opportunity and responsibility. Cuba has wrought a revolution and a government of the people.

"HOW HAS THE REVOLUTION CHANGED YOUR LIFE?": "COMPLETELY"

In the isolated mountains, the fertile plains, the provincial towns, the cosmopolitan city, I asked the people, "How has the revolution changed your life?" The answers differ, but all agree on one measure: "Completely." A sugar mill worker said the greatest change has been in freedom and integrity. Before, people were shot in the streets like dogs, and men were slaves to the management of the mill. Now people can walk the streets in peace and speak with the new managers with equality and dignity. A worker in the sugar cane fields said his cooperative is now planting corn, beans, and rice crops in addition to sugar, and they are building brick and concrete houses for the co-op members. So now he has work all year instead of four months, and his children have food and soon a decent place to live. A peasant with a couple of acres of coffee, so isolated in the mountains as to be inaccessible even by jeep, rolled me a cigar out of his home-grown tobacco and said he is no longer exploited by middlemen; the *Tiendas del Pueblo* have a much lower markup than the merchants who had a local monopoly, and if he sells his coffee through the government organization he is not cheated on price and quality, as he used to be. Now he can obtain agricultural credit to buy a cow, improve his crops, and for subsistence too; and when his child is sick he need no longer mortgage his farm and his family's future to an usurer or land speculator who wants to foreclose if he can.

An urban slum dweller said the Urban Reform Law is the best law of the new government; it makes all occupants owners of their dwellings in five to twenty years, depending on the age of the building; landlords received pensions up to $650 a month; and what was previously rent, now amortization receipts, are used to finance new low-cost housing, payments on which will not exceed 10 percent of the occupant's income (present payments average a quarter to a third of income). Taxi drivers no longer complain that army people use their taxis without payment. Students speak of opportunity, a Negro of the abolition of race discrimination, a minister of spiritual awakening, a housewife of justice for all, a worker of freedom from the United States ("Cuba—the first country in the Americas to be free") as the most important change. But all agree that the revolution is the dawn of a new day for *los humildes* ("the humble people"), a new day of opportunity, and work, and dignity, and justice and hope. The revolution created a future.

THE REVOLUTION IS OPPORTUNITY

The opportunity offered by the new future is represented variously: by new jobs from industrialization, new crops in cooperative farms, new credit for subsistence and small commercial farmers. But the opportunity and the desire to take advantage of it is nowhere so evident as in education. More impressive than the nearly 15,000 new classrooms is the sudden interest in, nay demand for, education among the people. In March 1959 the new superintendent of schools personally counted 340 school-age children of the poorest section of Sagua de Tánamo (population 5,000) without schooling. Why are all 340 in school now? Why has school attendance in Sagua County (population 75,000) jumped from 5,270 or 7 percent of the population in 1958, to 15,500 or 20 percent of the population in 1960? Because the revolution has created the opportunity. An opportunity not only to learn in one of the new 206 schoolrooms of Sagua (90 before, 296 now), the opportunity not only to learn under the tutelage of new teachers, but maybe more importantly, the revolution has created the desire to use that education to build a new life. Parents, and particularly poor parents, are now sending their kids to school and keeping them there longer because only since the revolution do children have the opportunity of a better life than their parents. Many of the parents, also, are suddenly going to school—to night school, to technical school, or just to learn to read and write in the adult classes which have been organized in town and country as part of the national campaign of "those who know teach those who don't." Teenagers and people in their early twenties are most insistent on obtaining more and more education, a highly valued commodity. As I asked young people what they most want to do, one after another answered "study" in high school, technical school, university, or abroad, whichever is next on his list of goals. "Then why didn't you study, or continue to study before?" "Because there was no future to study for." "Because industrialization since the revolution has created new work for engineers, the opportunity to better myself and serve Cuba at the same time."

REVOLUTION IS RESPONSIBILITY

The opportunity, the near-universal participation in the revolution, has its counterpart also in responsibility. Responsibility to use the new opportunities, to increase them and to extend them to others. Cubans have assumed a social responsibility for the common good as never before. To staff new classrooms, thousands of people have temporarily sacrificed their homes and careers to teach in the mountains and the countryside until the teacher shortage is eliminated. Young people from the cities, students, white-collar workers, others, are taking short intensive teacher-training courses to enable them to live in a straw hut in the hills and teach in a one- or two-room school as a member of the Voluntary Rural Teachers. Art, music, and other specialty teachers have left Havana to teach in towns like Sagua. One man leaves his family in Havana to live in a bunkhouse and earn $183 a month (most of which he sends home) as administrator of a cooperative farm which is only just beginning to break virgin land and build housing for its members. An accountant trades his $300 a month job at the U.S. Naval Base for a $100 one at the same co-op. The white-haired agricultural engineer in the hotel room next to mine left his family in Havana because wardestroyed Sagua has no available housing. He works 12 hours a day at the local branch office of INRA (Instituto Nacional de Reforma Agraria) and makes jeep trips into the mountains to explain the new agricultural credit facilities to peasants whose isolation and poverty used to exclude them from credit. As I try to talk with these people, they run off to this meeting or that, at all hours of the day and night, explaining that they are the *responsable* of the local youth group, or of the *Alfabetización* Committee of the 26th of July Movement, or of some political education committee, or of another one of the thousand other voluntary community service and educational organizations which work, not to run dances and picnics, but to advance the revolution and its work. All these same people and a million others also serve in the voluntary *milicia* (National Guard), buying their uniforms and their own guns, and giving their time and enthusiasm—meeting the responsibility they feel—not only to work for, but to defend the revolution, from the constant threat of invasion from abroad.

The full-time Rebel Army, unlike other armies, does not polish its boots and tidy its uniforms. It dirties them instead, building schools, hospitals, and housing in the mountains. The officers have no officer's clubs, but work like all others, wearing the same uniforms, with only the smallest insignia to identify their rank. Many of the officers serve in government departments such as INRA at nothing but their low army pay, an income much lower than the corresponding civilian salary. I have not heard a single complaint—not even by those unfriendly to the revolution—of corruption in the army or the government. On the contrary, people take pride in pointing out the difference between the corruption of before and the responsibility of today. In stark contrast to the armies of the South American and Asian countries supported and supplied by the United States, the Cuban Rebel Army, born in the revolution, is an army of the people, with responsibility for the people.

Not all people, however, have taken on the responsibility for the new Cuba. The "pillars," the "responsible citizens of our communities," the local merchants, small-town lawyers, and would be professionals—in a word the petite bourgeoisie—are in the forefront of those who have not felt the need to take on such social responsibilities. Why not? In one sense they do not understand the revolution, and in another sense they understand it only too well. A print shop owner (and small-town publisher on the side) and his merchant, lawyer, and engineer friends who form his social circle cannot empathize with the tide of work, education, freedom, equality, and dignity that is pouring out of the mountains which surround him; and he does not understand its source in misery and the knowledge that it can be overcome. Peasants leaving the land to work, and rural kids seeking an education in town—his town—are ruining the economy, that is only logical, he says; and his friends nod approval. True, the movement is inconsistent within the confines of his small world, and he understands only too well but cannot accept this change in structure and dimension of the world in which he lives—the small world in which he was a big fish, a responsible pillar of the community. And thus, like the petite bourgeoisie elsewhere, he and his circle are afraid of the emancipation of the peasant in Cuba and in the world, an emancipation that disturbs his social position in the community.

Another group trying to stay aloof from the revolution is the tourist industry in Havana—unfortunately the first and, for many, the only Cubans the visitor meets. Unlike the bourgeoisie, these people are workers and thus have no social position to lose (although some have been temporarily economically hurt). They just don't understand the revolution. Like the American abroad, they associate so much with the American tourists, and like the British butler who is more uppity than his master, the tourist workers seem to have taken on the attitudes and expectations of the tourists rather than their compatriots. For Cuba, the foreign tourist industry is no less colonial than the sugar industry, and maybe more so: it has corrupted some of her people—they can no longer assume responsibility in helping to build a new Cuba.

Although these people often do not support some of the work of the revolution, this does not mean they wish that the revolution, the overthrow of the Batista dictatorship, had not happened; nor does their fear or disapproval make them into counterrevolutionaries. The revolution is still in the process of finding itself, trying this and that. Inevitably, there are those people who react unfavorably to the uncertainty just as others, opportunists and fair-weather friends, respond to the social pressure and appeal for unity behind the revolution by jumping on the revolutionary bandwagon. The latter wave the Cuban flag while the former, trained by a generation of right-wing and Catholic Church propaganda, shout "Communist" with no more understanding of what communism, or socialism for that matter, is than their American Legion counterparts in the United States. The farther away from middle-class Havana one gets, and the closer to the heart of the Cuban peasant, the less opposition and fair-weather friendliness is to be found, and the more near-universal total participation and support.

A REVOLUTION OF THE PEOPLE, BY THE PEOPLE, AND FOR THE PEOPLE

Notwithstanding these reservations, were it possible to ask all Cubans whether there is popular support for the revolution and for the government, the answer would undoubtedly be a heartfelt, resounding, yes. No account such as this one can hope to capture the spirit of the revolution and the Movement of July 26, 1953 from which it was born. The spirit is embodied in the people who have spoken herein, in the eyes and the quiet voice of a mountain peasant, the devotion of a worker, the unending cheers of the young, The "Cuba-Sí, Yanquis, NO" (though a genuine friendliness toward the American people as distinct from the U.S. government and big business exists). It shows in the "Patria o Muerte" said and meant and in the tremendous personal loyalty to Fidel, "Somos Fidelistas." Probably no modern revolution, and certainly not the world-shaking American, French, Russian and Chinese revolutions had the depth and breadth of popular participation and support at their inception that the Cuban Revolution has. Let the doubters only consider the million civilian *milicia* members in all walks of life. No other modern government, not even the Swiss, and certainly no newly installed government has ever permitted so many or so large a proportion of its civilians (Cuban population is 6.5 million) to have arms. Imagine a highly armed population in Guatemala, Nicaragua, Vietnam, or another of the underdeveloped countries supported by the United States! And no U.S.-supported counterrevolution, regardless of the amount of aid given, can possibly reverse this tide of history that has so captured the Cuban spirit. "Patria o Muerte" is no idle slogan. No, Cuba's revolution will itself be world shaking, not only because "history is with us" but also because Cuba has truly created a revolution and a government of the people, by the people, and for the people.

22 Why Is Cuba Different?

Arthur MacEwan

Cuba is not like most other socialist countries. While formal institutions of economic, social, and even political organization in Cuba are similar to those in the Soviet Union and Eastern Europe generally, there are significant substantive differences. Outstanding symbols of these differences are the high degree of politicization of the Cuban people and the far-reaching social and economic equality that has been a hallmark of the Cuban Revolution. These are factors that endow Cuba's formal institutions of participation with far more than formal significance and go a long way toward limiting bureaucratic and repressive practices. Such practices are present in Cuba, but in much of the rest of the socialist world, bureaucracy and repression are dominant features of social life.

Cuba's difference is widely recognized. Among left-wing activists in both the Third World and the advanced capitalist nations, the influence and prestige of the Soviet Union has long been in decline. However, in spite of its close ties with the Soviets, Cuba is generally seen as a positive example of socialist development. While achieving substantial material successes—in the economy, in health care, and in education—the Cuban Revolution has also built some elements of a democratic social system. An electoral system, Poder Popular, was implemented during the 1970s. Also in the 1970s, the bureaucratic control of unions was relaxed, and they and other mass organizations became vehicles for popular discussion of social and political issues and for popular participation in local economic affairs. Moreover, Cuba has developed a court system that involves considerable mass participation, and the educational system encourages participatory social behavior, at least in terms of the ideology that guides it.

Even a very favorable interpretation of these structures of participation in Cuba would have to point out their limitations (and one should not ignore the significance of their formal similarity to Soviet structures). Organized opposition is not allowed in Cuba. Elections are contested in Poder Popular, but the range of dispute is limited. Whatever voice the workers and the community may have in the direction of an enterprise, managers are generally appointed from above and are formally accountable to the higher authorities. The Cuban government would not tolerate efforts to establish an independent union movement, and there is no question of compromise on the political hegemony of the Cuban Communist Party.

Nonetheless, in spite of these qualifications, economic and social organization in Cuba does not fit "the Soviet model." Cuba is different. But why is it different? Are there features of Cuban history (in the development of the Cuban Revolution) that help us explain Cuba's particular course of socialist development? It is politically important (as well as academically interesting) to explain why revolutions evolve as they do. Moreover, if a "Cuban difference" is consistent with Cuban history, it gives us more confidence in the reality and durability of that difference.

CAPITALISM AND IMPERIALISM

The first aspect of Cuba's history that needs to be noted is that at the time of the revolution Cuba was a thoroughly capitalist nation. Wage-labor relations dominated economic life, in agriculture as well as in industry and services. In part, the importance of wage labor was connected to the central role of sugar in Cuba's economy; generally, cane cutters were wage laborers, and the sugar mills were large and relatively modern capitalist enterprises (though located in rural areas). In addition, Cuban society was urbanized, with a majority of the population living in the cities by the early 1950s and thus engaged in relatively modern (i.e., wage labor) activity. In the countryside, where agriculture was carried out on peasant farms (as opposed to sugar plantations, cattle ranches, or other wage labor-employing activities), production was market oriented and relatively specialized.

In other countries where revolutions have led to efforts to establish socialist organization, fundamental material circumstances were very different. In Russia, China, and elsewhere, the modern capitalist sector was a small island in a sea of semifeudal and small, tradition-dominated peasant agriculture. Significant parts of agriculture, to be sure, were tied to a market in the modern sector—indeed, often to an international market. Thus, the entire economies of these other nations were connected to and affected by capitalist development. Wage-labor relations, however, were of decidedly secondary importance, and much peasant activity was still directed toward self-sufficiency. These economies were not capitalist; they were not urban; they were not modern. Cuba has the distinction of being the first and only capitalist nation to experience a socialist revolution.

While Cuba carries this distinction, nonetheless, like other nations that have experienced socialist revolutions, it was on the periphery of the international capitalist system. Yet, associated with its capitalist nature and also with its proximity to the United States, Cuban society had been much more thoroughly dominated by imperialism. This thorough domination had many facets, but its impact on Cuba's class structure is most central. The prolonged colonial status of Cuba, the continued presence of Spanish authority throughout the nineteenth century, was followed in the first half of the twentieth century by neocolonial status, including the infamous Platt Amendment and a series of interventions by the U.S. military. These conditions preempted the development of a cohesive and politically powerful bourgeoisie. Power within Cuba was dominated in the nineteenth century by a narrow and relatively isolated sugar oligarchy backed by the Spanish crown. In the first half of the twentieth century, even the role of the sugar oligarchy was undermined by U.S. penetration of the Cuban economy and of Cuban society generally. Formal power fell into the hands of a loosely knit group of *caudillos*, dictators, and demagogues, lacking any firm class base and ultimately dependent upon U.S. capital and the U.S. government.

THE STRUGGLE FOR POWER

Cuba's particular economic and social history—the nation's class structure and thorough domination by imperialism—had, of course, an extensive impact on the character of the political struggle that ultimately led to the triumph of the revolution in 1959. With considerable legitimacy, the revolutionary leadership traces its roots in that struggle over almost a century. From the 10 Year War beginning in 1868, through the battles that led to independence in 1899 and the uprisings of the early 1930s, Cuba experienced a connected, if not continuous, series of frustrated revolutions. The 10 Year War failed to bring independence from Spain, though it led to considerable transformation of both Cuban society and its international relations. The battles of the 1890s did achieve independence, but only an independence under the tutelage of the United States. In the 1930s while the dictatorship of Machado was ended, the U.S. government was able to manipulate the situation, install a regime favorable to its interests, and abort any far-reaching political or social transformation. The frustration of these revolutionary upheavals can be explained by several factors, but important among them is the fact that Cuba was so weak in relation first to Spain and later the United States. No Cuban class or set of classes was able to forge a successful movement.

In this context of frustrated revolutions, activists of each era saw themselves as the political heirs of those who had gone before, and at each stage there were those who carried on the experience of one generation of rebels to the next generation. In this sense, and contrary to the popular image, the revolution that came to power in 1959 was the product of a long struggle. A long struggle and connections between different eras of struggle would seem to have considerable impact on the character of the society that emerges from revolutionary conflict. Most importantly, a long struggle provides the experience that can be applied to the construction of new social institutions. It is the *struggle itself* that prepares people for running the new society, for building the institutions of socialism.

Moreover, in Cuba during the twentieth century, the experience of past struggles was embodied in organizations of the working class. Labor unions, in particular, played a significant role from the early decades of the century, as the working class, already well formed, expanded rapidly with the sugar boom of that period. Affected in their early years by an anarcho-syndicalist tradition inherited from Spain and then in the 1920s by the growth of a communist movement, unions played an increasingly important political as well as economic role. When Cuba's history is compared with the histories of other nations in which socialist revolutions have taken place, it is evident that unionization had a more thorough and extensive impact there than elsewhere. The Cuban working class in its size and importance provided the opportunity for unions to develop; in addition, the development of those unions gave the Cuban working class an organizational experience that was lacking elsewhere or much more limited.

It should be stressed that unionization in Cuba involved rural as well as urban-based workers. As the working class itself included a large segment of agricultural wage laborers and also industrial workers in rural areas (the mill workers), so too did the working class organizations span the rural-urban division. In 1917 there had been two distinct revolutions in the Soviet Union—one urban-based in the working class and one rural-based in the peasantry. When the Cuban revolutionary government came to power in 1959, not only was there a single revolution, but the unity of different segments of the population had a long-established organizational foundation.

Beyond the unions, the Cuban Communist Party also played a substantial role in providing organizational continuity for working class struggles. While it would be incorrect to view the Party as playing the leading role in the uprisings of the 1930s, its role and influence were substantial. The following passage from Ramón Ruiz's history of the revolution suggests the significance of the Communists and also underscores the advanced nature of the struggle:

> In August 1933, urban workers in Havana, again with Communists participating, launched their own strike, which in less than a month forced Machado to flee.... Demanding better working conditions, higher wages and recognition of their unions, 200,000 sugar workers joined the protest. On August 21, 1933, the workers seized a sugar mill in Camagüey Province; in less than a month, thirty-five other mills had fallen into their hands, and by early September, 30 percent of the country's sugar production was under workers' control. Meanwhile, rural Soviets made their appearance at Mabay, Jaronú, Senado, Santa Lucía and other *centrales* [sugar mill complexes]. Mill managers were held prisoner; labor guards at the mills wore red armbands for uniforms; strikers fraternized with soldiers and police; and, at Antilla, a red flag fluttered over city hall, while Communist-led demonstrations in Santiago forced the mayor and the provincial governor to flee their offices.

In 1934 the Communist-led Fourth National Labor Congress claimed 400,000 members, and union activity was on an industrial, rather than craft, basis. By 1940 Communist Party membership stood at 43,000 and would grow to 150,000 by the end of World War II, making it the largest Communist party in the Western hemisphere on a per capita basis and one of the largest in the world. According to the 1951 report of the World Bank, the Communists had "succeeded in attaining practically complete control of the Cuban labor movement" and had formed "a relatively compact and disciplined proletariat."

The point that deserves emphasis here is not the political role of the Communist Party. Indeed, the Party's membership rolls had been decimated by the late 1950s, its position in the labor movement greatly weakened, and its leadership compromised by reformist practices. The Party did not play a notable role in aiding the triumph of the revolutionary forces. What does deserve emphasis is that the Party made a substantial contribution to the organizational experience of the Cuban working class. When the revolution came to power, even though the immediate struggle had not involved widespread working class activity, the longer range struggle through the Communist Party and, more broadly, through the trade union movement, provided a foundation on which new participatory social institutions might be built.

When the revolution did triumph in 1959, it had a history of broad class alliances and extensive popularity on which to build. In this respect, Cuba's experience was unusual, if not unique, among socialist revolutions. Throughout "the one hundred years of struggle," Cuban regimes had been so isolated that opposition arose in virtually all social groups. In the nineteenth century, slaves, free workers, artisans, small farmers, and large land owners had all joined against the "Spanish yoke." In the twentieth century, both in the 1930s and in the 1950s, almost all segments of society supported the struggle against the dictatorships and U.S. domination. Whatever divisions would later emerge, the isolation of Cuba's government authorities and the role of imperialism had spawned a broad base and a popular revolution.

FORMING NEW INSTITUTIONS

Cuba's pre-1959 history of social and economic development and of political struggle did not determine what would happen after 1959. In periods of dramatic social upheaval, numerous factors intervene to affect the course of change, and it would be folly to attempt to draw precise connections between the historical factors discussed previously and later events. (In fact, on the basis of the historical circumstances, it would have been virtually impossible to predict the political triumph of the revolution—why did the U.S. government allow it?—let alone the course of social and economic events following the triumph.) Nonetheless, these historical factors provided the context for what happened after 1959, and they certainly affected the way new economic institutions influenced Cuban society.

Reflecting the broad social base of the revolutionary movement, the new economic institutions did not emerge from any well-devised, ideologically defined program for change. For example, in the first years following the triumph of the revolution, there was not a general move toward national economic planning, nor could the early change be seen as the systematic structuring of a socialist system. Instead, the new institutions amounted to an eclectic set of reforms, far-reaching and profound in their implications, but eclectic reforms nonetheless.

Among these reforms were the agrarian reforms, the employment laws (proscribing lay-offs), rent reductions, and great extensions of the education and medical care systems. Together these programs brought about a rapid and extreme equalization of income. Well before the socialist character of the revolution had been formed, the poorer classes saw their incomes shoot upward, often doubling in the span of a few months, in what amounted to a huge transfer from the propertied classes. Other socialist revolutions, of course, have also led to considerable redistribution of income, though seldom so great as that in Cuba. In any case, in Cuba the redistribution of income, mostly accomplished by 1963, would have a significant impact on events in subsequent years.

The material benefits that working people received from the revolution were very clear, and there is no doubt that in this sense the Cuban Revolution was a revolution *for* the working classes. At least in the early years, however, it was not a revolution *by* the working classes. The immediate struggle for power had not directly involved the masses of the people, and, by and large, the early reforms were instituted from the top down. Peasants and rural workers, for example, received the benefits of agrarian reform, but decisions were made and the process was directed at the center through the Instituto Nacional de Reforma Agraria.

The literacy campaign of 1961 did provide, at least in part, a notable exception. While the general form of the campaign was determined by the central authorities, its implementation involved mass participation. Many tens of thousands were responsible as teachers, to say nothing of the much greater numbers involved as students. With responsibility there always goes a certain amount of authority, and thus the literacy campaign established a model, however limited, for participation in programs of change and for the diffusion of power.

During most of the 1960s, however, the model was not applied. Economic affairs in particular were dominated by centralized decision making and were thoroughly encumbered by bureaucracy. Also, as is well known, the economic record of the 1960s was dismal. Yet, it is important to note that in spite of the extreme economic difficulties in the 1960s, political repression did not emerge as the solution to those difficulties. In the Soviet Union (during the 1920s and 1930s) and elsewhere, the trials of economic change were loaded onto the peasantry, control was gathered more and more thoroughly into the hands of centralized bureaucracies, and repression became the level of "progress." In Cuba, neither the private peasantry (which continued to operate some 30 percent of agriculture) nor the rural population generally was made to bear the brunt of the 1960s difficulties. The broad, historically-built social base of the revolution remained in place. There was a bureaucratization and militarization of the economy, but it was limited and did not become thoroughly institutionalized. At the beginning of the 1970s when the economic situation was of crisis proportions, divisive social conflict remained minimal; and the leadership continued to rely on its positive popularity, rather than on any extensive repression, to implement its programs.

Out of the crisis, the government might have moved in the direction of tightening bureaucratic control and relying on an incentive combination of large salary differentials and repression. Nonetheless, the *immediate circumstances*, the *conditions established* by the early reforms of the revolution, and the nation's longer *historical experience* all tended to push things in a different direction.

Immediate circumstances were characterized by cohesion among various social groups, a lack of antagonisms that would have been created by a period of sharp repression, and the continued popularity of the revolutionary leadership. This situation was one in which participatory programs—programs that could give responsibility in economic affairs to the people themselves—remained possible.

Among the *conditions established* by the early reforms, the extreme equality served to force the leadership away from a bureaucratic, repressive solution to the crisis. A move toward such a solution would have required the reestablishment of considerable income inequality, a major reversal of the earlier pay-offs of the revolution. Moreover, along with income equality, the revolution had established widespread social equality, which provides a firm basis for a participatory system of organization.

Even by 1970, the *historical significance* of the Cuban working class, its extensive involvement in organizational activity, had not been lost. Indeed, certain processes set in the 1960s had built upon and maintained this organizational experience; the growth of the educational system, including extensive adult education, and the expansion of mass organization are examples. This accumulation of experience provided a further basis for a participatory system of organization.

In this context, it is not surprising that Cuba moved toward the development of participatory institutions in the 1970s. Cuban history, both in the long run and over the period since 1959, favored this direction of development. It would be wrong to pretend that by citing the various elements of that history we can see a "determination" of the way economic and social institutions have evolved in recent years. It does seem, however, that by examining those factors we can find some basis for a "Cuban difference."

23 The Cuban Revolution: An Historical Perspective

James F. Petras and Morris H. Morley

The evolution of the Cuban Revolution—its successes and failures, the particular institutions that have developed, the policies and commitments pursued, the ideological synthesis and the nature of the relationships between civil society and the state—can be understood only in terms of the specific features that have been etched on the process over the past 25 years.

The specific features that define the Cuban Revolution include: (1) the country's geographic status as an island and the particular political consequences that this entailed; (2) the cultural-racial-historical matrix out of which the revolution emerged and its pivotal role in the shaping of an internationalist foreign policy; (3) the persistence of an economy that revolves overwhelmingly around the fortunes of a single agricultural commodity; (4) a perpetual state of siege due to the sustained hostility exhibited by the United States imperial state through seven administrations, Republican and Democratic, liberal and conservative—the longest blockade policy ever maintained by a dominant imperialist country; and (5) a political leadership whose formative experiences and political successes have been forged largely in social and political struggles, rather than in the organization of production. Analyzing the Cuban Revolution in terms of these factors contributes to our understanding of the policies pursued by the leadership and the institutions that have developed under its aegis.

ISLAND SOCIALISM

That Cuba is an island has significantly affected its ability to survive and to serve as a model for revolution in other Latin American countries. The absence of adjoining borders has limited the capacity of the United States to institute the kind of massive and ongoing counterrevolutionary effort that characterizes Washington's policy toward the Sandinista government in Nicaragua. While the White House and CIA have sponsored exile invasions, economic sabotage expeditions, and various forms of covert warfare, the absence of a common border between Cuba and another country that could serve as a base for the training and arming of counterrevolutionaries has meant that U.S.-supported political terrorism has not been a problem of great magnitude. Moreover, imperial policymakers have had to contend not only with Cuba's geography but also with its high level of military preparedness, facilitated by the advantages that a small island state offers for defense mobilization.

Although geography has favored the Cuban Revolution's survival, it has simultaneously contributed to its political isolation and curbed its ability to support (morally or otherwise) revolutions elsewhere in Latin America. Difficulties in communicating, traveling, and exchanging ideas and experiences have all played a role in limiting the multiplier impact of the Cuban experience on a regional level. The same body of water that shelters Cuba from external attacks has acted as a formidable barrier between the revolution and progressive developments in the rest of the hemisphere.

The political isolation of the "sheltered" revolution has profoundly shaped Cuban development. It has heightened relations with the socialist bloc in order to secure vitally needed defense equipment and energy goods; and it has curbed Cuba's access to markets and suppliers in the capitalist world, raising the costs of trade and putting strains on production. The global economic blockade and the reorientation of export and import markets to the socialist countries was accompanied by innumerable problems that negatively affected economic planning and production.

Nonetheless, the political isolation and its consequences have strengthened internal solidarity among Cubans. The common experience of survival and pressing need for self-reliance has reinforced national commitments and identification between the Cuban people and its political leadership. Cuba's nationalist consciousness has in large part been forged by both the country's political geography and the unremitting hostility of the United States. At the same time, the island's small size and the unusual accessibility of the political leadership to the populace has led to a continuous informal dialogue that is found in few other countries of the world. The absence in Cuba of elected representative bodies and of officials responsible to an electorate is partly counterbalanced by these direct informal exchanges that take place outside formal political institutions. The paradox, then, that confounds dogmatic critics is that the revolutionary government lacks formal channels through which popular consent can be registered, but it still enjoys the consent of the majority. Cuba's size and geography partly account for the character of Cuban socialism as mobilized, participatory, and nondemocratic.

CUBAN SOCIALISM AND THIRD WORLD STRUGGLES

Cuba's powerful commitment to the national liberation struggle in the Third World has been visibly displayed in its commitments in Southern Africa—commitments closely related to the island's own Afro-Caribbean roots. The strong consensus within Cuban socialism that embraces international solidarity has been particularly manifest in Havana's defense of the socialist MPLA government in Angola against the combined attacks of the South African armed forces and CIA-funded domestic counterrevolutionary forces.

The longstanding and substantial presence of Afro-Cubans has also greatly facilitated Havana's solidarity with governments in the Caribbean area attempting to define an independent path to socioeconomic development. Cuba's support for both the Grenadian revolution under the leadership of Maurice Bishop's New Jewel Movement and the nationalist Jamaican government of Michael Manley was rooted in complex regional, ideological, and racial bonds. What is clear from Cuban behavior is that racial and national consciousness have blended to yield a deep undercurrent of support for the nationalist and anti-imperialist movements that have emerged throughout the region. Furthermore, Cuba's leadership in the Nonaligned Movement and its consistent intervention on behalf of Third World interests has offered an alternate approach to the development-through-dependency pattern characteristic of the Caribbean area. Its ability to defend itself against U.S. military, economic, and political aggression, and to continue the revolutionary process serves to encourage all small island-states to pursue independent paths to development. Thus, while the Cuban Revolution has embraced universal goals, its experience is particularly rooted in, and relevant to, the immediate Caribbean context.

MONOCULTURE: THE ROOTS OF CLASS SOLIDARITY

One of the most striking features of the Cuban Revolution is the high degree of class solidarity and its sustained manifestation in mass mobilizations in defense of the revolution, in the proliferation and vitality of numerous mass organizations, and in the codification of that solidarity in the full-employment policies and other social policies that have emerged under the auspices of the Castro leadership.

This solidarity flows partly from a common work experience centered around the sugar industry. The occupational communities responsible for planting, harvesting, and processing sugar cane reinforce a common set of working class perspectives. In an even more fundamental sense the continued centrality of sugar to the Cuban economy has enhanced the position of the sugar workers in both production and regime ideology. In prerevolutionary Cuba, class solidarity was based on job insecurity due to the seasonal nature of the sugar harvest. Most of the wage workers employed in the sugar sector usually worked only at harvest time, which averaged around one hundred days a year.[1] Claes Brundenius notes that immediately prior to the overthrow of the Batista dictatorship "over half of the rural labor force of 900,000 workers were employed in the cane fields, and during the 'dead season' it has been estimated that more than 400,000 workers were unemployed, the majority of them sugar workers."[2] In postrevolutionary Cuba, solidarity has emerged from the social solidarity and full employment provided by the revolution. By the end of the 1960s, open unemployment was virtually eliminated. In its place was the new problem of "getting enough skilled people to do a particular job at a particular time."[3]

A PERMANENT STATE OF SIEGE: SOCIALIST FORTRESS MENTALITY

The Cuban Revolution, unlike any other socialist revolution, has never been recognized by the United States as a permanent reality. The antagonism between Havana and Washington has not been merely ideological—as was the case in U.S. relations with both the Soviet Union and China—but has frequently taken on a military character. Cuba has been the scene not only of a "cold war," but of American-initiated or American-threatened "hot wars." The White House and the CIA have sponsored a failed military invasion, covert economic sabotage, assassination efforts, global economic blockade, and active opposition to Cuba's internationalist foreign policy. The latest link in this long chain of sabre rattling and open hostility can be traced back to early 1981 when the Reagan State Department, as part of its Central America-Caribbean policy, requested the Pentagon to examine the possibility of taking various military actions against Cuba, including a show of airpower, a large naval exercise, a quarantine on arms shipments to the island, a naval blockade, and even a possible invasion.

The reality of U.S. invasions, CIA-sponsored terrorist activity, continual threats of military intervention, and the permanent presence of an American military base on Cuban soil have forced the Cubans to give priority to national security issues. The political system has largely been organized around the preponderant concern with creating the most effective military-preparedness system, one capable of dealing with any form of U.S. military aggression. Cuba's high defense expenditures and organizational readiness have deterred direct military intervention, as no American president has been willing to pay the price of the enormous casualties that would certainly accompany any such decision.

CLASS STRUGGLE AND ECONOMIC STAGNATION

The Cuban political leadership was forged largely in the arena of military confrontation and social mobilization—divorced from the organization of production. The guerrilla movement and the Rebel Army were the instruments to overthrow Batista; for the most part the massive transformation of the economy and society took place through governmental edict (around which popular support was generated). The history of "class struggle" in Cuba occurred mainly at the level of the state and, accordingly, is eminently a political struggle in which the contending class forces were subsumed in politico-military organizations. The revolutionary intervention of the political leadership preempted political action from below. The process of change characteristically involved successive expropriations (from national to foreign) and redistributive measures reflecting an extension and deepening of the class struggle. The revolution's popularity was built from the social changes and social struggles. By both temperament and experience the leadership was divorced from the problems of production and its organization. The discipline and commitment exhibited in the context of social and political struggle, and again in military organization, were lacking in the domain of production. The virtues of the social revolution were not transferable to the banality of everyday work. The energies unleashed in the struggle for social justice were not reproduced in the organization of production. While the Cuban Revolution has achieved a highly dynamic social transformation, it is attached to a rather mediocre economic performance attributable in part to the persistence of an agro-export economy.

The success of Cuba's political history weighs heavily on its economic record. The values of the past that stress struggle, solidarity, and militancy are continually reinforced and sustained by their values for protracted defense of the revolution and its achievements. Nonetheless, the exigencies of rationality, technology, and organization in the sphere of production cannot always be squared with the priorities of the class struggle.

CONCLUSION

Any serious evaluation of the Cuban Revolution must take into account the contextual factors and driving forces that together have shaped and influenced the trajectory of the island's socialism. In terms of its African roots, the revolution has been quite successful in expressing through practice the bonds of internationalist solidarity (with the notable exception of Eritrea where Cuba supported the efforts of a dictatorial military regime in Ethiopia to defeat a national liberation movement). As regards the defense of its own sovereignty against the sustained hostility of the U.S. imperial state, the revolution has thwarted military intervention, economic aggression, and political-diplomatic isolation efforts originating in Washington—efforts that sought, and still seek, to reconstitute a capitalist state, polity, and economy on the island. In the rest of the Caribbean region, however, Havana unsuccessfully opposed Washington's actions during the 1960s, 1970s, and 1980s to destabilize and undermine fraternal nationalist and/or socialist regimes.

To raise the question of the structure of Cuba in the world economy and the way in which this affects the position of the Cuban working class is to confront a fundamental fact that while the revolution has brought about a basic shift in the terms of exchange, it has done so without altering Cuba's role in the international division of labor. This means that Cuba's economic integration into the socialist bloc has had two major (and beneficial) consequences: (1) the costs of critical large-scale purchases from the Soviet Union and its allies, especially petroleum and military supplies, compare favorably with possible alternate sources in the West; and (2) the price paid for Cuban sugar by the bloc countries has remained significantly above that of the capitalist marketplace (the average annual world market price for sugar between 1959 and 1976, for example, was $6.76 per pound; the average annual price per pound paid by the Soviet Union for Cuban sugar during this same period was $9.42 per pound[4]). Even though Cuba still reaps the bulk of its foreign exchange earnings from a single commodity export, the social consequences of this sugar dependence have been vastly different since 1959. In place of large-scale and recurrent unemployment and underemployment, there are labor shortages in areas of sugar productions; in place of job insecurity, there is guaranteed lifetime employment. Clearly, the effects of Cuba's participation in the world market are decisively shaped by the island's organization of production and its internal class relations—a fact that should be highlighted in view of the monumental oversimplification that so-called center/periphery theorists of development make in subsuming all primary-product export countries under the same "peripheral" "dependency" category.

The Cuban Revolution has successfully organized a highly competent and effective security force that is second to none in the Third World. The level of professionalism and skill, the morale and combativeness—which has enabled the revolution to deter U.S. aggression—have frequently been acknowledged by allies and even enemies. On the other hand, the development of democratic institutions has fared less well. The nationwide experiment with Popular Power beginning in 1976—the popular election of legislative assemblies at the municipal, provincial and (indirectly) national levels—provided limited opportunities for direct participation.[5] But at the national level, notwithstanding this and other efforts at forms of local government and representation, centralized political control is the rule, and citizens are generally the objects of policy and not the protagonists. However, the overriding and necessary concern with the permanent siege constructed by the United States has led to overdeveloped institutions of national defense and underdeveloped institutions of democratic representation. The relevance of the Cuban Revolution for other countries is found in the superb organization of its defense system; its weakness lies in the leadership's inability to broaden the scope of citizen participation and debate.

The history of pre- and post-revolutionary Cuba has been a history of national liberation and class struggle. Over the past quarter century, perhaps more than any other postrevolutionary society, Cuba has sustained a revolutionary ethos in its relations with movements and governments throughout the Third World. While this continuity in revolutionary praxis is an important index of its success, the Cuban Revolution has been less triumphant in the areas of converting political energies into disciplined productive activity. The lag between high revolutionary achievement and uneven economic performance still confronts the Castro leadership with a significant problem. The question of how to combine militancy and productivity is an issue that will continue to demand the attention of revolutionaries in Cuba and elsewhere in the Third World.

NOTES

1. For an extended discussion, see Maurice Zeitlin, *Revolutionary Politics and the Cuban Working Class* (Princeton, N.J.: Princeton University Press, 1967), pp. 45-65.

2. Claes Brundenius, "Development Strategies and Basic Needs in Revolutionary Cuba," in Claes Brundenius and Mats Lundhal, eds., *Development Strategies and Basic Needs in Latin America: Challenges for the 1980s* (Boulder, Colo.: Westview Press, 1982), p. 146.

3. Ibid., p. 147.

4. William M. LeoGrande, "Cuban Dependency: A Comparison of Pre-Revolutionary and Post-Revolutionary International Economic Relations," *Cuban Studies/Estudios Cubanos* 9, no. 2 (July 1979), p. 25.

5. The Popular Power experiment is discussed in William M. LeoGrande, "Mass Political Participation in Socialist Cuba," in John A. Booth and Mitchel A. Seligson, eds., *Political Participation in Latin America, Volume 1* (New York: Holmes and Meier Publishers, 1978), pp. 114-28.

24 Impressions on Twenty-Five Years of Change

Philip S. Foner

When news of the triumph of the Cuban Revolution reached me on January 1, 1959, I was determined to visit the island as soon as I could to see concrete evidence of what changes were taking place in Cuban society. I had been in Cuba before the revolution and had studied Cuban history. I had spent time in the Caribbean, Central America, and South America. I knew that speeches pledging reforms in the lives of the people were quite usual following the overthrow of a dictator in Latin America. I also knew that speeches were not enough. Too often, the change in government meant not the slightest change in the oppressed state of the mass of the people. Would this be the same now in Cuba?

I arrived with my wife in Havana in March 1960. I brought with me a booklet by Carlos Rafael Rodríguez, published by International Publishers of New York City, and offering an evaluation of the thinking of José Martí, the Cuban "Apostle." Carlos Rafael Rodríguez, a leading Communist, had fought with the 26th of July guerrilla forces in the Sierra Maestra. He was then the editor of the Communist daily paper *Hoy*. I brought him the copy of his booklet, and he asked me how long I planned to stay in Cuba. At least five weeks, I told him. "Then," he said, "you should visit Oriente and see where the revolution began and what is being accomplished, especially in the more backward sections of our country."

So off to Oriente we went. And I did see with my own eyes the beginnings of real changes in the lives of the Cuban people. The vast majority of the people in the countryside still lived in *bohíos*, thatched roofed huts with dirt floors and no water or sanitation facilities. However, with the aid of the Cuban revolutionary army, people were beginning to build new homes already—homes with decent facilities and indoor plumbing. In Las Mercedes, a community in Oriente, I saw an entire new village being constructed. New houses, stores, schools, and other facilities were springing up from the barren surroundings. In several places there were no buildings, but there were signs indicating that soon there would be a theater, a cinema, and a clinic on these spots. When I returned to Las Mercedes a year later, these facilities were in place and functioning.

High above Las Mercedes at the top of the Sierra Maestra, I saw the early stages in the construction of a school city, soon to be named Camilo Cienfuegos in honor of the great revolutionary who had disappeared during an airplane flight. Soldiers of the rebel army were building the school city. Children were already beginning to study in the buildings that had been completed. These children had come from villages in the mountains where educational facilities had barely existed, and where there were few roads. They would be studying at the school for a few months before returning home, since travel was so difficult. A number of peasants, parents of the children, were present, and I asked them if they were concerned about the fact that their children would be absent for such a long time. At this particular time there was a strong propaganda campaign in the United States charging that the Cuban Revolution was engaged in taking children from their parents and sending them to the Soviet Union to be indoctrinated in communism. The peasants laughed when I told them of these reports and pointed out that it was impossible to transport their children to school on a day-to-day basis because of poor transportation facilities. They were happy that their children could obtain an education in the school now being constructed. Several years later when I again visited the school on top of the Sierra Maestra, I found 10,000 students studying in the vastly expanded facilities.

During a visit to Caimanera in Oriente in April 1960, I saw fishermen painting a sign on a truck; it read, "Cooperativa Pescadores Caimanera, INRA." Proudly they pointed out to me that this was a refrigerated truck that the revolutionary government had turned over to the cooperative so that the fishermen could furnish the people in the area with fish. Previously, because of the lack of refrigeration, they had

had to discard whatever fish they could not dispose of quickly. This, I was told, was the first refrigerated facility in Cuban fishing operations.

In later visits to Cuba, I saw Cuban vessels engaged in a vast fishing operation with refrigeration facilities for operations while at sea. In Havana I was present at the opening of a huge refrigeration plant built with the assistance of the Soviet Union. In a short period a fully developed fishing industry has emerged in Cuba. Before the revolution nothing of this sort really existed.

During my visits to Cuba since 1960 I have witnessed the struggle waged by the Cuban Revolution against racism and the emergence of a multiracial society that can truly be a model for many other countries. While writing a multivolume work, *History of Cuba and its Relations with the United States* and *Antonio Maceo: The "Bronze Titan" of Cuba's Struggle for Independence*, and editing a five-volume edition of the writings of José Martí (translated into English), I have studied the history of race relations in Cuban history. While there is a significant antiracist tradition among the Cuban people, racism has also been a powerful influence in Cuba's struggle for independence. In addition to the racism in Cuba already, U.S.-style racism was brought to the island after the victory over Spain and the occupation by North America. During the decades of U.S. domination over Cuba from the first occupation in 1899 to the revolution in 1959, segregation in jobs, housing, and public facilities grew in Cuba. But the tradition of antiracism—the tradition associated with Antonio Maceo, José Martí, and later the Communist Party of Cuba—continued. Two weeks after the rebel army entered Havana, Fidel Castro said:

> There doesn't exist in Cuba the same problem that exists, for example, in the South of the United States. There is racial discrimination in Cuba but on a much lower level. Our Revolution will try to eliminate these prejudices and injustices that remain.
>
> In our revolutionary struggle we have seen the absolute brotherhood and identification of people of all colors. In this sense, our thinking is that of Martí. We would not be revolutionaries or democrats if we were not to divest ourselves of all types of discrimination.

I witnessed how the new revolutionary government moved on the legal front to open up to black Cubans the facilities and services from which they had been totally barred. I saw how the new government made public all beaches, hotels, and restaurants. These facilities were ordered to admit blacks or have their doors closed. Neighborhood discrimination was ordered to cease, and all professions previously denied to blacks were declared open to all. But it was when unemployment was eliminated in Cuban life that the single most important blow against racism was delivered. With the elimination of unemployment, competition between workers for what had been a limited number of jobs was eliminated.

There are still racial prejudices among some Cubans. However, I am confident that this will ultimately disappear.

One of my most memorable experiences relates to the Isle of Youth. Previously called the Isle of Pines, the island is less than an hour's flight south of Havana. When I first visited the Isle in 1967 it was to accompany members of the Institute of History who had interrupted a series of lectures on American labor history I was delivering at the Capitolio in Havana to plant citrus trees on the isle. I went along to help and to lecture in the evenings, continuing the course that started in Havana.

At that time we visited the isle it was a fairly barren place with poor roads, where they existed, and few buildings apart from those constructed for rich American tourists who could come in their expensive boats or private planes. The isle also contained a prison where both José Martí and Fidel Castro had been incarcerated.

In 1982 I revisited the Isle of Youth. Roads covered the entire isle, and they were in fine condition. New apartment houses had been built for citrus workers and for workers in the ceramics industry. Schools were everywhere, and the former prison was now a museum. The Isle of Youth holds nearly 60 boarding schools for youngsters of high-school age. Over 20 are for non-Cubans. These are youngsters from Namibia, Mozambique, Angola, Nicaragua, and other Third World countries. The youngsters from Africa and Latin America are learning to prepare themselves for work in their own countries. While half the student body attends classes, the other half tends citrus groves—"to learn the dignity of work."

In a school for Nicaraguan youngsters, I spoke of the support in the United States from 1927 to 1933 for the guerrilla movement led by Augusto Nicolás Calderón Sandino and the opposition to the presence of U.S. Marines in Nicaragua. I left the Isle of Youth convinced that the Cuban Revolution was making many friends in the Third World.

During repeated visits to Cuba I could see how the U.S. embargo has caused economic hardships. By U.S. standards Cuba is still a poor country. Luxuries and many routine items are scarce, and staples are rationed. However, there are no beggars on the streets. People look healthy and well fed. Abject poverty has been abolished, something exceedingly rare in Latin America. There is, to be sure, little food diversity and the choices are fairly limited, but the average Cuban worker can go to special cafeterias that offer breakfast, lunch, and dinner at subsidized prices. Cubans can go into a good restaurant at least once a week with the family and enjoy a fine meal, and they now can go to the "free markets" where pork, beans, and other commodities are sold unrationed by farmers who produce a surplus after fulfilling their government quotas. Indeed, Cuba is succeeding in keeping rural incomes sufficiently high to encourage people to stay on the land and grow food.

There are still dingy, crowded flats in downtown Havana with no running water, but there is a master plan in operation to eliminate them. Despite a continuing housing shortage, more and more Cubans are enjoying adequate housing. Much of it is constructed by the Cuban people themselves, with government assistance, in the form of the famous "microbrigades."

I have personally witnessed the decline of malnutrition in Cuba, from a level of 40 percent to less than 5 percent. In 1960 when I first visited the new Cuba, the country spent 25.80 pesos per person in social services. In 1983, on my last visit, it spent 423 pesos per person.

I have visited Cuba 15 times since the revolution. I did so to engage in research in the Archivo Nacional and other libraries and historical societies in connection with research for my works on Cuban history and the relations between Cuba and the United States. I also came to teach American history, American labor history, and the history of black Americans at the University of Havana, the University of Las Villas, and the University of Oriente. In the course of my visits, I have traveled the length and breadth of the island over and over. I have been able to witness how small, underdeveloped Cuba eliminated hunger, illiteracy, and unemployment, how it provided education, medical facilities and adequate housing for great masses of its population, and how it effectively eliminated racism from its society.

25 Cuba: A Personal Overview

Margaret Randall

Cuba: a personal overview? What would that be? I had hoped to have time to write something more formal, perhaps a piece on Cuban women or on Cuban culture (the two areas about which I feel most qualified to speak), but the deadline coincided with my move back to the United States after 23 years in Latin America, and the extenuating circumstances made that more "formal" piece impossible. So, a personal overview—could that be of any use, in a book of this type? Perhaps it could.

I lived in Cuba from 1969 to 1980. My four children did a good deal of their growing up there. I wrote more than a dozen books while living there, two of them about Cuban women and one about a peasant playwright. I was a participant as well as an observer of the struggle of women in that country; and I was also closely involved in aspects of the cultural explosion that has characterized the Cuban revolutionary process.

My first contact with Cuba was through its poets. In Mexico of the sixties and through my editing of a bilingual cultural magazine *El Corno Emplumado*, I came in contact with what poets, writers, and graphic artists were doing on that blockaded island. *El Corno* devoted some of its pages to Cuban work for the first time in 1962, and in 1967 it published an entire issue (in Spanish and English) of Cuban artistic expression. That same year I visited the island for the first time, invited to a meeting of poets honoring the one-hundredth anniversary of Rubén Darío. In 1968 I returned, along with 600 others, to the Cultural

Congress of Havana; and in 1969, I went there to live—an experience that would last 12 years.

Looking back on that experience, I think one of its most valuable aspects for me was something many might find surprising, that is, the Cubans' extraordinary capacity to be experimental, open, and honest about their mistakes (often leaving themselves open to extremely ill-intentioned and unfair pokes in the process, especially in the early years). It always amazed me that foreign writers came to a place like Cuba, and after staying a week or ten days (occasionally a bit longer), they went off to write some "definitive" assessment of foreign or domestic policy, the economy, the cultural scene, women, the Church, agriculture, and any other of an endless series of subjects.

A people's revolution is made, essentially, by people. That may seem like a truism, but it sadly needs to be repeated and repeated. Certainly historic time and place are important, the reaction of other nations (especially powerful ones) can be deeply affecting, and world events often aid (or conspire against) certain plans; but the revolution comes from the people, their particular history, their needs, their dreams and culture, even the way the liberation war was waged. Those who have had to become adept and articulate at wresting state power, suddenly have that power in their hands. What to do with it?

And so the revolutionary process, that process of social change (based, of course, on economic and political change), is an experiment. One change is attempted; if it works, great, if it doesn't, it's dumped and something else is tried in its place. Inspiration, as well as lessons of all kinds, come from preceding revolutionary experiences. However, each nation must contend with its own history, needs, and vision. Sometimes mistakes are costly and set back a process more than is immediately apparent. In a context of honest searching, channels are gradually institutionalized through which experimentation becomes both creative and productive.

The deepest and most lasting impression of my Cuban experience is that Cubans have the capacity to see the trees *and* the forest, the ability to continually evaluate progress and be frank about errors, giving people a solid participation in solutions, that they share with the world information about what went wrong from time to time, as well as the revolution's extraordinary achievements.

The Cuban Revolution was able to educate its people (beginning with a literacy campaign that reduced illiteracy to under 3 percent of the population). It was able to almost entirely eradicate unemployment, launch a housing program that has given shelter—if not yet always adequate shelter—to everyone, slowly but surely develop one of the finest and most comprehensive (and free) public health systems in Latin America, distribute its food and commodities fairly, encourage art and culture in the most distant areas of the country, give dignity to blacks and to women for the first time in their history, and set an example of principled government and real internationalism through a quarter of a century of crisis.

However, the critics are quick to say that the Cuban Revolution made economic errors in the 1960s that cost the people years of comfort and progress. This is true. The ideological aspect of the women's struggle was slow to get off the ground in Cuba, and economic equality proved not to be enough to totally eradicate sex discrimination. This is true as well. Gays have been mistreated and harassed in Cuba. A revolutionary understanding of gay humanity is relatively new in the country, and homophobia still needs to be struggled against. All of that is also true.

But what does this mean? Simply that the Cubans, as well as ourselves, are women and men, ordinary humans who make mistakes and who have—by the way—conceived, won, and kept alive and growing the first socialist revolution on this continent. One without which all subsequent struggles, if not impossible, would certainly have taken much longer, perhaps centuries longer.

I feel fortunate, indeed privileged, to have lived in Cuba during those years of experimentation. Through my children, I experienced the changes in a nationwide educational system. No more than 50 percent of Cuban youths even went to school before the victory in 1959. Logically, the Cubans saw their first task to be that of sending all children to school—to makeshift classrooms under the shade of country trees, as well as to the incredibly complete and beautiful work-and-study units that almost from the beginning began to change their national landscape. First it was the general challenge, education for everyone, then came the particulars. Some thought the schools were too regimented, other thought the quality of education needed to be improved. I saw those things happen; I was involved in the discussions, the evaluations, the improvements.

Health care is another example. First, it was made available to everyone—at whatever painfully low level was possible. Then the more in-depth work began. I remember how in 1969 and 1970 family members had to attend to our ill in hospitals; there were not enough staff members—conditions were still minimal. (Half the nation's doctors had left the country in 1959, many lured by offers of excellent jobs in the United States). Gradually the health system improved, not only in the larger cities, but in the remote mountain regions as well. Even during the most difficult times, the concept engendered confidence. No one was going to operate, prescribe lengthy treatment, or pull a tooth for money. No money changed hands. Health care was based on what the individual needed. But the Cubans were not satisfied with even those internationally recognized strides. In recent years the general polyclinic system, which was developed during the 1960s has been replaced by a more personal approach. Once good basic health care had been made available to everyone, it was possible to look at psychological and integral implications. Now almost throughout the country teams of doctors and health workers attend to reduced areas of population; these professionals get to know their patients while healthy, not just while they are ill. Therein lies the possibility for more personal, in-depth attention.

In 1973, when the Cubans realized they needed more effective participation by workers in the decisions affecting their lives, they strengthened their union movement. Previously, no one had been all that sure how unions were supposed to work under socialism! When it became clear that the Party was inadvertently taking on administrative tasks, a people's democracy developed an electoral process that institutionalized popular participation in government, and Cuban "people's power" became a system of national, regional, and municipal assemblies with free elections and direct representation. When the Cubans realized they were losing ground in their struggle for women's liberation and integration, they took stock of the situation, went nationwide in popular discussion, and revised legislation affecting women's lives as well as intensifying ideological work around the social effects of sexism. When the Cubans saw that their attitude toward homosexuals was antiquated and unrevolutionary (indeed that there were problems in sex education in general), they brought in a team of German sexologists who, working with the Cubans, began to structure changes in that difficult area. Results included a widely distributed book on human sexuality that treats homosexuality as a "natural way of relating between so-inclined adults." When liberation theology began to make the power of its message felt throughout Latin America, the Cubans looked at their own difficult state-church relationship and made the first moves toward understanding and commitment on both sides.

Foreigners have gone to Cuba for the past 25 years. What they find there often depends on their own preconceived notions as well as on the particular moment in Cuban revolutionary history they are able to touch. And so they write differing reports—cautious, superlative, purely descriptive (no commitment is better than the wrong commitment), flip, cute, or insightful. What rarely emerges, is a recognition of the extraordinary task the Cubans have tackled and sustained, that is, the task of changing their society according to their needs, while constantly facing the active hostility of the strongest nation on earth (just 90 miles from their coast). Also, the amazing openness and renewal that has been a part of that process is rarely recognized.

While engaged in this multifaceted task, the Cubans consistently have been an example in internationalism. They have offered aid, ranging from technical advice, health and education support, and construction work, to the giving of many Cuban lives, to more than 30 other countries—countries of the Third World, which are poorer and less developed than Cuba.

Let this stand, then, as my personal overview: gratitude for the mistakes as well as the achievements, gratitude for the courage and creativity as well as the tenacity and resistance.

Index

Abortion, 83
Adventures of Juan Quin Quin, 140
Affirmative action, 88
Afghanistan, invasion of, 365
Agrarian Reform Law
   (1959), 200
   (1963), 201
Agriculture, 8, 12, 66, 186, 200, 201, 225, 263
   see also Farmers
Aguirre, Mirta, 161, 164
Almeida, Juan, 241
Alvarez, Santiago, 138, 141, 144
Alvor agreement, 341, 343
ANAP. *See* National Association of Small Farmers
Angola, 340-43, 365, 366, 372, 373, 377, 386
Antonio Echevarría, José, 102
Arce Martínez, Sergio, 108
Argenter, Miró, 236
Arias, 163
Arlt, Roberto, 160
Army of Working Youth, 190
Army. *See* Rebel Army
Arrufat, Antón, 164
Arrupe, Pedro, 101
Art, 10, 121
   literature on, 401
Art education, 121
Así en la paz como en la guerra, 162
Assets, redistribution of, 198-204
Authors. *See* Literature
Azicri, Max, 15

Barre, Siad, 344, 345
Bastarache, Yvon, 109
Batista, Fulgencio, 4, 97, 99
Battle of Chile, The, 151
Battle of San Juan Hill, The, 136
Bay of Pigs (film), 140, 141, 151
Bay of Pigs (invasion), 67, 99, 244, 337
   literature on, 399
Benedetti, Mario, 166
Benjamin, Medea, 4, 9, 12
Berman, Harold, 311, 312
Bernardo, Robert, 183, 198
Bibliography, of literature on Cuban Revolution, 402-12
Biblioteca Nacional José Martí, 160
Biografía de un cimarrón, 170
Birth control, 83
Bishop, Maurice, 373, 431
Blacks, 439, 444
   Education of, 31
   in film, 149
   literature on, 401
Bloom, Harold, 156
Boal, Augusto, 127
Bohemia, 124, 157, 163
Bolívar, Simón, 334
Bonsal, Philip, 335
Book production, 120
Borges, 155, 156, 163, 166
Boti, Regino, 160, 161
Bray, Donald, 17
Brecht, Bertolt, 127
Brundenius, Claes, 9, 12, 432
Buenaventura, Enrique, 127

Bueno, Salvador, 162, 163
Büntig, Aldo J., 109

Cabrera Infante, Guillermo, 159, 162, 171
Cabildo Teatral, 128
Caimán Barbudo, 124, 162
Canción de Rachel, 170
Canto General, 164
Capitán de cimarrones, 171
Caridad Colón, María, 87
Carpentier, Alejo, 118, 120, 158, 161, 164, 165, 166, 168, 170, 171, 172
Carrión, Miguel de, 160, 161
Carteles, 157
Carter, James, 343, 344, 349, 366
Casa de cultura, 124-25
Casa de las Américas, 120, 122, 159, 162, 166, 167
Castro, Fidel, 3, 6, 7, 16, 19-24, 36, 37, 67, 72, 80, 81, 82, 84, 86, 88, 94, 96, 98, 99, 101, 119, 121, 122, 177, 181, 186, 216, 217, 220, 236, 237, 238, 239, 241, 242, 244, 245, 251, 252, 253, 254, 157, 263, 266, 272, 274, 296, 297, 299, 302, 303, 314, 315, 322, 334, 335, 337, 338, 339, 341, 341, 343, 349, 354, 355, 356, 359, 360, 361, 368, 378, 439
Castro, Raúl, 241, 255, 256, 257, 274, 293
Catholic Church, 93-111
Cazabandido, 169
Central budgeting, 180-181, 183, 184
Centralization, 187-188, 273, 292
Cespedes, Msgr. Carlos Manuel de, 105
Chaple, Sergio, 160
Charcoal Worker, The, 137
Chávez, Rebeca, 149
Chronicles of War, 236
Ciclón, 157, 158
Cienfuegos, Camilo, 236, 238, 241, 242
Cine Cubano, 142, 150
Cinema. *See* Film
Cine Rebelde, 135
Civil code, 324

Class structure. *See* Social structure
Clothing, 196
Colina, Enrique, 150
Collins, Joseph, 4, 9, 12
Commission on Medicine in the Community, 53-55
Committees for the Defense of the Revolution (CDR), 262, 263, 359
Communism, 181-87
Communist Party, relationship with Organs of People's Power, 270-89
  see also Partido Comunista de Cuba (PCC)
Condenados de Condado, 169
Confederation of Cuban Workers (CTC), 262, 264-65
Conjunto, 160, 162
Conjunto Dramático de Oriente, 128
Consejo Nacional de Cultura (CNC), 120, 121, 123
Constitution (1976), 315, 320, 321-23
Construction, overseas, 374
Coppola, Francis Ford, 139
Cortázar, Octavio, 140
Cortázar, Julio, 155
Council of Ministers, 258, 259, 274, 275, 281, 282, 288, 322
Cristo vivo en Cuba, 108
Cuba Internacional, 163
Cuban Communist Party. *See* Patrido Comunista de Cuba (PCC)
Cuban Institute of Cinematographic Art and Industry (ICAIC), 120, 122, 135, 137, 140, 142, 143-52
Cuban Medical Federation, 46-47
Cuban Workers' Confederation (CTC), 291-303
Cuentos cubanos del siglo XX, 162
Cultural Congress of Havana (1968), 122
Culture, 9-10, 444
  government sponsorship of, 118
  literature on, 401
  see also Popular culture
  statistics, 23
Czechoslavakia, invasion of, 365

Daniel, Jean, 338
Danielson, Ross, 9
Day care centers, 31–32, 85
Death and Life in El Morrillo, 141
Death of a Bureaucrat, 134, 140
Desnoes, Edmundo, 156
Dewart, Leslie, 95
Dialéctica del espectador, 142
Diario de la Marina, 157
Díaz, Jesús, 149
Díaz, Martínez, Manuel, 165
Diego Cañizares, Fernando, 313
Diego, Eliseo, 126, 171
Direccíon de Cultura, Ministry of Education, 119, 120
Discusión, 157
Disease, 198
  statistics, 5, 60, 64
Dispensarization, 57
Divorce, 84, 85, 90
Doctors. *See* Physicians
Domînguez, Jorge I., 29
Dorticós, Osvaldo, 314

Eckstein, Susan, 17
Economic growth, 12, 22, 23, 204–208
Economic planning, 7, 10–11, 213–27, 427
Economic policy, 177–92, 434
Economy of Socialist Cuba: A Two Decade Appraisal, 213
Edelstein, Joel, 12
Eder, Dick, 338
Education, 5–6, 7, 8, 9, 22, 27–42, 120, 195–98, 415, 421
  art, 121
  of blacks, 31
  curriculum change, 39
  literature on, 401
  overseas, 374
  political, 233, 239, 240
  for rural population, 35–36
  statistics, 5, 23, 27, 30, 31, 34, 35
  testing, 39
  of women, 31, 83, 88
El Caimán Barbudo, 162

El ingenio, 167, 170
El Mégano, 137
El mundo alucinante, 170
El Nacional, 157
El recurso del método, 170
Employment, 5, 6, 8, 65, 66, 194–195, 196, 299, 432, 444
  statistics, 194–195, 196
  for women, 80, 83–84, 85–86, 88, 195, 196
  see also Labor force; Wage scales
Epstein, Erwin, 29
Escalante, Aníbal, 253, 254
Espín, Vilma, 83, 87, 89
Esta Tierra Nuestra, 135
Ethiopia, 372, 373

Family Code (1975), 86, 88, 315, 323, 324–25
FAR. *See* Fuerzas Armadas Revolucionarias
Farmers, 65, 262, 264
  markets, 72–73, 225, 263
  see also Agriculture
Federation of Cuban Women (FMC), 80, 82–83, 87–88, 262, 265–66
  see also Women
Feijóo, Samuel, 163
Fernández, José R., 33, 35, 40
Fernández Retamar, Roberto, 158, 159, 164, 165, 166, 171
Fighting With Our Boys in Cuba, 136
Film, 10, 120, 135–52
  literature on, 401
First Charge of the Machete, 141, 151
First Conference of Writers and Artists (1961), 121
Five Year Plan
  (1976–80), 121, 207
  (1981–85), 208
FNLA, 340, 341, 342
Foner, Philip, 17
Food
  consumption, 5
  distribution, 7, 12, 62–76, 195–98, **444**

prices, 69, 70, 72–73, 75, 76
rationing, 69–71, 73–76, 178, 183
statistics, 62
Ford, Gerald R., 341
Foreign relations
literature on, 399
with U.S., 17, 333–50
with U.S.S.R., 189–91, 208, 334, 352–68, 376–78
Foreign trade, 22–23, 379
Fornet, Ambrosio, 165
For the First Time, 140
Fraga, Jorge, 137, 141, 144, 148, 149
Frank, Andre Gunder, 17
Fuentes, Carlos, 154
Fuentes, Norberto, 169
Fuerzas Armadas Revolucionarias (FAR), 233
Fuller, Linda, 221

Gabaldón, Argimiro, 245
Galiano, Carlos, 150
Gálvez, William, 241
García, Alejandro, 125
García Espinosa, Julio, 135, 136, 137, 140, 141, 142, 144, 148, 150, 151, 152
García Márquez, 155, 368
García Marruz, Fina, 171
Genette, Gérard, 166,
Giral, Sergio, 149
González, Reynaldo, 170
González, Sara, 125, 126
Goytisola, Juan, 155
Grande Sertão Veredas, 164
Granma (newspaper) 106, 124, 150, 163, 256, 272, 277, 298
Granma (yacht), 238, 239, 244
Group of 77, 357
Grupo La Yaya, 129
Grupo Moncada, 126
Grupo Teatro Escambray, 129
Guevara, Alfredo, 135, 137, 142, 144, 145
Guevara, Ernesto "Ché," 65, 125, 169, 180, 215, 216, 236, 240, 241, 242, 243, 244, 245, 246, 252, 337, 339, 355, 356
Guillén, Nicolás, 158, 160, 165, 166, 171
Guimarães Rosa, 164
Gutiérrez Alea, Tomás, 134, 135, 137, 139, 140, 141
Gutiérrez, Gustavo, 93
Guzmán, Patricio, 151

Haig, Alexander, 366
Ham Reyes, Adolfo, 108, 110
Hart, Armando, 120, 122, 123, 150, 167
Hasta Cierto Punto, 141
Haydu, Jorge, 137
Health care, 5, 7, 8, 9, 22, 33–34, 45–60, 64, 195–98, 444–45
literature on, 401
overseas, 374
rural population, 5
statistics, 5, 23, 50, 60, 198–99
for women, 83
Herrera, José, 220
Herrera, Manuel, 140, 149, 151
Hicks, Norman, 206
Higher Institute of Art (ISA), 121
Hijacking agreement, 339–40, 347–48
Historias de la Revolución, 140
Historias de una Infamia, 141
History of an Infamy, 141
History of Cuba and its Relations with the United States, 439
Hollingsworth, Charles, 161
Hombres de Mal Tiempo, 141
Hospitals. *See* Health care
Housing, 5, 8, 84, 182, 195–98, 200, 220, 414, 444
statistics, 6, 23, 197, 381

ICAIC. *See* Cuban Institute of Cinematographic Art and Industry
Iglesias, Joel, 241
Illiteracy. *See* Literacy
Incentives. *See* Material incentives; Moral incentives

Income
  per capita, 62, 217
  redistribution of, 66, 193–210
  see also Wage scales
Infant mortality, 60, 63–64, 83, 198
Institute for Health Development, 59
Institute of Internal Demands, 225
Instituto de Lingüística y Literatura, 161
Internationalism, 372-88
Irakere, 126
Islas, 158, 159, 161, 162

Jørgensen, B., 280
JUCEPLAN. *See* Junta Central de Planificación
Judicial system. *See* Legal system
Judson, C. Fred, 15
Junta Central de Planificación (JUCEPLAN), 222, 223, 224, 225, 260, 275, 301
Juventud Rebelde, 124, 277

Kampuchea, invasion of, 365
Kennedy, John F., 338
Kirk, John M., 9
Khrushchev, Nikita, 337
Kissinger, Henry, 340, 341
Kristeva, Julia, 166

Labor force, 182–90, 220–21, 264–65, 291–303
  literature on, 401
  see also Employment
La consagración de la primavera, 168
La crítica literaria y estética en el siglo XIX cubano, 160
La expresión americana, 168
La fiesta de los tiburones, 170
La Gaceta de Cuba, 160, 162, 165, 166, 167
Las honradas, 160
Las impuras, 160
La Muerte de Artemio Cruz, 154
La Muerte de un Burócrata, 134
La Nación, 157
La noche de los asesinos, 171

La Pasión de Urbino, 159
Last Supper, The, 141
Latin American Economic System (SELA), 362
Latin American Film Market (MECLA), 150
La última mujer y el próximo combate, 164
La Vibienda, 135
Law 4, 320
Law 21, Penal Code (1979), 315, 323, 325–26
Law 1250, 318–20
Law 1289, Family Code (1975), 86, 88, 315, 323, 324–25
Law. *See* Legal system
Leante, César, 159, 171
Legal system, 307–27
Leiner, Marvin, 9
Lezama Lima, José, 158, 161, 164, 165, 166, 168, 171, 172
Libya, 373
Libraries, 121
Life expectancy, 60, 64
Literacy, 119
  statistics, 5, 29
Literacy campaign, 29, 41, 426, 443
Literary criticism, 158–59, 163, 167–68
Literature, 10, 154–72, 393–412
L/L, 160
López, Cofiño, 164
López, Rigoberto, 149
Los pasos perdidos, 164
Lucía, 140, 141, 150
Lugo, Ismael de, 99
Lunes de Revolución, 158

Maceo, Antonio, 235, 243, 439
MacEwan, Arthur, 17
Makhnenko, Aleksandr, 312
Malnutrition. *See* Nutrition
Maluala, 149
Manguaré, 126
Manual de Capacitación Cívica, 235
Marcha, 158
Marinello, Juan, 163, 164, 165, 167, 171

Martí, José, 3, 6, 89, 122, 134, 150, 160, 236–37, 244, 246, 334, 437, 439
Mass organizations, 261–66, 277, 293, 420
Mater el Magistra, 101
Material incentives, 215–216, 219, 221, 298
Mecham, J. Lloyd, 96
Medical Federation. *See* Cuban Medical Federation
Medicine. *See* Health care
Mella, 140
Memorias del subdesarrollo, 156
Memories of Underdevelopment, 134, 139, 140, 141, 144, 156
Men from Mal Tiempo, 141
Merryman, John H., 318
Mesa-Lago, Carmelo, 213, 224, 225
Microbrigades, 220
Mikoyan, Anastas, 98, 336
Milanés, Pablo, 125
Military Territorial Courts, 320
Ministry of Culture, 120, 122, 124, 130, 131
Ministry of Education, 119, 120, 123
Ministry of Public Health, 48, 51, 53, 55
Moral incentives, 183–90, 201, 215, 273, 292
Moreno Fraginals, Manuel, 167
Morley, Morris, 17
Movement of Nonaligned Countries, 357
Movies. *See* Film
Mozambique, 373
MPLA. *See* Popular Movement for the Liberation of Angola
Muerte y Vida en El Morrillo, 141
Municipal assemblies, 274, 275, 278–81
Museums, 121
Music, 10, 125–27, 131

National Assembly, 258, 259, 260, 274, 275, 279, 281–87, 288–89, 320, 322
National Association of Small Farmers (ANAP), 262, 264
National Congress of Culture (1962), 121
National Publishing House, 120
National Rationing Board (OFICODA), 68
National School of Art (ENA), 121
Nelson, Lowry, 28, 63
Neruda, Pablo, 164
Neto, Agostinho, 341
New Jewel Movement, 373, 431
New System of Economic Management and Planning, 222–25
New Theater, 127–30
New York Times, 338
Nicaragua, 109, 367, 374
Nicola, Nöel, 125
No Hay Sábado Sin Sol, 149
Novás Calvo, Lino, 162
Nuclear weapons, 354
Nuestro Tiempo, 137, 158
Nueva Trova, 125–27
Nuevo Teatro, 128
Nutrition, 5, 9, 41, 63, 64, 441

Octavio Gómez, Manuel, 141, 150, 151
One Way or Another, 141, 149
OPEC, 359, 360
Organization of African Unity, 341
Organization of American States (OAS), 336, 337, 339, 340
Organs of Popular Power (OPP), 189, 258–60, 320, 322
  relationship with Communist Party, 270–89
Oriente, 161
Orígenes, 157, 158, 171
Ortega, Daniel, 109
Ortega y Gasset, 156
Otero, Blas de, 155
Ortiz, Fernando, 118
Other Francisco, The, 140, 141
Our Times, 137
Overseas programs. *See* Foreign relations; Internationalism

Padilla, Herberto, 144, 164, 171
Padula, Alfred, 9
País, Frank, 238, 241
Para una teoría de la literatura hispanoamericana y otras aproximaciones, 164
Parallel market, 73-75
Parrales, Edgar, 353
Partido Communista de Cuba (PCC), 253, 254, 256, 257, 258, 259, 260, 265, 267, 270-89, 292, 293, 294, 320, 321, 421, 424
Pashukanis, E.B., 311
Patakin, 151
Paz, Octavio, 155, 163, 166
PCC. *See* Partido Communista de Cuba
Penal Code (1979), 315, 323, 325-26
People's Power, 120, 121, 124
People's Provincial Courts, 319, 320
People's Regional Courts, 319
People's Supreme Court, 319, 320
People's Tribunals, 308
Peral Collado, Daniel A., 324, 325
Pereira, Manuel, 168
Perfeccionamiento plan, 32
Peru, construction in, 374
Pérez, Amaury, 125
Pérez, Humberto, 224, 225, 259, 260, 261, 301
Pérez, Louis, Jr., 4, 17
Pérez Serantes, Msgr. Enrique, 97, 110
Pérez-Stable, Marifeli, 12, 15, 220
Physicians, 33-34, 46, 54-60
  see also health care; Polyclinics
  statistics, 45
Piché, Gisèle, 103, 104
Piñea Barnet, Enrique, 140
Plays. *See* Theater
Political education, 233, 239, 240
Political structure, 15, 251-67, 270-89
Politics
  literature on, 400
  women in, 86, 89, 265
Polvo Rojo, 149
Polyclinics, 48, 50-59, 445
Popular Councils of Culture, 121
Popular courts, 314, 317

Popular culture, 117-31
Popular Movement for the Liberation of Angola (MPLA), 340, 341, 342, 366
Popular Power, 222-23, 435
Population, 8-9, 65
Portrait of Teresa, 85, 141, 149
Portuondo, José Antonio, 161, 163, 164, 165, 166
Prebisch, Raúl, 356
Priests, 95
Programme of Action, 195
Prostitution, 80-81
Protestant Church, 95, 108
Provincial assemblies, 274, 275, 279, 281-82, 320
Pueblo y Cultura, 123

Quotas, production, 219

Radio, 121
Raising Old Glory Over Moro Castle, 136
Ramos, Eduardo, 125
Randall, Margaret, 17
Rapkin, Rhoda Pearl, 15
Rationing system, food, 68-70, 71, 73-76, 178, 183
Reagan, Ronald, 350, 364, 366-68
Rebel Army, 233, 235, 239-42, 416, 417
Red Dust, 149
Redistribution with Growth, 193
Relaciones, 128
Religion, 93-111
  literature on, 401
Rent Reform (1959), 200
Retrato de Teresa, 149
Revista Cubana, 157
Revista Cubana de Administración de Salud, 59
Revista Cubana de Derecho, 313
Revista de Avance, 157
Revista de la Biblioteca Nacional José Martí, 162
Revolución, 158
Revolucion y Cultura, 123-24, 163

Revolutionary, in *Verde Olivo*, 233–46
Risquet, 218, 220
Roa, Raúl, 101, 335
Roberto, Holden, 340, 341, 342
Robins, Carla Anne, 367
Rodríguez, Carlos Rafael, 215, 260, 264, 347, 348, 437
Rodríguez Feo, Jose, 171
Rodriguez, Silvio, 125
Rogers, William D., 340
Romero, Oscar, 107
Rosenkranz, Hernán, 220
Ruiz, Ramón, 424

Saderman, Alejandro, 141
Salas, Luis, 81
Sánchez, Rutilio, 106
Santamaría, Abel, 236, 237
Santiago, 159, 162
Sardiñas, Guillermo, 97
Sastre, Alfonso, 155
Savimbi, Jonas, 340, 341
School for Exact Sciences, 38
Schools. *See* Education
Schroeder, Susan, 6
SDPE. *See* New System of Economic Management and Planning
Second Party Congress (1980), 323
Seers, Dudley, 198, 206
Selassie, Haile, 344
Self-finance, 180–81
Sheer, Robert, 5
Siempre, 158
Sierra Maestra, 97, 238, 239, 240, 241, 244, 272, 437
Signos, 162
Silverman, Bertram, 181, 184
Simparele, 141
Smith, Lois, 9
Smith, Wayne, 3, 16
Social, 157
Social conditions, 5, 7
Social medicine, 46–48
Social structure, 5, 7
Sociedad Cubana de Administración de Salud, 59

Solas, Humberto, 149, 150
Son O No Son, 151
Sorel, 236, 242
Sports, women in, 87
Stockwell, John, 342
Stores, government owned, 69
Stories from the Revolution, 140
Sugar
  prices, 208, 297, 381, 435
  production, 179, 184, 186, 189, 206, 217, 254, 273, 292, 315, 432
Sur, 157
Sussex Institute of Development Studies, 193
Symbolism, 15

Teachers, 27, 28, 36–38
  see also Education
  statistics, 28, 37
Teatro de Participación Popular (TPP), 129
Teatro Experimental de Cali (TEC), 127
Television, 121
Theater, 127–30
There's No Saturday Without Sunshine, 149
Third World Nations, 17, 352–68, 372–88, 431–32
Third World, Third World War, 140
This is our Land, 135
Torres, Miguel, 141
Tourist industry, 121, 366, 417
Trade. *See* Foreign trade
Trade embargo (1960), 66–67
Trade unions, 15, 218–19, 221, 273, 291–303, 420, 423, 445
Tres tristes tigres, 159, 171
Tribunales Populares, 314, 317
Tribuna Médica, 46
Trujillo, Marisol, 149
Twelfth Workers' Congress (1966), 201

Unemployment. *See* Employment
Unión, 159, 162, 165
Unión de Jóvenes Comunistas (UJC), 277

UNITA, 340, 341
United Nations Conference on Trade and Development (UNCTAD), 356, 357, 358, 359
United Nations Economic Commission for Latin America (ECLA), 356, 358
Universidad de La Habana, 158, 159, 161, 162
Up to a Certain Point, 141
Urban Reform Law, 97, 414
U.S.-Cuban relations, 17, 333–50
U.S.S.R., 189–91, 208, 334, 352–68, 376–78

Valde, Oscar, 141
Valle, Sergio del, 33, 34
Vance, Cyrus, 344
Van Whiting, 312
Vega, 141, 149, 151
Vega, Belkis, 149
Veiga, Roberto, 264, 298, 301
Verde Olivo, revolutionary symbolism in, 233–46
Vertov, Dziga, 138
Vietnam, 374
Vilaris, Mayra, 149
Villapol, Nitza, 63
Virulo, 125, 126
Visión, 137
Vitier, Cintio, 158, 160, 171

Viva la República, 151
Vyshinsky, Á.Y., 311

Wage scales, 8, 65, 182, 201, 203, 216, 298
see also Income
With the Cuban Women, 140
Women, 9, 79–91, 444
education of, 31, 83, 88
employment for, 80, 83–84, 85–86, 88, 195, 196
in film, 149
health care for, 83
literature on, 401
in politics, 86, 89, 265
rights of, 126
see also Federation of Cuban Women (FMC)
in sports, 87
Woodford, Marjorie, 17
Workers' Theatre, 127
World Bank, 193
World Employment Conference (1976), 195
Writers, 121
see also Literature

Yabur, Alfredo, 314
Young, Andrew, 366

Zacchi, Msgr. Cesare, 100, 101, 104, 109
Zimbalist, Andrew, 12

About the Editors

SANDOR HALEBSKY is professor of sociology at Saint Mary's University, Halifax, Nova Scotia, Canada. He holds a B.A. in sociology from City College of New York and a Ph.D. in sociology from Cornell University. Professor Halebsky is the author of *Mass Society and Political Conflict: Towards a Reconstruction of Theory* (Cambridge, England: Cambridge University Press, 1976), which was translated into Portuguese and published in Brazil as *Sociedade de Massa e Conflito Politico* (Rio de Janeiro: Sahar Editores, 1978). He is the editor of *The Sociology of the City* (New York: Charles Scribner's Sons, 1973), and his work has also appeared in the *Administrative Science Quarterly* and the *Journal of Political and Military Sociology*.

JOHN M. KIRK is associate professor at Dalhousie University, Halifax, Nova Scotia, Canada. He holds a B.A. in Hispanic studies from the University of Sheffield, an M.A. in Latin American literature from Queen's University, Ontario, and a Ph.D. in Latin American Studies from the University of British Columbia. He is the author of *José Martí, Mentor of the Cuban Nation* (Gainesville, Fla.: University Presses of Florida, 1983) and the coeditor of *A Fist and the Letter: Revolutionary Poetry from Latin America* (Vancouver, B.C.: Pulp Press, 1977), and he has published articles in *Latin American Research Review, Cuadernos Americanos, Journal of Latin American Studies, North-South* and the *International Fiction Review*. He is currently studying the role of religion in revolutionary society, specifically examining Cuba and Nicaragua.

About the Contributors

MAX AZICRI is professor of political science at Edinboro University of Pennsylvania. He holds a Ph.D. and M.A. in political science from the University of Southern California, a Doctor of Laws (LL.D.) from the University of Havana, and a degree in journalism from the Havana School of Journalism, "Manuel Márquez Sterling." Dr. Azicri has written extensively on Cuban society and its politics, legal system, and international relations since 1959, as well as on cultural and political changes among Cubans living in the United States. His present work in progress includes a book-length manuscript, *Cuba: Politics, Economics, and Society*, to be published in the United States and England in late 1985.

MEDEA BENJAMIN works at the Institute for Food Development, where she is coordinator of the Central American program. For the last ten years she has lived and worked in Africa and Latin America (as a nutritionist and economist for the Food and Agriculture Organization of the United Nations and the Swedish International Development Agency). Ms. Benjamin holds an M.A. in economics from the New School for Social Research and an M.A. in nutrition from Columbia University. Together with Joseph Collins, she is the author of *No Free Lunch: Food and Revolution in Cuba Today*, to be released in early 1985.

DONALD W. BRAY, a specialist in Third World studies, is a professor of political science at California State University, Los Angeles. He is an editor of *Latin American Perspectives*. He is coauthor, with Timothy F. Harding, of the Cuba section in R. Chilcote and J. Edelstein, eds., *Latin America: The Struggle with Dependency and Beyond* (New York: John Wiley and Sons, 1974). He received his B.A. from Pomona College, an M.A. from the University of California, Berkeley, and a Ph.D. from Stanford University.

ABOUT THE CONTRIBUTORS

MARJORIE WOODFORD BRAY is coordinator of Latin American studies at California State University, Los Angeles. Dr. Bray is an editor of *Latin American Perspectives* and currently president of the Pacific Coast Council on Latin American Studies. She holds a B.A. from Pomona College and a Ph.D. in international relations from the Claremont Graduate School.

CLAES BRUNDENIUS is a research fellow at the Research Policy Institute of the University of Lund, Sweden. During the winter term of 1984, he was a visiting Mellon Professor at the Center for Latin American Studies of the University of Pittsburgh. He has written extensively on Cuba and is the author of *Revolutionary Cuba: The Challenge of Economic Growth with Equity* (Boulder, Colo.: Westview, 1984) and *Economic Growth, Basic Needs and Income Distribution in Revolutionary Cuba* (Lund, Sweden: Research Policy Institute, 1981).

JULIANNE BURTON, who teaches Latin American literature at the University of California, Santa Cruz, has published widely on historical and critical aspects of the new Latin American cinema movement. She received her Ph.D. in 1972 from Yale University and recently held a residential fellowship at the Woodrow Wilson International Center for Scholars in Washington, D.C. She is currently preparing a collection of interviews with Latin American media activists and an anthology on social documentary in Latin America.

JOSEPH COLLINS works at and is cofounder of the Institute for Food and Development Policy in San Francisco. He has traveled extensively in Latin American and has produced several books on development and food policies, including: *What Difference Could a Revolution Make?: Food and Farming in the New Nicaragua* (San Francisco: Institute for Food and Development Policy, 1982), (coauthor with Frances Moore Lappé); *Now We Can Speak: A Journey Through the New Nicaragua* (San Francisco: Institute for Food and Development Policy, 1982), (co-author with Frances Moore Lappé); *Food First: Beyond the Myth of Scarcity* (New York: Ballantine Books, 1979), (coauthor with Frances Moore Lappé). Together with Medea Benjamin, he is the coauthor of *No Free Lunch: Food and Revolution in Cuba Today*, to be released in early 1985.

ROSS DANIELSON has been a research investigator with Kaiser Permanente Health Sciences Research Center in Portland, Oregon since

1978. He has also taught sociology at several colleges. Dr. Danielson holds both a B.A. and a Ph.D. from the University of Pittsburgh. He has published widely in the areas of health care organization and health in Cuba, including the volume *Cuban Medicine* (New Brunswick, N.J.: Transaction Books, 1979), as well as articles in *Social Science and Medicine*, *Inquiry*, and the *International Journal of Health Services*.

SUSAN ECKSTEIN is professor of sociology at Boston University. She received her Ph.D. from Columbia University and is the author of *The Poverty of Revolution: The State and Urban Poor in Mexico* (Princeton, N.J.: Princeton University Press, 1977) and *The Impact of Revolution: A Comparative Analysis of Mexico and Bolivia* (Beverly Hills, Cal.: SAGE Professional Papers, 1976). She is currently writing a book on Latin American revolutions and a study of peasant protest in Latin America.

JOEL C. EDELSTEIN is associate professor of political science at the University of Colorado at Denver. He obtained his Ph.D. in political science from the University of California at Riverside. Dr. Edelstein is the coauthor with Ronald Chilcote of *Latin America: The Struggle with Dependency and Beyond* (Cambridge, Mass.: Schenkman, 1974), and the coauthor of the recently completed *Development and Underdevelopment in Latin America: Capitalist and Socialist Perspectives*.

PHILIP S. FONER needs no introduction to *cubanólogos*, largely because of his seminal studies on Cuban history. Dr. Foner obtained his M.A. and Ph.D. from Columbia University and has been publishing works of social history for more than 40 years. At present he is professor emeritus at Lincoln University. Among his best-known studies are: the four-volume *History of Labor Movement in the United States* (New York: International Publishers, 1947, 1955, 1964 and 1965); *History of Cuba and its Relations with the United States*, 2 vols. (New York: International Publishers, 1962–63); *The Spanish-Cuban-American War and the Birth of American Imperialism, 1895–1902*, 2 vols. (New York: Monthly Review Press, 1973); *Antonio Maceo: the 'Bronze Titan' of Cuba's Struggle for Independence* (New York: Monthly Review Press, 1977); Among his works on José Martí are his edition of *Inside the Monster: Writings on the United States and American Imperialism* (New York: Monthly Review Press, 1975); *José Martí, Major Poems: a bilingual edition* (New York: Holmes and Meier, 1982); *José Martí on Education: Articles on Educational Theory and Pedagogy, and Writings for Children from the Age of Gold* (New York: Monthly Review Press, 1979); and *Our*

America: Writings on Latin America and the Struggle for Cuban Independence, by José Martí (New York: Monthly Review Press, 1977).

ROBERTO GONZÁLEZ ECHEVARRÍA is professor of Spanish and chairman of the Department of Spanish and Portuguese at Yale University. He received his Ph.D. from Yale University. Dr. González Echevarría has published works on Golden Age Spanish literature, colonial and contemporary Latin American literature and criticism, including *Calderón y la crítica* (Madrid: Gredos, 1977); *Relecturas: estudios de literatura cubana* (Caracas: Monte Avila, 1976); *Alejo Carpentier: The Pilgrim at Home* (Ithaca, N.Y.: Cornell University Press, 1977); *Sola a su vuelo fugitivo: ensayos de literatura hispanoamericana* (1983); and *Alejo Carpentier: Bibliographical Guide* (Westport, Conn.: Greenwood Press, 1983).

ANDRÉ GUNDER FRANK, who received his Ph.D. in economics from the University of Chicago, is virtually a legend in the field of development studies. His writings have been published in 21 languages and include 20 books, more than 60 book chapters, and over 150 articles and essays. Among his many notable works are: *Capitalism and Underdevelopment in Latin America* (New York: Monthly Review Press, 1967); *Latin America: Underdevelopment or Revolution* (New York: Monthly Review Press, 1969); *Sociology of Development and Underdevelopment of Sociology* (Andover Mass.: Warner, 1967); *Lumpenbourgeoisie: Lumpendevelopment* (New York: Monthly Review Press, 1972); *On Capitalist Underdevelopment* (New York: Oxford University Press, 1975); *World Accumulation 1492-1798* (London: MacMillan, 1978); *Dependent Accumulation and Underdevelopment* (London: MacMillan, 1978); *Mexican Agriculture, 1521-1630* (Cambridge: Cambridge University Press, 1979); *Crisis: In the Third World* (New York: Holmes and Meier, 1981); *Reflections on the World Economic Crisis* (New York: Monthly Review Press, 1981); *Reflections on the World Economic Crisis* (New York: Monthly Review Press, 1981); *Dynamics of Global Crisis* (co-author, 1982); *The European Challenge* (1983); and *Critique and Anti-Critique* (1984). At present Dr. Frank is professor of development economics and social sciences at the University of Amsterdam and director of its Institute for Socio-Economic Studies of Development Regions (ISMOG).

C. FRED JUDSON is visiting assistant professor of political studies at the University of Alberta, Edmonton, Canada. He teaches on international relations, Latin American politics and society, and nuclear weapons. Dr. Judson holds a B.A. from Lewis and Clark College and an M.A. and Ph.D. from the University of Alberta. He has published work on Cuba, religion, and popular culture in Nicaragua, and on the Sandinista armed forces. A book on political education in the Cuban Rebel Army was published by Westview Press in 1984.

MARVIN LEINER is professor of education at Queen's College, City University of New York. A former elementary-school teacher, he obtained his doctorate in education at New York University. Dr. Leiner spent the 1968-1969 school year in Cuba with his family and has published extensively on the Cuban educational system. Among his works are *Children are the Revolution: Day Care in Cuba* (New York: The Viking Press, 1974) and *Major Developments in Cuban Education* (Andover, Mass., Warner, 1973).

ARTHUR MacEWAN is chairman and an associate professor of the Department of Economics at the University of Massachusetts, Boston. He has been a visiting professor at the University of Havana and has also worked at Harvard University and the Pakistan Institute of Development Economics. His articles have appeared in *Politics and Society* and *Socialist Revolution*. In addition to books on development economics and on economic alternatives for Pakistan, he has written the study *Revolution and Economic Development in Cuba* (New York: St. Martin's Press, 1981).

MORRIS H. MORLEY is senior research fellow at the Council on Hemispheric Affairs in Washington, D.C. He is the coauthor (with James Petras) of *The United States and Chile* (New York: Monthly Review Press, 1975) and *The Nationalization of Venezuelan Oil* (New York: Praeger, 1977). Dr. Morley has published articles on U.S.-Cuban relations in the *Journal of Latin American Studies*, *Comparative Politics*, and the *Canadian Journal of Political Science*.

ALFRED PADULA is associate professor of history at the University of Maine, Portland. Dr. Padula, a former foreign service officer, is a graduate of Holy Cross (B.S.), the University of the Americas, Mexico (M.A.), and the University of New Mexico (Ph.D.). His articles on Cuba and on multinational corporations have appeared in the *Caribbean Review*, the *Nation*, the *Revista/Review Interamericana*, and elsewhere. He is a member of the staff of the *Times of the Americas*.

LOUIS A. PÉREZ, Jr., is professor of history at the University of South Florida, with research interests in nineteenth—and twentieth—century Cuba. Dr. Pérez has published extensively on Cuban army politics and Cuban bibliographies. Among his works are: *The Cuban Revolutionary War, 1953-58: A Bibliography* (Metuchen, N.J.: Scarecrow Press, 1976); *Historiography in the Revolution: A Bibliography of Cuban Scholarship, 1959-1979* (New York: Garland, 1982); *Cuba Between Empires, 1898-1902* (Pittsburgh: University of Pittsburgh Press, 1983); and *Army Politics in Cuba, 1898-1958* (Pittsburgh: University of Pittsburgh Press, 1976).

MARIFELI PÉREZ-STABLE is an instructor of politics at the College of Old Westbury, State University of New York. She holds a B.A. and M.A. in political science from Rosemont College and the University of Florida, respectively, and is currently completing a Ph.D. in sociology at Stony Brook, State University of New York. Ms. Pérez-Stable has published articles on Cuba in *Latin American Perspectives, Cuban Studies/Estudios Cubanos,* and the *Latin American Research Review,* and an essay on the working class in Thomas W. Walker, ed., *Nicaragua in Revolution* (New York: Praeger, 1981).

JAMES F. PETRAS is professor of sociology at the State University of New York, Binghamton. He obtained his Ph.D. in political science at the University of California, Berkeley and has traveled extensively throughout Latin America. In addition to the works coauthored with Morris Morley (see Morley entry), Dr. Petras has published scores of articles and books, including: *Latin America: Reform or Revolution?* (Greenwich, Conn.: Fawcett, 1968); *Fidel Castro Speaks* (London: Allen Lane, 1970, coeditor); *Cultivating Revolution: The United States and Agrarian Reform in Latin America* (New York: Random House, 1971), coeditor; *Critical Perspectives on Imperialism and Social Class in the Third World* (New York: Monthly Review Press, 1978, co-author); *Political and Social Forces in Chilean Development* (Berkeley, Cal.: University of California Press, 1969); and *Politics and Social Structure in Latin America* (New York: Monthly Review Press, 1970).

RHODA PEARL RABKIN is currently a visiting scholar at the Latin American Studies Program, Cornell University. Dr. Rabkin's research interests include modern Cuba and U.S. policy toward Central America and the Caribbean. She has published in the *Journal of*

International Affairs and *Third World Quarterly*. Dr. Rabkin holds a B.A. from Cornell University and a Ph.D. in government from Harvard University.

MARGARET RANDALL is a poet, photographer, and political analyst. From 1969 to 1981 she lived and worked in Cuba. In addition to her recent works on Nicaragua: *Doris Tijerino: Inside the Nicaraguan Revolution* (Vancouver B.C.: New Star Books, 1978); *Sandino's Daughters* (Vancouver, B.C.: New Star Books, 1981); and *Christians in the Nicaraguan Revolution* (Vancouver, B.C.: New Star Books, 1983), she has published a number of works on Cuba, of which the best known are *Women in Cuba* (New York: Smyrna Press, 1981); *Cuban Women Now* (Toronto: The Women's Press, 1974); and *Carlota: Prose and Poetry from Cuba*.

ARCHIBALD R.M. RITTER is professor of economics at the Norman Paterson School of International Affairs at Carleton University, Ottawa, Canada. He received his B.A. from Queen's University, his M.A. from the University of Western Ontario, and his Ph.D. from the University of Texas. He is the author of several articles on Latin America, coeditor of *Latin American Prospects for the 1970s: What Kinds of Revolutions?* (New York: Praeger, 1973), and author of *The Economic Development of Revolutionary Cuba: Strategy and Performance* (New York: Praeger, 1974).

LOIS SMITH is a researcher in Latin America. She is currently working on projects concerning women in Cuba and Nicaragua and on the history of selected multinational companies. Her articles and reviews have appeared in *Cuban Studies, Times of the Americas,* and *Signs*. Ms. Smith has lived in Costa Rica and has recently visited Nicaragua. She has a B.A. in political science from the University of Maine, Portland.

WAYNE S. SMITH is a Senior Fellow at the Carnegie Endowment for International Peace and adjunct professor at the Johns Hopkins University's School of Advanced International Studies in Washington, D.C. A career diplomat for 25 years, Dr. Smith was the U.S. State Department's top expert on Cuba when he left the diplomatic service in 1982. He had served in Havana as third secretary of the embassy from 1958 until the United States broke relations in 1961 and as chief of the U.S. Interests Section from 1979 until 1982. Dr. Smith hold a Ph.D. from George Washington University and an M.A. from Columbia University. He also received his B.A. and an M.A. from La Universidad de las Américas in Mexico.

JUDITH A. WEISS, associate professor of Spanish at Mount Allison University, Sackville, New Brunswick, Canada, was visiting professor at the University of Maryland last year. She obtained her Ph.D. at Yale University. Included in her research on Cuban popular culture is her study, *Casa de las Américas: An Intellectual Review in the Cuban Revolution* (Chapel Hill, N.C.: Estudios de Hispanófila, 1977).

ANDREW ZIMBALIST is chairman of the economics department at Smith College. He holds a B.A. from the University of Wisconsin and an M.A. and Ph.D. from Harvard University. He has written several articles on the Cuban economy and has published four books, including *Comparing Economic Systems: A Political Economic Approach* (New York: Academic Press, 1984), with H. Sherman; and *Comparative Economic Systems: An Assessment of Knowledge, Theory and Practice* (The Hague: Kluwen-Nijhoff, 1983), editor. He is currently serving as a consultant on the Cuban economy to *Cubatimes*.